Kellogg
on
Branding

Kellogg on Branding

The Marketing Faculty of The Kellogg School of Management

EDITED BY
ALICE M. TYBOUT
AND
TIM CALKINS

FOREWORD BY
PHILIP KOTLER

WILEY

John Wiley & Sons, Inc.

Published by John Wiley & Sons, Inc., Hoboken, New Jersey.
Published simultaneously in Canada.

For general information on our other products and services please contact our Customer Care Department within the United States at (800) 762-2974, outside the United States at (317) 572-3993 or fax (317) 572-4002.

Designations used by companies to distinguish their products are often claimed by trademarks. In all instances where the author or publisher is aware of a claim, the product names appear in Initial Capital letters. Readers, however, should contact the appropriate companies for more complete information regarding trademarks and registration.

Wiley also publishes its books in a variety of electronic formats. Some content that appears in print may not be available in electronic books. For more information about Wiley products, visit our web site at www.Wiley.com.

Library of Congress Cataloging-in-Publication Data:
Kellogg on branding : the marketing faculty of the Kellogg School of
Management / edited by Alice Tybout and Tim Calkins ; foreword by Philip
Kotler.
    p. cm.
  ISBN-13 978-0-471-69016-0 (cloth)
  ISBN-10 0-471-69016-3 (cloth)
  1. Brand name products.   2. Brand name products—Marketing.   3. Brand name products—Management.   4. Customer relations—Management.   I. Tybout, Alice M. II. Calkins, Tim.   III. Kellogg School of Management.
  HD69.B7K46 2005
  658.8'27—dc22

2005007457

Printed in the United States of America.

13

CONTENTS

Section IV
BRANDING INSIGHTS FROM SENIOR MANAGERS

FOREWORD BY PHILIP KOTLER

In an age of hypercompetition, commoditization, globalization, and rapid technological obsolescence, marketers are struggling to find new conceptual bases on which to design and deliver their marketing programs. The haunting truth is that traditional marketing is not working. Top management now sees many mass advertising campaigns as losing money. They see sales promotion campaigns as boosting sales temporarily but being largely unprofitable. They experience direct mail campaigns as barely delivering a 1 percent response rate. Their new products are failing at a disturbing rate.

There are two answers to the marketing challenge facing today's companies. One is to know your customers better and to get closer to them. The other is to differentiate your offering through your branding work so that the offering stands out as relevant and superior in value to a clear target market.

The power of creative branding is visible to all. We are drawn to Starbucks, Harley-Davidson, Coca-Cola, Apple Computer, Singapore Airlines, Heinz, Gillette, Porsche. These companies have learned how to make their brands live in customers' minds and hearts.

Branding is much more than attaching a name to an offering. Branding is about making a certain promise to customers about delivering a fulfilling experience and a level of performance. Therefore, branding requires that everyone in the supply chain—from product development to manufacturing to marketing to sales to distribution—works to carry out that promise. This is what is meant by "living the brand." The brand becomes the whole platform for planning, designing, and delivering superior value to the company's target customers.

The Kellogg School of Management enjoys its ranking as the number-one business school and the number-one marketing department due to its relentless research and teaching regarding what helps companies become superior performers in the marketplace. We have taught the principles and practices of marketing and branding to countless generations of MBA students who are now plying their craft in the world's leading companies.

In this book, we offer our version of what goes into brewing successful brands. We have invited our experts to describe the foundations of branding, the strategies for building and leveraging brands, and the task of moving from strategy to implementation. As a *coup de grâce*, we have asked market leaders to describe their actual experiences in developing and marketing their brands.

Most companies take the easy road to marketing their brands by buying a lot of expensive advertising, making cliché claims, and spending lavishly on sales promotion. We see branding instead as the foundation of deep market planning. We offer this book as a treasure trove of ideas for bringing new life to your brands.

PREFACE

Prior to 2003, the Kellogg School of Management didn't offer any courses or executive education programs on the topic of branding. The issue wasn't that the faculty thought branding was unimportant. Rather, we thought branding was *so* important and encompassing that it was incorporated into almost every marketing class and executive education program offered by the school. So when people asked for a branding program, they were directed to consumer marketing, or business-to-business marketing, or another course based on their specific situation and need.

This changed in 2003, when the Kellogg School decided that the time was right to launch a program focused solely on issues related to branding. Interest in branding was high and growing, as companies recognized the critical role brands played in driving profitable, long-term growth. More important, it was clear that executives were looking for help on the specific topic of creating and managing brands. Many managers understood that brands were essential, but they didn't know where to turn for skills in this particular area. With this in mind, the Kellogg School introduced a new executive education program, Kellogg on Branding.

Response to the program was remarkably strong; the first sessions quickly sold out, and the participants were excited about the material. As we explored this response, we learned two things. First, branding is becoming a focus for more and more companies. The managers in our first sessions of Kellogg on Branding were remarkably diverse; they came from the pharmaceutical, financial services, apparel, building materials, and technology industries. Our participants included lawyers and doctors and teachers. Many of these individuals were being asked to think about brands for the first time. Second, while the world is full of branding agencies and branding books, there are few resources that combine academic theory and practical application. These two insights inspired us to develop this book.

xi

OVERVIEW

Kellogg on Branding is a book for managers who are responsible for creating and building brands. It is also a book for managers who are not directly responsible for branding decisions but want to deepen their understanding of and ability to support their firm's brand-building initiatives.

The book offers key theories and insights related to branding. It is unique because it combines theory and practice. The authors are both academic scholars from the Kellogg School of Management's marketing department and seasoned brand-builders from industry who are part of the larger Kellogg community. Together these authors present a diverse set of perspectives on branding—a rich conversation with multiple voices and views. The book is unified by a common belief in the power of brands.

Kellogg on Branding begins with an overview of the challenges confronting brand managers. The remainder of the book is organized into four sections. Section I, Key Branding Concepts, covers three topics. First, Alice Tybout and Brian Sternthal discuss the concept of brand positioning, which is the specific intended meaning for the brand in consumers' minds. Understanding a brand's positioning is the first task for most managers; it is difficult to make headway with a brand until you understand what you want the brand to be. Second, Bobby Calder presents brand design—the process of translating a positioning into a product—which includes important topics like name, colors, and graphics. Third, John Sherry reviews brand meaning and explains how brands begin to take on associations that are shaped partly by the company and partly by the consumer. These three chapters form a logical progression; a manager should first create a positioning, then design the brand, then track and monitor the brand's meaning in the market. Based on in-market learnings, the manager may then decide to revise the positioning or design.

Section II, Strategies for Building and Leveraging Brands, addresses issues related to managing brands in a dynamic environment. Greg Carpenter and Kent Nakamoto present the concept of customer learning and discuss how an understanding of learning processes can be leveraged when building either a pioneer brand or a later entrant. Bridgette Braig and Alice Tybout review approaches to leveraging an established brand through launching line and category extensions. Finally, Tim Calkins explores the challenges associated with managing a portfolio of brands over time.

Section III, From Strategy to Implementation, covers a diverse set of topics. The section starts with two chapters on brand communications. Brian Sternthal and Angela Lee provide an overview of developing effective brand advertising, and Ed Malthouse and Bobby Calder explain how customer relationship management (CRM) can play a role in building relationship brands. The next three chapters cover branding in specific industries. James Anderson and Greg Carpenter review branding in the business-to-business environment. Amy Ostrum, Dawn Iacobucci, and Felicia Morgan look at branding in services industries. Mohanbir Sawhney discusses branding in high-tech organizations. Scott Davis then describes how managers can bring a brand to life inside a company. Finally, Don and Heidi Schultz highlight why measuring the value of brands is important but challenging and present three approaches for doing so.

Section IV, Branding Insights from Senior Managers, is a collection of insights from senior corporate executives, each with years of experience building and growing brands. The first four of these chapters focus on issues related to building brands in consumers' minds. Mark Goldston, chairman, CEO, and president of United Online, presents the story of building the NetZero brand, which successfully challenged much larger, better funded Internet service providers and established a strong market presence in a mere five years. Mark Shapiro, principal at the New England Consulting Group, discusses why frame of reference is such an important part of a brand's positioning and illustrates creative ways to leverage the frame of reference. Carol Bernick, chairman of the Alberto-Culver Company, describes the importance of brand names and offers illustrations of successful and unsuccessful naming efforts. Betsy Holden, president of global marketing and category development at Kraft Foods, discusses how to combine the best of global and the best of local marketing to create brands that thrive around the world.

The final three chapters focus on building the right brand culture within the organization. Gary Mecklenburg, president and CEO of Northwestern Memorial HealthCare, highlights the role of culture in building a hospital brand. David Coolidge, vice chairman of William Blair & Company, describes how his company built a financial services brand through its people. Ed Buckley, vice president of marketing at UPS, and Matt Williams, senior vice president at the Martin Agency, review how UPS used branding to drive organizational change.

HOW TO USE THIS BOOK

This book is designed so that it can be used in several ways. Someone new to the topic of branding will likely benefit from reading the foundational chapters in Section I first and then moving on to more specialized topics. Those with a background in branding may approach the book with a specific topic or goal in mind. There are six themes that cut across the book.

The first theme is *brand positioning.* A reader interested in this topic should begin with Brand Positioning (Chapter 1) and Competitive Brand Strategies (Chapter 4). The concepts in these chapters are further developed with an emphasis on consumer goods in Marketing Leverage in the Frame of Reference (Chapter 15), Building Brands through Effective Advertising (Chapter 7), and Using Positioning to Build a Megabrand (Chapter 14). For those interested in brand positioning in a business-to-business context, Brand Strategy for Business Markets (Chapter 9) is an appropriate follow-up.

The second theme is *brand design.* Here, Designing Brands (Chapter 2) provides a foundation and Brand Portfolio Strategy (Chapter 6) elaborates on this topic. Finding the Right Brand Name (Chapter 16) complements these chapters.

The third theme is *brand meaning.* The chapter on Brand Meaning (Chapter 3) provides a broad overview of the range of meanings that may be associated with a brand. Building Global Brands (Chapter 17) then illustrates the challenge of understanding and adapting brands to cultural differences around the globe.

The fourth theme is that of *leveraging a brand.* This concept is introduced in Brand Positioning (Chapter 1) and is elaborated in Brand Extensions (Chapter 5) and Brand Portfolio Strategy (Chapter 6). Using Positioning to Build a Megabrand (Chapter 14) provides a detailed illustration of the growth of the NetZero brand.

The fifth theme is that of *creating a brand-driven organization.* Two chapters, Services Branding (Chapter 10) and Building a Brand-Driven Organization (Chapter 12), make a compelling case for the role that employees play in creating brands. The general points outlined in these chapters are further developed in Branding and Organizational Culture (Chapter 18), Branding and the Organization (Chapter 19), and Internal Branding (Chapter 20).

Finally, three chapters offer guidance on *measurement* issues. Designing Brands (Chapter 2) suggests ways to assess whether a brand design embodies the intended brand concept. Building Brands through Effective Advertising (Chapter 7) discusses the adequacy of various measures for evaluating the effectiveness of brand advertising. Finally, Measuring Brand Value (Chapter 13) presents three approaches to calculating the value of a brand.

Throughout the book, the authors offer frameworks, checklists, and other tools to assist the manager. We hope that these tools will be useful and that the perspectives will be thought-provoking to all who share our fascination with brands.

ALICE M. TYBOUT
TIM CALKINS

ACKNOWLEDGMENTS

Many individuals contributed to this book and warrant our thanks. It is impossible to mention everyone who helped, but a few people stand out.

This book is a product of the entire Kellogg School community. The faculty embraced the project and readily agreed to participate. Our executive contributors took time from their busy schedules to assemble thoughtful and insightful chapters. Kellogg School of Management Dean Dipak Jain was supportive of the project from the start. The marketing department administrative team provided invaluable assistance, as they do every day. James Ward and Subarna Ranjit deserve our special thanks. Judy Piper and Peggy Morrall kept the first Kellogg on Branding executive education programs on track. Perhaps most important, our students in the MBA and executive education programs gave us both insight and inspiration.

Several other people made invaluable contributions. Our editor at John Wiley & Sons, Richard Narramore, was supportive and encouraging throughout the project. Isidora Lagos at William Blair & Company, Dan Stone at the Alberto-Culver Company, and Kristina Hedley at Northwestern Memorial HealthCare all played critical roles in their respective chapters. Sally Saville Hodge provided valuable assistance on Chapter 12, Building a Brand-Driven Organization. Rebecca Lindell deserves a special thanks for her assistance with early drafts of the chapter on global branding.

The entire book benefited from the deft touch of Patty Dowd Schmitz, who reviewed and edited each chapter and provided invaluable feedback with directness and sensitivity.

Above all, we thank our families for their support and encouragement.

A.M.T.
T.C.

INTRODUCTION

THE CHALLENGE OF BRANDING

TIM CALKINS

In August 2003, more than 100,000 leather-clad bikers rumbled into Milwaukee, Wisconsin, to celebrate Harley-Davidson's one-hundredth birthday. For three days, the city was transformed into a massive biker–birthday party; there were concerts and festivals and celebrations, including a parade featuring more than 10,000 motorcycles. Harley-Davidson aficionados traveled from 47 different countries to attend the event.

The birthday celebration was a powerful demonstration of the strength of the Harley-Davidson brand. Harley-Davidson isn't unique because it makes good motorcycles; there are many companies in the world that make good motorcycles. Harley-Davidson is unique because it has a powerful brand that connects with its customers. The brand transcends the product.

More broadly, the Harley-Davidson birthday celebration was an example of the power of brands to create customer loyalty and insulate companies from competition. By building strong brands, companies can build strong businesses. Harley-Davidson, for example, has delivered exceptional financial results—2003 was the eighteenth consecutive year of revenue and earnings growth for the company.

A brand is a set of associations linked to a name, mark, or symbol associated with a product or service. The difference between a name and a brand is that a name doesn't have associations; it is simply a name. A name becomes a brand when people link it to other things. A brand is much like a reputation.

The Coca-Cola brand, for example, has associations including cola, refreshment, red, the Real Thing. The Dom Perignon brand brings to mind celebrations, luxury, champagne, France, and expensive. Las Vegas quickly conjures up gambling, fun, shows, and sin.

Brands are not always a positive; associations can be positive or negative.

1

One-time energy giant Enron, for example, has associations including financial mismanagement, fraud, and bankruptcy due to its 2001 implosion into financial scandal. Similarly, ValuJet, a discount airline, developed associations including dangerous, reckless, and poor maintenance after one of its planes crashed in the Florida Everglades.

Virtually any type of product or service can be branded; brands are not just for luxury goods or consumer packaged goods. Indeed, it is difficult to come up with a product or service where brands don't play a role. There are hundreds of brands of water, including Evian, Perrier, Dasani, and Aquafina. Medical device and pharmaceutical companies have built strong brands, developing associations in the minds of patients and health-care professionals—Viagra, Lipitor, Vioxx, and Claritin are all brands with clear associations, some positive and some negative. Business-to-business companies have developed exceptionally powerful brands such as McKinsey, Goldman Sachs, and Baker & McKenzie. Entertainers are brands; the Rolling Stones, Britney Spears, and Andrea Bocelli all bring clear sets of associations. Nonprofit organizations are brands, religious groups are brands, and every person is a brand.

BRANDS AND PERCEPTION

Brands have a remarkable ability to impact the way people view products. Consumers rarely just see a product or service; they see the product together with the brand. As a result, how they perceive the product is shaped by the brand.

Perceptions, of course, matter most—how people perceive something matters far more than the absolute truth. The question generally isn't which product or service is best; the question is which product or service people *think* is best. Is Dom Perignon the best champagne in the world? Does Tiffany sell the finest diamonds in the world? Does McKinsey do the best strategic thinking? Perhaps so, perhaps not; however, many people think so, and perceptions matter most.

The presence of a well-known brand will dramatically affect how people view a product or service. If people see a premium brand name on a product, they will likely view the item as high quality, exclusive, and expensive. If people see a discount name on a product, they will probably perceive the item to be low quality and cheap.

Brands function like prisms (Figure I.1); how people regard a branded product is shaped both by the actual product, such as specific features and attributes, and by the brand. The brand can elevate or diminish the product.

To demonstrate the power of a brand to shape expectations, I conducted a

Figure I.1
Brand Prism

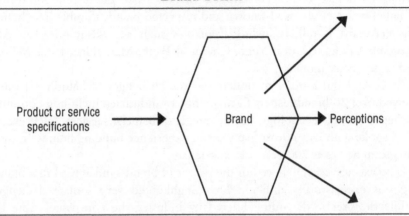

simple study with MBA students. I first asked a group of students what they would expect to pay for a pair of good-quality, 18-karat-gold earrings with two 0.3-carat diamonds. I asked a second group of students how much they would pay for the same earrings, only this time I added the words "From Tiffany." I asked a third group the same question, but this time changed "From Tiffany" to "From Wal-Mart."

The results were striking. The average price for the unbranded earrings was $550. With Tiffany branding, the average price increased to $873, a jump of almost 60 percent. This increase was solely due to the addition of the Tiffany brand. With the Wal-Mart branding, the price expectation fell to just $81, a decline of 85 percent from the unbranded earrings and a decline of 91 percent from the Tiffany-branded earrings.

The study highlights the power of the brand to shape perception. "Good quality," for example, means something entirely different when it comes from Tiffany rather than from Wal-Mart. In addition, the experience of wearing earrings from Tiffany is different from the experience of wearing earrings from Wal-Mart. The distinction between the brands is not just conspicuous consumption; you can't tell a Tiffany earring from a Wal-Mart earring from a distance.

BRANDING CHALLENGES

Branding looks easy. Nike is a powerful brand. Starbucks and Pepsi and Goldman Sachs and Steinway are all distinctive and well known. Building a brand appears to be straightforward; a manager just needs to come up with a good name, an attractive logo, and a catchy slogan.

In reality, creating and building brands are two of the greatest challenges a manager will face. For every Starbucks or Nike, there are dozens and dozens of failed brands. Even well-known and respected brands stumble. The branding graveyard is full; it includes notables such as Oldsmobile, Pan Am, pets.com, ValuJet, Chiffon, Yugo, Chemical Bank, MarchFirst, PaineWebber, and many, many more.

In 2003, I did a study to understand the challenges of branding. I interviewed over 30 brand leaders from a range of industries, including consumer packaged goods, technology, health care, and financial services. Each executive I spoke with had at least five years of experience building brands. In total, the group had over 200 years of experience.

The executives all believed in the power of brands, and agreed that branding was exceptionally difficult. They highlighted very similar challenges. While the precise dynamics differed by industry, the core issues were the same. Three key challenges emerged from the study: *cash, consistency*, and *clutter*. These are the "three *C*'s" of branding.

Challenge 1: Cash

The challenge of cash, or dealing with short-term financial concerns, is the biggest single challenge brand leaders face. It is driven by a very simple conundrum: Executives need to deliver short-term financial results, but brands are long-term assets. Executives who hit quarterly profit targets are rewarded, and those who exceed them are often rewarded handsomely. Although it is important to make headway on long-term initiatives such as building a strong brand, hitting the short-term financial targets matters most. As one of my former colleagues at Kraft Foods noted frequently, "Good numbers don't guarantee your success, but bad numbers will get you every time."

Brands are long-term assets. If managed properly, a brand can live for decades or centuries. For example, Harvard, Moet & Chandon, and Pepsi were created in 1636, 1743, and 1898, respectively. All of these brands continue to be vibrant and valuable today.

Virtually all of a brand's value resides in the future; the current-year financial returns are a very small part of the total. If a brand delivers a steady stream of cash flow in perpetuity, less than 5 percent of the value of the brand resides in the first year, assuming a discount rate of 5 percent.

However, if a manager is forced to choose between investing in a brand and missing short-term financial targets, most managers will choose to hit the short-term numbers. It's usually the career-optimizing decision. And in a supreme bit of irony of business, a manager who boosts short-term profits while damaging the long-term health of a brand is often rewarded, while a manager who invests in a brand at the expense of short-term results is often penalized. The cost-benefit analysis on a brand-building initiative highlights the tension. The benefits are difficult to quantify, uncertain, and in the future. The costs are quantifiable, certain, and immediate.

It is astonishingly easy for brands to get caught in a "branding doom loop." The doom loop begins with a manager struggling to deliver a short-term profit target. To boost sales and profits, the manager deploys programs that have a significant short-term impact, such as a price promotion. To fund these programs, the manager reduces spending on programs with smaller short-term returns, such as brand-building programs. These moves are usually successful in improving short-term results, and with better results, the manager survives to fight another day.

However, the plan that was so successful in the short run may well have created negative long-term issues. First, the plan might prompt a competitive response. Second, customer pricing expectations may shift, as customers are now accustomed to the promoted prices. A buy-one-get-one-free offer is motivating and exciting the first time, and perhaps the second time. But eventually customers come to expect it, so companies must cut prices further to create excitement and drive sales. And third, the brand may weaken because brand-building programs were cut. (See Figure I.2.)

Combined, these factors put the brand in a weak position, with disappointing sales. And this, of course, forces the manager to implement more short-term programs, continuing the doom loop and sending the brand into a dangerous downward spiral.

Figure I.2
Price Promotion Doom Loop

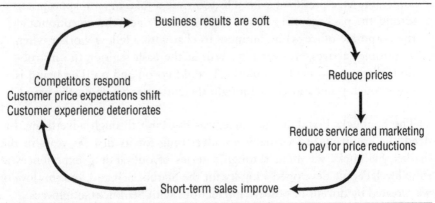

Dealing with short-term financial constraints, then, is one of the most critical challenges of branding. Managers must balance driving short-term numbers with building a long-term brand. Without understanding the challenge of cash, executives undertaking branding programs are certain to encounter trouble. They will invest in their brand without setting proper expectations, and if short-term results are weak, these managers may not survive in their position long enough to see the benefits of their investment.

Challenge 2: Consistency

The second great challenge of branding is consistency, or getting an entire organization to embrace the brand and live up to the brand promise over time. Crafting the perfect brand positioning and developing the ideal brand portfolio are both noble tasks. However, if the organization doesn't understand, believe in, and *own* the brand—if the message, the brand, and the product are not consistent—the vision will remain unfulfilled.

Brands are created through a wide range of touch points; every time customers interact with a brand they form associations. This means that almost everyone in a company has an impact on the brand, from the receptionist to the advertising manager to the customer service representative.

One marketing executive put it this way:

A brand is the feel of your business card, the way the company's phone is answered, the assistant coordinator who's had one too many after work yet has handed out her business card while at the bar, the disgruntled salesman who complains to his family and friends that the company he works for is really ripping people off for big profits on the products he sells, the tone of a letter, the employee who doesn't help the customer, the vice president who tells too rude a joke in an inappropriate setting, the package that's almost impossible to open, the receptionist at the corporate office who continues to chat with a fellow worker when a customer arrives, an over-long wait at the cash register, the instructions that are too hard to follow....I could go on and on. The brand is every touch point and every thought the customer has about the brand.

The Starbucks brand, for example, was not built through advertising. Indeed, the company did virtually no advertising for its first 30 years in the market. Starbucks was built through a series of outstanding experiences at store level. People developed a loyalty for the Starbucks brand, and this loyalty was created by dozens of positive interactions with Starbucks employees.

Conversely, the Lands' End brand was damaged after it failed to live up to its brand promise. Lands' End, a direct retailer with a reputation for outstanding customer service, was acquired by Sears in 2002 for $1.9 billion. Sears quickly began selling Lands' End products in Sears stores. However, the customer service provided by Sears was poor. This disappointed Lands' End customers and tarnished the once powerful Lands' End brand.

In short, Starbucks and many other great brands succeed by offering their customers a consistent experience with their brands at every customer touch point by engaging their entire organizations. Consistency matters, and it matters at every turn.

Challenge 3: Clutter

The third great challenge facing brand managers is clutter. Simply put, consumers are bombarded every day by hundreds and sometimes thousands of advertisements and promotions. From the moment we awake until the second we drift off to sleep, we are the recipients of messages and marketing appeals. It makes the local flea market seem positively serene.

Consider the number of media outlets now available to consumers. With satellite or cable access, people can watch over 200 different television stations. XM Satellite radio alone offers over 120 channels. There are millions of web sites to browse at every hour of the day. An exceptionally popular primetime network television show may reach 15 million people, which is only 5 percent of the U.S. population.

Breaking through this cluttered environment is exceptionally difficult. It's hard to get anyone to pay attention to your brand, and harder still to form meaningful associations.

To stand out, brands need to be focused and unique; great brands mean something distinct for customers. This is why brand positioning is so important. Almost every great brand has a clear set of associations. Wal-Mart stands for low prices. Tiffany is synonymous with luxury and exclusivity. BMW defines performance driving. Vanguard offers low-price mutual funds, especially low-price index funds. Viagra is all about erectile dysfunction. Red Bull stands for energy and excitement.

Weak brands, however, are bland; they don't stand for anything in particular, and so they mean essentially nothing. Weak brands struggle because they have no focus and they don't stand out. Sears is a weak, diffuse brand, for example; it is not particularly cheap and not particularly high quality. It's not just about tools and it's not just about apparel. Ford's Lincoln brand of vehicles has no obvious associations; it is simply another brand. Charles Schwab, once the leader in low-cost online trading, has lost its distinctiveness; it is neither high service nor low cost.

Having a clear positioning is a good start, but it is not sufficient; brands need to be creative in the market to attract attention. Great advertising is important, but advertising alone is no longer enough, due to the high levels of media fragmentation. Marketers must identify and execute creative ideas that are unique and attract attention. Red Bull enlisted influential college students to promote its drink. BMW's Mini attached one of its cars to the roof of a large SUV and drove around major cities.

Strategic focus and out-of-the-box creativity has become essential: without both a brand will be lost in the clutter.

SUMMARY

Brands are sets of associations linked to a name or mark associated with a product or service. The associations can be positive or negative, and anything can be branded, even water, cities, and people. In addition, brands have the ability to shape how people perceive products—they can elevate a product or diminish a product. As a result, brands are critically important; a brand with negative associations will hurt a company, and a brand with positive associations will help.

While branding looks easy, creating and building brands is exceptionally challenging. Effective brand managers must understand the challenges of cash, consistency, and clutter and focus on overcoming the issues specific to their brand.

Above all, managers must believe in the power of brands. Ultimately, brands are built by people who passionately believe in their brands. Indeed, many of the world's best brands can be linked to a single person: Howard Schultz created Starbucks, Steve Jobs built Apple, Pleasant Roland formed American Girl, Richard Branson developed Virgin, and Phil Knight was the driving force behind Nike. Brand builders understand and believe in the power of brands.

Tim Calkins is clinical associate professor of marketing at the Kellogg School of Management and co-director of the Kellogg on Branding program. He consults with companies around the world on marketing strategy and branding issues. Prior to joining the Kellogg faculty, Tim worked at Kraft Foods for 11 years, managing branding including A.1.® Steak Sauce, Miracle Whip, and Taco Bell. He received a BA from Yale University and an MBA from Harvard Business School.

SECTION I

KEY BRANDING CONCEPTS

CHAPTER 1

BRAND POSITIONING

ALICE M. TYBOUT and BRIAN STERNTHAL

When TiVo launched its digital video recorder (DVR) system in 1999, the leading technology market research firm Forrester predicted, "These hard-drive machines will take off faster than any other consumer electronics product has before." Forrester projected that there would be greater than 50 percent household penetration by 2005. They were optimistic because TiVo allowed viewers to store a library of shows tailored to their preferences, pause or rewind live TV, and quickly skip through commercials. In addition, TiVo was easy to program. In its initial advertising, TiVo announced that it would revolutionize television by empowering viewers to "Watch what you want, when you want."

Although TiVo aficionados love it and recommend it with an almost evangelical zeal, sales have fallen far short of Forrester's (and others') enthusiastic initial forecasts. As of January 2005, only 2.3 million households (slightly less than 2 percent) had TiVo. At the same time, the adoption rate of DVRs was increasing as cable companies began to embrace the technology and offer their own systems. But TiVo's future remained uncertain. We contend that a critical factor in TiVo's lackluster performance was the absence of a clear brand positioning.

Brand positioning refers to the specific, intended meaning for a brand in consumers' minds. More precisely, a brand's positioning articulates the goal that a consumer will achieve by using the brand and explains why it is superior to other means of accomplishing this goal. In the case of TiVo, the brand was positioned as empowering consumers, but how and why it accomplished this goal was never clear. Was TiVo like a VCR in allowing consumers to record programs for playback at a later time? If so, what made it a superior means of performing this function? If TiVo wasn't a better version of the

VCR, then what was it and why was it uniquely empowering? Advertisements used to launch TiVo failed to answer these questions.

Summary

This chapter addresses the challenge of developing a strong brand positioning. We begin by outlining the key elements of a brand's position. These include the goal that the customer can expect to achieve by using the brand (frame of reference) and an indication of why the brand is superior in achieving the goal (point of difference). This is followed by a more detailed assessment of how to select an appropriate customer goal, create a superiority claim, and orchestrate these elements to develop an effective position. We conclude by discussing how a brand's positioning can be evolved over time.

POSITIONING FUNDAMENTALS

A statement of a brand's position is typically developed by the brand manager. Ideally, it is grounded in insight about the goals and perceptions of a targeted group of consumers. Managers develop formal positioning statements to ensure a shared vision for the brand throughout the organization and to guide tactical thinking. Accordingly, a brand positioning statement may be distributed widely within the firm and even shared with the firm's partners (i.e., advertising agency and retailers). Although the positioning may be written in consumer-friendly language, consumers are not expected to read the positioning statement. Rather, the consumer will see the end results of this positioning statement—the brand design, pricing, communications, and channels of distribution.

Formats and terminology for presenting a brand's position vary by company, but certain components are generally viewed as critical:

1. A brief description of the *targeted consumers* in terms of some identifying characteristics, such as demographics and psychographics (activities, interests, opinions). These target characteristics are typically selected on the basis of category and brand usage.
2. A statement of the target's goal that will be served by consuming the brand, commonly referred to as the *frame of reference*. The frame of reference may guide the choice of targets, identify situations in which the brand might be used, and define relevant competitors (i.e., brands that claim to serve the same goal).
3. An assertion regarding why the brand is superior to alternatives in the frame of reference, referred to as the *point of difference*.
4. Supporting evidence for claims related to the frame of reference and point of difference, referred to as *reasons to believe*. This final element is

more important when the claims are relatively abstract (credence claims) versus concrete (verifiable) because concrete claims often are their own reason to believe.

These items may be represented in a formal positioning statement. To illustrate, consider the following positioning statement for Black & Decker's De-Walt line of power tools:

> To the tradesman who uses his power tools to make a living and cannot afford downtime on the job (*target*), DeWalt professional power tools (*frame of reference*) are more dependable than other brands of professional power tools (*point of difference*) because they are engineered to the brand's historic high-quality standards and are backed by Black & Decker's extensive service network and guarantee to repair or replace any tool within 48 hours (*reasons to believe*).

The above positioning targets the tradesman and focuses on his goal of generating a reliable income by practicing his trade. DeWalt promises to help the tradesman achieve this goal more effectively than other brands of power tools by being more dependable. The essence of this positioning was captured in communications to the tradesman that promised "No downtime with DeWalt."

If Black & Decker had instead wished to target the Do-It-Yourselfer (DIY), a different frame of reference and point of difference would have been necessary. Here, the goal might be to complete home repair projects in a professional manner, and DeWalt might claim superiority to other power tools in achieving that goal by noting that its tools are the tools of choice by the professional tradesman. This alternative approach is illustrated below.

> To the Do-It-Yourselfer who takes pride in achieving a professional result when doing home improvement projects, DeWalt power tools are superior to other power tools in helping you create a high-quality finish because they are engineered for and chosen by tradesmen, who depend on their tools to make a living.

Occasionally, a brand is positioned to more than one target. Indeed, a common growth strategy is to seek additional targets when demand within the initial target becomes saturated. For example, once DeWalt strongly established the brand among tradesmen, Black & Decker might attempt to grow the brand by targeting DIYs with the positioning just described.

However, adopting such growth strategies requires caution. Although DIYs may wish to identify with professional tradesmen, the reverse is unlikely to be true. Thus, when attempting to reach multiple targets, it is important to consider whether one target will be aware of the other target's consumption of the brand and, if so, how feelings about the brand will be affected.

In fact, the introduction of the DeWalt line of professional power tools was motivated by the need to manage the perception of two targets for products marketed under the Black & Decker brand. The tradesman was the target for Black & Decker branded Professional Power Tools, and consumers were the target for a less rugged line of Black & Decker branded power tools, as well as small appliances (i.e., Black & Decker popcorn poppers, waffle irons, and Dustbuster). As consumers' acceptance of Black & Decker branded products grew, tradesmen's acceptance of the brand declined. Apparently, tradesmen preferred power tool brands (such as Makita and Milwaukee) that were not in their customers' tool boxes or their wives' kitchens. Black & Decker only regained its dominant position with tradesmen when it launched a separate (DeWalt) brand targeted solely at tradesmen.

FRAME OF REFERENCE

When developing a brand position, the frame of reference can be represented in many ways. These frames of reference fall into two general categories: frames that are depicted in terms of product features and frames that are represented by more abstract consumers' goals.

Frame of Reference Based on Product Features

A brand can establish a frame of reference by claiming membership in a product category. This strategy assumes that the consumer will understand (infer) that the brand serves the goal that is associated with the product category. Thus, DeWalt might use the professional, portable power tools category as a frame of reference, implying that DeWalt competes with other power tool brands offering professional quality performance. Coca-Cola uses soft drinks as a frame of reference, conveying that it is a beverage that tastes good with casual meals. And Subway uses fast-food restaurants as a frame of reference, signaling that it offers quick, tasty meals to be eaten on the go.

Another means of conveying a brand's frame of reference is to single out a specific competitor that has features exemplifying the goal a brand wishes to achieve. DeWalt might compare itself to Makita, and Subway might compare itself to McDonald's. A specific competitor may be chosen as the frame of reference when consumers view that competitor as the gold standard for the category goal or benefit. For example, at the time that DeWalt was launched, Makita was widely seen as *the* tradesman's power tool brand. Thus, comparing DeWalt to Makita would have been an efficient, concrete way for DeWalt to convey that it too offered professional quality performance.

Choosing category membership or a specific competitor as the frame of reference implies that the brand competes with firms that share a number of concrete features. Thus, Subway has positioned itself as a fast-food restaurant chain, conveying that it is similar to other fast-food restaurants, such as McDonald's and Burger King. Like its category competitors, Subway provides quick service, numerous, convenient locations, and low prices. The features that are shared by members within a category are referred to as *points of parity*.[1]

Presenting points of parity to customers offers yet another means of representing the frame of reference. This approach is viable when the target customer is well aware of the relationship between a set of features and a specific category but is unfamiliar with the brand itself. For example, highlighting that Subway has the features associated with the fast-food category would help customers infer that Subway is a fast-food restaurant.

Caution is warranted in using points of parity to define the frame of reference. If a brand does not possess attributes associated with a category, obviously it cannot use parity to align itself with that category. For example, when Motorola launched its personal digital assistant, Envoy, the product served the goal of wireless communication that was associated with pagers. However, it would not have been credible for Envoy to claim that it was an enhanced version of a pager because it was too big (the size of a VHS tape) and too expensive (initially $1,500); it did not belong in the pager category, and consumers knew it.

Nevertheless, there are circumstances in which brands use product categories with which they have little feature overlap as the frame of reference because they offer a clear way of highlighting the goal. For example, when Invisalign launched a new approach to straightening teeth, traditional braces served as the frame of reference. Although there is little or no feature similarity between traditional braces and Invisalign, consumers associate traditional braces with the goal of achieving a perfect smile. Invisalign promised to achieve this goal more effectively than metal braces by using clear, molded plastic trays that are invisible during the adjustment process.[2] However, there are risks associated with such an approach. The lack of feature similarity allowed orthodontists who were skeptical about Invisalign to question whether the system would in fact achieve the same goal as traditional braces. (Additional discussion of the frame of reference concept appears in Chapter 15.)

Consumer Goals as the Basis for the Frame of Reference

Although frames of reference are often represented in terms of product features, there are times when it is appropriate to choose a frame of reference based on abstract consumer goals. In the DeWalt power tools example described earlier in the chapter, launching the brand with the professional power tools category as the frame of reference made sense. It clearly categorized the brand and highlighted a point of difference that was meaningful to the tradesman—"no downtime" on the job. However, once the brand was established in the professional power tools category, a more abstract frame of reference related to the emotional goals of tradesmen might have been employed. Tradesmen (like most people) seek the acceptance and regard of their peers. This goal-based frame might be communicated by placing the power tools in the context of a job site and showing a group of tradesmen asking advice from the alpha male on the site, who is using DeWalt tools. Here, DeWalt tools would help tradesmen achieve the goal of fitting in. Having the "right" tools would help to achieve this goal, just as would driving the right truck, or hanging out at the right bar.[3]

A consumer goal–based frame of reference may also be helpful in planning the marketing strategy because it typically identifies potential competitors beyond those in the category where the brand holds membership. For example, the frame of reference for Coca-Cola might be soft drinks. However, the goals associated with the soft drink category—being refreshed or sociable—also may be met by non–soft drink competitors such as bottled waters or sports drinks. Focusing on consumers' goals in selecting the frame of reference might help Coca-Cola to assess the threat to the soft drink posed by these competitors, and if it is substantial, to select points of difference that address this threat.

When launching a truly new product, it is often tempting to employ an abstract frame of reference because the product is likely to lack the points of parity necessary to claim membership in an established product category. As noted earlier, Motorola's Envoy served the goal of wireless communication, but it lacked sufficient points of parity to claim membership in the pager (or any other established) category. Thus, an abstract frame of reference of staying in touch while on the go was employed. Envoy failed, in part, because consumers did not understand Envoy's role in relation to the many other products they might use to stay in touch when on the go (e.g., pagers, cell phones, and e-mail).

TiVo followed a strategy similar to that of Envoy and had similar difficulty gaining customers. TiVo was positioned as serving the abstract goal of viewer freedom and was not associated with a specific product category. Ads depicted a person engaging in self-expressive acts such as removing parking meters and driving the wrong way down a one-way street to represent the feeling of freedom that comes from owning TiVo. Although TiVo did enhance personal freedom, the viewer was left to conjure up the TiVo features that would accomplish this goal. The slogan "TiVo, TV your way" indicated that the freedom pertained to television watching, but it was a mystery to consumers just how TiVo accomplished this goal. A more successful strategy might have involved comparing TiVo to a familiar category. For example, TiVo might have been compared to the home video category, which represents the freedom to choose your own movie whenever you like.

Thus, when introducing a new product, a frame of reference based on abstract consumer goals is likely to be inappropriate. Framing the brand concretely using other products and product features is necessary because consumers learn about new brands by relating them to familiar ones. Palm Pilot understood this point. In contrast to Envoy, this personal digital assistant was launched using electronic organizers as a concrete frame of reference. The claim that Palm Pilot was an electronic organizer was credible because Palm Pilot only served the key functions associated with electronic organizers. It was an address book, a date book, and a to-do list. In contrast to Envoy and TiVo, Palm Pilot enjoyed rapid adoption, selling more than one million units in its 18 months on the market.

More generally, whether a frame of reference is based on product features or abstract consumer goals depends on the decisions at hand. When developing a broad strategic plan, the positioning may be discussed in relatively abstract, visionary terms. When executing the plan, the positioning is more likely to be articulated in terms of a specific target, product category, and point of difference. Translating the abstract consumer goal-based positioning into more specific terms assists retailers, who must decide where to shelve the brand. It also provides guidance to consumers, who must locate the brand in order to purchase it. Kraft's 2003 launch of the easy-to-prepare dinner kit FreshPrep illustrates the importance of having a concrete frame of reference when making tactical decisions. Both grocers and consumers were uncertain about whether the product belonged at the meat counter, in the deli case, or in the dairy section, and this confusion was a contributing factor in the product's failure to gain acceptance in the marketplace.

POINT OF DIFFERENCE

The point of difference indicates how the brand is superior to other alternatives within the frame of reference. Like the frame of reference, the point of difference can be expressed at various levels of abstraction. Some brands claim relatively concrete, functional benefits such as superior performance or greater economy. Other brands promise more abstract, emotional benefits related to how important, special, or good the consumer will feel as a result of using the brand. Attribute, image, or attitude information provides a reason for believing the functional or emotional benefit.

Functional Benefits

In many categories, brands can be distinguished by their functional benefits. Gillette has traditionally differentiated its razors from those of its competitors by claiming to provide a closer, more comfortable shave. In contrast, BIC has focused on superior economy in terms of saving time and money. BIC promises a good (enough) shave more conveniently and less expensively than competing brands.

Superiority on functional benefits gains credibility when it is supported by reasons to believe. This support may take the form of tangible product features. In 2005, Gillette's M3Power was the only wet shaver that had battery-powered vibration to stimulate hair, which lent credence to the claim that it provided a closer, more comfortable shave than Schick's Quattro. In our earlier DeWalt example, the brand's extensive service network and the promise to replace any tool that could not be repaired in 48 hours made the claim of "no downtime with DeWalt" believable. Likewise, with fast-food chain Subway, nutrition information posted in stores and printed on napkins provided a reason to believe Subway's assertion that it offered healthier fast food than its competitors. And at Wal-Mart, out-of-the-way locations and a no-frills atmosphere reinforced the retailer's differentiation on the basis of low prices.

The product attributes presented as reasons to believe a functional benefit are not always technically relevant.[4] Alberto-Culver added real silk to its Silkience shampoo to reinforce the claim that the shampoo left hair silkier than other shampoos. Although adding silk to the shampoo was irrelevant to how silky it left hair, it reinforced the association between silkiness and the shampoo in consumers' minds. Similarly, Folgers supported its claim of superior taste by noting that its coffee beans were mountain grown. The claim was accurate but largely irrelevant to the functional benefit, because most coffee is mountain grown.

Superiority claims also can be supported by the brand image, which is represented by who uses the brand and when it is used. For example, a person with expertise in a product category may support a claim of superior performance. When golf champion Tiger Woods endorsed Nike, he was providing a compelling reason to believe that Nike offered superior gear for golfers. An endorsement by someone known for being tight with a dollar (comedians Jack Benny and Minnie Pearl had this reputation) would lend support to a claim involving superior economy. Similarly, associating a brand with use on occasions of special significance (i.e., a wine being consumed at a wedding in a Paul Masson ad) may support claims of superior performance, whereas associating a brand with use on occasions when cost is likely to be an issue (i.e., the need to feed a band of teenage boys, as depicted in a Wal-Mart ad) may support claims of superior economy.

Emotional Benefits

Differentiating a brand in terms of functional benefits is attractive because such benefits are relatively concrete and, thus, can be communicated to consumers and trade partners simply and clearly. However, functional benefits are typically linked to more abstract benefits that provide a basis for making an *emotional connection* with the brand. For example, McDonald's promoted its cleanliness and good-tasting food as a basis for implying that eating at McDonald's was fun.

Emotional resonance sometimes emerges independent of an underlying functional benefit. Himalaya perfume claimed to make women feel refreshed and enticing. Emotional benefits shift the emphasis from the brand and its functions to the user and the feelings to be gained by using the brand. These benefits are related to enduring, basic human needs and desires.

Some brands promise emotional benefits that revolve around self-presentation and a person's relationship with others. Motorcycle manufacturer Harley-Davidson promises its customers that they will be seen as strong, rebellious, and independent and will enjoy membership in a club of like-minded others (i.e., the Harley Owners Group (HOG)). Abercrombie promises peer acceptance to its teen market because the company has historically offered hip or trendy clothing styles. The Tiffany blue box that arrives on Valentine's Day is a powerful message that is likely to evoke an affectionate response from the recipient. Brands that promote this type of emotional benefit are sometimes referred to as image or "badge" brands, reflecting their role in communicating with others.

Other brands claim to offer emotional benefits that are more internally focused. These benefits may be related to consumers' desire for self-expression, personal growth and achievement, and self-determination. Starbucks makes a great cup of coffee, but the brand has been built on much more than the functional benefits that it delivers. Starbucks' regulars have traditionally ordered their cup of java in highly personalized ways ("one Venti, decaf, skim cappuccino, dry") and enjoy their drinks in comfy chairs with smooth jazz in the background. A trip to Starbucks promises self-expression and self-indulgence in an otherwise unfulfilling day.

Like functional benefits, emotional benefits are often grounded in product attributes or the image that is represented by the people and occasions of use. The unique, powerful (and trademarked!) sound of a Harley motorcycle conveys rebelliousness, and Starbucks' background music and upholstered couches signal self-indulgence.

In addition, some brands rely on depicting the feeling experienced by brand users as a means of supporting their point of difference. Apple's iPod is positioned as a carefree, fun-loving brand. This positioning is supported by its bright colors, easy downloading, and wearable styling. However, the most compelling support for the point of difference may be the attitude of iPod users, which is depicted in the dancing silhouettes in the company's ads—these folks are obviously having a blast grooving to their music! The Gap has embraced a similar carefree, casual chic positioning in the clothing category. Not surprisingly, it too has supplemented information about product features (i.e., bright colors and relaxed fit) with communications that represent the attitude of the clothing wearer. Ads have included khaki wearers dancing to popular tunes and fashion maven Sarah Jessica Parker playfully accessorizing her Gap gear.

SUSTAINING A POSITION OVER TIME

Once a brand position is well established, focus centers on sustaining the position. In a few instances, a brand's frame of reference and point of difference can be sustained without change. Along these lines, Marlboro has not altered its cigarette positioning since the mid-1950s. The position is empowerment, which is supported by masculine imagery such as cowboys and race cars. For many years, Charmin's has positioned its brand of toilet tissue as squeezably soft. In these cases, a critical motivation for using the brand and the context in which it is used have not changed, and thus it has not been necessary for the brand to change in order to maintain its relevance.

In most cases, however, some modification of the position is needed to sustain a brand over time. Two classes of strategies can be used to enhance a

brand's position. The first is fortifying the brand position, which entails maintaining the same brand and position but embellishing the positioning. The
second approach involves leveraging, where a positioning is used to extend
the brand equity to new products.[5]

Fortifying Strategies

Two strategies may be employed to fortify a brand. One approach is to mod-
ernize the way in which the brand is presented to the consumer. An alternative approach is to represent the positioning in a more or less abstract manner
than previously, using a technique called "laddering."

Modern Instantiation   Once a brand has a well-established point of difference, it is difficult to change. Dash was a superior detergent that was positioned as performing well in front-loading washing machines because of its
low level of suds. When front-loaders declined in popularity, so did the demand for Dash. An effort was made to reposition the brand by featuring other
attributes such as its deodorizing capability. But years of positioning Dash as a
low-suds detergent could not be overcome. Reebok was initially positioned
as a women's athletic shoe. This positioning was supported by offering comfort as the point of difference—the shoes were manufactured using soft garment leather. Despite extensive marketing efforts over the past 20 years to
change that image by using male celebrities and depicting athletic male pur-
suits, Reebok's persona has remained feminine, and today the brand is still
considered a women's shoe.

If an established brand cannot readily change its position to accommodate
changing consumer tastes and competition, it needs to sustain the relevance
of its already-established position. In most instances, this is achieved by identifying modern ways to represent the brand. For example, Special K historically positioned itself as the ready-to-eat cereal that offered a healthy way of
keeping fit. For many years, fitness was defined in terms of being slender.
However, in the face of growing displeasure with the objectification of
women, a modern representation of fitness was needed. Special K sustained
the fit-functional benefit by redefining it as athletic and active rather than
thin. Supermodel Cindy Crawford served as the spokesperson to personify
the fit benefit. In effect, Special K's benefit was not changed. But it received a
contemporary depiction in order to sustain the brand's franchise.

In some instances a contemporary representation requires adjustments
beyond changing the spokesperson and the advertising. It also requires
changes in other elements of the marketing mix. For many years, per capita

consumption of milk had declined in the United States and many other parts of the world. Efforts were made to reverse this trend through advertising. In a national print campaign during the mid-1990s, celebrities were shown with a milk mustache endorsing the nutritional value of milk. And at about the same time in California, a television campaign was aired that illustrated the consequences of running out of milk. The "Got milk?" slogan became so popular in California that it was used to promote milk in other countries. By the late 1990s, the campaigns were merged and featured celebrities with a milk mustache asking, "Got milk?"

As creative as these campaigns were, they weren't ultimately successful in reversing the per capita decline in milk consumption. People already knew that milk was nutritious. They were avoiding milk because it contained fat, and low-fat diets had become immensely popular. Thus, a contemporary representation of nutrition required consumers to understand that milk could be nutritious, taste good, *and* be low-fat. Developing a contemporary package was a first step in developing a modern version of a healthful beverage. When the category finally provided a low-fat, vitamin-enriched milk that tasted good, the decline in consumption began to slow by 2003.

Laddering   Pantene shampoo was a minor brand in the early 1990s when it was acquired by Procter & Gamble. Pantene's ingredient, ProV, served as a basis for claiming that the brand would offer shiny hair, which implied that it would ensure healthy hair. Within several years, this positioning propelled Pantene to the leading share brand in the category.

The Pantene strategy illustrates the effective use of another fortifying strategy called laddering. One way to ladder is to give multiple reasons to believe a brand's functional benefits. Pantene's position as providing the healthiest hair was supported not only by its ProV ingredient, but also by the fact that it had different shampoos to make hair softer or feel thicker. Thus, *laddering down* can serve as a means of sustaining a brand's position by presenting additional reasons to believe the brand's functional benefit.

Pantene not only laddered down by supporting its shiny hair benefit in terms of the Pro-V and other reasons to believe, but it also used shiny hair to imply a more abstract emotional benefit, healthy hair. In turn, healthy hair might be used to imply a feeling of self-confidence among Pantene users. Thus, a ladder is established with tangible features at the bottom that offer a reason to believe the functional benefit, which indicates what the brand does for the consumer. In turn, the functional benefit provides a basis for inferring emotional benefits, which describe how the functional benefit makes the consumer feel. Laddering up from a tangible feature to a functional benefit to an emotional benefit provides a means of sustaining a brand's position.

In summary, laddering up entails the transformation of the marketing effort from focusing on the brand to focusing on the customer. At the lowest level of the ladder, attribute information is used to depict the unique features of the brand. At the highest level of the ladder, the focus is on the person rather than the brand. Emphasis is given to how the target customer feels as a result of using the brand. In so doing, a brand may distinguish itself from competitors even if other brands eventually achieve attribute parity.

However, laddering does not imply that the goal is necessarily to sustain a brand position by moving to the top of the ladder. For some products, most consumers are unlikely to develop a deep emotional attachment to the brand. For example, lightbulbs are perceived as functional by many segments of the population. Brand positioning to such a target entails specifying a functional benefit (convenience due to long bulb life) and perhaps sustaining the brand position by presenting multiple reasons to believe the benefit (Philips Halogena offered a two-year guarantee) or by developing a modern instantiation of the benefit's application (Philips ran advertisements showing their lightbulbs outlasting a young man's four years at college). In other instances, only the emotional benefit might be appropriate to present. For example, image products such as luxury goods and fragrances are not marketed on the basis of tangible features or functional benefits, but rather on the emotional benefits that resonate with consumers, such as feeling empowered or unique. (Further discussion of laddering for business to business brands appears in Chapter 9.)

Leveraging Strategies

Whereas fortifying strategies involve bolstering a current brand's position, leveraging strategies entail using some aspect of the brand's positioning as the basis for launching new products. These new products may broaden the brand's frame of reference or demonstrate the relevance of the brand's point of difference in a new category.

Broadening the Frame of Reference   Oreo is a cookie sandwich made with two chocolate cookies and a vanilla creme filling. Its frame of reference has traditionally been that of a special treat (see Chapter 15). To increase the demand for the brand, Oreo was extended to a larger snack position. This entailed producing mini Oreos that were sold in a snack pack. Not only were these cookies distributed in the grocery aisle of the supermarket, but the new mini Oreos package was also frequently available at checkout, which is consistent with a snack offering. And like other snack products, the line was extended so that it came with dark filling and creme cookies as well as many other flavors. The result was a substantial increase in Oreo sales. Thus, extensions of the Oreo brand expanded its frame of reference from special occasions to more frequent snacking.

When broadening the frame of reference, it is important not to undermine customers' initial motivation for buying the brand. For example, a diet aid was positioned as a lunch substitute (eat two diet wafers in lieu of lunch). In an effort to increase demand, the brand was also marketed as a snack. This confused users about the product's appropriate usage. If it was a snack, then surely it wasn't adequate as a meal substitute. The result was reduced lunch consumption. In the case of Oreo, Kraft is presumably willing to compromise the "special treat" aspect of Oreo in order to generate more frequent consumption through everyday snacking.

Leveraging the Point of Difference in New Categories   Dove is a bar soap that has traditionally dominated its category. Its point of difference is superior moisturizing in a cleansing context. Dove leveraged this equity by launching Dove brand shampoos and conditioners, which extended the moisturizing point of difference into other cleansing categories. A line of deodorants was also launched. This extension had the advantage of a strong point of difference from other deodorants, which did not feature the moisturizing point of difference. Here the challenge was to demonstrate the relevance of moisturizing for the category. Consumers were assured that Dove deodorant was effective in keeping users dry and was better than other brands in limiting razor burn. (Further discussion of how brands can be extended to new categories appears in Chapter 5.)

CHANGING A POSITION

It is difficult to change the position of a well-established brand. Most efforts to reposition a long-lived brand fail. However, when a brand is entering a new category, change is necessary as competitors arrive on the scene. For example, when Miller introduced the first light beer, the frame of reference was regular beer, and the point of difference was that light beer was less filling than regular beer. When Bud Light entered the category about a decade later, there were now two brands making the claim of less filling. As a result, the "less filling" benefit now was a point of parity that served as the frame of reference for what had become known as the light beer category. In effect, Bud Light's entry into the category turned Miller Lite's point of difference into a point of parity in the new light beer category. We refer to this repositioning as *reframing* because it is the frame of reference that requires change.

The decline in Miller Lite's sales can be traced in part to its failure to reframe. Lite continued to be represented as less filling. Focusing on this parity claim provided Budweiser with the opportunity to distinguish itself from Lite by claiming that Bud Light was the superior-tasting light beer and using the Budweiser heritage as the reason to believe that benefit.

SUMMARY

Brand positioning plays a key role in the building and managing of a strong brand by specifying how the brand is related to consumers' goals. It can be thought of as answering three questions: (1) Who should be targeted for brand use? (2) What goal does the brand allow the target to achieve? and (3) Why should the brand be chosen over other brands that achieve the same goal?

The frame of reference is an important and often overlooked element of a brand's position. Viewing the frame of reference as the goal that a brand promises to achieve allows a company to consider competition and growth opportunities outside the brand's own category. The frame of reference also offers guidance about the points of difference that are likely to be meaningful in goal achievement. Once a frame is established in customers' minds, it is difficult to change. However, reframing is necessary when a pioneer brand is faced with a viable second entrant into a category.

A brand's point of difference indicates why it is a superior means of achieving a goal. Points of difference may take the form of functional or emotional benefits. These types of benefits might be closely related in that the implication of a functional benefit (easy to use) serves as the basis for an emotional benefit (free time to explore a passion). Points of difference gain credibility by presenting reasons to believe their veracity. This entails presenting tangible evidence for the benefit, which can take the form of brand attributes, people who use the brand, or the contexts in which a brand is produced or used.

A sustained position provides a barrier to competitive entry. A position may be sustained by fortification of the brand through the development of a modern instantiation of the brand's position or by laddering from more functional to more emotional benefits. Alternatively, leveraging may be used to sustain a brand. This entails a disciplined broadening of the position or the development of extensions that share the brand's position. (For a more detailed discussion of brand extensions, see Chapter 5.)

Perhaps the most important contribution of a sound brand positioning is to offer guidelines for the execution of marketing strategy. Hallmark's greeting cards focus on superior quality in communicating sentiments. The "superior quality" point of difference guides the choice of materials (quality paper and verse), price (high), distribution (Gold Crown stores), advertising (carefully crafted two-minute emotional ads), and media (quality family programming). The "communicating sentiments" frame of reference provides a direction for growth that is based on the brand's heritage. It suggests that in addition to greeting cards, other vehicles for communicating sentiments should be offered, including flowers, candies, and stuffed animals. Thus, effective positioning not only charts the strategy a brand pursues, but directs the choices among alternative ways to execute the strategy.

Alice M. Tybout is Harold T. Martin Professor of Marketing and chairperson of the Marketing Department at the Kellogg School of Management. She is also co-director of the Kellogg on Branding Program and director of the Consumer Marketing Strategy Programs at the James L. Allen Center. She received her BS and MA from The Ohio State University and her Ph.D. from Northwestern University.

Brian Sternthal is the Kraft Professor of Marketing and a past chairperson of the Marketing Department at the Kellogg School of Management. He received his BS from McGill University and his Ph.D. from The Ohio State University.

NOTES

1. Keller, Kevin Lane, Brian Sternthal, and Alice M. Tybout (2002), "Three Questions You Need to Ask About Your Brand," *Harvard Business Review* (September), 80–89.

2. Coughlan, Anne T., Julie Hennessy, and Andrei Najjar (2004), "Invisalign: Orthodontic Unwired," Northwestern University Case #5-104-008.

3. Tybout, Alice M. and Brian Sternthal (2001), "Brand Positioning," in Dawn Iacobucci (ed.), *Kellogg on Marketing*, New York: John Wiley & Sons, pp. 31–57.

4. Carpenter, Gregory S., Rashi Glazer, and Kent Nakamoto (1994), "Meaningful Brands from Meaningless Differentiation: The Dependence on Irrelevant Attributes," *Journal of Marketing Research*, 31 (August), 339–350.

5. Keller, Kevin Lane (2003), *Building, Measuring, and Managing Brand Equity*, Upper Saddle River, NJ: Prentice Hall.

CHAPTER 2

DESIGNING BRANDS

BOBBY J. CALDER

The psychology of consumer perception is fundamental to creating strong brands. It should be the basis for *designing brands*. To design a brand, marketers must make a number of critical decisions regarding the use of names, colors, symbols, and the like to help consumers perceive a product in a way that is consistent with the intentions of the brand. Often this process is referred to as packaging, but this term does not do justice to its marketing importance. It is better to think of this activity as *designing the brand*. It is a key step in transforming a brand's internal marketing description into something tangible that consumers can relate to. To illustrate this process, it will be helpful to begin by defining the word *brand* in psychological terms, helping us understand why the psychology of perception is fundamental to creating strong brands.

BRANDS AS CONCEPTS

Suppose that a friend at a party suggests you try a new dip for chips and crackers. You like it. It's light and creamy, with a satisfying rich taste. Later you see an ad reinforcing the richness and dairy heritage of the product. Through these combined experiences with this product, you've just formed a *concept*.

Consumers experience a brand or a product as a concept, which is a set of properties and associations that give that product a specific meaning. In our example above, the concept of the new chip dip is that it is light and associated with dairy richness. A concept is the way in which we differentiate a certain item among all the things we experience. In psychological terms, a chair is not a chair—a chair is a concept that we apply to a piece of wood or plastic based on its fit with the properties and associations that make up our idea of what a

27

chair should be. Your kitchen chair probably fits this concept very well. Conversely, a tree stump on a camping trip might not fit your concept of a chair quite as well, but out of necessity it serves the purpose. As humans, if we did not think in terms of concepts, everything we encountered would need to be thought of anew each time we experienced it. Our minds would be quickly overloaded, and we would go crazy merely finding a place to sit.

As marketers we want our product to be meaningful and different from other things. In the language of psychology, we want consumers to have a well-developed and positive concept of the product. The word marketers give to this process is *brand*. But if you ask what a brand is, the answer is most often long (sometimes book-length!), and it usually varies greatly across companies, consultants, and different writers. Some define the word *brand* as a *positioning* that relates the product to a particular category of products while differentiating it from other products in that category. Others define a brand as a *promise* by the company to consumers about what the product will do for them. Others refer to the abstract personal and emotional *essence* of the brand. Still others point to a brand as the *value* the brand provides relative to its cost. All of these definitions can be useful ways of describing a given brand, but they are not very good answers to the question of what a brand actually is.

Fundamentally, a brand is a concept. Consumers form concepts of products just as they do with anything else they experience. But with products, marketers attempt to influence the properties and associations that go into a consumer's concept of a given product. For this reason, I find it useful to refer to *brand concepts* as a way of reinforcing the nature of brands. Positioning, promise, essence, and the like are best thought of as formats for describing brand concepts.

Defining a brand as a concept helps us understand a critical aspect of branding that deals with perceptions. Consumers are constantly forming and using concepts. The consumer is actively trying to categorize products. Crucial to this categorization is the psychological process of perception. And an understanding of perception is critical for designing brands. It is through the process of brand design that the marketer can influence perceptions that result in one concept versus another. To return to our party dip, the use of the color white could lead the consumer to have a concept of the product as associated with dairy richness.

PERCEPTION

We have established that brands are concepts resulting from the categorization of products. Whenever we encounter a product, we attempt to categorize it as a concept, which we do by using the cues that accompany the product or its uses. This is the psychological process of perception—the immediate use of cues to form and recognize concepts.

For example, let's say that you are driving down the street and hear a loud noise in the distance. You see blinking lights. Then a large object becomes apparent. It is red. Using these audio and visual cues, you immediately perceive the large object to be a fire truck. In most cases the object would in fact turn out to be a fire truck (and not a blinking red sign in front of a car dealership). Perception is the immediate use of cues to form and recognize concepts (where misperception is also a possibility).

Perception occurs very quickly, and ordinarily it is automatic (it happens outside of our conscious awareness). In the example above, you don't consciously think about the noise and the lights—the concept of fire truck just takes shape in your mind from the preconscious perceptions. The cues that are present cause you to categorize. Size implies something bigger than a car. Blinking lights and the color red imply something dangerous. The cues lead the categorization process toward fire truck. If you did not know what a fire truck was, the cues would help you to acquire the concept.

Look at the cube in Figure 2.1. It is a simple line diagram. Stare at it. Don't let your eyes move until you see something. When you see it you will be aware that perception is taking place. The cues in this figure are ambiguous as to the orientation of the cube. Yet we want to categorize the cube as having an orientation. Since two orientations fit equally well, perception is interrupted and we become aware of our mind attempting to categorize the cube. Normally we are not aware of forming perceptions. Perception uses cues, immediately and without our awareness, to begin to form and recognize concepts.

What does perception mean for branding? It means that brands, as concepts, depend heavily on cues that surround the product. These cues can

Figure 2.1
Experiencing Perception

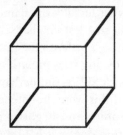

dramatically affect how a product is categorized. If we see that the party dip is in a fire-engine red container, we perceive it in a certain way. The color cue leads us to categorize the dip as dangerous, probably something hot. If this is what the marketer intended, the cue helps in leading the consumer to the right concept. If not, marketing has made it more difficult to convey the intended brand concept through advertising and other consumer contacts. Eventually consumers *could* form the concept that the dip is a rich dairy product, but the use of red in the brand design does not facilitate this categorization.

Marketers need to consider carefully how perception will affect the categorization process of a product. Perception dramatically impacts how easy it is for consumers to get the intended brand concept. This means that the sensory cues surrounding a brand should be designed to lead to desired perceptual categories. This in no way obviates the need for good design in a traditional graphic arts or industrial design sense, but design objectives should also focus on design elements as cues that lead to perceptual categories.

CUES AND PERCEPTUAL CATEGORIES

The implication is that any marketing description of a brand objective should be accompanied by a specific set of desired perceptual categories. These categories should facilitate perception of the brand concept. The marketer should then focus on how cues can be designed into the product to lead consumers to perceive it in terms of these categories.

Naming is one such cue, and we will focus on it here to illustrate the approach. All marketers realize that naming is important. There is even a small industry devoted to helping companies name products. Certainly design firms pay considerable attention to product names. All too often, however, names are not fully appreciated as cues that affect product categorization. Consider the name of a car that received a great deal of attention in this regard when it was introduced—the Porsche *Cayenne*. It is a short name, perhaps memorable. It holds up across languages. But how does it function as a perceptual cue? What perceptual categories does it entail? In this regard the name seems limited. Somewhat literally the name suggests hot and spicy, but not much else. Now consider that Porsche has selected this name for its SUV product. No doubt the main reason Porsche entered the SUV category was to take advantage of the increasing sales growth of the category. The Porsche brand is not an obvious fit with SUVs. But perhaps there is room for the concept of a *really* sporty SUV. If this were the intended brand concept, then the car's name should help consumers to categorize it as such. *Cayenne* says "hot and spicy," but this connotation does not help much with the intended concept, and in fact, it may induce a negative reaction in that it may detract from "high performance." Instead, the name should convey authenticity, speed, and flare. According to Alex Frankel (2004; see note 1), Porsche used the name *Sportility* in development as disinformation for competitors. Though obviously prosaic, this name might well have more perceptual impact against authenticity and speed than *Cayenne*. The *Porsche Sportility* conveys a really sporty SUV better than *Porsche Cayenne*.

Frankel, in his interesting book on product naming, provides an example of one name that was wonderfully thought out in terms of its value as a perceptual cue, the *BlackBerry*. In development, the team at Research in Motion called the product the *PocketLink*, and described the brand concept along these lines:

> For businesspeople on the go, *PocketLink* is a portable communication device for sending and receiving e-mail anywhere that has a quick and responsive personality that ensures interactive accessibility.

In describing the brand, the team at Research in Motion was also very clear about the perceptual categories that the name should convey. The objective was a name that would imply categories like:

Connected
Fast
Friendly
Fun
Approachable
Vital

The name *PocketLink* implied *connected* but did not cue the other desired perceptual categories.

A team from the naming firm Lexicon developed a number of names to try to improve on *PocketLink*. These included: *AirWire, Badge, Banter, Combio, ComTop, eBox, GamePlan, Geode, Hula, LiveRide, Mica, Nemo, Photon, Reon, Slide, Sling, Tailwind, Tecton, TelTop, Transite, Veon, Verb, Waterfall, Wheels, WorldTop*.[1] The name *BlackBerry* was chosen over these because it was judged to do a better job against the perceptual categories. *BlackBerry* implies something live, growing on a vine, and therefore connected and vital. As a fruit, a blackberry is friendly and approachable, not intimidating at all, and as a small, more unusual fruit, it is fun. Plus as a small fruit it is fast as well as easy to use. Even the sound of the name helps. *BlackBerry* is pronounced fast, and the alliteration of the *b*'s shortens the word. (All this probably assumes that most consumers do not actually pick blackberries, which are full of thorny weeds.)

Not only did the name help consumers form the intended brand concept, but it continued to reinforce that concept once the brand became successful. But other cues apart from naming were important as well. Both the color and the shape of the *BlackBerry* helped to convey the intended perceptual categories. *BlackBerry* became synonymous with being addicted to staying in touch through quick message bites.

Now that we understand the psychology of perception and its role in brand design, let us now consider a complete case of successful brand design, one that uses a variety of perceptual cues to influence the consumer's brand concept of the product.

DESIGNING A BRAND

Brand design is a step between the articulation of the brand concept and the creation of advertising and other contacts with the consumer. Ideally it should employ a wide array of cues. It is easiest to see this by looking at one particular brand.

The *Philadelphia* brand of cream cheese has been a successful product for almost 100 years. Over the years, the intended brand concept has been refined so that the essence of the brand can be stated very succinctly.

Philadelphia is a touch of heaven every day.

Advertising in the mid-2000s showed consumers as angels enjoying *Philadelphia* as a heavenly treat. The usage of the product was ordinary, but the result was transformative—a special moment of active enjoyment.

A number of cues surrounded the *Philadelphia* brand in order to affect relevant perceptual categories. The categories included:

Rich
Creamy
Authentic
Special reward
Accessible every day
Creative

The name *Philadelphia* is a legacy name that dates back to the origin of the brand. It might seem to be useful only because of its familiarity. Otherwise, it is a long name with no obvious connection to cream cheese. But from the point of view of the above perceptual categories, there is more to the name than its longevity. As a place name, Philadelphia suggests accessibility. It is a place you can get to. Philadelphia also connotes authenticity. It is a real place, and a city with an important historical heritage. While it might not be the best name for a new product, it is a strong name against the categories of authenticity and accessibility.

The name, moreover, can be rendered in a typography that makes it even more authentic-looking. As shown in Figure 2.2, when *Philadelphia* is done in plain, all-capital, bold letters, it suggests authenticity and accessibility even more strongly. The bold letters particularly suggest that the product needs no artifice—you recognize the name; you have come to the source.

Other cues were used in designing the *Philadelphia* brand. One is the name used for the *product* category. The name of the generic category provides an additional cue for perception. The product category name used for the basic brick version of *Philadelphia* is *cream cheese*, thereby reinforcing authenticity and creamy. The category name for the tub unit is *cream cheese spread*, implying

Figure 2.2
Philadelphia Brand Design

that this version is more accessible (though at some cost to authenticity). The category name is much bolder on the brick version than the spread, cueing more authenticity (or a special reward) for the brick version.

Corporate identity functions as a perceptual cue as well. Identity names the source of a product. *Philadelphia* is identified as a Kraft product. Since Kraft has historically connoted cheese, this contributes to authenticity.

It is useful to think of all the words that routinely surround a product as forming a *verbal lexicon* of brand cues. One word that appears prominently with the brick version of *Philadelphia* is *Original*. Such words might seem inconsequential, but they are more important than they seem as perceptual cues. *Original* connotes authenticity. And authenticity along with accessibility is accentuated by using more of a script rendering of the word *Original*. Contrast this with the word *Regular* that appears on the basic tub version—by using the word *Regular* on the tub version, *Philadelphia* incurs some cost to authenticity. Other brand lexicon words that routinely appear with *Philadelphia* are *Dairy* and *Rich, creamy taste*. These words bolster the desired perceptual categories.

Beyond verbal cues, visual cues should be given equal attention in designing brands. *Illustrations* are especially effective in this regard. Illustrations can be thought of as realistic or fanciful pictures that imply perceptual categories. For example, consider a picture of a cloud. What perceptions would a cloud imply if we used it in designing a brand? Softness, to be sure. But also natural and authentic. Clouds also suggest rising above the everyday—something special, more creative. Accordingly, a cloud illustration seems just the right visual cue for the *Philadelphia* brand. The only danger is that it might seem too aspirational. This is mitigated in the *Philadelphia* design by perspective: The cloud is at the bottom of the container, implying that *Philadelphia* easily rises above the clouds. The picture looks like clouds viewed from above in an airplane.

Visual symbols can be used in the same way as illustration in designing brands. They have the advantage of being more flexible and less literal to work with. It is often more difficult, however, to relate symbolic visualizations to perceptual categories. As in art, symbolism is often more powerful than realistic depiction, but it can be more difficult to understand. The *Philadelphia* brand uses a powerful symbol, the oval. The oval is used to frame the brand name. It is a classical shape that connotes authenticity. As used, it has a badge-like quality that implies the desired special-reward perceptual category. Yet it is done simply, even plainly, so that everyday accessibility is preserved.

Color itself is another important visual cue. Color triggers categories above and beyond the use of illustration and symbols. The background color for *Philadelphia* is silver. Silver indicates richness and special reward. Yet silver is not the ultimate, gold level, so that a measure of accessibility is preserved. Silver furthermore sparkles and shines, indicating creativity. An important consideration for the *Philadelphia* brand design was to make sure that the silver background is not overly dominating. A design that sparkled too much could inhibit the perception of everyday accessibility.

The foreground color in the *Philadelphia* design is white. The cloud illustration is white, and the oval framing the name is white. This strongly suggests creaminess and richness. And the white against the silver background cues a special treat. Blue completes the color palette of the brand and complements the cloud (sky) imagery. It also fits the oval and lends itself to blue-ribbon authenticity.

Finally, the *functional forms* of the different versions of *Philadelphia* are themselves perceptual cues. The brick form emphasizes creaminess and authenticity. The tub versions highlight everyday accessibility. The form itself affects the perceptual categories that enter into the brand concept.

In sum, *Philadelphia* is a good example of designing a brand with specific objectives about perceptual categories in mind. The goal is to get consumers to form and recognize the brand concept by categorizing the product in ways that facilitate the concept. The intended concept is: *Philadelphia* is a touch of heaven every day. The design uses the cues we have discussed: brand name, product category name, corporate identity, verbal lexicon, illustration, visual symbols, color palette, and functional form to affect how the product is perceived. It does so by mapping the impact of the cues on specific perceptual categories—in this case rich, creamy, authentic, special reward, everyday accessibility, and creativity. Getting the consumer to categorize the product in this way, through perception of the cues, goes a long way toward ensuring that the consumer thinks about the product as a touch of heaven every day. (For further discussion of the Philadelphia brand, see Chapter 17.)

EVALUATING BRAND DESIGN

In order to design brands the way we have described, *it is critical that marketers separate brand design from product design*. Ultimately the two will be intertwined in the marketplace, but they must be evaluated separately. With product design, we should be concerned about how the product itself is physically experienced. In the case of cream cheese, we can consider factors such as how creamy the product actually is. This is likely to be measured in terms of product characteristics such as consistency or cohesiveness. Most often, measurement is best accomplished with panels of people who are trained to detect and describe these product characteristics and who experience the product in environments that eliminate perceptual cues. The last thing we would want to do is to provide perceptual cues such as names if we wanted to focus on product design.

On the other hand, if we are concerned with evaluating a brand design, we should try to minimize information about the physical product. It is best to use actual consumers and expose them to the entire design (or alternative designs) or separate individual cues (e.g., the brand name). Since the goal is to evaluate perceptual impact, consumers should be exposed very briefly (a few seconds) to the design. It is important that they react in a perceptual mode—fast and automatically. More considered responses tend to obscure actual perceptual responses. One of the worst methods of brand design evaluation is to give consumers in a focus group (or in other types of open-ended interviews) a design and let them comment on it. Such settings are very likely to stimulate people to think about the design in all kinds of ways (including playing design expert) that obscure the design's real perceptual impact.

The best technique for brand design evaluation is to expose the design briefly and then measure the attention given to various design cues by asking consumers about what they remember seeing—names, colors, and the like. Alternatively, research can track the actual path of eye movements (*eye fixations*) across these cues during exposure (although this requires special equipment). Even more important than measuring what consumers look at, however, is to ask consumers to rate the design, or specific cues, on seven-point scales that reflect the desired perceptual categories. For *Philadelphia*, we would ask consumers to rate how rich, creamy, and authentic they think the product would be. (Note that even if consumers are familiar with the product, their rating would still reflect the recency of seeing the design, as opposed to just their past experience with the product). It is possible in this way to obtain a perceptual profile of a design across all the perceptual categories that are the objectives of the design. The result is both useful evaluative and diagnostic information.

It is necessary to isolate the brand design as described above to evaluate its pure perceptual impact (separate from the experience of the product per se, insofar as this is possible given prior experience). This does not mean that even a good design cannot be undermined by a poor product design. In the marketplace, perception and the experience of the product itself will come together. It may well be that a strong brand design can facilitate a positive brand concept even in the face of a weak product design. It might be possible to cost-reduce the product quality of *Philadelphia* and maintain the brand concept through perception via brand design. It is also possible in doing this to undermine the brand design so that consumers react adversely to misleading perceptions.

BRAND SYSTEMS

Intimately related to the focus here on the design of individual brands is the issue of systems or portfolios of related brands. Brand systems and portfolios must also be considered through the lens of managing perceptions and concepts across categories. The classic case of this is extending brands through flavors and sizes. Companies increasingly count on taking successful brands into new forms, alternatives, and categories. The original brick *Philadelphia* has been taken into a spreadable form and various lower-calorie alternatives. And it has been taken into new categories such as snack bars and salad dressing. David Aaker[2] and others provide ways of thinking strategically about managing such systems of brands. (See Chapter 5, Brand Portfolio Strategy, for more on this topic.)

In thinking about these systems, it is important to keep in mind the basic fact that a brand is always a concept. What permits a brand to become a system or portfolio of products is a brand concept that is broad enough to allow different product versions to be categorized as fitting the concept. And, as with a single product, the perceptual categories implied by the brand design can facilitate this categorization.

The party dip your friend recommended earlier is a *Philadelphia* brand. Is this a smart marketing decision? Yes, the brand concept of a touch of heaven every day is a positive way of categorizing a dip. Applying the brand design to the dip so that it is perceived as *rich, creamy, authentic*, a *special reward, everyday accessible*, and *creative* facilitates the concept. The danger here is that the dip product category name might suggest artificiality, which could compromise Philadelphia's perception of authenticity. But emphasizing the other perceptual categories can probably compensate for this.

Could *Philadelphia* be a line of frozen cheesecakes? The brand concept fits, and brand design would be easy. Could *Philadelphia* be a canned cold beverage? The concept might just be broad enough, and a really good brand design suggesting rich and creamy could go a long way here. But the cold beverage category and the can form would be a problem. So what about a hot beverage? Can you begin to see a brand design?

The fundamental question with brand systems is thus the same as with individual brands. Can we get the consumer to categorize the product in terms of the brand concept? And specifically, does the brand design facilitate this?

CONCLUSION

A brand design is essentially a mechanism for helping consumers categorize a product in terms of a desired marketing concept. In this chapter we have outlined a process for using the design activities that are always associated with a brand to create such a mechanism. The process can be summarized as series of steps.

Step 1. Realize that brands are concepts, and begin with a strong articulation of the brand concept. How do you want the consumer to categorize the product?

Step 2. Identify a small set of perceptual categories that will facilitate the brand concept if they are used by consumers.

Step 3. Consider specific cues in the design process that can affect the perceptual categories. Be sure to include the brand name, product category name, corporate identity, verbal lexicon, illustration, visual symbols, color palette, and functional form.

Step 4. Ideally, evaluate the resulting brand design (or alternative designs) with consumers who are exposed to them briefly and who react by rating the design(s) on the perceptual characteristics.

Step 5. Extend the brand to other products (a brand system) by considering the fit of each product with the brand concept. Give special consideration to the ability of the brand design to support the concept for that product.

This chapter has focused on the process of designing brands and the importance of perception. It recommends an approach that is different from that followed by many companies. Put simply, it is more consumer-focused. Brand design is not just one of the four P's or one type of marketing communication activity. It is an integral part of getting consumers to perceive the brand concept. As Calder and Reagan[3] point out, this contrasts with approaching branding more as an internal planning exercise or as a byproduct of the creation of advertising. Focusing on brand design forces more attention on the consumer.

Bobby J. Calder is the Charles H. Kellstadt Distinguished Professor of Marketing and professor of psychology at the Kellogg School of Management, Northwestern University. He is also a professor of journalism at the Medill School of Journalism. In addition, he serves as director of research for the Media Management Center at

Northwestern University and is co-director of the media MBA program at Kellogg. Previously, he taught at the Wharton School, University of Pennsylvania, and the University of Illinois. He is co-editor of Kellogg on Integrated Marketing *(Wiley).* He received his BA, MA, and Ph.D. degrees from the University of North Carolina at Chapel Hill.

NOTES

1. Frankel, Alex (2004), *Word Craft*, New York: Crown Publishers, p. 71.

2. Aaker, David A. (2004), *Brand Portfolio Strategy*, New York: Free Press.

3. Calder, Bobby J. and Steven J. Reagan (2001), "Brand Design," in Dawn Iacobucci (ed.), *Kellogg on Marketing*, New York: John Wiley & Sons.

CHAPTER 3

BRAND MEANING

JOHN F. SHERRY, JR.

Imagine this chapter as an exercise in brandthropology. As an anthropologist who uses ethnographic methods to conduct cultural analysis, my view of branding departs from the conventional marketing perspective. Traditionally, marketers have framed branding as a cognitive or structural enterprise in models of strategic management, slighting the lived experience consumers have of brands, neglecting the cultural complexity that animates brands in so many distinctive ways, and treating the consumption experience as a reactive, idiosyncratic after-effect of marketers' efforts.[1]

Over the past two decades, work in consumer culture theory has encouraged practitioners to understand marketing as a semiotic venture. That is, the principal obligation of the marketer—and at once its chief source both of unintended and unanticipated consequence—is to shape the experience of stakeholders engaged in transactions. That marketers are behavioral architects or social engineers is denied as often as decried, but it is the central tenet of our discipline. Marketers, consumers, public policy makers, and consumerists are engaged in a perpetual game of discovering, creating, translating, transforming, and reconfiguring meaning. This quest for meaning drives marketplace behavior.[2]

The brand is a principal repository of meaning in consumer culture, in both a residential and generative sense. It is both a storehouse and a powerhouse of meaning.[3] In a universe of functional parity, as we move beyond a features-and-benefits understanding of our offerings to plumb their collective experiential soul, the way meaning is managed becomes crucial to the brand's success. The art of meaning management, as well as the detection of its antecedents and consequences, are exercises in applied anthropology—in brandthropology—driven by a narrative view of the brand that braids the filaments of everyday empirical and eternal truth into a common strand. That braiding is a communal effort, the plait a joint outcome of stakeholder negotiation.

In this chapter, I argue that we have always lived, and will always live, in an experience economy, despite the recent volume of the imagineering brand-wagon.[4] I illustrate how brands help make the categories of culture stable and visible, facilitating change in the bargain, an especially important consideration in an increasingly globalized marketplace.[5] I describe branding as a holistic combination of marketers' intentions, consumers' interpretations, and numerous sociocultural networks' associations, a co-creation and co-production of stakeholders from start to finish. I assert that brands shape and reflect cultural trends. Finally, I emphasize throughout the chapter that the foundations of brand meaning are personal, tribal, and mythic.

ETYMOLOGY, DEFINITION, AND ROOT METAPHOR: A PERSPECTIVE

A treatise on meaning rightfully begins with a lexical focus. The word *brand* has a tripartite etymology. One emphasis clusters around *burning*, with connotations both of fiery consummation and of banking the domestic hearth. A second emphasis clusters around *marking*, with connotations of ownership and indelibility, as well as paradoxical allusions to intrinsic essence, whether of merit or stigma. A third emphasis clusters around the delivery of, or deliverance from, danger (stoke, anneal, cauterize; conflagration, possession, aggression). The brand embodies the transformative heat of passion, properly tended. It is bestowed, and it is earned. The brand bespeaks the forging of family.

Definitions are another direct avenue into meaning. A brand is a differentiator, a promise, a license to charge a premium. A brand is a mental shortcut that discourages rational thought, an infusing with the spirit of the maker, a naming that invites *this* essence to inhabit *this* body. A brand is a performance, a gathering, an inspiration. A brand is a semiotic enterprise of the firm, the companion spirit of the firm, a hologram of the firm. A brand is a contract, a relationship, a guarantee; an elastic covenant with loose rules of engagement; a non-zero-sum game; improvisational theater at best, guerrilla theater at worst. As perceived vessels of exploitation, brands provide the impetus for generics and voluntary simplicity, as well as targets for demonstrations of cultural nationalism. McDonaldization, Coca-Colonization, and Disneyfication are simultaneously courted and countered, imported and deported.[6] The *swooshtika* becomes a badge of infamy, Ronald McDonald is toppled and graffitoed, and iPod adverts are morphed with images from the infamous Abu Ghraib prison to protest the war in i-Raq.[7] The brand demands an antiphonal, overlapping call-and-response patterned singing among communicants. It requires collusion, collaboration, and the willing suspension of disbelief.

As a brandthropologist, I am attuned to marketing mythopoeia, the creation and perpetuation of deep meaning through narrative. Marcom is most effective when it resonates with the universal types and motifs of folklore, with archetypal patterns in poetry, with the deep play of cultural forms, as each of these is grounded at the local level and revealed, not through simple anthrojournalism, but through ethnography.[8] My present understanding of branding is best conveyed by a root metaphor.

Imagine the brand as a Thai spirit house. A ubiquitous structure in residential and commercial neighborhoods, often mistaken by tourists as a bird house, this tiny building resembles a temple, and acts as a dwelling for spirits of the land and household, who are plied with offertory gifts by petitioners in search of favors or assuring pledges. The spirit house is often piled high with gifts of flowers, food, and currency, left by suppliants in hope of intercession by the residents. As will be evident in the following pages, I view branding as the creation of household gods, the mythic charter of our consumer culture. The brand is also a habitat in which consumers can be induced to dwell. In that dwelling, consumers domesticate the space, transforming it, and themselves, to essence. The resulting glow emanating from the dwelling is the brand's aura.

As the marketer's offering moves from undifferentiated homogeneity to distinctive difference—that is, as the brand individuates—consumers experience both therapeutic and salvific results, and grace is returned to the firm in the forms of consumers' willingness to pay a premium, and to repeat purchase over time. Thus, the brand is both a physical and metaphysical presence, an economic and festive fixture that binds stakeholders in a multifaceted relationship. It is the corporeal and noncorporeal webwork of postmodern existence.

BIOSOCIAL PSYCHOLOGY OF BRANDS

A thumbnail sketch of brands in evolutionary perspective is instructive. An early hallmark of humanity resides in the symbiotic co-evolution of the thumb and the brain. Over millennia of manipulating objects in the environment, our reach eventually exceeded our grasp. In short, the opposability of our thumb allowed us to interact with the material world in a way that enhanced enormously the sophistication of our brain. Manual dexterity and sapience potentiated one another, our paleolithic technology eventually permitting people to make themselves. Materiality is intrinsic to this process.

As humans evolved, we developed an extremely plastic conception of the self. In particular, our perceptions of our body's boundaries grew very fluid. This fluid body boundary, so evident at the subatomic level of electron sharing, when, for instance, we rest our palms upon a desktop, has eventually come to be described as a cybernetic self. We regard technology and its traits as extensions of ourselves, and we incorporate the material world into our sense of self.[9] As acculturated creatures, we are not simply sentience borne in meatsacks, nor wetware encased in hardware. We are cybernetic systems, simultaneously of and in the environments we manipulate. We are the art effects of artifacts.[10]

Artifacts are instrumental and expressive manifestations of our humanity. Humanity is predicated upon artifactuality, our ability to make things the vehicles of projection and introjection. Perception—or, rather, apperception, as anthropologists understand the culturally mediated interpretation of sensory input, the theory-ladenness of our facts—has a prelinguistic foundation. Artifactuality is the bedrock of apperception. Things literally shape our ability to think. Things make the categories of culture stable and visible.[11] Artifacts are sedimented behavior with which, in turn, we furnish our minds, providing us views of realities and endless opportunities for remaking ourselves.[12]

As we have moved from flint-knapping to imagineering, our mental infrastructure has become essentially postmodern paleolithic. We live less in a natural world than we do in a supermediated world, where goods have become "good to think."[13] That is, we interpret our realities through a screen of images arising largely from the artifacts—material and virtual—that marketers have proliferated. Among our primary artifacts, hence apperceptual furniture, in contemporary life, are brands. Our built environment is suffused with brands.[14] We literally see the world through branded lenses. Brands have become powerful material vehicles of thought and emotion.[15] Brand names are among children's earliest lexical acquisitions. These lenses are long-lived as well.

Recall, if you can, the climactic encounter of the Ghostbusters (from the eponymous film[16]) with Gozzer, the demon who demands they choose the form of their own destruction, wherein Bill Murray instructs his comrades to let their minds go blank, so they might avoid annihilation. To Dan Aykroyd's dismay, the image of the Stay-Puft Marshmallow Man pops, unbidden, to mind, and thence materializes on the streets of New York to wreak havoc. The marketecture of Aykroyd's mind mirrors our own. In an era where the aphrodisiacal Green M&Ms brand character runs second in recognition only to Santa Claus (himself a brand incarnation and patron saint of consumption), and a parade of brand icons (Ronald McDonald, Tony the Tiger, Mr. Peanut, Miss Chiquita, Mr. Clean, and others) in Times Square kicks off Advertising Week 2004 in New York, it is easy to imagine the household gods of Aeneas, borne out of Troy to ease the burden of his exile, having been transmogrified into this symbolic economy of reassurance. Brands are the used gods that facilitate our accommodation and resistance to the culture of consumption.[17]

BRANDS AS SECULAR RITUAL

Brand-based behaviors are the principal forms of secular ritual in contemporary social life.[18] To a large extent, the brand has been the ritual substratum of consumer behavior from time immemorial. Insofar as culture is reproduced in and through material objects, branding has always been a vehicle of human agency. Again, an evolutionary perspective is instructive.

The original hallmark of humanity was once believed to be the ability to use tools. From the handprints in blown ochre on the prehistoric cave paintings at Pêche Merle, to the signed casting blocks of the Meidum Pyramid, to the rabbit *hao* brand of the Northern Song (A.D. 960), to the medieval European trademarks of guild hegemony, makers have marked their creations as distinctive.[19] Gradually, the mark defined the maker. Eventually, *Homo faber*—people who make things—was demoted, as tool use was discovered throughout the animal kingdom.

Homo narrans—people who tell stories—has been promoted as our true hallmark. Storytelling is now regarded as our signature talent. Consequently, a narrative theory of branding is emerging among consumer researchers. Effective brand management involves the discovery, creation, and constant revision of stories. The brand is regarded as an allegory, suffused with aura and touched by paradox, that lives in the oral tradition of interpretive communities to the extent that the brand remains relevant to consumers' core cultural concerns.[20]

Theorizing ranges from top-down models of culture industry hegemony to bottom-up models of brand community creativity.[21] Product placement advances story lines (and avoids consumer ire) even as it returns marketers to the early days of television advertising. American Brandstand tracks brand mentions in *Billboard*'s Top 20 Singles chart, as rappers embellish their lyrics with verisimilar references. The polymorphously perverse Axeman sends consumers on a hermeneutic quest for the essence of deodorant. Members of the iPod brand community post images of themselves on the Internet morphing into MP3 players or lamenting the death of their machines, or they post images of their playlists titled with the names of ex-girlfriends or nostalgic hometowns. Authors such as Alex Shakar, William Gibson, Max Barry, Victor Pelevin, and Jonathan Dee, among others, push K-Mart realism to its limits, writing as evocative and insightful analyses of brand dynamics as can be found in the scholarly literature.[22]

Revision of reception theory to recognize the active production of consumption by consumers formerly regarded as passive (or worse, miscomprehending) has led to yet another contender for hallmark status in our bid to define human agency. *Homo ludens*—people who play—is an interesting hybrid of the ancestors.[23] When playfulness is seen as agentic motive, consumption as bricolage, and lifestyle as mosaic, marketers must build space into their offerings within which consumers can create, innovate, and deviate in pursuit of satisfaction.[24] Themed flagship brand stores that harness the interactive power of retail theatre and retail therapy capitalize effectively on this ludic impulse.[25]

Despite the dominant developmental sequence I have presented, each of these modes of agency has been active through time, and, as a result, marketers have engaged brand ethos selectively. These agentic motives have been trained primarily on three ritual domains: brand as fetish; brand as totem; brand as kinship alliance. Again, these ritual domains have been invoked throughout time, and none has a monopoly on consumers' imaginations. Each, however, implies a distinctive orientation toward brand management.

As a nation of unchurched seekers for whom denominational religion has become increasingly unsatisfying, and yet for whom the idea of a spiritual quest continues to provide direction to life, Americans have elevated the brand to the status of fetish, and not simply the commodity fetish that conceals the symbolic codes of capitalism from consumers.[26] Recall photographic images of Freud in his consulting room, surrounded by hundreds of African fetish statues, some of which he would fondle in contemplation as his clients held forth on problems. Brands have been invested with the numinous, as the interiority of the artifact has been more effectively unpacked. As a making sentient of the external world, the brand has become a portal to exalted experience. Consumers employ brands to achieve the experience both of transcendence and immanence, to infuse their lives with a lived experience of the sacred. The blurring of the boundary between conventional religion and secular consumption, a paraprimitive postmodern paradox of the first order, is at once a source of cultural stability and cultural dislocation, as ideologies contend on a global stage.[27]

As a totem, the brand performs the crucial social function of symbolic classification. It acts as both a beacon and a badge, a dashboard and a billboard.[28] Imagine the majestic Kwakiutl totem poles of the Pacific Northwest, whose carved frogs, whales, ravens, wolves, or bears embody not just the identity of the clans, but their relationship to one another. Now imagine those figures replaced by the swoosh, the helios, the mermaid, the bull's-eye or the bull, performing those identical classificatory operations. Brands assist individuals in the achievement of their own individual identity projects.

This assistance may not stop at simple brand loyalty or evangelism. Enthusiasts have literally tattooed the logos of Harley Davidson, Gibson Guitars, and Apple, among others, on their skin, effectively embodying the brand. (At least one surgeon stands accused of branding the logo of his alma mater—the University of Kentucky—on the uteruses of his unwitting patients).[29] Brands promote and proclaim group affiliation. These groups range from grassroots, populist brand communities that thrive in cyberspace, to autonomous subcultures of consumption that commune IRL, to marketer-sponsored user groups that interact at commercially created brandfests.[30] Finally, the brand comprises every action the firm undertakes, effectively encapsulating the company and presenting it to the world as a hologram. This is an especially important concern in business-to-business markets, where, to a large extent, the firm's reputation is the brand.[31]

The third ritual domain enacted through the brand, while related to the others, acts essentially as the replication of a template for the formation of relationships. This secular ritual has to do with kinship and the formation of alliances. It is less about the political imposition of order from the culture industries (advertising, cinema, and the like) than it is about the negotiation of harmony in the domestic sphere. To the extent that consumer-brand relations mirror the relationship between people in the social order, consumers imagine brands existing on a continuum from intimacy to estrangement, from kinship (or kithship) to enmity; brands may be consanguines, affines, friends, strangers, or adversaries.[32] Erosion of brand loyalty in the United States corresponds to the pattern of serial monogamy that is the dominant marital profile of the day.[33] The demographer-identified trend of *starter marriages*—25 percent of first marriages terminating within five years without children—portends further brand loyalty adjustments.[34]

LIVED EXPERIENCE AS MEANING PLATFORM

No matter its type—parity, niche, mega, or quintessential; elite, dowager, or new peer; cult or iconic; fast-moving consumer goods or business-to-business— every brand depends for its longevity on the skillful management of customer experience.[35] Further, the status of *customer* must be granted to every stakeholder in the brand's franchise, whatever the provenance. And while touch points are efficient occasions of observation and intervention, prospective touch points are just as essential to the process of experience management. Remember that brands are suspended in webs of significance only partially of marketers' own making. The lived experience of customers, from which all those meanings relevant to the brand arise, provides the platform from which brand strategy can be launched. Let us prefigure discussion of pre-launch dynamics with a brief example.

Consider the recently heralded birth of the *bling* finger. For decades, DeBeers has successfully promoted a link between diamonds and romantic love, and, in particular, diamond rings and marital engagement. DeBeers spends $200 million annually to provide consumers with both mythic appeal and economic guidance (diamonds are "forever," and the price of the ring should be equivalent to two months of the groom's salary). The company has traditionally marketed diamonds as gifts bought by men to be given to women.[36]

Predictably, marketing mythopoeia has become confounded with a feminist critique of patriarchy (the symbolic branding of women as chattel), with a shifting pattern of marital stability (increased divorce rate and numbers of female singletons), with geopolitical intrigues in sourcing ("war," "conflict," or "blood" diamonds), and with the gradual erosion of gendered economic inequality (more women controlling greater disposable income). Couple these changes with the rising trend in monadic giving—women buying gifts for themselves, to be given "to me, from me," as a proactive consequence of the perceived failure of their significant others to give them gifts that indicate that "he really 'gets' me" (men often being eleventh-hour order-fillers at best, and bearers of lingerie and appliances at worst).[37] Add a downward tick in ring-share of jewelry, and early sightings of fashionistas wearing diamonds on the ring finger of the right (that is, mythopoetically *incorrect*) hand, and DeBeers is faced with a branding opportunity.[38] Can the brand colonize new territory by claiming the right ring finger? Recent ads stressing female empowerment, individual autonomy, and self-worth encourage women to buy these bling rings (a folk locution lifted from fashion-forward rap culture for a product designed to look different from an engagement ring) for themselves. "Your left hand says 'We,' Your right hand says 'Me'" begins one appeal; "For me, myself and I" begins another.[39]

The sources of meanings to be managed in this particular case (a business-to-business example, as DeBeers sells to the trade, and thence to consumer, via J. Walter Thompson advertising) are instructive, as they illustrate the kind of orchestration involved in the invention of tradition. Sociodemographic, geopolitical, and cultural-historical forces are all implicated in the negotiation of identity projects. To the extent that marketers are aware of the multistrandedness of the experiential warp through which they must wend their managerial weft, the fabric that is the brand can be woven more effectively.

TRIANGULATING BRAND MEANING

The principal sources of brand meaning arise in three primary domains. While these domains intergrade and overlap in their animation of one another, they are discrete enough for pedagogical purposes to provide strategic guidance. By tacking between these sources, the marketer can effectively triangulate the meanings that must be managed if the brand is to become, and remain, relevant and resonant in customers' experience. These sources are brand image, brand essence, and brandscape.

Brand image is the external form and observable characteristics of the marketer's offering. This is the artifact as offered. It is the embodiment of the marketer's offering. Image is the operational meaning of the brand. It is the meaning the marketer has been able to infuse into the brand, and it is the most susceptible to strategic manipulation.[40]

In current practice, marketers are able to create (through repeated introspection, intuition, and insight) a brand mantra, which, through repeated incantation, reminds the brand's champion of the grail of which the firm is in quest.[41] This fabulous formula focuses attention on the outcome toward which all effort, strategic and tactical, should be directed. Nike professes "Authentic Athletic Performance." The University of Notre Dame promises "Life, Sweetness, and Hope" (*Vita Dulcedo Spes*). Burning Man urges "Radical Self-Expression." Starbucks prizes "Rewarding Everyday Moments." All of the meaning that stewards are able to harness in the realization of the mantra, as enacted through every traditional design element of brand identity (from name through fit and finish to point of experience), serves as input to the creation and maintenance of brand image.

Brand essence, on the other hand, is the meaning that arises in the customer's creative engagement with the marketer's offering. It is the internal form of the offering that must be elicited on the ground. It is the meaning that is co-created and co-produced by customers. Consumers' interpretations of the brand (along with all other aspects of their active reception of marketers' efforts) may not have been intended or anticipated by the marketer, but they must be thoroughly understood, if not embraced. Brand essence is exegetical meaning.[42]

Like Tiv tribesmen struggling to convey the true meaning of Shakespeare's *Hamlet* to the resistant, classically trained anthropologist, consumers try ever to alert marketers to the polysemic character of products and services.[43] A transformation occurs in the remaking of a brand from an image to an essence, from *your* brand (the marketer's) to *my* brand (the consumer's).

While essence is perhaps most effectively elicited ethnographically, often consumers will telegraph their ownership directly in the nativizing or taming of the brand. Coca-Cola becomes *Coke*. Federal Express becomes *FedEx*. McDonald's becomes *Mickey D's*.[44] Target becomes *Tarzhay*. Consumers *google* and *tivo*. They keep abandoned brands alive (Newton). They write new episodes for media brands and circulate them in online communities (*Star Trek, Xena*).[45] They appropriate intellectual property as a sign of esteem (or disdain) for the brand, as much as for monetary gain. Finally, customers may prompt marketers to explore the paradoxical essence of the brand that permits apparently opposing desires to be sated concurrently, such as the VW Beetle's yoking of irony and earnestness, or Muzak's evocation of eternity and transcience.[46]

Image and essence are suspended in webs whose filaments anchor and nourish them, and whose constant plucking encourages these modes of meaning to cross-pollinate and hybridize. Collectively, these webs constitute the *brandscape*. The brandscape is all about positional meaning, as it casts brands in relationships with one another, and with the culture industries at large, to create entire networks of associations that consumers use to limn their lives.[47] In cultural terms, the brandscape is the material and symbolic environment that consumers build with marketplace products, images, and messages, that they invest with local meaning, and whose totemic significance largely shapes the adaptation consumers make to the contemporary world.[48] As marketing and other cultural forms—art, education, religion, politics, technology, journalism, and so on—grow increasingly imbricated and globalized, the meaning-bank from which all stakeholders draw grows larger and more variegated by the moment.[49]

Let us ground the brandscape for a moment in Chicago, the home of numerous evocative flagship brand stores, which compete not only with each other and with retail outlets of more modest stature, but also with tourist attractions of all manner of description. On a stroll through Nike Town, you would ascend from the natural world, through the cultural world to the supernatural world, as you moved through successive venues that evoked the experience of being outside, on the street, in the marketplace, in an art gallery, in a museum, and, ultimately, in a sacred place of worship. Your sense of Nike-ness would be suffused with the aura of each of these different domains, whose meanings interpenetrate and synergize one another.[50]

On a visit to ESPN Zone, you might spend time in the screening room before a huge television monitor flanked by banks of slightly smaller monitors, bracketed and surmounted by crawlers, providing you with images of and information about an enormous array of sports contests worldwide. You might feel like you were in a Las Vegas sports book (and possibly engage in a bit of illegal gambling), or a theatre, or possibly even at home in your den. Should you occupy the front row Throne Zone, in a plush leather recliner tricked out with surround-sound stereo and armrest control panel to adjust the audio feed, and gaze at the images while female servers ply you with food and drink, you might lose yourself regally in alternating phallic and uterine fantasies, or feel like Captain Kirk on the bridge of the Starship Enterprise or Archie Bunker in the La-Z-Boy, or wish you could buy a seat license as you would in an NFL stadium. ESPN Zone-ness would be about quenching carnal desire through multiple senses and media in quintessentially American male fashion. Once again, the brand would be amplified and constellated across a range of meaning domains.[51]

Finally, on a pilgrimage to American Girl Place, you might watch young girls play with dolls meticulously supplied with authentic cultural biographies and period-appropriate outfits. These dolls themselves might have smaller dolls of their own, dressed in identical fashion. The girls who own the dolls might be dressed identically to the dolls themselves. Mothers accompanying the girls might be dressed in identical fashion. Grandmothers along for the trip might be dressed like the mothers who are dressed like the girls who are dressed like the dolls' dolls. These female kin units wander the store, shopping, playing, reading, dining, conducting grooming rituals, talking and telling stories, teaching and learning, and documenting their outings with photos and video. You would be observing memory in the service of practice. The site is alive with the intergenerational transfer of female energy, the constant reproduction of domesticity and the laying down—most frequently by grandmothers—of a template for making family that will become a living legacy. Doll merchandising serves as the object of contemplation, evoking concepts of gender and family that range from retro-ethnicity to futuristic genetic engineering, from Eden to Stepford. American Girl-ness would be about convergence and individuation in gender projects as they bear on culture-making, once again ramified through multiple genres of narrative.[52]

In each of these examples, the marketer and the customer draw from numerous cultural wellsprings of meaning to inform their understandings of the brand, while the brand itself is fungible or syncretic in terms of the meaning floating freely in the experiential portfolio of the culture. Aligning the meanings across stakeholders and domains to ensure consistent interpretation, or coordinating the differences in meanings across segments when consistency is deemed irrelevant or counterproductive require painstaking attention to the brandscape in which the managed meaning will eventually have to play.[53] A meaning audit can enhance this management immeasurably.

CONDUCTING A MEANING MANAGEMENT AUDIT

While a comprehensive grasp of all the sources of meaning available to the marketer will prove elusive (and probably illusive as well), it is possible to specify some most likely prospects for nuanced understanding. I identify seven categories and corresponding practices that can assist in a conscientious audit of brand meaning. These practices can then be mapped against conventional canons of brand analysis (e.g., brand equity, function, ideal design) to probe the ways in which standard accounts and metrics might be narratively enriched. As the meaning manager inevitably strategizes *in medias res*, and because the print medium prevents the simultaneous presentation of these coequal categories (on a Mobius strip, as I would prefer), I treat them cumulatively, not serially, in the following pages.

Archetypal Mythography

This is an ultimate source of brand meaning, and requires the strategist to *cosmologize*. That is, the meaning manager must learn to coax an *implied spider*—those foundational experiences all humans share and which storytellers have, from time immemorial, used as the very stuff of myth-making—to spin filaments that wire the brand into our way of apprehending reality.[54] We must be reminded constantly of the ways in which brands are woven through the fabric of our experiential universe.[55] Meaning managers imbue the brand with archetypal qualities (e.g., find the hero in Nike, the outlaw in Harley, the lover in Hallmark), metaphysical presence (e.g., the demonstration of Coke as the Real Thing, Allstate as the Good Hands, Visa as Everywhere You Want to

Be), and primal narrativity (Apple as irresistible forbidden knowledge, American Express as companion spirit, ConAgra as cornucopic abundance).[56] They synthesize the deep memes that become myth and help customers discern eternal from merely empirical truth.

Cultural Biography

Cultural biography is the local source of meaning in a global marketplace, a diachronic account of the brand as it evolves in concert with the forces of social life. It is a life history narrative.[57] It requires the strategist to *historicize*. That is, the meaning manager must have a panoramic view of the brand as it evolves over time, and a deep understanding of the changing sociocultural dynamics that shape the brand's role in the lives of consumers. Here, a generational or genealogical metaphor may guide insight; a metaphor based on *zeitgeist* or *épistème* may also be appropriate.[58] The guiding principle is simply that temporal ethos affects profoundly the way a brand is interpreted.

Trademarks, reference figures, and spokespersons are instructive in this regard. Betty Crocker, the human face of General Mills, has changed markedly (although she is still within the bounds of effective integrated marketing communication) over generations. Through an early twenty-first-century lens, her incarnations have included an apparently stern, matronly grandmother, a lighter-hearted motherly June Cleaver look-alike, a competent and slightly coquettish businesswoman, and, in her current visage, a computer-morphed composite Anglo/Afro/Hispanic/Asian American. This metamorphosis reflects the change in culinary styles from time-consuming nutritious cooking from scratch to the ascendance of comfort foods, to the modular cooking meal-solutions era, to the rise of ethnic and fusion foodways. Social forces such as decreasing and increasing rates of female participation in the paid labor force, involvement of males in household cooking responsibilities, time famine, ethnic resilience, and the need for projective identification in an era of multicultural diversity are also reflected in these changes. Aunt Jemima, the syrup icon, has undergone a similar metamorphosis as the climate of class, race, and gender relations has changed over time. So also have the Brawny Man and countless others.

Everyday Ethnography

Everyday ethnography is the phenomenological source of brand meaning, a synchronic account of the brand as it figures in the quotidian life of the customer. It requires the strategist to *contextualize*. That is, a grounded understanding of behaviors as they actually occur—not, as is most often the case, as managers believe they occur, or as consumers recall they occur—as the brand comes into play in customer experience. Here meaning arises in the course of day-to-day living, and it is here that the lived experience of the brand is revealed.[59]

Ethnographic consumer research reverses the anthropologist's mandate to make the strange *familiar* (i.e., interpret the exotic behavior of distant others): The brand strategist must make the familiar *strange*. Everyday reality must be viewed through a novel lens, highlighting the taken-for-granted and translating *consumer* behavior into *human* behavior. Grooming and purification rituals inform interaction with faucets and fixtures, detergents and emollients. Palpating, hefting, sniffing, and tasting behaviors characteristic of the produce aisle are reproduced (often covertly) by anxious new mothers in the baby food aisle, suggesting modifications to packaging and labeling. The efficacy of branding for doors can be strengthened by drawing on consumers' earliest experience of doors, which is characterized by feelings of isolation, anxiety, and anomie, by depicting doors in advertising in an open condition, with people on the other side of the threshold.[60] Refrigerators, ethnographically reconceived as being only secondarily about refrigeration and storage, become the soul of the smart house. The context in which brand behavior unfolds is embedded with meanings essential to the customer's personal narrative.

Utopian Cartography

This is an important aspirational source of brand meaning, a projective account of the brand as it attempts to colonize the future. It is arcadian in character, and represents a fantastic ideal (the consumption imaginary, such as the American Dream) to which the brand acts as a portal. It requires the strategist (with apologies both to Bob Dylan and Don King) to *prophesize*, to give consumers what they really want.[61] Whether it is called trend spotting, cool hunting, futurology, or scenario planning, it tasks the strategist to read shifts in values and levels in the aesthetic edge in an effort to anticipate the trajectory of the culture's worldview and ethos.[62]

The strategist must answer Microsoft's query, "Where do you want to go tomorrow?", today, and build the response into the brand. Can the brand speak to Bobos in a transformational future?[63] Can it reconcile the priorities of Boomers, Thirteeners, and Millennials, or must it assume a multiphrenic image to prosper?[64] Will the drivers of New Luxury founder on the shoals of mass affluence?[65] Shouldn't soul searching, cultural infidelity, bunkering, and values vertigo affect the financial services industry as much as the tourism industry?[66] Might the twenty-first-century contest between crusaders and jihadis alter the roles of marketing and consumption in the evolution of cultural nationalism?[67] To what extent can all brands, regardless of industry, heed the directive to nurture nature?[68] Perhaps the most instructive example of arcadian meaning mapping on the contemporary marketing scene is the rise of retro branding, as exemplified by the success of such brands as the VW Beetle, the Star Wars franchise, Quisp cereal, Airstream trailers, Charlie cologne, and most recently, Sting Ray bicycles, in going back to the future.[69]

Brand Iconography

Brand iconography is an immediate source of meaning, an instance of Kant's "thing in the thing." It is the affecting presence of the brand, as manifested in the totality of design dimensions that render the marketer's offering as it is.[70] It requires the strategist to *tangibilize*. That is, the experience of the brand must be made palpable for the consumer; the virtual must become actual.

A tangibilized brand has both a cognitive and visceral reality for the apprehender. Sensation helps reify the brand. Visualize Big Blue. Smell Chanel No. 5. Touch the grips of Oxo tools. Taste Altoids. Hear the sound of Intel inside. The more senses the brand engages, the more tangible its existence is to the customer. Visit any flagship brand store for comprehensive sensory engagement. A brand has numerous affordances, those points of mental and emotional acquisition. Artifactuality, name, tag line, logo, packaging, web site, corporate architecture, retail atmospherics, advertising, and communication media are just a few of these affordances.[71]

Semiotic Choreography

Semiotic choreography is an intimate source of meaning, arising from and tailored to the experience of individuals in a segment. It requires the strategist to *customerize*. In order to suit the identity projects of segment members, the brand must resonate with authenticity, with the abiding rightness of its fit with a customer's lifestyle. It is customer relationship management (CRM) at the individual level, the soul of the database that touches the tails as well as the curve. It is the stickiness that facilitates projection and introjection, the mirroring that catalyzes the transformation of *a* brand to *my* brand. It is the reinforcing of the identity project at every touch point.[72]

This semiosis is successful when the consumer regards the brand and says "It's me"; the blue-collar integrity of Carhartt work garments, supported with populist advertising; the upscale exoticism of J. Peterman fashion garments, supported with the ironic advertising copy that reads like a bodice ripper; the ingenious engineering of Victoria's Secret lingerie, supported with the erotic advertising imagery that enflames desire across genders; Amazon's prompting of other books you might like, based on current purchase profile; Starwood's retention of guest preferences for the customizing of repeat booking; loyalty programs. These examples each embody the effective tailoring of the brand to the individual. Sometimes semiotic redaction is the proper corrective to pursue, especially when the culture experiences seismic shifts in meaning domains. In the wake of popular animated films such as *Antz* and *A Bug's Life*, which effectively repositioned household pests as lovably personified quasi-pets, pest controllers Orkin found it necessary to reanimate insect intruders, endowing them with horrific and ferocious qualities, in order to overcome children's objections that their parents were engaged in cute-icide.

Moral Geography

Moral geography is the primary communal source of meaning. It is the tribal dimension of authority. It requires the strategist to *evangelize*. That is, the meaning manager must harness the collaborative and consultative potential of brand co-creation and -production, to facilitate the emergence of proselytes among customers, and to abet the flourishing of brand communities and subcultures on the ground and in the ether.[73]

In narrative terms, this abetting can take two forms: the theft of fire and the gift of starter dough. The former entails a passive monitoring and recycling of meaning elements to the group, allowing it to maintain its populist autonomy and nonmarket ethos. The latter entails an active involvement with the group, an encouraging of the group to accept the firm as a partner, and engagement that borders on sponsorship. Illicit lurking in chatrooms, flying false flags on bulletin boards, and other unwelcome interaction from the firm can be viewed as, and occasionally results in, a hostile takeover by *the* brand of *our* brand, a co-optation of community by corporation that subverts the moral authority the brand desires to tap.

Mapping these meaning management directives against traditional templates of brand dynamics can provide very specific guidance for the strategist. For example, a thorough audit of the brand's composite meaning—its "_____ -ness" (e.g., Coke-ness, Chevy-ness, Sony-ness, etc.) quintessentially distilled— might begin with an analysis of the dimensions of equity, as suggested in Figure 3.1.[74] The Good Humor brand might prospect for narrative power along

Figure 3.1
"_____-ness" through Equity

Audit Item / Equity Dimension	Loyalty	Awareness	Perceived Quality	Associations	Proprietary Assets
Cosmologize					
Historicize					
Contextualize					
Prophesize					
Tangibilize					
Customerize					
Evangelize					

the proprietary asset dimension, by focusing analysis and interpretation on its delivery trucks (a tack UPS might follow in a distinctly different direction):

Divinity
Horn of Plenty
Pandora's Box
Pied Piper
Ubiquity
Instant gratification
Iceberg
Oasis
Nostalgia
Retro
Holistic sensory engagement
Diversity
Neighborhood
Infantile regression
The good parent
Altered consciousness
Buzz
Children becoming market criers and pitchers

Each cell affords a distinctive way of imagining brand meaning.

A strategist might seek deep insight into the functional quality of a brand's appeal, as suggested in Figure 3.2.[75] Asking the analytical question, "What is the brand supposed to do?" and expecting a pithy response, a meaning manager might probe the seduction dimension for its narrative power in under-wiring the Victoria's Secret brand:

Paradox goddess
Angel
Succubus (or incubus)
Pygmalion
Happy hooker
Happy housewife
Mom
Models and modes
Foundation and façade
Engineering marvel
Prosthetic
Second skin
Mystery and fantasy
Chrysalis
Catalog as wishbook redux
Buzz

Commercials and webcasts spark discussion and debate. Some catalog models become celebrities, others are endowed by male readers with pet names and storylines.

Figure 3.2
"_____-ness" through Function

Audit Item / Functional Dimension	Information	Differentiation	Seduction
Cosmologize			
Historicize			
Contextualize			
Prophesize			
Tangibilize			
Customerize			
Evangelize			

Designing an ideal brand might involve the strategist in a detailed exploration of the aesthetic dimension of meaning, as suggested in Figure 3.3.[76] Narrative power for a brand like Evian might be derived from artistic exploration of meaning:

Fundamentality
Aboriginality
Aqua vita
Purity
Oceanic merger
Mountains
Glaciers
Carved ice
Cerulean vastness
Homophonic with "avian," hence associations with winged grandeur
Anagrammatic stigma: naïve
Luxury and indulgence
Conspicuous consumption
Milk baths and bathtub gin
Facial spritzers and personal fan-atomizers
Buzz from *affecté* to *de rigeur*

Figure 3.3
"_____-ness" through Ideal Design

Audit Item \ Design Dimension	Functions	Behaviors	Aesthetics
Cosmologize			
Historicize			
Contextualize			
Prophesize			
Tangibilize			
Customerize			
Evangelize			

Bottles come in multiple sizes imprinted, incised, and engraved to convey all these meanings, surmounted with a pink cap, to recall our ultimate source of refreshment, replenishment, and indulgence: Mom.

Whatever template is chosen, brand meaning is most thoroughly explored by mapping the meaning practices systematically against the template's meaning dimensions. Alternatively, a simple free listing of domain-specific meanings, accompanied by a kind of spreading activation charting of the association evoked (denotatively and connotatively) by the listing, will also prove enlightening, as will a subsequent cross-domain charting of overlaps and meaning migrations.

For example, the Levi's brand is cosmologically anchored in an explorer archetype.[77] It encompasses entrepreneurial Americana, from the Gold Rush through the cultural revolution of the 1960s, to the nanotech cyborg millennium of smart fabrics. It comprises individuality, authenticity, and the quintessential extended self. It anticipates and reinforces disruptions such as the casual workplace, and it must creatively respond to ones such as the emerging *masstige* market. It shapes and reflects the human form with stylish fit and finish. It marries its models to personal narrative of great projective power, tapping cultural narratives of sexiness across the spectrum of gender (straight, gay, and androgynous). It is emblematic of youth subcultures, working class subcultures, and intelligentsia subcultures, investing the concept of a uniform with the paradoxically customized cast. The brand's core values—empathy, originality, integrity, and courage—radiate from each meaning code and ramify throughout the constellation of meanings, in ways that suggest a multitude of management options.[78]

In summary, the practical outcome of an audit is a comprehensive inventory of meanings, clustered by category, that managers can use to guide the design, positioning, communication, and rejuvenation of the brand at any point in time. This guidance might be particular, as in a simple adjustment of nuance in a single category, or holistic, as in a thoroughgoing overhaul across all categories; it might be devoted to a single brand or an entire portfolio. Let me illustrate the audit outcome with one last example.

Coffee has perennially straddled the commodity–brand boundary, the tune of its dialectical dance called by imaginative marketers. Coffee is among the key symbols of contemporary consumer culture.[79] It is principal among our household gods, and the ritual substratum of much of our interpersonal interaction. The meanings available to manage any particular brand's ownership of *coffee-ness* can be conveniently chunked.

Cosmologized, coffee is foundational and fundamental. It is *prima materia*. It is *sui generis*. It is *aqua vitae*. Historicized, coffee has ranged from a sacramental aid to prayer, to a call for communitas, to a tonic stimulant fueling work, to a sedative hypnotic promoting relaxation and escape, to a personal indulgence on the order of reward and therapy. Contextualized, coffee is a site magnet and a beacon product, emplacing homeyness and domesticity, and sacralizing third places; it embodies sociality and bonding, even as it serves as a rite of passage in a consumer's individuation. Prophesized, coffee is the quintessential gift, to others and to oneself; it is a vessel of the donor's essence. Tangibilized, coffee is a politically correct psychotropic, awakening, engaging, and challenging all the senses, inviting a cult of connoisseurship to unpack and appreciate its complex character. Customerized, coffee is a Rorschach roast, the touchstone of identity whose intimate idiosyncrasies are rediscovered with each sip; it is the sensory stimulation driving the guilty pleasure of a "*$", or the quest for the "godshot." Evangelized, coffee is a global–local lightning rod of third-world emancipation/immiseration, of independent/franchised freehold; it is a primer of cabal, klatsch, and convocation.

Thus inventoried, coffee admits of many brands, distinctly positioned. Meaning clusters abound; sacramentality, sociality, sensuality; individuality, idiosyncrasy, indulgence; cost, class, connoisseurship; pace, place, politics; time, transformation, therapy. Any particular meaning may suit the brand's image and essence; any particular cluster may be invoked to locate and fix it in the brandscape. Recall one last time that meaning management is a dynamic process that must incorporate the creative input of consumers.

Failure to check the marketing imagination against consumer creativity can tarnish the brand. Toyota outraged an entire segment of consumers by presenting a putative homage ostensibly to their hip users, a gold miniature RAV 4 sport utility vehicle embedded in the front tooth of an anonymous African-American smile, as the knowing wink of a street-smart partner. Consumers objected strongly to the rap–ethos allusion as an exercise in stereotypification, rather than as an exercise in insider bonding. So also did American Girl in 2005 evoke the ire of Hispanic critics in Chicago, who resented the implications of a biographical detail of its latest doll, Marisol Luna. Marisol's home neighborhood of Pilsen, a Mexican-American enclave in Chicago, was characterized by her mother as a dangerous place for children to grow up; the family subsequently moved to the suburbs. A well-intentioned acknowledgment of demographic trends in the service of verisimilitude quickly and rightly becomes a flashpoint for identity politics in a plural society. Marketers must recognize that meaning is highly contextual, and that triangulation is essential to avoid alienating those consumers they long most ardently to woo.

CONCLUSION

In twenty-first-century perspective, brands are an experiment in memetic engineering. They encode and engender the meanings that sustain our culture of consumption. To a very substantial degree, human behavior *is* marketplace behavior. Inevitably, Brands R Us, with all the social, political, and ethical complications such identification implies.

Brand stewards must become astute meaning managers, if their charges are to become the kinds of cultural building blocks that ensure not only mere profitability, but also the long-term adaptability of the species itself. Accommodating and resisting this management are the principal preoccupations of our postmodern era.

Let me return to the ritual and evolutionary orientations with which I began this chapter, to bring these themes full circle. A persuasive case has recently been made for the emergence of a new hallmark of humanity: *homo quaerens*, that is, people who seek, or search.[80] Wisdom, handiness, storytelling, and playfulness may ultimately be harnessed in the service of our intrinsic inclination to quest. While questing may assume many forms, the quest for meaning is preeminent among them. This particular quest is a journey that brands were bred to undertake. Brands shape and reflect our quest for meaning. They are often the lodestar and the destination in our nomadic walkabouts. Brands reinforce and challenge our foundational notions of the real. Brands fix and focus our search for meaning, as we parse our seeking across the institutions of culture.

The wellsprings of brand meaning are both finite and inexhaustible. These sources are readily identified and tapped. Harnessing them in the service of marketing strategy is the manager's challenge. By tapping the narrative and performative power inherent in these sources in a collaborative fashion with stakeholders, marketing managers can create and sustain truly meaningful brands.

John F. Sherry, Jr., a professor of marketing at the Kellogg School of Management for the past two decades, is currently the Ray W. and Kenneth G. Herrick Professor of Marketing at the University of Notre Dame. He received a BA from the University of Notre Dame and an MA and Ph.D. in anthropology from University of Illinois at Urbana-Champaign.

NOTES

1. Aaker, David (1991), *Managing Brand Equity: Capitalizing on the Value of a Brand Name,* New York: Free Press; Aaker, David (1996), *Building Strong Brands,* New York: Free Press;

Kapferer, Jean-Noel (2001), *[Re]inventing the Brand: Can Top Brands Survive the New Market Realities?*, London: Kogan Page; Keller, Kevin (2002), *Strategic Brand Management: Building, Measuring and Maintaining Brand Equity*, Englewood Cliffs, NJ: Prentice Hall.

2. Levy, Sidney J. (1978), *Marketplace Behavior: Its Meaning for Management*, New York: Amacom; McCracken, Grant (1986), *Culture and Consumption: New Approaches to the Symbolic Character of Consumer Goods and Activities*, Bloomington, IN: Indiana University Press; McCracken, Grant, (1993), "The Value of the Brand: An Anthropological Perspective," in David Aaker and A. Biel (eds.), *Brand Equity and Advertising: Advertising's Role in Building Strong Brands*, Hillsdale, NJ: Lawrence Erlbaum, pp. 125–139; McCracken, Grant (2005), *Culture and Consumption II: Markets, Meaning and Brand Management*, Bloomington, IN: Indiana University Press; Sherry, John F., Jr. (1995a), *Contemporary Marketing and Consumer Behavior: An Anthropological Sourcebook*, Thousand Oaks, CA: Sage.

3. Turner, Victor (1967), *The Forest of Symbols*, Ithaca, NY: Cornell University Press; Turner, Victor (1974), *Dramas, Fields and Metaphors*, Ithaca, NY: Cornell University Press.

4. Pine, Joseph and James Gilmore (1999), *The Experience Economy: Work Is Theatre and Every Business a Stage*, Boston, MA: Harvard Business School Press; Schmitt, Bernd (1999), *Experiential Marketing: How to Get Customers to Sense, Feel, Think, Act, Relate to Your Company and Brands*, New York: Free Press; Schmitt, Bernd (2003), *Customer Experience Management: A Revolutionary Approach to Connecting with Your Customers*, New York: Wiley; Wolf, Michael (1999), *The Entertainment Economy: How Megamedia Forces Are Transforming Our Lives*, New York: Random House.

5. Aaker, David and Erich Joachimsthaler (1999), "The Lure of Global Branding," *Harvard Business Review* (November–December), 137–144; Douglas, Mary and Baron Isherwood (1979), *The World of Goods*, New York: Basic Books; Gregory, James and Jack Weichman (2002), *Branding Across Borders: A Guide to Global Brand Marketing*, New York: McGraw-Hill; Tobin, James, ed. (1992), *Remade in Japan: Everyday Life and Consumer Taste in a Changing Society*, New Haven, CT: Yale University Press; Watson, James, ed. (1997), *Golden Arches East: McDonald's in East Asia*, Stanford, CT: Stanford University Press.

6. Flusty, Steven (2004), *De-Coca-Colonization: Making the Globe from the Inside Out*, New York: Routledge; Holt, Douglas (2002), "Why Do Brands Cause Trouble? A Dialectical Theory of Consumer Culture and Branding," *Journal of Consumer Research*, 29 (June), 70–90; Klein, Naomi (1999), *No Logo*, New York: Picador; Ritzer, George (1993), *The McDonaldization of Society*, Thousand Oaks, CA: Sage.

7. Codrington, Andrea (2004), "Dark Shadows," *I.D.* (November), 34.

8. Aarne, Antti and Stith Thompson (1973), "The Types of the Folktale," *FF Communications*, 184, Hilsinki: Academia Scientarium Fennica; Bodkin, Maud (1948), *Archetypal Patterns in Poetry: Psychological Studies of Imagination*, Oxford: Oxford University Press; Geertz, Clifford (1973), *The Interpretation of Cultures*, New York: Basic Books; Geertz, Clifford (1983), *Local Knowledge*, New York: Basic Books; Thompson, Stith (1955), *Motif Index of Folk Literature*, Bloomington, IN: Indiana University Press; Winsor, John (2004), *Beyond the Brand*, Chicago, IL: Dearborn.

9. Belk, Russell (1988), "Possessions and the Extend Self," *Journal of Consumer Research,* 15(2), 139–168; Belk, Russell (2004), "Possessions, Self and the Sacred," in Abbie Griffin and Cele Otnes (eds.), *The Sixteenth Paul D. Converse Symposium,* Chicago: American Marketing Association; Sherry, John F., Jr. (2004), "We Might Never Be Post-Sacred: A Tribute to Russell Belk on the Occasion of His Acceptance of the Converse Award," in Abbie Griffin and Cele Otnes (eds.), *The Sixteenth Paul D. Converse Symposium,* Chicago, IL: American Marketing Association.

10. Bateson, Gregory (1972), *Steps to an Ecology of Mind,* New York: Ballantine; Bateson, Gregory (1991), *Sacred Unity: Further Steps to an Ecology of Mind,* New York: Cornelius & Michael Bessie Books.

11. Csikszentmihalyi, Mihaly and Eugene Rochberg-Halton (1981), *The Meaning of Things: Domestic Symbols and the Self,* Cambridge: Cambridge University Press; Douglas, Mary and Baron Isherwood (1979), *The World of Goods,* New York: Basic Books; Levi-Strauss, Claude (1962), *Totemism,* London: Merlin Press; Levi-Strauss, Claude (1979), *Myth and Meaning: Cracking the Code of Culture,* New York: Schocken Books.

12. Childe, V. Gordon (1981), *Man Makes Himself,* Bradford-on-Avon: Moonraker Press; Richardson, Myles (1987), "A Social (Ideational-Behavioral) Interpretation of Material Culture and Its Application to Archaeology," in Daniel Ingersol and Gordon Bronitsky (eds.), *Mirror and Metaphor,* Lanham, MD: University Press of America, pp. 381–401.

13. Douglas, Mary and Baron Isherwood (1979), *The World of Goods,* New York: Basic Books; Levi-Strauss, Claude (1962), *Totemism,* London: Merlin Press; Levi-Strauss, Claude (1979), *Myth and Meaning: Cracking the Code of Culture,* New York: Schocken Books.

14. Sherry, John F., Jr. (1995a), *Contemporary Marketing and Consumer Behavior: An Anthropological Sourcebook,* Thousand Oaks, CA: Sage; Sherry, John F., Jr. (1998), "The Soul of the Company Store: Nike Town Chicago and the Emplaced Brandscape," in John F. Sherry, Jr. (ed.), *Servicescapes: The Concept of Place in Contemporary Markets,* Lincolnwood, IL: NTC Business Books, pp. 109–146.

15. Geertz, Clifford (1973), *The Interpretation of Cultures,* New York: Basic Books; Turner, Victor (1967), *The Forest of Symbols,* NY: Cornell University Press; Turner, Victor (1974), *Dramas, Fields and Metaphors,* Ithaca, NY: Cornell University Press.

16. Aykroyd, Dan and Harold Ramis (1984), *Ghostbusters,* a film directed by Ivan Reitman, Columbia/Tristar Pictures.

17. Coombe, Rosemary (1997), "The Demonic Place of 'Not There': Trademark Rumors in the Postindustrial Imaginary," in Akhil Gupta and James Ferguson (eds.), *Culture, Power, Place: Explorations in Critical Anthropology,* Durham, NC: Duke University Press, pp. 249–276; Coombe, Rosemary (1998), *The Cultural Life of Intellectual Properties: Authorship, Appropriation and the Law,* Durham, NC: Duke University Press; Marling, Karal, ed. (1998), *Designing Disney's Theme Park: The Architecture of Reassurance,* New York: Flammarion; Sherry, John F., Jr. (1995a), *Contemporary Marketing and Consumer Behavior: An Anthropological Sourcebook,* Thousand Oaks, CA: Sage.

18. Sherry, John F., Jr. (1986), "Cereal Monogamy: Brand Loyalty as Secular Ritual in Consumer Culture," paper presented at the *Seventeenth Annual Conference of the Association for Consumer Research*, Toronto, Canada.

19. Hamilton, G. and C.K. Lai (1989), "Consumerism without Capitalism: Consumption and Brand Names in Late Imperial China" in Henry Rutz and Benjamin Orloue, (eds.), *The Social Economy of Consumption*, Latham, MD: University Press of America, pp. 253–279; Mollerup, Per (2001), *Marks of Excellence: The History and Taxonomy of Trademarks*, New York: Phaidon.

20. Brown, Stephen, Robert V. Kozinets, and John F. Sherry, Jr. (2003a), "Teaching Old Brands New Tricks: Retro Branding and the Revival of Brand Meaning," *Journal of Marketing*, 67(3), 19–33; Brown, Stephen, Robert V. Kozinets, and John F. Sherry, Jr. (2003b), "Sell Me the Old Old Story: Retromarketing Management and the Art of Brand Revival," *Journal of Customer Behavior*, 2(2), 133–147; Williamson, Judith (1978), *Decoding Advertisements*, New York: Boyars.

21. Holt, Douglas (2003), "What Becomes an Icon Most?" *Harvard Business Review* (March), 43–49; Holt, Douglas (2004), *How Brands Become Icons: The Principles of Cultural Branding*, Boston, MA: Harvard Business School Press; Muniz, Albert and Thomas O'Guinn (2001), "Brand Community," *Journal of Consumer Research*, 27(3), 412–432.

22. Barry, Max (2003), *Jennifer Government*, New York: Doubleday; Dee, Jonathan (2000), *Palladio*, New York: Vintage; Gibson, William (2003), *Pattern Recognition*, New York: Putnam; Pelevin, Victor (2000), *Homo Zapiens*, New York: Viking; Shakar, Alex (2000), *Savage Girl*, New York: Harper Collins.

23. Huizinga, Johan (1955), *Homo Ludens: A Study of the Play Element of Culture*, Boston: Beacon.

24. Kozinets, Robert V., John F. Sherry, Jr., Diana Storm, Adam Duhachek, Krittinee Nuttavuthisit, and Benet Deberry-Spence (2004), "Ludic Agency and Retail Spectacle," *Journal of Consumer Research*, 31(3).

25. See note 24.

26. Marx, Karl (1990/1867), *Capital*, Vol. 1, Harmondsworth: Penguin; Taussig, Michael (1980), *The Devil and Commodity Fetishism in South America*, Chapel Hill, NC: University of North Carolina Press.

27. Arnheim, Rudolph (1987), "Art Among the Objects," *Critical Inquiry*, 13(4), 677–685; Belk, Russell, Melanie Wallendorf, and John F. Sherry, Jr. (1989), "The Sacred and Profane in Consumer Behavior: Theodicy on the Odyssey," *Journal of Consumer Research*, 16(1), 1–38; Forty, Adrian (1986), *Objects of Desire*, New York: Pantheon; Rappaport, Amos (1982), *The Meaning of the Built Environment*, Beverly Hills, CA: Sage; Sahlins, Marshall (1976), *Culture and Practical Reason*, Chicago: University of Chicago Press.

28. Hartman, Harvey (2003), *Reflections on a Cultural Brand: Connecting with Lifestyles*, Bellevue, WA: The Hartman Group; Holt, Douglas (2004), *How Brands Become Icons: The Principles of Cultural Branding*, Boston, MA: Harvard Business School Press; McCracken, Grant (1993),

"The Value of the Brand: An Anthropological Perspective," in David Aaker and A. Biel, (eds.), *Brand Equity and Advertising: Advertising's Role in Building Strong Brands,* Hillsdale, NJ: Lawrence Erlbaum, pp. 125–139; Twitchell, James (2004a), *Branded Nation: The Marketing of Megachurch, College, Inc. and Museum World,* New York: Simon and Schuster; Twitchell, James (2004b), "An English Professor Thinks About Branding," *Journal of Consumer Research,* 31(2), 484–487.

29. Taylor, Louise and Greg Kocher (2003), "Doctor Is Sued Over Branding Uterus," *Lexington Herald Reader* 25 (January), 1.

30. McAlexander, James and John Schouten (1998), "Brandfests: Servicescapes for the Cultivation of Brand Equity," in John F. Sherry, Jr., (ed.), *Servicescapes: The Concept of Place in Contemporary Markets,* Lincolnwood, IL: NTC Business Books, pp. 377–402; McAlexander, James, John Schouten, and Harold Koenig (2002), "Building Brand Community," *Journal of Marketing,* 66 (January), 38–54; Muniz, Albert and Thomas O'Guinn (2001), "Brand Community," *Journal of Consumer Research,* 27(3), 412–432; Schouten, John and James McAlexander, (1995), "Subcultures of Consumption: An Ethnography of the New Bikers," *Journal of Consumer Research,* 22 (June), 43–61.

31. Barlow, Jenelle and Paul Stewart (2004), *Branded Customer Service: The New Competitive Edge,* San Francisco: Barrett-Kohler; Minett, Steve (2002), *B2B Marketing,* New York: Pearson Education.

32. Fournier, Susan (1998), "Consumers and Their Brands: Developing Relationship Theory in Consumer Research," *Journal of Consumer Research,* 24 (March), 343–373.

33. See note 18.

34. Paul, Pamela (2002), *The Starter Marriage and the Future of Matrimony,* New York: Random House.

35. Atkin, Douglas (2004), *The Culting of Brands,* New York: Penguin; Holt, Douglas (2004), *How Brands Become Icons: The Principles of Cultural Branding,* Boston, MA: Harvard Business School Press; LaSalle, Diana and Terry Britton (2003), *Priceless: Turning Ordinary Products into Extraordinary, Experiences,* Boston, MA: Harvard Business School Press; Levy, Sidney [compiled by Dennis Rook] (1999), *Brands, Consumers, Symbols and Research,* Thousand Oaks, CA: Sage; Ragas, Matthew and Bolivar Bueno (2002), *The Power of Cult Branding: How 9 Magnetic Brands Turned Customers into Loyal Followers (and Yours Can, Too!),* Roseville, CA: Prima; Schmitt, Bernd (1999), *Experiential Marketing: How to Get Customers to Sense, Feel, Think, Act, Relate to Your Company and Brands,* New York: Free Press; Schmitt, Bernd (2003), *Customer Experience Management: A Revolutionary Approach to Connecting with Your Customers,* New York: Wiley; Vincent, Laurence (2002), *Legendary Brands: Unleashing the Power of Storytelling to Create a Winning Market Strategy,* Chicago: Dearborn.

36. Hart, Matthew (2001), *Diamond: The History of a Cold-Blooded Love Affair,* New York: Penguin.

37. Sherry, John F. Jr., Mary Ann McGrath, and Sydney Levy (1995), "Monadic Giving: Anatomy of Gifts Given to the Self," in John F. Sherry, Jr. (ed.), *Contemporary Marketing and Consumer Behavior: An Anthropological Sourcebook,* Thousand Oaks, CA: Sage, 399–432.

38. Walker, Rob (2004), "The Right-Hand Diamond Ring," *New York Times Magazine* (January).

39. The first excerpt is part of the current Diamonds Are Forever campaign, the second from an advertisement for the Lazare diamond ring.

40. Gardner, Burlegh and Sidney Levy (1955), "The Product and the Brand," *Harvard Business Review,* 33(2), 33–39; Thaler, Linda and Robin Koval (2003), *Bang! Getting Your Message Heard in a Noisy World,* New York: Currency Doubleday; Turner, Victor (1974), *Dramas, Fields and Metaphors,* Ithaca, NY: Cornell University Press.

41. Bedbury, Scott (1997), "What Great Brands Do," *Fast Company* (August–September), 97–100; Bedbury, Scott and Stephen Fenichell (2002), *A New Brand World: 8 Principles for Achieving Brand Leadership in the 21st Century,* New York: Viking.

42. Cornfeld, Betty and Owen Edwards (1983), *Quintessence: The Quality of Having It,* New York: Crown; Knapp, Duane (2000), *The Brand Mindset,* New York: McGraw Hill; Locke, Christopher (2001), *Gonzo Marketing: Winning Through Worst Practices,* Cambridge, MA: Perseus; Taylor, David (2003), *The Brandgym,* New York: Wiley; Turner, Victor (1974), *Dramas, Fields and Metaphors,* Ithaca, NY: Cornell University Press.

43. Bohannan, Laura (1966), "Shakespeare in the Bush," *Natural History,* 75, 28–33.

44. Atkin, Douglas (2004), *The Culting of Brands,* New York: Penguin; Ragas, Matthew and Bolivar Bueno (2002), *The Power of Cult Branding: How 9 Magnetic Brands Turned Customers into Loyal Followers (and Yours Can, Too!),* Roseville, CA: Prima; Vincent, Laurence (2002), *Legendary Brands: Unleashing the Power of Storytelling to Create a Winning Market Strategy,* Chicago: Dearborn.

45. Muniz, Albert and Hope Schau (2005), "Religiosity in the Abandoned Apple Newton Brand Community," *Journal of Consumer Research* (March), forthcoming; Schau, Hope and Albert Muniz (2004), "If You Can't Find It, Create It: An Analysis of Consumer Engagement with *Xena: Warrior Princess* and the Creation of Consumer Generated Fest," in Barbara Kahn and Mary Fances Luce (eds.), *Advance in Consumer Research,* 31.

46. Shakar, Alex (2000), *Savage Girl,* New York: Harper Collins.

47. Gobé, Marc (2001), *Emotional Branding: The New Paradigm for Connecting Brands to People,* New York: Allworth Press; Gobé, Marc (2002), *Citizen Brand: 10 Commandments for Transforming Brands in a Consumer Democracy,* New York: Allworth Press; Pavitt, Jane, ed. (2000), *Brand New,* London: V&A Publications; Turner, Victor (1974), *Dramas, Fields and Metaphors,* Ithaca, NY: Cornell University Press; Williams, Gareth (2000), *Branded?,* London: V&A Publications.

48. Sherry, John F., Jr. (1995a), *Contemporary Marketing and Consumer Behavior: An Anthropological Sourcebook,* Thousand Oaks, CA: Sage.

49. Twitchell, James (1996), *Adcult, USA: The Triumph of American Advertising,* New York: Columbia University Press.

50. Sherry, John F., Jr. (1998), "The Soul of the Company Store: Nike Town Chicago and the Emplaced Brandscape," in John F. Sherry, Jr. (ed.), *Servicescapes: The Concept of Place in Contemporary Markets,* Lincolnwood, IL: NTC Business Books, pp. 109–146.

51. See note 24; Sherry, John F., Jr. (2003), "Bespectacled and Bespoken: The View from Throne Zone and Five O'Clock and Head," in Stephen Brown and John F. Sherry, Jr. (eds.), *Time, Space and the Market: Retroscapes Rising,* New York: M.E. Sharpe, pp. 19–34.

52. Sherry, John F. Jr., Robert Kozinets, Nina Diamond, Mary Ann McGrath, Albert Muniz, and Stefania Borghini (2003), "Girl of Many Lands: Seeing the World Through the . . . Eyes of Your American Girl Today," paper presented at the *Ninth Annual Cross Cultural Research Conference,* Rose Hall, Jamaica.

53. Sternthal, Brian and Alice Tybout (2001), "Segmentation and Targeting," in Dawn Iacobucci (ed.), *Kellogg on Marketing,* New York: Wiley; Tybout, Alice and Brian Sternthal (2001), "Brand Positioning," in Dawn Iacobucci (ed.), *Kellogg on Marketing,* New York: Wiley, pp. 31–57.

54. Doniger, Wendy (1998), *The Implied Spider: Politics and Theology in Myth,* New York: Columbia University Press.

55. Randazzo, Sal (1993), *Mythmaking on Madison Avenue: How Advertisers Apply the Power of Myth and Symbolism to Create Leadership Brands,* Chicago: Probus.

56. Floch, Jean-Marie [trans. Robin Bodkin] (2001), *Semiotics, Marketing and Communication: Beneath the Signs, the Strategies,* New York: Palgrave; Mark, Margaret and Carol Pearson (2001), *The Hero and the Outlaw: Building Extraordinary Brands Through the Power of Archetypes,* New York: McGraw Hill.

57. Kopytoff, Igor (1986), "The Cultural Biography of Things: Commoditization as Process," in Arjun Appadurai (ed.), *The Social Life of Things,* New York: Cambridge University Press, pp. 66–91.

58. Holt, Douglas (2004), *How Brands Become Icons: The Principles of Cultural Branding,* Boston, MA: Harvard Business School Press; Olsen, Barbara (1995), "Brand Loyalty and Consumption Patterns: The Lineage Factor," in John F. Sherry, Jr.(ed.), *Contemporary Marketing and Consumer Behavior: An Anthropological Sourcebook,* Thousands Oaks, CA: Sage, pp. 245–281; Smith, J. Walker and Anne Clurman (1997), *Rocking the Ages,* New York: Harper; Strauss, William and Neil Howe (1992), *Generations,* New York: Perennial; Strauss, William and Neil Howe (1997), *The Fourth Turning,* New York: Broadway.

59. Sherry, John F., Jr. (1995a), *Contemporary Marketing and Consumer Behavior: An Anthropological Sourcebook,* Thousand Oaks, CA: Sage; Sherry, John F. Jr. and Robert V. Kozinets (2001), "Qualitative Inquiry in Marketing and Consumer Research," in Dawn Iacobucci (ed.), *Kellogg on Marketing,* New York: Wiley, 165–194.

60. Rapaille, G. Clothaire (2001), *7 Secrets of Marketing in a Multicultural World,* Provo, UT: Executive Excellence Publishing.

61. Brown, Stephen, Robert V. Kozinets, and John F. Sherry, Jr. (2003a), "Teaching Old Brands New Tricks: Retro Branding and the Revival of Brand Meaning," *Journal of Marketing,* 67(3), 19–33; Brown, Stephen, Robert V. Kozinets, and John F. Sherry, Jr. (2003b), "Sell Me the Old Old Story: Retromarketing Management and the Art of Brand Revival," *Journal of Customer Behavior,* 2(2), 133–147; Eliade, Mircea (1954), *The Myth of the Eternal Return,* Princeton, NJ: Princeton University Press; Levitt, Theodore (1984), *The Marketing Imagination,* New York: Free Press.

62. Abrahamson, Vickie, Mary Meehan, and Larry Samuel (1998), *The Future Ain't What it Used to Be: The 40 Cultural Trends Transforming Your Job, Your Life, Your World,* New York: Riverhead Books; Samuel, Larry (2003), *The Trend Commandments: Turning Cultural Fluency into Marketing Opportunity,* New York: Bang Zoom Books; Schwartz, Peter (1991), *The Art of the Long View,* New York: Currency.

63. Brooks, David (2000), *Bobos in Paradise: The New Upper Class and How They Got There,* New York: Simon & Schuster.

64. Strauss, William and Neil Howe (1992), *Generations,* New York: Perennial; Strauss, William and Neil Howe (1997), *The Fourth Turning,* New York: Broadway.

65. Nunes, Paul and Brian Johnson (2004), *Mass Affluence: Seven New Rules of Marketing for Today's Consumer,* Boston, MA: Harvard Business School; Silverstein, Michael and Neil Fiske (2003), *Trading Up: The New American Luxury,* New York: Penguin.

66. Samuel, Larry (2003), *The Trend Commandments: Turning Cultural Fluency into Marketing Opportunity,* New York: Bang Zoom Books.

67. Sherry, John F., Jr. and Robert V. Kozinets (2004), "The Comedy of The Commons: Nomadic Spirituality at Burning Man," unpublished working paper, Kellogg School of Management, Northwestern University, Evanston, Illinois.

68. See note 66.

69. Brown, Stephen, Robert V. Kozinets, and John F. Sherry, Jr. (2003a), "Teaching Old Brands New Tricks: Retro Branding and the Revival of Brand Meaning," *Journal of Marketing,* 67(3), 19–33; Brown, Stephen, Robert V. Kozinets, and John F. Sherry, Jr. (2003b), "Sell Me the Old Old Story: Retromarketing Management and the Art of Brand Revival," *Journal of Customer Behavior,* 2(2), 133–147.

70. Armstrong, Robert (1974), *The Affecting Presence: An Essay in Humanistic Anthropology,* Urbana, IL: University of Illinois Press; Neumeier, Marty (2003), *The Brand Gap,* Indianapolis, IN: New Riders; Roberts, Kevin (2004), *Lovemarks: The Future Beyond Brands,* New York: PowerHouse Books; Simmons, John (2003), *The Invisible Grail,* New York: Texere; Van Auken, Brad (2003), *Brand Aid,* New York: Amacom.

71. Perry, Alycia and David Wishour (2003), *Before the Brand: Creating the Unique DNA of an Enduring Brand Identity,* New York: McGraw Hill.

72. Floch, Jean-Marie [trans. Robin Bodkin] (2001), *Semiotics, Marketing and Communication: Beneath the Signs, the Strategies,* New York: Palgrave; Thaler, Linda and Robin Koval (2003), *Bang! Getting Your Message Heard in a Noisy World,* New York: Currency Doubleday.

73. Ragas, Matthew and Bolivar Bueno (2002), *The Power of Cult Branding: How 9 Magnetic Brands Turned Customers into Loyal Followers (and Yours Can, Too!),* Roseville, CA: Prima; Tarlow, Mikela and Philip Tarlow (2002), *Digital Aboriginal: The Direction of Business Now: Instinctive, Nomadic and Ever-Changing,* New York: Warner Books; Vincent, Laurence (2002), *Legendary Brands: Unleashing the Power of Storytelling to Create a Winning Market Strategy,* Chicago: Dearborn.

74. Aaker, David (1991), *Managing Brand Equity: Capitalizing on the Value of a Brand Name,* New York: Free Press.

75. Atkin, Douglas (2004), *The Culting of Brands,* New York: Penguin.

76. LaSalle, Diana and Terry Britton (2003), *Priceless: Turning Ordinary Products into Extraordinary Experiences,* Boston, MA: Harvard Business School Press; Levy, Sidney J. and John Czepiel (1974), "Marketing and Aesthetics," in R.C. Curhan (ed.), *Combined Proceedings,* Series 35, Chicago: American Marketing Association, pp. 386–391; Schmitt, Bernd and Alex Simonson (1997), *Marketing Aesthetics: The Strategic Management of Brands, Identity and Image,* New York: Free Press.

77. Mark, Margaret and Carol Pearson (2001), *The Hero and the Outlaw: Building Extraordinary Brands Through the Power of Archetypes,* New York: McGraw Hill.

78. http://www.levistrauss.com/about/vision/.

79. Kozinets, Robert V. (2002b), "The Field behind the Screen: Using Netnography for Marketing Research in On-line Communities," *Journal of Marketing Research* 39 (February), 61–82; Sherry, John F., Jr. (1995b), "Bottomless Cup, Plug-in Drug: A Telethnography of Coffee," *Visual Anthropology,* 7, 351–370; Thompson, Craig and Zeynep Arsel (2004), "The Starbucks Brandscape and Consumers' (Anticorporate) Experiences of Glocalization," *Journal of Consumer Research,* 631–642.

80. Pasternak, Charles (2004), *Quest: The Essence of Humanity,* Hoboken, NJ: Wiley.

STRATEGIES FOR BUILDING AND LEVERAGING BRANDS

CHAPTER 4

COMPETITIVE BRAND STRATEGIES

GREGORY S. CARPENTER and KENT NAKAMOTO

Competitive brand strategies are created based on an implicit understanding of the competitive process. Traditionally, that process is presumed to be driven by rational buyers: Buyers know what they want, brands compete to satisfy buyers, and competitive advantage arises from meeting consumer needs better, faster, or at a lower price than competitors. Competition, in the traditional sense, is a race to build the proverbial better mousetrap.

Despite the powerful logic and appeal of this process, however, mounting evidence suggests that the view of buyers embodied in the traditional competitive process is at odds with actual buyer behavior. Buyers do not always consider all the options, weigh them carefully, and reach a deliberate choice in the conventional sense of rationality.[1] Moreover, buyers do not always know what they want. Instead, individuals *learn* what they like, and they learn how to choose. Indeed, buyer learning is a life-long process. We are born without preferences for any brand or product and, through our lives, develop preferences for thousands of products. As part of that learning process, we learn how to choose—impulsively in some cases, driven by emotion in others, and deliberately at other times.

Consumer learning suggests a fundamentally different view of competition. In the traditional view, strategies respond to what buyers want. But when buyers learn, the strategies create the experiences and observations on which buyer learning is based. By providing the raw material for buyer learning, competitive strategies shape buyers' experiences and observations and, therefore, they shape what buyers learn. And by shaping what buyers learn, organizations shape the rules of the competitive game depending on the buyer. Rather than a race to meet buyer needs, competition becomes a battle over the rules of the game, and competitive advantage arises from winning that battle.

In this chapter we examine how successful brands use competitive strategy to shape the rules of the game. We consider a market at two stages of development. First, we consider a market at its inception—when a "pioneer" creates an emerging market. In these cases, buyers are ill-informed, may have difficulty evaluating products, and may even have yet to form an opinion about what is important in a product. We outline how buyers learn their preferences and how that process affects choice and competition as well as how it creates an advantage for pioneering brands. Second, we explore competitive brand strategies for a mature market (late entrants). We consider brand strategy options that reflect buyer learning that has occurred as the market has developed. In some cases, for example, one brand has emerged as the standard of comparison. This affects options for late entry, which are very different under this evolutionary view of consumer choice and competition.

PIONEERING ADVANTAGE

Many pioneers outsell later entrants for years, and sometimes for decades. Market pioneers Coca-Cola, Levi's, and many others remain the best-selling brands in their categories today. Empirical research shows that these pioneers are not atypical. But risks must be overcome before a pioneer can successfully enter a new market: The firm must successfully educate buyers; it must make the right (perhaps lucky) technology choice; and it must have sufficient funding. If pioneers are successful, however, they enjoy market share advantages in many markets, including consumer goods, industrial goods, and services.[2]

The nature of that advantage is illustrated in Figure 4.1. It shows brands' market share relative to the pioneer, based on the order of entry.[3] To understand the importance of these results, it helps to compare what one might expect with what the data show. One would expect, based on the classical competitive process, that if rational consumers consider two brands, and believe both are equally attractive, priced equally, available in an equal number of outlets, and advertised with equal intensity, then both should obviously receive equal market share. But Figure 4.1 suggests that such logic is flawed. It shows that, adjusting for differences in brands' strategies, consumers do not judge early and late entrants alike. Instead, consumers prefer the pioneer.

Figure 4.1 illustrates the magnitude of that advantage by showing the market shares of brands arranged by order of entry, relative to the market share of

Figure 4.1
Order of Entry and Relative Market Share

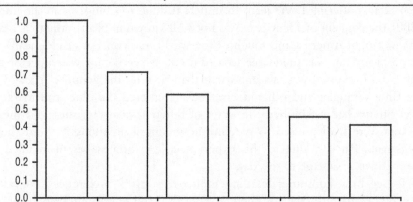

the pioneer after adjusting for differences in brand strategies. So, the figure shows that, by definition, the pioneer receives 100 percent relative to itself. But the second brand to enter, on average, receives only 75 percent of the pioneer's share, the third entrant less than 60 percent of the pioneer's share and so on until the sixth entrant receives less than half the share of the pioneer despite being equally attractive.

This effect creates a significant competitive advantage for the pioneer. To match a market pioneer's share or exceed it, for example, a sixth entrant (or any later entry after the first) would need to offer something more than the pioneer. It would need to spend more aggressively on advertising, be available in more outlets, or be priced below the pioneer. These additional costs impose a burden on later entrants that pioneers do not bear, creating *pioneering advantage*.

There are several sources of pioneering advantage. All are derived from the pioneer's unique role in creating the category, in defining the dimensions on which brands compete, and in influencing the importance buyers attach to perceived differences. Simply put, the pioneer plays a unique role. It is perceived differently from others, and that perception is valuable in several ways.

Preference Formation

One of the most powerful advantages the pioneer enjoys is derived from its impact on how buyers value brand attributes. By establishing the category, the pioneer gains a very important advantage. It can help influence the relative importance of product attributes. Consider the market for blue jeans. Prior to Levi Strauss offering Levi's jeans to miners rushing to California in the mid-1800s, the concept of a blue jean was not well known in North America. Levi Strauss taught America and much of the world one concept of blue jeans— that a baggy cut was preferable to a slim cut, heavy denim was superior to light, and low price was less important than owning the genuine article. By the time Wrangler and other denim makers entered the blue jean market, Levi Strauss had established the value of different characteristics, and these makers were hard pressed to redefine how Americans thought about their blue jeans. Partially due to this experience, Levi Strauss has maintained a competitive advantage to this day.

To see how consumer learning influences buyers' preferences, consider preferences prior to trial and then through trial and repeat purchase. Prior to trial, consumer preferences are weakly formed because the category is novel to the buyer. Even if buyers have objective information on brand attributes, the value of an individual attribute or the superiority of one attribute combination over another may not be obvious. For that reason, individuals may be indifferent to alternatives over some range. Buyers sample a brand in the category—most likely the pioneer. Lacking information to the contrary, the consumer can attribute a successful trial to the unique attribute combination of the pioneer. In doing so, buyers develop a naive theory relating brand features to value, which advertising and repeat purchase reinforce. Thus, buyers learn through trial how to value attribute combinations, but trial favors the pioneer, so buyers learn to like the pioneer and the combination of attributes it offers.[4]

The introduction of Vaseline petroleum jelly illustrates this preference formation process and the competitive advantage it creates. Vaseline was introduced in 1880 and was advertised as a healing agent of unsurpassed purity. By sampling Vaseline—a translucent, highly pure gel—buyers learned that its attributes produced an effective wound preparation. They generalized from this observation and concluded that the effectiveness of petroleum jelly lies in its translucence and purity (in contrast to the competing black coal tar derivatives of the time). And of course, subsequent trials and advertising confirmed this conjecture. Thus, translucence came to be favored over opacity and gained more importance in brand evaluation. Moreover, because Vaseline pioneered the product, all later brands were compared to it, and they were found wanting even if they were identical, simply because they were not Vaseline.

Category Association

A pioneer can become the *standard* against which later entrants are judged simply by establishing the category and being viewed as the near-ideal product. This strong association with the product category means that virtually all other products in the category are now judged by the established standard. Standards in markets take at least two forms—psychological standards and technological standards. Technological standards, such as the QWERTY keyboard, Microsoft Windows, and Lego children's building blocks, create *architectural standards.* Brands that control the architecture therefore can exert enormous control over competitors, as Microsoft demonstrates vividly and others such as Lego do more quietly.

Psychological standards also play a very important role in many markets. Levi Strauss, Coca-Cola, and Jell-O are the standards against which later entrants are judged. For years, Cadillac represented the epitome of the luxury car, Porsche the essence of the sports car, and Volkswagen the pure concept of the economy car. Some brands are even synonymous, and thus inseparable, in the minds of consumers with the product category. For many years, Xerox has been both a brand name and a verb used to describe the act of photocopying. The confection known as a Tootsie Roll is difficult to describe without using the brand name, and in China a Motorola is a pager.

Being a psychological standard has enormous competitive value. In most product categories, buyers consider only a subset of all brands in the market, often called a *consideration set.* This consideration set typically consists of a reasonably small number of brands (around three to five), relative to the complete set of brands available and even to the full range of brands known to buyers. For example, hundreds of brands of beer are available in the marketplace. A typical consumer may be aware of 10 brands of beer, but that same consumer may only seriously consider three to five brands for consumption. Research has shown that a brand that is the psychological standard will, for most buyers, be included in their consideration sets. The other brands often vary. However, because the pioneer is often the psychological standard, it will be chosen more often simply because it is considered more often. Thus, a psychological standard will gain an advantage over other brands.[5]

Awareness and Recall

Pioneering affects the buyer's memory in other ways. Buyers do not recall all brands equally often or with equal ease. We know more about some brands than others, and we recall those better-known brands more easily and more often. When walking down a grocery store aisle, consumers have only a moment to make a brand choice. Consumers typically include only a small number of brands in their consideration set—and more than likely the set will consist of the most vivid brands. The pioneer is likely the most vivid of any brand in the category. Being the category standard, it is often recalled first or more often than rivals. For example, in one study subjects recalled the pioneer brand most often, and they also recalled the pioneer brand more positively than others.[6]

A pioneer brand is novel. We devote cognitive effort to understanding the product and what it does. When we experience the next version of that product, some aspects are novel, others redundant. By the time we observe the sixth or tenth brand, redundancy increases, novelty decreases, and we devote much less effort to understanding new brands and what they do. The pioneer, having received the most attention early on, is most easily and most positively recalled. This results in the pioneer brand being chosen most often over others, giving it a competitive advantage.

Preemptive Positioning

Preemptive positioning in the category translates into an important competitive advantage for the pioneer. As a standard, the pioneer can become strongly associated with one perceived position in the market. Coca-Cola offers a unique mix of sweetness and carbonation, and Levi's offers a particular cut. These strong associations make the pioneer's position very difficult to assail. A me-too product (identical to the pioneer but with a lower price) will suffer in comparison despite its similarity to the pioneer: the more similar the me-too and pioneer, the greater the relative prominence of the pioneer. This happens because the me-too brand derives its identity from the pioneer, and greater similarity reduces the distinctiveness of the me-too brand. As such, the me-too brand differs from the pioneer simply because it is not the pioneer, but it remains inferior because it has no distinctive competence. Thus, positioning near a pioneer brand and also close to the ideal point of the market can actually *increase* the relative market share of the pioneer and *decrease* the relative share of the entrant.[7]

The powerful preemptive position of the pioneer can affect the ability of later entrants to use price to attack the pioneer. In one study, experimenters created an emerging market. In the experiment, consumers observed as a pioneer brand was followed by no later entrant, by a differentiated brand (priced at the same level as the pioneer), or by a me-too brand (priced below the pioneer). Consumers were then given a set of brands with differing prices to rate. All consumers rated the same brands at the same prices.[8] These ratings help us deduce price sensitivities and differences based on the position of the later entrant. The results show that the pioneer followed by the me-too brand is least price sensitive; the pioneer followed by no entrant is the most price sensitive; and the pioneer followed by the differentiated entrant is midway between the two other cases. By adopting a me-too position, the later entrant signals to buyers that the pioneer is indeed in the best position. The me-too brand implicitly admits this position by adopting it and then advertising it as such. This strategy reinforces the dominance of the pioneer and can lead to increases in its market share. One example of this occurred in the cola market, when Pepsi attacked the pioneer, Coca-Cola, in the famous Pepsi challenge. As a result of that attack Coca-Cola's market share rose, despite Pepsi's claim of superior taste.

Risk

Any perceived risk to consumers when making a brand choice can sustain the pioneer's advantage in the face of objectively superior alternatives. Inherently, a buyer has more information about the pioneer. It works. The other brands remain untested. That doubt makes the untried alternative risky, and thus buyers will favor the known alternatives, even paying a premium for them. Essentially buyers are paying a premium to avoid risky alternatives.

This effect is particularly important for so-called *experience* goods (i.e., products or services that buyers must experience to evaluate). For example, tires, aspirin substitutes, and barbecue sauce are all experience goods—hard to evaluate before consumption but easy to assess afterwards. Most products offer some value in terms of experience. Automobiles, for instance, differ in terms of performance, styling, and price, which can be easily assessed before purchase. But reliability is more difficult to determine unless the model has a long track record. In the case of experience goods, experience creates knowledge about a brand that has significant value; trial reveals critical information about the brand to the buyer.

The knowledge that buyers gain through trial can contribute to a pioneer's advantage. Imagine a new product, an experience good, such as a razor blade. The pioneer offers it, buyers try it, and they learn that it either works well or it does not. If it does work well, consumers now have valuable information. When they return to the store, they may find the pioneer's brand alongside other new rivals. But they will most likely choose the pioneer product they have already tried, rather than risking the trial of a new competitor.

Risk has even more dramatic consequences at the retailer level. Consider a grocer stocking the successful razor blades. Inevitably a new competitor will offer its own brand, and one of these new entrants may create a clearly superior product. The retailer faces a choice: Should space devoted to the current well-selling brand (or to some other known profit generator) be reduced to try the new brand of razor? The retailer faces reducing a known income stream and replacing it with an uncertain one.

As a result, in either the consumer or retailer case, non-pioneers must offer consumers or retailers something extra to overcome the risk of the potential loss associated with a new-brand trial. But having to offer something extra places the new entrant at a disadvantage, sustaining the success of the pioneer.[9]

Buyer Entry

Pioneering advantage appears long-lived. In fact, many pioneers continue to dominate their markets long after initial consumers have ceased buying their products. For example, Lipton traditionally has dominated the tea business since 1893, and Gold Medal has dominated the flour market since 1890. Certainly, very few if any of the consumers and retailers these brands influenced through pioneering their markets still buy tea and flour. But if the pioneering advantage relies in some measure on personal experience, how can a pioneering brand retain its advantage with subsequent generations of consumers?

By dominating a market, the pioneer secures important long-lived advantages that enable it to shape future buyers' knowledge of the category. One such advantage is distribution. For example, if Coca-Cola can dominate the restaurant channel, then a greater number of new consumers will experience Coca-Cola in restaurants relative to Pepsi and other competitors. By encountering Coca-Cola first and possibly more often, these new consumers' experience will yield many of the same advantages as does pioneering in the more conventional sense.

Another important asset for the pioneer is previously loyal customers. If Coca-Cola has many loyal buyers, more young consumers will grow up in households where Coca-Cola is consumed regularly. Their first experience with a cola may very well be Coca-Cola, and through that initial experience, Coca-Cola can begin to define the market for these new buyers as well, influencing perception, forming preferences, and building the other advantages associated with pioneering.[10]

LATE-ENTRY STRATEGIES

Although pioneers do indeed dominate many markets, many late entrants overtake pioneers. Karl Benz invented the automobile, but Ford Motor Company and later General Motors took the lead in that industry. Amana created the microwave oven, but in 2005 Samsung led the market. Star was the pioneer in safety razors, but Gillette took over from the pioneer. Diet Coke has dominated the diet cola market pioneered by that well-known brand Lirsch. What enabled these late entrants to overcome the disadvantages associated with late entry?

Unlike new-to-the-world markets, mature markets have well-educated buyers with well-defined perceptions, strong established preferences, and tried-and-true strategies for brand choice. The risk associated with technology is relatively low (even if it is evolving), and the competitive set is well defined. A mature market challenges a late-entry product with an established set of players, a known technology, and well-informed buyers. The rules of the game clearly exist and are often difficult to break. In such a situation a late entrant has a nearly infinite variety of strategic options. But we can identify three broad categories:

1. A *fast-following* strategy relies on playing the game the pioneer has created, but doing so better or with more resources than the pioneer. Fast followers do not challenge the logic of the pioneer's efforts to create the market. In fact, they embrace that logic and seek to capture the profits associated with it.
2. A *differentiation* strategy recognizes the power of the pioneer and seeks to define the later entrant as fundamentally different from the powerful pioneer. This effort relies on the power of the pioneer to establish a unique position.
3. An *innovation* strategy seeks to redefine what buyers know or perceive about the established brand and the market. This strategy renders obsolete the knowledge created through the interaction between buyers and the pioneer, allowing the innovative later entrant to redefine the nature of the competitive game.

Fast-Following Strategy

Fast following is one of the most effective routes to beating the pioneer at its own game. Many pioneers start a game without the resources to win it. With too few resources, the pioneer will be unable to influence preference formation and will struggle to become the standard in the category. Without adequate resources, the pioneer will be unable to gain high brand awareness or become the low-risk choice. Sometimes the pioneer may be able to establish such a position among only a small portion of the market (e.g., Apple Computer). When too few resources are devoted to a pioneering brand, a quick, well-funded later entrant can move quickly to pick up where the pioneer falters. This fast-following later entrant then gains all of the advantages associated with pioneering without actually being the pioneer.

The success of fast followers was investigated in a historical analysis of 50 product categories, including frequently purchased consumer goods, consumer durables, and industrial products.[11] Golder and Tellis categorized the 50 brands based on their timing of entry as the *market pioneer* (the first to market the product), *early followers* (those that entered soon after the market pioneer), and *later entrants*. Analysis of those 50 markets shows that market pioneers, on average, fare less well than might be imagined. In the 50 markets examined, the typical pioneer retained its leadership position for just five years. Early followers, on the other hand, failed only 8 percent of the time. Moreover, fast followers led in 53 percent of the markets examined.

To examine how fast followers overtake pioneers, researchers have examined how entry timing affects the sales of pioneers and later entrants. In one study, researchers examined ethical pharmaceuticals in six markets. Over many years, 29 different brands entered these six markets; the researchers categorized the brands as pioneers, growth-stage, or mature-stage entrants.[12] Based on this categorization, they built a statistical model explaining each brand's sales as a function of the brand's stage of entry (pioneer, growth-stage entrant/fast follower, or later entrant); the marketing activities of each brand; and the cumulative previous sales of the brand and its rivals. Examining the pattern of sales for three brands showed that growth-stage entrants (fast followers) enjoyed three advantages compared to other entrants:

1. *Brand growth rates.* Fast followers, or growth-stage entrants, grow faster throughout their entire life span than either pioneers or mature-stage entrants. Pioneers, in fact, grow most slowly. Quite possibly they bear the burden of building the category, which may have longer-term consequences. Mature-stage entrants, on the other hand, grow faster than pioneers, but they grow more slowly than growth-stage entrants. The research also showed that growth-stage entrants are not (as was thought) eclipsed by faster-growing later entrants. In fact, these fast followers catch the wave at the right time and are able to ride that wave to faster growth in the long run. By comparison, mature-stage entrants are

even more disadvantaged than was previously thought: Not only do they reach a lower sales level than other entrants (pioneers, for example) but they do so more slowly than others. They are doubly disadvantaged.

2. *Buyer response to marketing activities.* In the case of buyer response to product quality, buyers are most responsive to changes in quality levels by fast followers. The pioneer faces a skeptical market of relatively uniformed buyers; buyer response to changes in quality will be correspondingly poor. But buyers of growth-stage entry products (fast followers) are more knowledgeable about the newly created marketplace, making these consumers more responsive to changes in quality levels. By comparison, mature-stage entrants face buyers who may be locked into more of a routine, making them once again less responsive to quality changes by late entrants. Interestingly, the research results also showed that with respect to marketing expenditures, growth-stage entrants have no advantage relative to pioneers, but they do have an advantage relative to brands that enter in the mature stage.

3. *Competitive impact.* Fast followers, or growth-stage entrants, enjoy a unique level of insularity from competitors that others do not share. Research results show that in the long run pioneers are hurt by the growth of competitors' sales and that mature-stage entrants are not helped by that same competitor growth. Fast followers appear able to create more unique identities than other later entrants, leading to greater insulation from competition. They enjoy some measure of uniqueness and, like the pioneer's uniqueness, that has competitive value.

In summary, brands that enter quickly after the pioneer appear to have a number of advantages. Although they bear risks, they do not bear the *same* risks as the pioneer. Fast followers grow faster than all other entrants. Fast followers have the greatest response to change in their quality levels and are insulated from any negative effects of the growing sales of rivals. In addition, their buyers are more responsive to marketing spending than those brands that enter later in the life of the market.

Differentiation Strategy

After a pioneer becomes established, one classically successful avenue to market entry is *differentiation*. Successful brand differentiation requires that a brand offer some sort of unique value in a category. The challenge in differentiating from a pioneer is that, as already mentioned, greater differentiation increases market share. But a product can also run the risk of being so different as to be irrelevant. Being too close to the pioneer runs the risk of being overshadowed—or worse yet, copied—by the pioneer. It appears that late entrants face a differentiation dilemma. How can this be resolved?

Differentiating from Pioneers Research reveals one option.[13] In the study, the authors examined buyer preferences for pioneering brands and differentiated later entrants using two categories, automobiles (Jeep, Porsche, and Mitsubishi) and soft drinks (Coca-Cola, 7-Up, and Hanssens). In each category, subjects were shown late-entrant brands that were differentiated from the pioneer (e.g., 7-Up and Hanssens cola); they also tested brand extension of the pioneering brands to assess their ability to imitate differentiated later entrants (e.g., a Jeep sports car). The results, summarized in Figure 4.2, show buyer preferences for pioneers and later entrants based on the differences between the parent brand (e.g., Coca-Cola) and the differentiated late entrant.

The results show that the key to differentiation is to position a new entrant just far enough to be out of the reach of the pioneer's imitation. Here's the logic: For both pioneers and later entrants, brand extensions that are more similar to the original brand are more highly valued. That effect, however, is

Figure 4.2
Pioneer and Late-Entry Brand Preference

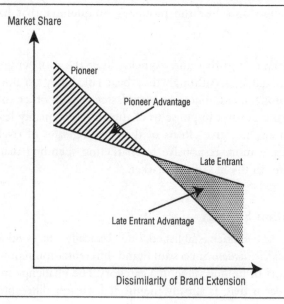

more dramatic for pioneers than for late entrants. When a pioneer extends its brand with a similar new product, the preference for the pioneer's new product far exceeds a similarly positioned later entrant. That situation is shown in Figure 4.2 as *pioneering advantage*. In this case, the pioneer's brand is clearly preferred to the later entrant's. For a pioneer's brand extension, being strongly associated with its original position makes it more unassailable by a later entrant. But there are also drawbacks for the pioneer: Being strongly associated with the original position also means that when the pioneer strays too far under its own brand, buyers see those new products as inconsistent with the pioneer's original position.

Therefore, when the later entrant offers a brand that is sufficiently far from the pioneer's original position, buyers prefer the later entrant's product to the pioneer's. That situation is shown in the right-hand side of Figure 4.2 and is labeled *late entrant advantage*. In this case, the later entrant has identified a weakness associated with the pioneer's advantage. As was stated above, the key to differentiation for later entrants, then, is to position just far enough to be out of the reach of the pioneer's imitation.

The degree of differentiation chosen by the late entrant depends on the power of the pioneer. In some cases, the pioneer is strongly associated with the category, so the late entrant can move in closer to the pioneer's original position.[14] If the pioneer is weaker, it can reach further afield, so a late entrant needs to position further from the pioneer to be safe from competitive imitation. A weaker pioneer, however, is more vulnerable to direct attack—it is less protected by a set of powerful, unique perceptions that define it. At some point, when the pioneer becomes sufficiently weak, a direct attack can be the best alternative. Whatever precise position is chosen, high-profit differentiation strategies are supported by high prices (as opposed to pricing to be a me-too to the pioneer) and high advertising support (as opposed to being a no-name rival).

Differentiation is a classic competitive strategy, and typically the term is used to indicate simply offering something different from another brand. In the context of challenging a pioneer, however, the term takes on a more specific meaning. It suggests using the power of the pioneering advantage to the advantage of the later entrant. Every competitive advantage has a corresponding competitive weakness. The pioneer's great strength is its unique, powerful association with one valuable position in the market. Its corresponding weakness is strategic inflexibility. A differentiation strategy in this context draws on the same sources that create pioneering advantage—preference formation, perception formation, category associations, and risk—to create a differentiation advantage for the later entrant.

Innovation Strategy

Innovative late entrants have eclipsed many a pioneer. Innovation takes many forms, but one way to create a new standard is through product innovation. Gillette has built a powerful position in the razor market through product innovation, overtaking the market pioneer, Star, and other later entrants.[15] Innovation plays a central role in low-technology markets as well. The U.S. laundry detergent market, pioneered by Dreft, has become dominated by Tide, for example. But in all these cases, these late entrants displaced the pioneer as the standard of comparison and created a new standard.

Using innovation to overtake a pioneer is risky. Unlike pioneering, the risks arise from a combination of concerns about consumer acceptance and competitive reaction. In addition, an innovative late mover faces a dominant, well-established competitor. That competitor can be strongly associated with the category, having exerted great influence in the formation of brand preferences. The pioneer competitor will have high brand awareness, have extensive distribution, and be seen as a low-risk choice. All of these pioneering advantages create a daunting challenge for an innovative late mover. But an innovative late mover also faces many of the same risks that a pioneer does. The product is new-to-the-world (at least to a significant degree); the technology producing it can be untried; and consumer knowledge about it is very low. Even so, many late movers succeed. So what is it about innovation that can create such a powerful advantage?

One study provides insights into the sources of late-mover advantage created by innovation.[16] The study focuses on 13 brands of ethical pharmaceuticals launched into two separate markets. In both markets, late entrants followed a pioneer. Some of the late entrants were innovative; others were not. But innovative late movers overtook pioneers in both cases. The study examines the sources of the innovative late-mover's advantage relative to the pioneer and the non-innovative late entrants. To do so, the authors examined the impact on each brand's sales of its marketing effort, the sales of rivals, and the potential market it created.

The results show that non-innovative late movers suffer considerable disadvantages: Buyers are less responsive to their marketing spending, and buyers are less loyal as compared to pioneers and more innovative late entrants. Pioneers have larger potential markets than non-innovative late entrants, and the growth of these competitors' sales does not affect the sales of the pioneer. Pioneers enjoy a number of advantages compared to non-innovative later entrants. These results suggest that non-innovative late movers must play by the rules created by the pioneer. By doing so, they suffer while the pioneer prospers. Non-innovative late movers have access only to a portion of the same market; their buyers are less loyal; and they need to spend more to have the same impact through marketing.

For innovative late movers, however, the story is quite different. Innovative late movers grow faster, have larger potential markets, and have more loyal buyers than other entrants—pioneers included. These findings suggest that the innovative later entrant can take advantage of the investment others have made to establish the category and, by virtue of its innovation, expand that market beyond what others have been able to achieve. The result is faster growth and more loyal buyers.

The entry of an innovative late mover affects the success of other brands in a more direct way as well. In the two markets examined, growth of the innovative late entrant actually slowed the growth of the pioneer and reduced the effectiveness of its marketing spending. Therefore, success of an innovative late entrant can diminish the advantages associated with pioneering. By comparison, growth of non-innovative later entrants had no such effect. Innovation coupled with late entry enables a brand to impose costs on its rivals, creating an advantage associated with late entry and a disadvantage associated with pioneering.

Innovative late entrants clearly enjoy advantages over other later entrants. Late movers enter a market that is entirely different from the one faced (created) by the pioneer. The rules of the game are very well established; the set of competitors can be clearly identified, buyers are knowledgeable, and some risks are low. Taking the low-risk path, however, appears to produce relatively poor results. Being a non-innovative late entrant yields a lower potential market, greater costs associated with marketing spending, and less loyal buyers. By contrast, the greater risk associated with innovation appears well rewarded. More important, innovative late entrants enjoy advantages over the pioneer. In fact, innovative late entrants appear able to redefine the competitive game and, drawing on the same process that creates pioneering advantage, create a late-mover advantage.

CONCLUSION

All buyers learn. Competitive strategies play a central role in the learning process by creating, in part, the observations and experiences that fuel buyer learning. Through their role in consumer learning, competitive strategies influence the fundamental rules of the competitive game—how buyers perceive alternatives, what they value, and how they choose. Successful brands, from pioneers through late entrants, use competitive strategy to shape that learning process. By doing so, they create the rules of the competitive game and create competitive advantage in the process.

Pioneers have the obvious opportunity to establish the rules of the game. With sufficient skill, resources, and insight, a pioneer can create a category, become strongly associated with it, and create a distinctive brand that is insulated to a significant degree from rivals. Late movers face a less obvious opportunity. From the advantages of the pioneer arise disadvantages for that same pioneer. Clever late entrants can leverage the weaknesses of the pioneer. By fast following, an entrant can exploit the innovation of the pioneer and its lack of relative resources. By differentiating, a later entrant can exploit the pioneer's relative inflexibility. Innovative late entrants can restart the learning process and use it to their own advantage, overtaking the pioneer and placing it in the role of follower.

The branding implications of these competitive findings are profound. Adopting a dynamic and long-term perspective on the evolution of a brand is critical. Building a strong brand is not enough. Innovative late entrants can overtake even the most successful brands—pioneers and followers alike. Mastering the dynamics of competition means that brands must constantly evolve to preempt competitors and reinforce the uniqueness of the brand.

Some have argued that this process can be so difficult as to defy even the best management. Christensen[17] argues, for example, that no firm that dominated the computer market during one era has successfully maintained its dominance into the next. While this may be true, firms like Harley-Davidson owe their continued survival, in significant measure, to the strength of their brands. From a conceptual standpoint, these findings suggest significant limitations of traditional analyses of marketing strategy, which are largely static. The fact that firms' activities change consumer perceptions not only of brands but also of categories means that industries evolve. This in turn means that long-term successful strategy hinges on recognition of dynamic evolutionary processes of brand revision, redefinition, and even reinvention.

Gregory S. Carpenter is James Farley/Booz Allen Hamilton Professor of Marketing Strategy and director of the Center for Market Leadership at the Kellogg School of Management. He served on the faculties of the University of California, Los Angeles, Columbia University, and the Yale School of Management before joining the Kellogg School faculty in 1990. Carpenter received a BA from Ohio Wesleyan University and an MBA, MPhil, and Ph.D. from Columbia University.

Kent Nakamoto is R.B. Pamplin Professor of Marketing and head of the Market-
ing Department at the Pamplin College of Business, Virginia Polytechnic Institute and
State University. Previously he held academic positions at the University of Colorado–
Boulder, the University of Arizona, and UCLA. He received a BS from the California
Institute of Technology, an MS from the University of Wisconsin–Madison, and a
Ph.D. from Stanford University.

NOTES

1. Kahneman, Daniel and Amos Tversky (1979), "Prospect Theory: An Analysis of Decision under Risk," *Econometrica,* 47, 263–291.

2. Robinson, William T. and Claes Fornell (1985), "Sources of Market Pioneering Advantages in Consumer Goods Industries in Consumer Goods Industries," *Journal of Marketing Research,* 22, 305–18; Robinson, William T. (1988), "Sources of Market Pioneering Advantages: The Case of Industrial," *Journal of Marketing Research,* 25, 87–94; Urban, Glen L., Theresa Carter, Steven Gaskin, and Zofia Mucha (1986), "Market Share Rewards to Pioneering Brands: An Empirical Analysis and Strategic Implications," *Management Science,* 32, 645-59.

3. Urban, Glen L., Theresa Carter, Steven Gaskin, and Zofia Mucha (1986), "Market Share Rewards to Pioneering Brands: An Empirical Analysis and Strategic Implications," *Management Science,* 32, 645–59.

4. Carpenter, Gregory S. and Kent Nakamoto (1989), "Consumer Preference Formation and Pioneering Advantage," *Journal of Marketing Research,* 26, 3 (August), 285–298.

5. See note 4.

6. Kardes, Frank R. and Gurumurthy Kalyanaram (1992), "Order-of-Entry Effects on Consumer Memory and Judgment: An Information Integration Perspective," *Journal of Marketing Research,* 29, 343–57.

7. See note 4.

8. See note 4.

9. Schmalensee, Richard (1982), "Product Differentiation Advantages of Pioneering Brands," *American Economic Review,* 72, 340–65.

10. See note 4.

11. Golder, Peter N. and Gerard J. Tellis (1993), "Pioneering Advantage: Marketing Logic or Marketing Legend?," *Journal of Marketing Research,* 30, 158–170.

12. Shankar, Venkatesh, Gregory S. Carpenter, and Lakshman Krishnamurthi (1999), "The Advantages of Entry in the Growth Stage of the Product Life Cycle: An Empirical Analysis," *Journal of Marketing Research,* 36, 2 (May), 269–276.

13. Carpenter, Gregory S., Donald R. Lehmann, Kent Nakamoto, and Suzanne Walchli (1993), "Pioneering Disadvantage: Consumer Response to Differentiated Entry and Defensive Imitation," working paper, Kellogg School of Management, Northwestern University.

14. Carpenter, Gregory S. and Kent Nakamoto (1990), "Competitive Strategies for Late Entry into a Market with a Dominant Brand," *Management Science,* 36, 10 (October), 1268–1278.

15. See note 11.

16. Shankar, Venkatesh, Gregory S. Carpenter, and Lakshman Krishnamurthi (1998), "Late Mover Advantage: How Innovative Late Entrants Outsell Pioneers," *Journal of Marketing Research,* 35, 1 (February), 54–70.

17. Christensen, Clayton M. (1997), *The Innovator's Dilemma: When New Technologies Cause Great Firms to Fail,* Boston: Harvard Business School Press.

CHAPTER 5

BRAND EXTENSIONS

BRIDGETTE M. BRAIG and ALICE M. TYBOUT

Successful companies understand that brands are assets. And successful managers seek to leverage these assets when they use an established brand name to launch new products. These *brand extensions* are termed *line extensions* when they are in the same product category as the parent or flagship brand, and they are termed *category extensions* when they are in a different category than the parent brand.

Consider the Ivory Soap brand, which was introduced to the marketplace by Procter & Gamble in 1879. Since that time, the brand has been used to launch line extensions, such as Ivory Liquid Hand Soap and Ivory Aloe Bar. These products leverage the Ivory equity of purity, mildness, and gentleness while helping to maintain the relevance of the brand in an evolving marketplace. Ivory Liquid Hand Soap offers consumers greater convenience and sanitation when washing hands. Ivory Aloe Bar reinforces and updates the claim that Ivory is pure and gentle by incorporating an ingredient that consumers associate with soothing and healing skin.

The Ivory name also has been extended into other cleansing-related categories, such as dishwashing liquid (Ivory Dish Soap) and detergent (Ivory Snow in Powder and Liquid), where gentleness is a benefit. Ivory Dish Soap is positioned as "Mild on Hands, Hard on Grease." Ivory Snow, long recognized as being mild enough for washing baby clothes, now claims a broader position as the detergent for all gentle-cycle garments ("Go ahead, wash it with Ivory Snow").

Ivory's disciplined approach to line and category extensions has been a key factor in keeping the brand viable in a dynamic marketplace for more than 125 years. Looking forward, what further extensions might leverage and support the brand? Should Ivory add versions of the bar that include popular skincare ingredients such as vitamin E? Should the brand be taken into other cleaning categories, such as shampoo or carpet cleaner? Would it be wise to consider co-branding to expand the reach of the brand (i.e., Marriott bed linens washed in Ivory Snow)? In this chapter, we address questions such as these that every company must ask when deciding to extend its brands.

We begin by discussing the rationale underlying brand extensions. We then present a framework for anticipating how consumers will respond to brand extensions. We conclude by considering the benefits and liabilities of brand extensions and provide a checklist of questions to answer prior to launching an extension.

WHY DO COMPANIES EXTEND BRANDS?

A primary engine for business growth is launching new products and services. New products and services address neglected consumer needs and respond to changing tastes and new competition in the marketplace. At the same time, the business of launching new products is both costly and risky. Establishing a new brand typically requires millions of dollars and a significant amount of time. Moreover, the vast majority of new products fail (9 out of 10 is a commonly referenced percentage) and are withdrawn from the market within a year.

Brand extensions can help manage the costs and risks associated with launching a new product. A familiar, trusted brand name signals quality to consumers and increases the likelihood that they will try the product. Anticipated consumer interest, in turn, increases retailers' willingness to stock the product. Further, an established brand name typically reduces advertising cost (consumers are already informed of the brands' many features and benefits). In fact, consumers' knowledge of the brand and its benefits may be automatically transferred to new products that are perceived to be compatible with the parent brand.

Appropriate brand extensions also benefit the parent brand. They sustain the brand's relevance as consumers' needs and competitors' offerings evolve (as in the Ivory example), and thereby motivate continued consumer and retailer interest in the brand. Finally, brand extensions may allow a firm to hedge its bets by reducing dependence on a single product flavor, form, or category, which may fall out of favor with consumer tastes.

Nevertheless, the use of an established brand by no means ensures a successful product launch. Many brand extensions fail to garner sufficient consumer acceptance to survive beyond the launch year. Thus, it is important to have a framework for anticipating how consumers will respond to brand extensions.

HOW DO CONSUMERS EVALUATE BRAND EXTENSIONS?

In general, consumers' response to a brand extension depends on the level of fit that they perceive between the parent brand and the extension.[1] The key question thus becomes, "What determines perceptions of fit?" The answer lies in understanding consumers' associations to and beliefs about a brand, many of which emanate from the brand's core *point of differentiation* or benefit. Consumers gauge fit by determining whether these associations make sense in the context of the extension.

Diet Coke is a good fit with the parent brand, Coke, because the two products differ primarily in the type of sweetener used and not in features such as taste, which are central to the product benefit. By contrast, Crystal Pepsi flopped, in part due to the poor fit with the parent brand, Pepsi. Launched as a clear cola, Crystal Pepsi's point of difference contradicted a key association to the parent brand—the traditional cola color. Similarly, BIC was able to extend its pen brand into the cigarette lighter and shaver categories through BIC's associations with "cheap," "plastic," and "disposability." But these same associations undermined consumer acceptance when the brand ventured into perfume, where these attributes have negative connotations.

The Role of Brand Positioning in Judgments of Extension Fit

Although *any* brand association may affect perceptions of fit, not all associations are created equal. The parent brand's positioning helps identify the associations that are most likely to influence perceptions of a brand extension's fit. We adopt the positioning framework detailed in Chapter 1; a brand's positioning specifies the target customer, the frame of reference (FOR), point of difference (POD), and reasons to believe (RTB) the claimed point of difference.

Target The targeted customer (user) is sometimes a potent association for the brand. For example, the image of the Harley-Davidson biker is an integral part of the Harley brand. Harley may both launch line extensions that serve the needs of this customer base (i.e., clothing, motor homes) and enter new categories, such as temporary tattoos, where the imagery of the tattooed biker lends an aura of authenticity to the product for consumers unwilling to commit to the real thing.

Of course, associations related to the brand user can also restrict brand extensions. Kimberly-Clark successfully extended the Huggies brand from babies to toddlers when it launched Huggies Pull-ups. However, when the company launched adult incontinence products, it developed an entirely new brand—while a Huggies diaper product could serve adults equally well, it was associated with children, not adults. Thus, the Depends brand is used for adult incontinence and the Poise brand addresses the needs of post-40-year-old women who experience occasional loss of bladder control.

Frame of Reference Companies work hard to build strong associations between a brand and its frame of reference. As discussed in Chapter 1, these associations may be relatively concrete (a product category or a key competitor) or abstract (a goal such as empowerment or achievement). When a brand is strongly associated with a specific product category, as is the case with Coke and *soft drink* and McDonald's and *fast food,* it may be challenging to extend the brand into categories that have dissimilar features. For example, line extensions such as Diet Coke and Cherry Coke may fit the parent brand, but forays into categories such as clothing may be perceived as stretching the brand beyond its associations. Thus, ironically, a brand's strength in the flagship category can become a limitation when trying to leverage the brand in other categories.

The Ralph Lauren brand avoided this pitfall by employing a more abstract FOR. Although the brand was launched in the clothing category, the FOR has been the goal of achieving a timeless sense of style, rather than a particular product category. As a result, extensions of the Ralph Lauren brand into a wide range of categories related to this lifestyle, including linens, furniture, and even cuisine (i.e., Ralph Lauren restaurant), are perceived to fit the brand.

Point of Difference A brand's defining benefit or POD may be the most potent association for a brand. Hence, it can often have the greatest influence on the perceived fit of a brand extension. Once again, the range of extensions that consumers will view as fitting the parent brand is influenced by whether the POD has been represented in a concrete or abstract manner.

Consider Bounty paper towels, which are differentiated from other brands in terms of superior absorption (i.e., "The quicker picker-upper!"). Bounty's POD might be used to enter other product categories where the absorption benefit is relevant (i.e., sponges). However, it is difficult to think of many such categories, especially when the hygiene category is excluded due to Bounty's association with cleaning rather than personal care.

By contrast, consider the Virgin brand. Virgin spans categories from airlines to music stores to colas. This works because Virgin's POD is its *attitude*. Virgin is the scrappy underdog that challenges the established players in a market with an iconoclastic attitude that is personified by the company founder, Richard Branson. This POD is equally relevant and resonant with consumers whether they're considering an airline, a music store, or a cola.

Reasons to Believe   Brands that claim an abstract POD typically support their claims with reasons to believe (RTB). These more concrete attributes also may influence the perception of fit. For example, Coors beer claims a unique crisp, clean taste. This POD is supported by noting that the beer is brewed in the Rocky Mountains of Colorado. This association might encourage consumers to view other products that would benefit from the Rocky Mountains point of origin (perhaps bottled water) as fitting the Coors brand.

An Illustration: Extending the Apple Brand

Apple Computer has successfully launched a variety of brand extensions based on a clear understanding of the brand's positioning. Apple's POD is empowering creativity and productivity. The POD has been the basis for extending the company's line of computers into professional desktops and mobile computers (iMac, iBook, G3, G4). It also has allowed the company to successfully launch products that empower consumers to play as well as to work (iPod, iTunes).

Apple's claim of empowering creativity and productivity is supported by user-focused aesthetics, form, and interface. These reasons to believe Apple's POD have been leveraged when the brand has entered categories such as monitors, where cutting-edge design sets Apple apart from its competitors. In the future, Apple's association with elegant design could support extensions into additional categories such as printers, speaker phones, and CD/DVD, where design has traditionally taken a back seat to function.

Although Apple has worked to establish a broad customer base in both office and home computer markets, it enjoys particular strength in the education segment. This association might allow it to extend into other education products and services, such as electronic textbooks or interactive distance learning programs. Such extensions would leverage not only the association with the education target, but also the POD of empowerment. However, although these extensions might be perceived to fit the brand, they also might undermine the goal of broadening the brand's reach beyond the education niche. Thus, it is important to remember that while an extension's fit with the brand's associations is necessary for consumers' acceptance, consumer acceptance is only one consideration in the decision to launch an extension.

The genius of Apple founder Steve Jobs arguably comes not only from his status as a technological visionary, but also from his insight about brand positioning and brand extensions. With each new product launch, Jobs (and Apple) have leveraged the core (no pun intended) associations to Apple. This strategy has allowed Apple to expand significantly without dilution or damage to the brand. Quite the contrary, Apple has grown beyond its former cult, taking empowering creativity and productivity to high-end shopping malls and standalone retail locations with its successful launch of Apple Stores.

Influencing the Perceived Fit between an Extension and the Parent Brand

Often, consumers more readily accept brand extensions that fit with the parent brand than those that do not. However, extensions with less obvious connections to the parent brand can also succeed if consumers are provided with the information and the motivation necessary to discover a basis for fit.

For example, advertising might present an unknown connection between the flagship brand and the extension. In the case of Porsche's entry into the SUV market with its Cayenne model, consumers might be more inclined to see Cayenne as fitting the Porsche brand if they knew that the company was one of the first auto manufacturers to make an all-wheel drive vehicle (in 1904). Similarly, consumers might view Jack Daniel's Charcoal as better fitting the whiskey brand if they knew that the charcoal is a by-product of filtering the whiskey through charcoal.

Context can also help consumers make sense of the brand extension associations. If a Guess? watch ad appears in a fashion magazine, consumers might be more likely to recognize that the watch is more a trendy accessory (leveraging the brand's fashion status) than a precise timepiece. Media vehicles might also confer a halo of credibility. Placing an ad for the new Cadillac CTS in GQ or *Vanity Fair* might encourage consumers to consider the luxury rather than the geriatric associations to the parent brand.

Also, a brand's shelf placement might help consumers recognize how the brand fits with a new category or usage situation. Almond Accents, a line of flavored sliced almonds for use in salads and other recipes, grew to a $100 million business when placed in the produce section of grocery stores (rather than in the salad dressing aisle).

In addition, consumer characteristics also play a role in the acceptance of extensions that are distant from the parent brand. Highly involved or motivated consumers are better able to make sense of distant extensions than less-involved consumers. In fact, the more involved and knowledgeable consumers are, the less likely they are to see a disconnect between the parent and the extension—these consumers have a greater number of associations to the parent brand, so they can find rationales for the extension more easily. Similarly, when consumers are in a positive mood, they are better able to see connections between a parent brand and a distant brand extension. Consequently, marketers may enhance a distant extension's chances by using advertising strategies, such as humor, that both engage consumers' interest and create a positive mood.

While it is optimal for an extension to fit with the most apparent associations to the parent brand, sometimes a moderate level of incongruity can be beneficial.[2] Consider again the example of Jack Daniel's Charcoal, an extension that lacks an obvious fit with the parent brand, whiskey. An issue like this can sometimes create a marketing buzz. Consumers might ask, Why did the company enter the category and what advantage might the brand offer relative to others? If these questions can be answered to consumers' satisfaction, they may exhibit increased interest and engagement with the brand extension (beyond what might have been achieved with an obvious fit).[3]

WHAT ARE THE RISKS IN EXTENDING A BRAND?

Although extensions can be beneficial, they also can be costly if not managed carefully. Thus, it is important to recognize the risks associated with brand extensions and weigh them against the benefits.[4]

Extensions are often motivated by the desire to address additional or different consumer needs. For example, line extensions may be introduced in response to consumers' desire for variety in flavors, forms, and package sizes. The logic is that it's better to get consumers to switch within the brand franchise than to lose the consumer to a competitors' product. Skippy Peanut Butter clearly would not want to risk losing the crunchy consumer to rival Jif, so its line includes both crunchy and smooth versions to attract consumers who prefer each type of peanut butter.

But caution is required. Although it's tempting to create a brand version to fit the specific needs of every consumer, a plethora of versions can confuse consumers about which version is the right one for them, sending them searching for a brand with fewer options. Consider a woman seeking a good moisturizer for her dry skin. If she wants an Olay facial moisturizing product, she must figure out whether Olay Total Effects Moisturizer, Olay Age Defying Cream, Olay Active Hydrating Fluid and Cream, or Olay ProVital Moisture Cream is the best one for her skin.

Household cleaners are no more disciplined than health and beauty aids. They have product variations for each surface and room in the house as well as a variety of forms for each (trigger spray bottle, wipes, concentrate, etc.). In contrast, Simple Green touts itself as the strong cleaner that is good for everything. Although it is unlikely to unseat 409 and Fantastik in the all-purpose cleaner category, Simple Green has consistently been in the top-10 SKUs in sales and total units, suggesting that its simple premise holds appeal. Lever 2000 has pursued a similar approach in the bar soap category, and it also has enjoyed success.

Line extensions may be attractive to managers because the R&D and production costs to introduce them are typically lower than those associated with entry into a new product category (regardless of whether an established brand is used). In many cases, existing suppliers and production lines can be readily adapted. Often, the product's label is the most complex change needed to produce a line extension. However, line extensions can possibly dilute associations to the parent brand and thereby make its appeal less apparent to consumers. Further, line extensions may divert intellectual resources from projects with higher-margin potential. For example, tweaking a pharmaceutical product from a three-times-a-day to a once-a-day dosing regimen (e.g., Wellbutrin-XL vs. Wellbutrin-SR) could take time from pursuing promising larger leaps in drug innovation.

In addition, although line extensions have been documented to deliver sales spikes, if they are driven by fads or represent only a cosmetic change readily copied by competitors, the sales gain may be short lived. For example, licensed character products, such as SpongeBob Square Pants cereal, are viable only as long as the character sustains consumers' interest. Likewise, the competitive advantage of Pledge cleaning wipes was erased when Endust quickly followed with a similar product. In such situations, line extensions only make good business sense when the cost structure allows profitability in the short-term *and* includes a clear plan for exiting the market when profits erode.

Line extensions also may be introduced in order to gain additional shelf facings from retailers. Gaining more retail space is attractive both because it can contract the space available for competitors' brands and because it can increase the visual impact of the extended brand at the point of sale. In addition, advertising and promotions for the flagship brand can benefit all extensions of the line, allowing one campaign to pack a bigger punch. A case in point is General Mills's extensions of the Cheerios brand to Honey Nut Cheerios and Frosted Cheerios. Each extension increased the shelf presence of the brand, and the promotional dollars spent on the flagship brand and the Honey Nut extension allowed the Frosted extension to capture half a share point in the multibillion-dollar cereal category in its first week of national distribution.

Although the potential efficiencies of line extensions are tantalizing, they are not always realized. The competition for shelf space is intense, and retailers often prefer to reserve additional facings for their own store-branded products. As a result, shelf facings for a line extension may be cannibalized from the existing brand allotment and are likely to be quickly withdrawn if the line extension fails to generate sufficient volume. And, the space lost to a failed line extension may be difficult to regain. Further, if the extension enjoys consumer acceptance, the retailer may quickly introduce a store-branded version to capture higher margins, which dilutes the sale of the original extension. In addition, adding SKUs (stock keeping units) through extensions also makes brand management more complex. Managers must track production, marketing programs, forecasting, shelf sets, plan-o-grams, and sales, and they must share results for each SKU individually as well as for the brand overall.

Category extensions are subject to many of the same risks as line extensions. However, the move to a new category adds some unique benefits and challenges. One rationale for taking an established brand into a new product category is that it may bring new users to the franchise by providing multiple points of entry into a relationship with the brand.[5] Over time, Nike has successfully drawn in consumers via running shoes, basketball, golf, fashion, and more. Once consumers experience the brand's performance-oriented sports gear in one category, they may be more likely to turn to the brand in other categories.

However, if the brand performance in the new category is disappointing because the company lacks the same level of expertise in that category that it has in the parent brand category, backlash may occur and damage the brand. Even if the category extension lives up to consumer expectations, dilution is a risk. As noted earlier, stretching a brand into other, more distant categories may weaken the linkage to the originating category, which in turn may weaken the brand's equity. Further, advertising efficiencies attributed to line extensions are less likely to be realized with category extensions. Category extensions typically require separate campaigns to establish brand membership in the new category and to demonstrate the new relevance of the POD.

On the positive side, research has found that the use of sub-brands might mitigate negative backlash from distant extensions. Sub-brands appear in a variety of forms, but they usually introduce a new name linked to the existing brand name, such as the Sony Walkman. When the Walkman hit the United States in the late 1970s, Sony was best known for higher-end stereo equipment and televisions. The portable radio and tape player was a new category and sported a far lower price point than Sony's previous offerings. The Walkman sub-brand addressed several issues. First, if the Walkman failed, the sub-brand name would absorb much of the failure and protect the Sony parent brand. Second, the Walkman name separated the new, lower-priced product from the higher-end Sony brand. Finally, the Walkman name helped educate consumers about the nature of the new product (i.e., that it was for mobile use).

The Walkman was hugely successful and became the generic category term for all portable music devices with headphones. As a result, Sony has been able to launch brand extensions in additional lower-end categories (e.g., videotapes, CDs, Discmans, Watchmans, etc.) as well as higher-end categories (e.g., DVD players, large-screen TVs, personal computers, etc.). Hence, while the sub-brand strategy initially protected the Sony brand against potential failure of the extension, the success of the Walkman extension gave Sony permission to stretch the brand even further. (For more discussion of sub-brands, see Chapter 6.)

CONCLUSION

When executed properly, a broad brand—one that has extended into a variety of product categories—is *stronger* than a narrower brand.[6] As brand breadth increases, favorablity toward subsequent brand extensions and confidence in its benefits and associations also increase. This has the effect of enriching core brand associations while building market share in multiple categories. However, brand expansion cannot proceed unchecked. Extension planning must be tempered by the reality of what consumers will accept as fitting with the parent brand. The framework that we have outlined suggests that consumer acceptance is more likely when managers observe three guidelines in launching brand extensions:

1. *Go slow.* Introduce extensions that draw the brand outward from its core category step by step.
2. *Facilitate perceptions of fit.* Use elements of the marketing mix, such as advertising and retail product placement, to help consumers make sense of brand extensions.

3. *Assess extension impact on the parent brand.* Any extension necessarily alters consumers' perceptions of the parent brand. Therefore, it is critical to ensure that the effects are consistent with the long-term goals for the brand positioning.

Further, managing a portfolio of line and brand extensions requires vigilant monitoring. From a business perspective, each version of the brand must have a clear reason for being and a plan for profitability. If a particular brand extension fails to turn a profit in the short term, managers must determine how long to give it before making the decision to pull the plug. From a brand positioning perspective, managers must also examine the impact of each extension on consumers' associations to the core brand.

KEY QUESTIONS TO ASK WHEN EXTENDING A BRAND

Brand extensions are more likely to succeed when managers ask the right questions and think hard about their answers. Below are seven key questions to consider. They are illustrated by the Ivory brand discussed at the outset of the chapter.

1. How is the parent brand currently positioned? (The Ivory brand stands for pure and gentle cleansing for delicate skin and fabrics.)
2. What elements of my positioning do I want to extend? (Ivory might leverage its association with babies (Ivory Snow), cleansing, purity, or gentleness in launching a new product.)
3. Will consumers automatically understand the logic for the extension? If not, how can the marketing plan help to lead them to such an understanding? (If Ivory introduced an Ivory bar with vitamin E, the connection to cleansing and purifying might be explained in advertising.)
4. Is the parent brand association valued by consumers in the new extension category? (If Ivory launched a carpet cleaner, would the association to gentleness be meaningful in this category? Consumers might seek products that promise "tough, deep-down cleaning" rather than gentleness in this category.)
5. What is the impact of the extension on the parent (backlash)? (Would the addition of an Ivory bar with vitamin E dilute Ivory's association with purity and gentleness?)

6. What is the impact of the extension on other existing extensions? (Will an Ivory bar with vitamin E merely steal market share from the already-introduced Ivory bar with aloe?)

7. What is the impact of the extension launch on <u>consumers' evaluation of competing brands</u>? That is, has the extension strategy served to reposition or alter associations to competitors? (Ivory's introduction of Liquid Hand Soap removed convenient dispensing as a point of difference for competitors such as Dial.)

There are no particular right answers to these questions. However, their careful consideration should improve the odds that brand extensions will leverage and support the parent brand rather than undermine it.

Bridgette M. Braig is an independent marketing consultant. Earlier in her career she was assistant professor of marketing at the University of Colorado's College of Business and Administration and a consultant with the Sterling-Rice Group, a brand consulting firm based in Boulder, Colorado. She received her BA and Ph.D. from the Kellogg School of Management.

Alice M. Tybout is Harold T. Martin Professor of Marketing and chair of the Marketing Department at the Kellogg School of Management. She is also co-director of the Kellogg on Branding Program and director of the Consumer Marketing Strategy Programs at the James L. Allen Center. She received her BS and MA from The Ohio State University and her Ph.D. from Northwestern University.

NOTES

1. Aaker, David and Kevin Lane Keller (1990), "Consumer Evaluations of Brand Extensions," *Journal of Marketing,* 54, 27–41; Barone, Michale, Paul W. Miniard, and Jean B. Romeo (2000), "The Influence of Positive Mood on Brand Extension Evaluations," *Journal of Consumer Research,* 26, 386–400; Park, C. Whan, Sandra Milberg, and Robert Lawson (1991), "Evaluation of Brand Extensions: The Role of Product Feature Similarity and Brand Concept Consistency," *Journal of Consumer Research,* 18, 185–193.

2. Meyers-Levy, Joan, Therese A. Louie, and Mary T. Curren (1994), "How Does the Congruity of Brand Names Affect Evaluations of Brand Name Extensions?" *Journal of Applied Psychology,* 79, 46–53; Maoz, Eyal and Alice M. Tybout (2002), "The Moderating Role of Involvement and Differentiation in the Evaluation of Brand Extensions," *Journal of Consumer Psychology,* 12, 119–131.

3. Maoz, Eyal (1995), "Similarity and the Moderating Role of Involvement in the Evaluation of Brand Extensions," unpublished doctoral dissertation, Northwestern University.

4. Quelch, John A. and David Kenny (1994), "Extend Profits, Not Product Lines," *Harvard Business Review* (September–October), 153–160.

5. Swaminathan, Vanitha, Richard A. Fox, and Srinivas K. Reddy (2001), "The Impact of Brand Extension Introduction on Choice," *Journal of Marketing,* 65, 1–15.

6. Dacin, Peter A. and Daniel C. Smith (1994), "The Effect of Brand Portfolio Characteristics on Consumer Evaluations of Brand Extensions," *Journal of Marketing Research,* 31, 229–242; Mervis, Tom and Chris Janisewski (2004), "When Are Broader Brands Stronger Brands? An Accessibility Perspective on the Success of Brand Extensions," *Journal of Consumer Research,* 31, 346–357.

CHAPTER 6

BRAND PORTFOLIO STRATEGY

TIM CALKINS

Building a single brand is a challenge. Determining the correct positioning, optimizing the brand's design, and managing the brand's meaning over time—all while developing and executing business initiatives that deliver profits—is a difficult undertaking. Indeed, most of this book is devoted to the topic.

Managing a brand portfolio, or a group of different brands, takes the challenge to another level. When dealing with brand portfolios, the challenge isn't building a single brand. The challenge is building a collection of brands, each with different strengths and limitations. Decisions that are optimal for one brand might not be optimal for another. Building a successful brand portfolio strategy is all about trade-offs and tough choices.

In today's challenging business climate, portfolio strategy is receiving focus and attention from corporations around the globe, as senior executives realize that building strong brands does not guarantee long-term financial success on its own; a company needs a powerful brand portfolio. Indeed, every company and organization faces brand portfolio questions. Even if a company has only one brand, it may launch or acquire a new brand or extend its current brand, and these moves impact the portfolio.

This chapter first defines brand portfolio strategy and highlights key brand portfolio questions, then reviews why portfolio strategy is so critically important. The chapter presents the two most significant brand portfolio models (house of brands and branded house), and highlights five keys to success.

104

BRAND PORTFOLIO STRATEGY DEFINITIONS

A brand portfolio strategy outlines how a company will use different brands and branding elements to drive profitable growth. Brand portfolio strategy helps companies address questions such as:

- Should we add a brand to the portfolio?
- How do we prioritize our brands?
- Do we have too many brands? Should we get rid of brands?

Portfolio strategy also helps companies determine how to develop the optimal brand structure, potentially using elements such as sub-brands, endorser brands, and branded ingredients or services.

Before proceeding too far in a discussion of brand portfolios, it is important to cover a few key definitions.

Primary Brand

The primary brand is the main brand name on a product or service. This is generally the largest branding element on a product package or in a piece of communication. This is what people refer to when they talk about the brand. Every brand has a primary brand.

The very simplest branding structures have just a primary brand and product description. Brands such as McDonald's restaurants, Starbucks coffee, Marlboro cigarettes, and Prozac antidepressant medication are all examples of a primary brand followed by a product description.

Sub-Brand

Sub-brands are secondary branding elements that fall below the primary brand in prominence but usually above the product description. The primary brand continues to be the most prominent branding element. Sub-brands are usually employed to set apart a group of products or service offerings that are different in some meaningful way from the primary brand. General Electric, for example, uses sub-brands in its appliances business; GE Monogram is a line of designer appliances and GE Profile is a line of high-quality appliances.

Sub-brands can vary substantially in prominence. Some sub-brands are very small branding elements; the primary brand clearly dominates the brand structure. Other sub-brands become very prominent, getting close to the primary brand in overall impact. There is a limit to how important the sub-brand can become; if the sub-brand is more prominent than the primary brand, then the sub-brand is actually the primary brand.

Sub-brands are best used when there is a need to clearly distinguish between products sold under a particular brand. Importantly, there must be a compelling reason to have a sub-brand; each sub-brand creates complexity and requires both attention and marketing support.

Barilla, for example, used a sub-brand on a new line of premium pasta sauces it launched in the United States in 2004. The new line was substantially different from the existing line of sauces; it was superior in quality and higher priced, and it needed to be cooked differently. As a result, Barilla needed to clearly distinguish between the new sauces and the existing sauces. Barilla used the sub-brand Restaurant Creations to differentiate these items from the rest of the line.

Endorser Brand

Endorser brands are secondary branding elements. When an endorser brand is present, a primary brand and a product description will also be present. Endorser brands are used to link the primary brand to another brand. Endorser brands are often used to communicate the parent company of the primary brand, but this is not always the case—sometimes an endorser brand simply links to another brand in the portfolio. Generally, endorsers are used to bring credibility to the primary brand while letting the primary brand establish its own identity. Apple, for example, is an endorser brand on iPod.

Endorsers can vary substantially in prominence, ranging from very slight endorsement to very strong endorsement. Like sub-brands, endorser brands can never exceed the prominence of the primary brand; if the endorser brand is the largest branding element, then it is actually the primary brand, not an endorser.

Ingredient or Service Brands

Ingredient and service brands are used to brand, and in turn claim ownership to, a particular product component or service. Ingredient or service brands help differentiate products by giving the product a distinct point of difference—a distinction that is not easy for competitors to match. A vague phrase, such as "heavy duty" or "high quality," is easy for competitors to copy. A branded ingredient or service is not, because it is legally protected. For example, Glad trash bags employed a branded ingredient to differentiate; Glad added a fragrance to their bags and created a branded ingredient, FreshScent. FreshScent wasn't part of the product name, but it was prominently featured on the package. Similarly, Chrysler created an ingredient brand around an engine, the Hemi, indicating a high level of performance. In hotels, Westin introduced the Heavenly Bed as a branded service.

Ingredient brands and service brands are not part of the official product name. The product will have a primary brand and a product description that will be independent of the branded ingredient or service.

THE CHALLENGE OF BRAND PORTFOLIO STRATEGY

In the simplest scenario, a company owns a brand, which exists in a category as a product. There is one company, one brand, one category, and one product. The company and the primary brand share the same name. Figure 6.1 shows this simple brand structure.

Figure 6.1
Simple Brand Portfolio

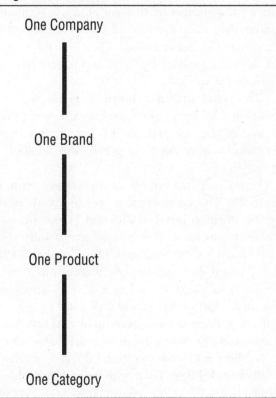

One Company

One Brand

One Product

One Category

Red Bull, for example, is a company with a simple brand portfolio. The company has only one brand. The company was founded in 1984 with just one product, an 8.3-oz energy drink. Red Bull didn't introduce another product for almost two decades—in 2003, the company brought Red Bull Sugar Free to market. But the portfolio continued to be simple: one company, one brand, one category, and two products. Despite the narrow product line, the company has delivered remarkable results—in 2004 it sold over one billion cans, providing evidence that simple brand structures can deliver strong performance.[1]

With a simple brand structure, the business challenge is clear: Drive short-term sales of the brand while building the brand for the long term. If the company optimizes the brand results, it will optimize the company results. This is not always easy to do, but there is little question about the basic objective.

Life, however, is rarely simple, and this is particularly true with brand portfolios. Few companies have just one brand and one or two products. Companies usually own a number of different brands. Each of these brands often has a number of different products, sometimes in several different categories. Very often each brand will have a brand structure that includes sub-brands and endorser brands. The company may have several brands playing in the same product category, and it may have different brands in different parts of the world.

The brand structure shown in Figure 6.2 shows the frequent reality of brand portfolios. In this example, the company has four different brands. Three of the brands have sub-brands, and one has a sub-sub-brand. The brands play in multiple categories, with multiple brands playing in the same categories.

PepsiCo is an example of a company with a large and complex brand portfolio. The company manages hundreds of different brands around the globe. PepsiCo lists 180 different brands on its web site, but it notes that these are just some of its best-known brands.[2] The company's brand portfolio is complex. For example, PepsiCo owns Frito-Lay. Frito-Lay is the primary brand on a number of different products, such as Frito-Lay nuts and Fritos corn chips. Frito-Lay is also an endorser brand on brands such as Doritos. Doritos has sub-brands such as Edge, which highlights low-carb offerings. Edge is a sub-brand that cuts across a number of different Frito-Lay brands, including Doritos and Tostitos. On the Doritos Edge product, then, there is an endorser brand (Frito-Lay), a primary brand (Doritos), and a sub-brand (Edge). Each of these branding elements is also present on mul-

Figure 6.2
Typical Brand Portfolio

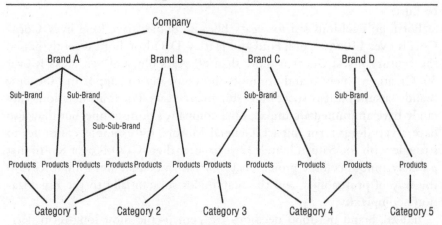

tiple other products. And all of them are owned by PepsiCo. It is a very tangled web.

The complexity of some brand portfolios can be staggering. Nestlé has 8,000 different brands. Newell–Rubbermaid has 500 brands. Kraft Foods has 59 different brands with over $100 million in annual revenue.

THE IMPORTANCE OF PORTFOLIO STRATEGY

Portfolio decisions are exceptionally important because they have a major impact on revenue and profitability. The profit of a company is ultimately the sum of profits from different brands in the portfolio. In the long term, if the portfolio includes profitable and growing brands that have little overlap, the company will do well. If the portfolio is made up of poorly performing brands that compete with each other, the company will struggle.

Brand portfolio decisions directly drive results. For example, a new product will have a dramatically different financial profile depending on whether the company launches it as a new brand or as an extension of an existing brand. A new product introduced as a new brand will likely be highly incremental. It will require substantial marketing spending and will meaningfully increase the complexity of the organization. The same new product launched under an existing brand will be less incremental. However, it will require less marketing spending and will create less organizational complexity. The new product will now pose some risk for the existing brand; if the new product disappoints consumers, the existing brand will be hurt.

Portfolio decisions last for years, because brands have long lives. Coca-Cola is over 110 years old; Ford and Harley-Davidson both recently passed the century mark. Gucci is more than 80 years old, and Starbucks is over 30. Creating a new brand commits the company to supporting the new brand—assuming it is successful—for many years. Portfolio decisions certainly have an immediate impact on a company's bottom line, but they also have a very long-term impact. General Motors, for example, continues to struggle with the Saturn brand, 22 years after then-CEO Roger Smith first publicly announced the project in 1983. Saturn contributes little to GM in the way of profitability, and the brand adds substantially to the organization's complexity.

Indeed, brand portfolio decisions are perhaps the most long-term decisions a manager will make. Advertising creative changes, sometimes remarkably quickly; some brands run several different advertising campaigns in a year. Promotions come and go, with some only lasting a day or a week. Pricing moves can certainly have long-term effects, but pricing is ultimately a flexible tactic. Even some branding moves are short term. Brand design elements can evolve—updating a logo is a significant move, but not one the company is stuck with for decades. Tag lines come and go. Portfolio decisions, however, last for years.

Portfolio decisions are also exceptionally hard to reverse. Once a decision has been made regarding the brand portfolio, it is difficult (and sometime impossible) to change course. Relaunching a failed new product under a different brand name is usually futile, because the opportunity to be new is gone—a product can only be new once. In addition, competitors are quick to respond to new products, so the relaunch of a failed new product will likely face increased competition. Bringing a discontinued brand back to life is costly and difficult; the brand must regain distribution and win back customers.

Portfolio decisions are not easy. The decisions have both short-term and long-term implications, so balancing the two perspectives is difficult. For example, launching a new brand might be the optimal move for short-term incremental volume, but it might not be the optimal long-term move because it creates complexity in the portfolio and stretches the organization. Portfolio decisions also require trade-offs between brands; optimizing the portfolio often requires sacrificing efforts on one brand to support growth on another. Building all of the brands simultaneously and maximizing the portfolio in total are often very different things; the best way to build a portfolio is often to focus on some brands at the expense of others.

Portfolio decisions also can become emotional. The team leading a brand is often very attached to it; the brand may even give the team a sense of identity, just as some brands give their customers a sense of identity. As a result, people working on a brand will often fight very hard to defend it, lobbying for resources and attention even when the moves might not be right for the company as a whole.

Most challenging, perhaps, is the fact that there is rarely a clear answer to a portfolio decision, and in most situations there are no analyses that will conclusively prove that one decision is right and another is wrong. Portfolio decisions are affected by many variables, making it difficult to construct a financial model that will clearly indicate which path will lead to the most long-term profitability. The results are dependent on the assumptions that go into the analysis. There are tools that can help; understanding a brand's meaning, for example, will help determine how far it can extend (see Chapter 3). Concept tests of new products under different brand names can shed light on the impact of different branding moves. Long-term financial modeling can help show the potential impact of different options. Ultimately, however, none of the analyses will decisively determine the right answer. The decisions have to be based on strategic thinking and good judgment.

While portfolio questions are challenging, they cannot be ignored. Every company must constantly monitor its brand portfolio. Some executives attempt to gloss over the topic, dodging the tough strategic and political issues. A senior executive at Kraft Foods, for example, frequently rallied his team by proclaiming that every brand should and could flourish, stating, "I don't believe in portfolio strategy." This, of course, ignores the obvious: Managers are always making portfolio strategy decisions. Each time a company launches a new product it makes a portfolio decision, and each time a company sets financial targets or allocates spending it makes a portfolio decision.

Optimizing each individual brand, in the absence of a broader perspective, is a bit like worrying about each particular color in a painting; the individual colors may be nice, but they must work together to create a beautiful piece.

BRAND PORTFOLIO MODELS

There are two basic models for brand portfolios: house of brands and branded house. Both models are widely employed by companies, and both have strengths and weaknesses. Importantly, most companies do not follow either model exclusively; they use elements of both models depending on their situations.

House of Brands

The classic and most powerful model for a brand portfolio is the house of brands. With this model, a company will own a number of different brands, possibly with several different brands in the same category. Each brand exists on its own. The company minimizes cannibalization and redundancy by creating a distinct positioning for each brand. In a particular category, for example, one brand may target price-sensitive customers and compete on low price, while another brand targets performance-oriented customers and competes on technical features. Companies employing the house of brands model often use a distinct corporate name. As a result, consumers are often unaware that a company's brands are all owned by the same parent.

Procter & Gamble is a classic example of a company employing a house of brands approach. The company owns dozens of different brands including Ivory, Tide, Pampers, Old Spice, Swiffer, Pringles, and Olay. Each brand is distinct; the Procter & Gamble brand is not used on any of the products. Indeed, the only way a customer would know the brands are owned by Procter & Gamble is by studying the fine print on the back of the label. Marketing efforts for each brand are largely independent, and brands are managed by distinct teams. In some categories, Procter & Gamble uses different brands to target different consumer groups and meet different consumer needs. In laundry care, for example, P&G has nine primary brands in the United States, including five brands of laundry detergent: Tide, Cheer, Gain, Dreft, and Ivory.

LVMH Group is another example of a company embracing the house of brands model. LVMH owns more than 50 different luxury brands across categories including fashion, wines and spirits, and watches. LVMH brands include Louis Vuitton, Donna Karan, Moet & Chandon, Dom Perignon, TAG Heuer, Zenith, and many others. Each brand is distinct; LVMH owns and manages the brands but plays no role in each product's branding. There is no LVMH store, no LVMH credit card, and no LVMH frequent buyer program.

The house of brands structure has a number of compelling advantages. The most obvious advantage is that each brand can be precisely targeted to a group of consumers with a distinct product offering and positioning. There is no need to stretch a brand beyond its positioning; if an opportunity is compelling but the brands in the portfolio are not appropriate, the company can acquire or launch a new brand. When PepsiCo saw a need for a carbonated drink to compete with Coca-Cola's Sprite, for example, it expanded its portfolio by launching a new brand, Sierra Mist, targeted precisely at the oppor-

advantages

tunity. This made perfect sense; extending the Pepsi brand into lemon-lime soda would have created confusion about the new product and confusion about Pepsi.

Similarly, a house of brands strategy makes it easy to build a global business, because brands can play in countries where they are most relevant. If a brand is not meaningful in one country, for example, the parent company can acquire or launch a brand that is relevant. Alternatively, if succeeding in a country requires a low-price, low-quality product, the company can create a distinct brand for the opportunity rather than risk damaging one of its more premium brands.

The house of brands model also lets a company create a distinct corporate brand. This has two advantages. First, the corporate brand can create a meaning distinct from the brands it owns. Second, a distinct corporate brand makes it easy to manage the portfolio; the company can buy and sell brands without having to change the corporate brand.

Altria Group provides an example of the value of having a distinct corporate brand. Altria is a classic house of brands; it is one of the world's largest companies, with 2004 revenues of over $89 billion. The company consists of 400 different brands playing in categories ranging from cigarettes to steak sauce. However, prior to 2003, the corporation was named Philip Morris. Using the Philip Morris brand created two problems. First, it tightly linked the corporation to the tobacco business, because the Philip Morris brand was tied to tobacco due to its long heritage in the industry. As David Sylvia, director of corporate identity at Altria, noted in a speech to the American Marketing Association, "People heard 'Philip Morris' and, rightfully so, thought 'tobacco.' "[3] This association was inconsistent with the corporation's business—tobacco was only one part of the portfolio. The association created a negative image for the company, linking the corporation to the unpopular tobacco business. Second, using the Philip Morris brand limited the corporation's flexibility to manage the entire portfolio, because the parent corporation would need to change its name if it ever spun off the tobacco business. Sylvia stated, "As we consider acquisitions and new financial transactions . . . it's important for the parent company, the publicly traded entity, to have a clear and distinct identity from its subsidiaries."[4]

The house of brands approach also minimizes risk because the company has a number of different brands it can rely on. If one of the brands loses favor or is tarnished by scandal, the company can focus on its other brands. Procter & Gamble, for example, faced a crisis in the early 1980s when Rely, its brand of tampon, was linked to toxic shock syndrome, a potentially deadly ailment. P&G was forced to pull the Rely brand from the market. However, since *disadvantages*

Rely was a distinct brand, the crisis had relatively little impact on the rest of the P&G portfolio.

The house of brands approach does have downsides. First, a house of brands can be a challenge to manage due to its complexity. Each brand needs to make decisions about pricing, new products, advertising, and other matters. With a large brand portfolio, senior management cannot focus on each brand individually. If a company doesn't have an entrepreneurial culture, a house of brands approach can lead to debilitating complexity. Second, this model can be inefficient. Since each brand markets its products independently, there is limited synergy. Indeed, if a company pursuing a house of brands model isn't careful, it can end up with a large number of small brands, each one lacking the scale needed to drive substantial profits. Third, a house of brands requires disciplined positioning to ensure that brands in the portfolio stand for different things. If a house of brands becomes a house of redundant brands, each one competing with the others, the company has a major problem indeed.

General Motors provides a vivid example of the risk of a house of brands strategy. General Motors is a classic house of brands; the company was formed in 1908 by William Durant, who saw the power of the house of brands strategy and brought together a number of leading automobile brands. Today, 97 years later, the company has nine different brands in the United States: Cadillac, Chevrolet, Buick, Oldsmobile, Pontiac, GMC, Hummer, Saturn, and SAAB. At one point, each of the brands in the GM portfolio had a distinct positioning. Over time, however, the brands have become more and more similar. In a bid to increase efficiency, the company came to sell essentially the same car under several different brand names. Today, GM has a portfolio of redundant brands. How is a Pontiac different from a Buick? Is Saturn really different from Chevrolet? What makes GMC unique? No one is really sure. As a result, GM's brands compete with each other, the company is forced to divide its resources, and the portfolio loses ground to the competition. Indeed, GM has consistently lost market share over the past decade. GM's recent decision to discontinue the Oldsmobile brand—once one of the strongest automobile brands in the United States—highlights the extent of the problem.

Finally, the house of brands model forces companies to devote resources to marketing the corporate brand. Since the corporate brand is distinct, it needs dedicated support to have any meaning. Corporate brands play an important role; investors, business partners, and employees are all important audiences. Royal Bank of Scotland provides an example. After a series of acquisitions including National Westminster Bank and Citizen's Bank, the Royal Bank of

Scotland is one of the largest banks in the world, ranking number five in market capitalization. The bank employs a house of brands strategy, with 22 different brands around the world. With each acquisition, the company retained the acquired brand and merged back-end activities. Unfortunately, RBS has found that few people are aware of the company's size and scope; the company needs to aggressively market its corporate brand in the business community.

Branded House

The second model for brand portfolios is the branded house. In this model, a company takes a single primary brand across multiple products and categories. Purely executed, all of the products a company produces are sold under a single brand name. Most often the corporation has the same name as the primary brand.

Dell is an example of a branded house. The company, founded by Michael Dell in 1984, operates virtually entirely under the Dell brand. The company uses the Dell brand for desktop computers, notebook computers, servers, monitors, professional services, printers, and training programs. In its 2004 fiscal year, the company had revenues of over $41 billion, making Dell one of the largest brands in the world in sales.

Virgin Group is another example of a branded house. The brand was created by British business leader Richard Branson in 1971. The company first operated a music store in London, and then gradually expanded into new businesses. The company created a record label, an airline (Virgin Atlantic Airways), and a cellular phone company. By 2005, the Virgin Group operated across a vast collection of categories. The Virgin web site noted, "We are involved in planes, trains, finance, soft drinks, music, mobile phones, holidays, cars, wines, publishing, bridal wear—the lot!"[5] The Virgin brand was used across almost all of these categories, making Virgin one of the most broadly applied brands in the world.

The branded house has a number of advantages. Perhaps most importantly, a branded house creates focus on the brand. Since there is one brand, it receives an enormous amount of senior management attention. Indeed, building the brand is essential because without a focus on the brand, the company, by definition, will not succeed. Senior management focuses on important branding decisions, and this (one hopes) results in better decisions. Richard Branson is deeply involved in the Virgin brand, for example, and Michael Dell worries about the Dell brand.

In addition, a branded house maximizes scale. In the branded house

advantages

So is one model or another really better globally? (margin note)

model, all of the marketing efforts fielded by the company support the primary brand. This scale can lead to efficiency in marketing efforts. It also makes it more likely the company will achieve the spending scale needed to succeed globally. Samsung, another company embracing a branded house strategy, spent over $10 billion marketing the Samsung brand between 1999 and 2004.[6] This would not have been possible had Samsung been splitting its spending across many individual brands. In addition, with scale a company may be able to undertake marketing activities that have a high fixed cost and require a broad scope of business to amortize the costs. Samsung, for example, was a primary sponsor of the 2004 Summer Olympics.

disadvantages (margin note)

Nonetheless, the branded house presents several substantial challenges that make it inappropriate for many organizations. Perhaps the biggest challenge is that the brand can become unfocused and lose its power to differentiate. *dilution* (margin note) There is an inherent pressure in a branded house structure to extend the core brand in multiple directions; since the company has no interest in launching new brands, every new product and initiative has to fit under the primary brand. This can lead to a weak brand positioning, with the brand targeting essentially everyone and promising nothing in particular. This is a clear recipe for trouble.

The branded house model can also constrain innovation and growth. If all ideas must fit under the one primary brand name, a company may not pursue good ideas simply because they don't fit. Alternatively, a company might find that new ventures are not successful because the core brand isn't a positive in the new category.

In addition, a branded house can be risky, because the company depends on only one brand. If the brand gets into trouble, the company will follow. When the Arthur Andersen accounting firm was caught in a scandal due to the actions of a few unethical employees, for example, the entire company was affected; there were no other brands to fall back on. Similarly, when Martha Stewart was convicted of securities fraud her company was hurt. Martha Stewart Living Omnimedia, with almost $300 million in revenue, was a branded house based on the Martha Stewart brand, and the brand took a major hit when Martha got into legal trouble.

KEYS TO SUCCESS IN BRAND PORTFOLIO STRATEGY

There is no one magic formula for creating a strong brand portfolio. Each company and situation is unique, with dynamics that require a deep strategic assessment of the particular situation. The answer that works in one situation will not necessarily work in the next. There are, however, some keys to success for developing and managing a successful brand portfolio.

Key to Success #1: Build and Extend Core Brands   *advantages*

The first and most important lesson in portfolio strategy is that it is always best to start with the core. If a company doesn't have a set of strong, core brands, it will be impossible to invest in new brands. As a result, establishing a strong base is priority number one.

Extending brands is a classic growth strategy for companies. Brands have meaning in the minds of customers, and this meaning often is relevant and motivating beyond the core business of a brand. There are very few brands that cannot be extended in some manner; companies should always be looking for opportunities to extend brands.   *Porsche?*

There are two basic ways brands can extend. First, brands can extend within their current category through line extensions. For example, Coca-Cola launched Diet Coke, and Palm introduced Palm II, both classic line extensions. Second, brands can extend into new categories through brand extensions. For example, Nike moved from athletic sneakers into apparel and sporting equipment while State Farm extended its brand from insurance into mutual funds and financial planning. These moves are brand extensions.

There are compelling reasons to extend brands. Indeed, Brad Kirk, chief marketing officer of Jergens, writes in his book *Lessons from a Chief Marketing Officer,* "Today's marketing economics make line extensions an unavoidable necessity."[7] The most powerful reason to extend a brand is growth; by extending within or across categories, companies can grow their brands. Within a category, an extension can reach new customers, increase buying rate with existing customers, increase margins, address changing customer needs and technology, and deal with competitive moves. Indeed, the faster the rate of change in a category, the faster a brand needs to extend. In technology markets, for example, where the rate of change is exceptionally high, brands need to introduce a steady stream of new products to keep up with changing technology. This makes extensions particularly important, because introducing a new brand in response to each technical improvement would be costly and inefficient.

Line extensions are appealing because they are relatively low-risk ways to drive growth. Since the brand already has awareness and a base of customers in a category, getting trial on the new item will be relatively easy. Brand extensions—where a brand enters a new category—open new markets to a company and provide significant incremental growth. By leveraging an existing brand to enter a new category, it is easier for a company to build awareness and trial. Both line extensions and brand extensions can also contemporize a brand and provide news. Brands thrive on news, and extensions provide this.

There are many examples of brands that have successfully extended beyond their core business. Gerber provides an example of a brand that has extended far beyond its base. Gerber was originally a line of baby foods; in 1927 Dorothy and Daniel Gerber began marketing strained peas, prunes, carrots, and spinach. They quickly extended the brand, first with line extensions and then with brand extensions. After a series of line extensions, the line now consists of 190 different baby food products. And after several major brand extensions, Gerber plays in baby skin-care products, shampoos, and utensils. Today the Gerber brand is used on a wide range of products, with all of the products unified by a focus on infants.

Importantly, extending a brand can sometimes be a bad idea. Extending a brand too far creates two problems. First, extensions can weaken a brand. Every extension of a brand shapes the brand's meaning. Expanding a brand into unrelated categories, then, can create confusion about what the brand means and make it harder to differentiate the brand. Extending the Gerber brand into frozen pizzas, for example, would weaken the meaning of the brand. As Jack Trout writes in *Differentiate or Die,* "The more things you try to become and the more you lose focus, the more difficult it is to differentiate your product."[8]

Second, extending a brand too far is unlikely to be successful. If a brand is not relevant to a category, it will not add anything to a new product, and it may well detract. There are hundreds of examples of ill-conceived brand extensions. Coors launched a line of spring waters. Harley-Davidson developed wine coolers and perfume. Jack Daniel's introduced Jack Daniel's mustard. Levi Strauss created Levi Strauss Tailored Classics, a line of suits. BIC developed both a perfume and a line of women's underwear. Smith and Wesson launched a line of mountain bikes. In all of these cases the extensions did not fit with the base brands, and the extensions failed.

It is useful to ask three questions about any line extension. First, will the existing brand help the new product? The existing brand must be an asset for the new product, but this is not always the case—as noted above, existing brands can sometimes diminish the appeal of a new product. Using the Clorox brand on a new line of salad dressings, for example, will not help sales of the new product. The Clorox brand is associated with bleach, which is obviously not a positive in the world of salad dressing. Similarly, using Kikkoman, a well-known brand of soy sauce, to launch an airline will simply create confusion.   *reinforce one another*

Second, will the new product help the existing brand? The new product must be a positive for the base brand. Damaging a strong brand by launching a poor-quality or confusing extension makes little sense.

Third, is the new product a good business idea? It may be possible to extend a brand into a new category, but the idea must make good business sense. Simply because a product can expand into a new category doesn't mean it should. Entering an existing, well-established category with a nondifferentiated item is not likely to be successful, regardless of how compelling the brand is.

Key to Success #2: Add Brands to the Portfolio to Address Major Opportunities

Expanding the brand portfolio by adding a brand, either by acquiring a brand or launching a new brand, is one of the most important moves a company can make. Each new brand brings opportunity, risk, and complexity. Companies should always consider adding a brand to the portfolio when targeting a new market or launching a breakthrough new product.

One of the most obvious times to launch a new brand is when the company is going after a new market—either a new segment of an existing category or an entirely new category. If the brands currently in the portfolio are not well aligned with the new opportunity, it may make sense to add a new brand to the portfolio rather than extend a current brand.

BMW Group provides an excellent example of appropriately introducing new brands. The BMW brand is a strong, well-defined brand, positioned around performance: the ultimate driving machine. According to the company, "Since its inception, the BMW brand has stood for one thing: sheer driving pleasure."[9] In 2001, BMW Group entered the small-car market in the United States, introducing an inexpensive two-door car. BMW Group wisely decided to introduce a new brand to the market: the Mini. By creating a new brand in the United States, the BMW Group preserved the integrity of the BMW brand and let the new brand, Mini, define itself. In 2003, BMW Group entered the luxury car market by acquiring rights to the Rolls-Royce brand. Again, the company leveraged a new brand to address a distinct market opportunity. The BMW Group now has three distinct brands, each positioned at a different segment of the market.

There are even times when it makes sense to launch the same product under different brand names, if the product is positioned against different

Porsche model?

uses. In the pharmaceutical industry, for example, compounds are occasionally introduced under different brand names to address different needs. GlaxoSmithKline introduced the molecule bupropion under the brand name Wellbutrin as a treatment for depression. The company later introduced the molecule as Zyban for smoking cessation. GSK wisely used a new brand to launch the anti-smoking product to maximize the opportunity.

When a company has a breakthrough technology or new product idea, it should carefully consider whether it is best to extend an existing brand or to introduce a new brand. Launching the new product idea under an existing brand will give the product a set of initial associations, and this may actually limit its long-term appeal. As Harvard marketing professor John Quelch noted, "By bringing important new products to market as line extensions, many companies leave money on the table. Some product ideas are big enough to warrant a new brand."[10]

By contrast, using the opportunity to introduce a new brand could drive high levels of incremental volume and lead to long-term growth. Importantly, a new brand can create its own identity. This is particularly important when the existing brands have limited appeal. As Bob Lutz, vice chairman at General Motors, noted, "When you're making a big change and you want to wipe the psychological slate clean, you change the name."[11]

Of course, launching a new brand is a costly undertaking. It is expensive and challenging to get a new brand established in the market. In addition, if technology rapidly changes, the primary point of difference of the new brand could become irrelevant down the road, leaving the new brand adrift. Sanka, for example, was introduced as a line of decaffeinated coffee. When the decaffeinated benefit was adopted across the category, the primary benefit of Sanka went away. Today Sanka is a weak, fading brand.

When evaluating adding a brand to the portfolio, a company must do three important things: It must ensure that the new brand is distinct from the brands currently in the portfolio; it must be sure that the financial returns are positive; and it must ensure that the organization has the resources to manage the new brand.

Key to Success #3: Proactively Prune Weak and Redundant Brands

Pruning is an essential part of managing the brand portfolio, and as such a company must look for opportunities to prune its portfolio just as it looks for opportunities to grow.

Brand portfolios tend to expand over time due to acquisitions and new product introductions. Few companies deliberately set out to create unwieldy brand portfolios—but it is the natural result of expansion without disciplined pruning.

Redundant brands are a particularly difficult problem for companies; it is exceptionally difficult to manage multiple brands in the same market space. Redundant brands inevitably compete with each other. This is inefficient—a company should focus on taking business from its competitors, not from itself. Trading sales between brands, often at great cost, is not a good way to do business. Inevitably, redundant brands also create internal conflicts; each management team, motivated by the need to deliver strong business results, will fight for sales attention, marketing spending, and new product ideas.

Pruning a portfolio has two benefits. First, it helps strong brands grow. By pruning a portfolio, management can focus its time, attention, and resources on its most profitable and most promising brands. Second, it eliminates brands that will likely never play a meaningful role in the company portfolio. Pruning a brand portfolio is a bit like pruning a tree; the pruning ultimately leads to a stronger, more vibrant tree.

Unilever provides a great example of a company aggressively pruning its portfolio. In 2000, following its acquisition of Bestfoods, Unilever found itself trying to manage 1,600 different brands around the world. Senior management concluded that this was simply too many brands for the organization to manage, as it led to unfocused and inefficient marketing efforts. In addition, the level of complexity was too high—each brand had to conduct research, develop programs, introduce new products, and track results.

As a result, Unilever decided to undertake a major project to streamline its brand portfolio. The company announced a program it called "Path to Growth." This program included reducing the number of brands from 1,600 to 400, then concentrating resources, time, and attention on these remaining power brands. Unilever combined brands, sold brands, and purchased brands, all in an effort to build a portfolio of large, high-performance brands. According to a Unilever press release, "The cornerstone of the plan is the focus of product innovation and brand development on a portfolio of around 400 leading brands, which will lead to less fragmentation of resources and bigger hit innovations."[12]

Unfortunately, there are few incentives to prune the brand portfolio. Pruning is not glamorous work and not the sort of activity that leads to public acclaim. At most companies, the rewards go to people who launch new initiatives and create new brands, not to people who identify and prune the deadwood. John Quelch accurately observes, "In many companies, removing an SKU is harder than introducing a new one."[13]

Pruning is a difficult decision. It is final, absolute, and, for those who have come to have an emotional connection with the brand, very sad. Decisions to prune a portfolio should be made with care, as it is hard to reverse the decision, and eliminating a brand means disposing of a key company asset. It can also be costly in the short run, as the company may be forced to liquidate inventory. Within a product category, companies should study the relative strength of different brands and the amount of positioning overlap. It may make sense to retain and invest in two strong brands that have little overlap, for example, while there is little reason to retain a weak brand that is very similar to a stronger primary brand.

Once a decision has been made to prune a brand, there are several ways to accomplish the task. First, brands can be divested, or sold to another company. This likely maximizes the value of the brand, but it could create a new competitor. As a result, it should be done with care. Second, brands can be harvested, or managed solely for short-term profits. Third, brands can simply be discontinued, or pulled off the market. This needs to be done carefully to ensure that the trademarks are not picked up by another company. Procter & Gamble, for example, lost control of its bathroom tissue brand White Cloud when the company discontinued the brand in order to focus its efforts on its primary bathroom tissue brand, Charmin. Wal-Mart eventually secured rights to the White Cloud trademark and relaunched the brand. Today White Cloud remains in the market, but it is now a competitor to P&G in the company's biggest customer, Wal-Mart.

Finally, brands can be combined. The goal for combining brands is to keep customers with the company while reducing redundancy in the portfolio. In this scenario, brands are gradually brought together, with the company transitioning customers over time. Generally, there is one primary brand at the end of the combination process. For example, Nestlé folded its Contadina line of refrigerated pastas into the Buitoni brand. Nestlé made the change very gradually, first adding Buitoni to the package as an endorser, then making Buitoni the primary brand and Contadina the sub-brand, and finally dropping the Contadina name entirely. Nestlé maintained category leadership during the transition.

Merging brands is easier said than done, however. It is easy to drive customers away from one brand, but it is far harder to ensure they are picked up by the other brand in the portfolio and not by the competition. In general, it is easier to merge brands with frequent purchase and relatively low brand involvement, because there is an opportunity to move consumers over time.

Key to Success #4: Keep Things Simple

Complexity is almost always a problem. In branding, this is particularly true; a complex brand portfolio is a challenge to manage. Each bit of complexity makes it harder to develop and execute business plans. Every brand must be managed and tracked.

Brand structures, in particular, can become very complex. In an effort to capture the best of all worlds, managers have an incentive to introduce many sub-brands and endorsers. The result, though, is that customers sometimes have no idea what any brand stands for. Here is a good rule of thumb: If you can't explain a brand structure in one minute, it is too complex.

Every branding element requires investment. Introducing a sub-brand that is meaningless to customers, for example, simply creates needless complexity. A company must invest in creating a meaning around a branding element; otherwise it should simply use a product descriptor.

Consider, for example, the complex brand structure of Purina. In just dog food, Purina is an endorser on a broad collection of brands including Dog Chow, Alpo, Beneful, Hi Pro, Mighty Dog, Kibbles and Chunks, Moist & Meaty, and One. Each brand has different flavors and varieties, and many of the brands have sub-brands. Fully understanding the options would take hours; the portfolio is simply too complicated.

Key to Success #5: Involve Senior Management

Brand portfolio decisions should be made at the very highest levels of an organization. This is true for three reasons. First, as discussed earlier, portfolio decisions are enormously important—there are few decisions that will have as important an impact as a brand portfolio decision.

Second, portfolio decisions require a long-term perspective, because the decisions will affect the company for years to come. Managers charged with delivering short-term financial targets obviously have an incentive to maximize short-term results. However, short-term thinking shouldn't drive a portfolio decision. It might make little sense to discontinue a brand in the short-term, for example, because the move could possibly have a negative short-term financial impact, either in lost sales or inventory write-offs. However, in the long-term, discontinuing the brand might be the optimal approach. Similarly, launching a new product under an existing brand might optimize short-term results but substantially underdeliver the long-term potential.

Third, portfolio decisions often require trade-offs between brands. The goal in managing a portfolio is maximizing the total, not maximizing the parts. The managers responsible for delivering results for a particular brand are not interested in hurting their own brand's results to help another brand in the portfolio. Senior management has to be the decision maker.

CONCLUSION

Managing brand portfolios is one of the great challenges in branding. As hard as it is to build a strong brand, it is even harder to build a portfolio of great brands. The answers are seldom clear, and the tradeoffs are significant. Still, a company must focus on the portfolio challenge in order to prosper. Results don't come from strong brands—results come from strong brand portfolios.

Tim Calkins is clinical associate professor of marketing at the Kellogg School of Management and co-director of the Kellogg on Branding program. He consults with companies around the world on marketing strategy and branding issues. Prior to joining the Kellogg faculty, Tim worked at Kraft Foods for 11 years, managing branding including A.1 steak sauce, Miracle Whip, and Taco Bell. He received a BA from Yale University and an MBA from Harvard Business School.

NOTES

1. Red Bull web site (2004).

2. PepsiCo web site (2004).

3. Speech by David Sylvia, Director, Corporate Identity, Altria to American Marketing Association, Chicago Chapter (February 27, 2003).

4. Ibid.

5. Virgin web site (2004).

6. Ramstad, Evan and Geoffrey A. Fowler (2004), "Marketing Chief at Samsung Departs for Intel," *Wall Street Journal* (September 7, 2004), B1.

7. Kirk, Bradford C. (2003), *Lessons from a Chief Marketing Officer,* New York: McGraw-Hill, p. 158.

8. Trout, Jack (2000), *Differentiate or Die,* New York: Wiley, p. 171.

9. BMW web site (2004).

10. Quelch, John A. and David Kenny (1994), "Extend Profits, Not Product Lines," *Harvard Business Review* (September–October), 155.

11. Welch, David (2003), "Headed for that Showroom in the Sky: GM's Pontiac Grand Am and Chevy Cavalier Are History," *BusinessWeek Online* (July 21, 2003).

12. Unilever web site (2004).

13. See note 10, p. 160.

SECTION III

FROM STRATEGY TO IMPLEMENTATION

CHAPTER 7

BUILDING BRANDS THROUGH EFFECTIVE ADVERTISING

BRIAN STERNTHAL and ANGELA Y. LEE

$\mathbf{F}$or the past several years, media analysts have predicted the demise of advertising—television advertising in particular. In today's world, media are fractured. With so many media choices, it is often difficult to attract a substantial audience for any one vehicle. Network television that once reached over 90 percent of Americans now reaches less than half that number. In 1965, 80 percent of Americans could be reached by three TV spots, whereas today it would require 97 spots. Magazines have proliferated, custom publishing has flourished, signage has grown substantially, and new media such as Internet advertising have emerged.

Not only are viewers' media choices more diverse, but the audience is more diverse as well. African Americans, Asians, and Hispanics now account for approximately 30 percent of the American population, and often have unique consumption habits and motivations. Another recent trend is the decline in television viewing by the key 18- to 34-year-old market and the daytime viewing audience. And even among those who have sustained their viewing habits, TiVo and other digital video recording devices make it easy to skip the normal viewing of commercials.

Despite these concerns, advertising expenditures have been growing at a steady rate. In 2004, ad spending growth was about 8 percent, while Internet and cable television advertising spending saw double-digit growth. Thus, it appears that the forecasted demise of advertising runs afoul of fact. However, the advertising landscape is definitely changing. Growing numbers of advertisers with large budgets are focusing their spending on building relationships with current heavy users of their brands. This strategy has greatly affected media choices, leading to the emergence of custom publishing materials and other direct marketing vehicles, the use of event marketing and other personal contact approaches, and the increasing and more selective use of product placement.

These developments mean that all advertisers must be concerned about the effective use of their advertising dollars. Customer insight is one starting point for developing effective advertising strategy. These insights pertain to *what* customers think and *how* people use information to evaluate products and make brand choice decisions (see Chapter 3).

In this chapter, we focus our attention on the *how* element of this equation—how people process advertising messages. We describe a processing model for advertising exposure, then discuss how advertising influences customers' product judgments and brand choices. We then present an analysis of media strategies that help brands shout with a dominant voice. In the final section, we discuss approaches to measuring advertising effectiveness.

AN INFORMATION-PROCESSING MODEL OF ADVERTISING EXPOSURE

Although it seems intuitive that consumers would choose a brand based on an objective evaluation of the information they receive about a product, this is not always the case. People may purchase a brand because it comes to mind most readily, or because it is the brand their mother always bought, or because the brand is the easiest to justify to others.

Advertising content is thought to influence brand judgments through a two-stage process. As is schematically depicted in Figure 7.1, advertising information is first encoded and represented more or less faithfully in the short-term memory store. This information reflects what a consumer is thinking at the moment when he or she sees an ad. The short-term memory store has a limited capacity—it can only hold a limited amount of information for a short period of time. If there is no further processing of the advertising message, the information will be lost.

With sufficient elaboration or repetition, the information in the short-term store will be transferred to the long-term memory store, which is the repository of all processed information. The long-term store's defining characteristic is its organization. Information in long-term memory is stored in clusters known as networks of associations. Each piece of information is called a node; for example, brands are stored in long-term memory as brand nodes. Nodes are hierarchically organized into categories and subcategories.

Figure 7.1
An Information–Processing Model of Advertising Exposure

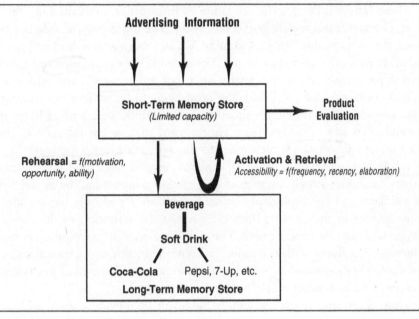

For example, Coca-Cola is represented in memory by a particular node. This node is a member of the category *soft drink*, which in turn is a member of the superordinate category *beverage*. Each brand and category can have different kinds of associations. The associations that advertisers often focus on to infer the brand's benefits include attributes (e.g., caramel color), users (e.g., young adults), and occasions of use (e.g., sports events).

The content of an advertising message is usually encoded in short-term memory. The encoding typically involves the automatic activation of prior knowledge from long-term memory that is part of the associative network. These associative inferences help people make sense of the message. However, not all information from the long-term store is activated. This occurs because long-term memory is the repository of *all* information that a person has processed, but the short-term store has a highly limited capacity to receive information. Therefore, only certain nodes of the long-term store are activated and represented in short-term memory. This raises the question of what prior knowledge might be activated when a person is first exposed to an advertising message. Answering this question is critical for marketers: If an advertiser can determine what references a consumer might call up when exposed to an advertising message, then ads can be most effectively created for maximum impact and long-term association.

Three factors influence the activation of information from the long-term store. The first is the *frequency* of its processing: The more often a node is activated, the more readily it comes to mind. We all recognize that leading brands are easier to recall than minor brands. The second factor is the *recency* of information processing: Memory operates on a "last-in, first-out" basis—the most recently processed information is the most likely to be retrieved from long-term memory into short-term memory. For example, we are more likely to remember an ad that we saw last night than one that we saw last month. The third factor is *elaboration*, which refers to the associations a person makes to a brand. For example, an airline's convenience may be associated with several factors, including a high number of sought-after destinations, the availability of e-tickets, and the option of curbside check-in. By elaborating on these conveniences in the ad, an airline can prompt the activation of the convenience node in consumers' minds. Through these associations, customers may conclude that flying with the airline is convenient, although convenience is not explicitly mentioned in the ad. And information elaborated in short-term memory will be transferred to long-term memory.

Thus, advertising affects consumers' judgment by providing them with information that in turn triggers the retrieval of prior knowledge. Once advertising content and accessible prior knowledge are represented in short-term memory, people may actively process these different pieces of information and form attitudes and opinions about the product by relying on (1) the information presented in the advertising appeal, (2) prior knowledge, or (3) the associations made through processing both advertising and prior knowledge. An understanding of how information from these different sources is used to make decisions offers further insights into how to develop effective advertising.

THE IMPACT OF MESSAGE CONTENT ON JUDGMENTS

The information-processing model of advertising provides the basis for several strategies advertisers can use to optimize the impact of messages advertising their brand.

Aspirations

People are inferential, and they make judgments about advertising based on their aspirations, not on literal information. Thus, a brand's advertising should reflect consumers' aspirations. Because advertising information triggers an individual's own repertoire of relevant information (from short- and long-term memory stores), product judgments are outcomes of *inferential* rather than *literal* processing. Inherently, consumers are *inferential* when they are exposed to advertisements—they infer meaning beyond what is literally presented in an ad. These inferences come from consumers' own *judgments* about the information presented; they are often a reflection of consumers' *aspirational* selves—the things that each person aspires to in his or her life. Thus, successful advertising often depends on whether individuals' aspirations are promoted in advertising and not on the information that is literally presented.

For example, older consumers are typically more persuaded by advertising that depicts younger people, and younger children are often persuaded by advertising showing older children. These ads play to the aspirations of their respective audiences (i.e., older people want to be younger; younger people want to be older). In Hallmark greeting card ads targeted at men in their twenties, preteen boys were depicted pondering the dilemma of the best way to ask for a date. This approach reminds the 20-something men how it felt to be younger and just starting to date (without making the ad so emotional that it would make them uncomfortable).

Prior Beliefs

People process advertising with their own filters, and thus advertising content should resonate with prior beliefs. Consumers respond to advertising by activating their own repertoire of knowledge, associating advertising content with the information already in their memory. Thus, it is easier to persuade consumers when advertising information resonates with their accepted beliefs. If consumers believe that honey offers better nutrition than sugar, it is easier to market a brand of cereal that coincides with this category belief (e.g., Honey-Nut Cheerios) than to try to change the belief. This is not to say that attitude change should not be a goal of advertising. But prompting change is likely to require a larger ad budget than strengthening accepted beliefs.

Consumer Goals

People are goal-driven when processing information, and thus advertising content should resonate with existing goals. Effective advertising is not simply a matter of featuring content that is compatible with consumers' prior beliefs. Effective advertising also involves presenting content that is consistent with consumer goals—*and* presenting it in a way that corresponds to these goals. People have consumption goals, such as the need to buy a car, a shirt, or a copying machine. Not surprisingly, consumers are more likely to pay attention when advertising helps them pursue these consumption goals.

The term *self-regulatory focus* refers to people's internal motivation that governs and regulates their attitudes and behavior as they pursue their consumption goals.[1] Two such orientations (or regulatory foci) are important in understanding how people make decisions. One involves the presence and absence of desirable outcomes (termed *promotion focus*), and the other involves the presence and absence of undesirable outcomes (termed *prevention focus*). People who are promotion focused have an orientation toward accomplishment, growth, and aspirations, and they pursue their consumption goals with eagerness. These consumers typically view information through the lens of what they will gain or not gain (they are looking to gain). By contrast, those who are prevention focused have an orientation toward safety, security, and responsibilities, and they pursue their consumption goals with caution and vigilance.[2] They typically view information through the lens of what they will lose or not lose (they are looking not to lose).

This distinction is important because an individual's regulatory focus affects the resonance of different types of brand claims. Consider advertising for tampons. One execution shows women swimming and biking and doing other everyday activities during their period (i.e., a promotion-focused message), whereas another shows the accidents that are avoided by using the advertised brand (i.e., a prevention-focused message). Often such executions are aired as part of the same campaign. This practice glosses over an important distinction. If the audience is concerned with aspirations and achievement, the first spot resonates with their promotion focus and is more effective than the second spot. However, if the audience is concerned about safety and security, the second spot appeals to their prevention focus, and thus is more persuasive.[3]

The distinction between promotion and prevention focus is also useful when deciding how the advertising message should be framed. The way that a message is presented affects its resonance with consumers' self-regulatory focus and in turn determines how persuasive it is. A promotion message is more persuasive when it emphasizes gain (e.g., eat right and get energized) than when it emphasizes nongain (e.g., you won't get energized if you don't eat right), and a prevention message is more persuasive when it emphasizes loss (e.g., you will have clogged arteries if you don't eat right) than when it emphasizes nonloss (e.g., you won't get clogged arteries if you eat right).[4]

Brands often compete by focusing on either a promotion or prevention goal. In the liquid bleach category, for example, Clorox presents its brand as the one that gives the purest clean by providing a brilliant white. Thus, the emphasis is on a promotion goal. By contrast, OxiClean focuses on prevention by positioning the brand as the one that cleans without being harsh on clothes. How the two brands perform in the marketplace depends on how well their message resonates with the regulatory focus of their target audience.

People's regulatory focus may reflect their individual disposition, their cultural orientation, or cues in the environment. Recent research shows that people from a western culture (e.g., Americans) are more likely to be promotion-focused, whereas those from an eastern culture (e.g., Chinese, Japanese) are more likely to be prevention-focused.[5] People may also adopt different regulatory foci for different consumption goals. For example, consumers shopping for home-security systems are inherently prevention-focused, but they may be promotion-focused when shopping for flat-screen televisions. An individual's regulatory focus may also change over time as changes in the environment occur. For example, with the economic decline in 2000, the environment for investors (and hence many large investment firms that serve them) changed from one where growth and achievement were the prevailing goals to one where financial safety and security was paramount.

THE IMPACT OF THE DECISION PROCESS ON JUDGMENTS

Message content is not the only factor that affects judgments. People may reflect on how they feel about the decision process and how they process information, and these feelings may influence judgments as well. Consider two ads for car-maker BMW. One ad shows a picture of a BMW and the headline, "There are many reasons to drive a BMW. Can you think of one reason?" The other ad is identical except that the headline asks "Can you think of 10 reasons?" If people use the reasons they generate to guide their decision, the more reasons they generate based on the request in the ad, the more favorable their evaluation should be. However, if people are reflecting on the ease (or difficulty) of generating reasons, then the ad that asks for more reasons may prompt less favorable evaluations since generating 10 reasons is presumably more difficult than generating one reason. Indeed, in a recent study, individuals exposed to the one-reason ad exhibited a more favorable disposition toward the car than those exposed to the second ad. The 10-reasons ad prompted the inference that if it is hard to think of reasons to drive a BMW, it must not be as good as one thought.[6]

Thus, a critical question arises: When will people rely on what they know about the brand (i.e., ad content plus prior knowledge) as the basis of their judgment, and when will they rely on the perceived ease of processing the information? The key lies in the perceived ease of processing that they experience and the inference they make based on their experience, both of which may be a function of their expertise in the brand or the category.[7] In the BMW example, consumers who have significant knowledge about the brand would recognize that generating even a substantial number of reasons is not difficult, and therefore, processing ease is not important to their decision. Similarly, those who have very limited knowledge of the BMW brand would realize that generating even a few reasons is difficult, and hence would not base their decision on processing difficulty. It is those who fall between these knowledge extremes who may rely on their experience as the basis of brand evaluation.

Because consumers monitor their processing experience and use it as the basis for judgment, advertisers must strive to make the decision process a positive experience. Indeed, in the BMW study, when the respondents were asked to *imagine* 10 reasons to drive one (thus making the *process* more enjoyable), their evaluation of a BMW became more favorable.[8] Framing the task in terms of a pleasant experience made the task seem easy and thus prompted a positive evaluation of the BMW.

The fit between an individual's regulatory goal and the content of the advertising's message is another source of positive feelings. Promotion-focused individuals find information relating to growth and achievement easier to process and remember, and prevention-focused individuals find information relating to safety and security easier to process and remember. In addition, individuals with a promotion focus have a more abstract perspective that deals with *why* something is done, whereas those with a prevention focus have a more concrete perspective that deals with *how* something is done. Thus, brand advertising targeting those with a promotion focus is more persuasive when it specifies why something is done rather than how it can be done. Conversely, brand advertising targeting those with a prevention focus is more persuasive when it describes how something is done rather than why it should be done.

In sum, there are two key factors that influence brand evaluations in response to advertising messages. People use the content that is presented in the ad and personal associations that the ad conjures up. They also monitor their decision-making experience and reflect on this experience as a basis for their judgments. Perceptions such as how easy it is to make a decision and how right the decision feels can have significant impact on the judgments individuals have about advertising.

ADVERTISING EXPOSURE AND BRAND CHOICE

Our analysis to this point has focused on how advertising affects brand evaluations. Although such judgments are often a key determinant of choice, this is not always the case. People often make purchase decisions based on what is available in the marketplace, what products or brands come to mind, or which packaging catches the eye when they are in the store. Advertising may play an important role in influencing what comes to mind or what catches the eye. To gain further insight into how advertising may influence brand choice decisions, it is useful to distinguish between memory-based and stimulus-based choice situations.

Memory-Based Choice

Many brand choices are memory-based in that a customer chooses a brand based on information retrieved from memory. Restaurant and store choices, for example, are often based on what comes to mind. Once in the restaurant, patrons may also be ordering their beverages in a memory-based context. Shoppers who make up their shopping list prior to their shopping trip are also making brand choices based on alternatives in memory. In these situations, a brand name must be retrieved from long-term memory to be chosen. Thus, a brand that comes to mind more readily has a greater chance of being chosen. Frequent as well as recent exposures to advertising will make a brand more accessible in memory, as will ad copy that encourages elaboration on the brand, such as the featuring of benefits that resonate with the audience.

Stimulus-Based Choice

In stimulus-based situations, information relevant to the decision is readily available in the physical environment. Many supermarket purchases are stimulus-based, where shoppers make their selection from an array of alternatives displayed on the shelves. Other stimulus-based choices may be made when individuals browse through the newspaper's movie section, surf the Internet, or flip through the pages in a catalog. In the absence of strong preferences, a brand that stands out on the shelf, a movie title that catches the eye, and items that pop out from the screen are more likely to be chosen. In these situations, prior advertising exposures that render a brand more easily recognizable and identifiable will benefit choice. And contrary to conventional wisdom, ad copy that promotes attention and elaboration of the brand may not necessarily help with visual identification. Rather, it is the visual match between the product in the ad and the product on display at the time of brand choice that ensures brand choice among several competitors. Thus, an effective ad copy strategy for the stimulus-based customer may be one that features just the product in its original package or the brand name, unencumbered by other information.[9]

DEVELOPING EFFECTIVE MESSAGE CONTENT

An effective ad for a brand makes the content of the message accessible at the moment of choice. Message content accessibility occurs when the brand benefits are elaborated and linked to the brand name. Below we examine a variety of approaches that facilitate the elaboration of benefits. We also review factors that may either undermine or facilitate the linkage of the benefit to the brand name.

Prompting Elaboration

Here are some strategies to encourage people to elaborate on the benefits of the brand.

Hard Sell   An explicit link between the brand name and its benefits is perhaps the most straightforward strategy to prompt people to consider a brand. This approach, termed the *hard sell,* was popularized by the Ted Bates advertising agency in the 1950s. Hard-sell advertising says, "Buy this brand, get this benefit." Advertising for Visa credit cards ("It's everywhere you want to be") and Bounty paper towels ("The quicker picker-upper") illustrate this hard-sell approach. By associating the benefit to the brand through an effective tag line, the advertising provides an additional cue to help people remember the brand name. The effectiveness of hard sell depends on whether the benefit featured in the advertising is important to potential customers and whether it distinguishes the brand from its competitors.

Big Idea   The *big idea,* developed by the Leo Burnett advertising agency, offers an alternative strategy to help customers link a benefit to a brand. This approach involves giving customers a variety of reasons to believe that a brand owns a specific benefit. For example, in the airline industry, the big idea might be *convenience.* An initial ad for Delta Airlines might describe its online boarding pass. In subsequent executions, Delta could describe its curbside check-in and its greater number of hubs for easier connections. In each ad, Delta's big idea—convenience—is emphasized through each benefit. Thus, the big idea approach links different sub-benefits as multiple reasons to believe in a primary benefit.

Story Grammar   Story grammar involves using a series of episodes to present a problem or a goal, followed by some progress toward the goal, and finally an outcome. This approach attempts to persuade consumers by dramatizing the benefits of a brand in a setting that consumers might experience. For example, Dynaco, a producer of industrial doors, developed a print ad that included three photographs. In the first, a high-speed door was shown striking a person who was passing under the door as it closed. The second photograph made it evident that the person who was struck was not injured. And the third demonstrated how easily the door reset on track again. The irony is that while the drama captures people's attention, sometimes the audience may become so absorbed in the story that they fail to link the benefit to the brand.

Celebrity Spokesperson   On some occasions, a spokesperson is the best choice to increase elaboration of the brand's benefits. This approach is most effective when the spokesperson's character can be used to personify the brand's benefit. For example, world-champion cyclist Lance Armstrong's endurance and speed were effectively used to personify the benefits that the U.S. Postal Service wished to convey.

Facilitating Effective Elaboration

Whatever the strategy used to prompt elaboration of a brand's benefits, its effectiveness ultimately depends on whether the consumer is willing to hear the message. People will listen if they have the motivation, ability, and opportunity to do so.

Advertisers can encourage elaboration by repeating the message, which offers consumers more opportunities to receive information. Using print media rather than radio or television also allows consumers to process information at their own pace, which is particularly important when the target audience includes the elderly or when the information is complex.

Humor is another device that can be used to stimulate elaboration of a brand's benefit. Humor motivates people to pay attention to the message content. The caveat is that when humor serves as the motivational device, the ad may wear out after relatively few exposures. Because humor can be distracting, the humor must be closely tied to the key benefit of the brand. For example, if the point of difference for a brand of glue is that it dries more quickly than other glues, humor can be used to show the consequences of this benefit. Alternatively, humor can be used to show the consequences that can result from *not* using the advertised brand. Dr. Scholl's depicted the consequences of not using its foot deodorant by showing dead fish rising to a lake's surface when someone dangled his nonpowdered feet into it. Finally, humor can be used to highlight a competitor's shortcomings. Lee Jeans successfully used humor to depict the difficulty people had fitting into other brands of jeans, suggesting that a person's next pair should be Lee's. By drawing attention to the fact that Lee understood the consumer's problem, the advertising implied that Lee was likely to be the solution.

Threats to Brand Linkage

An ad might not persuade even when the message elaborates on a benefit that is both important to consumers and differentiates the brand from competitors. *A key to effective advertising is the linkage between the benefit and the brand name.* As critical as brand linkage is, for many advertising campaigns, the audience can play back the message, but they either do not relate it to the advertised brand, or they relate it to a competing brand. For example, ads for Eveready batteries were remembered as ads for Duracell.

Late Identification   Late identification of the brand name can undermine the effective linkage of the benefit to the brand in TV advertising. The brand and its product category are typically identified early in a commercial; otherwise, customers may not readily associate the message with the brand. Sometimes late IDs are used to build suspense, in hopes of capturing attention and encouraging elaboration. However, use of this tactic requires caution. By withholding the brand name until the end of the ad, the audience is invited to make its own associations throughout the ad's duration. The result is that consumers may associate the commercial with another brand or even with another category. In most cases, presenting the brand name at the end of the commercial does not correct the erroneous association. This occurs because correcting judgment, even at a nonconscious level, requires cognitive resources, and people typically do not find it worthwhile to exert the effort needed to make the correction.

Despite their potential liability, late IDs are useful when an individual's disposition toward the brand is unfavorable, because it encourages people to process the current message rather than focus on their own prior (negative) thoughts about the brand. For example, Gallo had the reputation of being a mass-market winery. When the company introduced its first high-end wine, Gallo of Sonoma, it used late ID in the ad. In the initial ad exposure, consumers heard about the virtues of the brand before knowing the brand name.

This allowed consumers to approach the product with a fresh eye—they had no idea what the brand was while they were being introduced to its positive benefits. Without a late ID, people might have dismissed Gallo of Sonoma because of their prior opinion of the Gallo brand.

Me-Too Executions   Execution devices that are too similar to those of competitors or other advertisers can also undermine the link between the benefit and the brand. This is particularly problematic when the advertisers are from the same industry and the ads appear in the same medium. This problem is apparent in advertising for consulting firms, which typically place their advertising in leading business publications such as *Fortune* and *BusinessWeek*. The frequent use of metaphors to describe their point of difference by most firms renders their advertising very similar.

MEDIA STRATEGY: BREAKING THROUGH THE CLUTTER

In developing media strategy, the goal is to present brand information by supporting the brand's position and cutting through the marketplace clutter. Two media-related strategies are typically used to achieve these goals. One involves the selection of media. This entails deciding whether to use broadcast (radio, television), print (newspapers, magazines), Internet, outdoor, events, product placement, or some other venue. The second strategy involves media scheduling to maximize the signal strength of the communication to the target.

Media Selection

Two factors should be considered when making media selection decisions.

Intimacy   Media selection entails understanding the level of intimacy appropriate for an ad's message content. A message's intimacy level can range from impersonal (where the focus is on the brand) to intimate (where the focus is on the target customer). When an ad's goal is to convey information about the brand, little intimacy is needed. As such, mass media such as television, radio, magazines, and newspapers are appropriate. In recent years, there has been a growing trend to be highly selective in choosing the mass media vehicles for an ad. For example, retailer Saks Fifth Avenue began custom publishing the magazine *5* and mailing it to its best customers to inform them about gifts, events, destinations, and people. Mass-market retailer Sears achieved selectivity by featuring its products including tools, appliances, and furniture on the TV reality show *Extreme Makeover: Home Edition.*

In some instances, an advertising goal may be to highlight the common interests a brand shares with the customer beyond the product category. For example, by sponsoring NASCAR driver Ward Burton's car #0, NetZero Internet service showed potential and current customers (in this case, racing fans) that they have a shared interest—speed. Similarly, TiVo advertised its personal video recorder in magazines such as *Architectural Digest, Golf Digest,* and *The New Yorker* to underscore the values the company held in common with upscale consumers.

At the most intimate level, media are sometimes selected so that a brand directly communicates with its customers individually, attempting to meet these individuals' particular needs. For example, Lucky Strike cigarettes sent teams to support smokers taking cigarette breaks outside office buildings by serving beverages and providing folding chairs. W.W. Grainger, an industrial products supplier, provided its customers with a customized price list on its web site that reflected the individual contractual arrangements each customer had with Grainger.

Some advertisers use multiple media to attain different levels of intimacy. Along these lines, the U.S. Army aired television advertising to tell people about the army, then directed them to the web site. In turn, the goarmy.com web site allowed potential recruits to gain a more intimate understanding of the army experience by viewing profiles of current personnel (of all genders, races, and ethnicities). The prospect could click on the person they were most interested in, and view that person's typical day, their skills, and their challenges. At an even greater level of intimacy, army recruiters often talked to prospects on a one-on-one basis.

Timing   There is a growing trend toward selecting media that will reach a brand's target at a specific brand- or category-relevant time. For example, products such as No Doz (an anti-sleep aid) might be advertised on nighttime radio or on billboards in order to reach prospects when they are most likely to need the category.

Caution is warranted when attempting to optimize timing, as some audiences might perceive such deliberate customized advertising to be intrusive. For example, Health Club TV offered fitness and sports programming while people were exercising, interspersing health- and fitness-related advertising in the programming. Whittle Communications presented advertising for health products in custom magazines they developed for doctors' offices. The same firm later placed TVs in doctors' offices that showed health-related programming and advertising. All these ventures failed, suggesting that people might not appreciate being the targets of advertising messages at times when they are most vulnerable.

Media Scheduling

Once the media are selected, the next step is to develop a media schedule. This involves deciding on the number of exposures within each month and the number of exposures over the year. When considering the monthly exposure schedule, a choice is made between the percentage of the target who will be exposed to advertising at least once per month (reach) and the average number of times an individual will be exposed during that month (frequency). In considering the schedule for the entire year, the issue is whether to sustain advertising throughout the year (continuity) or to advertise in some months but not in others (concentration).

These decisions are related, because the media budget can be viewed as trading off reach, frequency, and continuity. Different trade-offs are made based on the marketing objectives for the brand. For example, when introducing a new product, the goal is to reach every person in the target and to expose them to the advertising a number of times. However, the budget trade-off to achieve reach and frequency might mean that a product cannot be advertised for several months during the year. In introducing a new cereal, for example, brands often spend as much as 40 percent of their budget in the first three months after launch. This delivers the reach and frequency needed to prompt the desired level of trial and repeat purchase. This introductory effort is often followed by several months with no ad support. A similar concentration strategy often occurs as small brands compete with their more substantial rivals by alternating between months of advertising and months of hiatus.

reach > frequency

Reach and Frequency A long-standing, critical question for advertisers is, What is the right number of monthly exposures for advertising? For many years, the answer offered by the trade association for advertisers and other industry experts was three or more. However, this conventional wisdom has more recently been challenged by the belief that perhaps one exposure is optimal. The rationale is that reach may be more important than frequency: It is better to reach one additional person than to reach a person an additional time.

It is important to recognize that neither of these recommendations offers a useful guideline to developing a frequency strategy. The optimal number of monthly exposures depends on the longevity of the brand's position, the creative strategy used, the extent to which the advertising presents news, the competitors' spending level and creative strategy, and many other factors. In short, the optimal frequency level is an empirical question.

Wear-Out   As ads are repeated over time, eventually consumers begin to realize that they are no longer receiving new information. This leads to a phenomenon called wear-out. Wear-out occurs when people start thinking about their own experiences with the brand, which might often be less favorable than information presented in the advertising message. Wear-out is most likely when the cost of media is low and companies concentrate their media buying in a small number of vehicles. These conditions often exist in business-to-business advertising where only a few books are dedicated to each industry (called vertical books), and the cost of space in these business-to-business publications is relatively low. Thus, a firm that sells grinding wheels may have limited outlets in which to advertise its product; and because advertising in these vehicles is relatively inexpensive, multiple insertions in each issue of each book are common. Often the result is wear-out. Similarly, in consumer marketing, the same spots are often aired repeatedly on the few radio stations that best fit the target demographic. Because consumers typically listen to just a few radio stations, they may hear the same ad over and over, prompting rapid wear-out.

Wear-out can be forestalled by a number of strategies. Perhaps the most obvious is to reduce the number of ad exposures or to vary the spacing of ad repetitions. When successive ads appear closely together and the message is relatively simple, people quickly begin to assume they know the ad without paying much attention. Increasing the spacing between exposures reduces consumers' sense of familiarity and makes them more likely to pay attention. When the content of a message is complex, ad exposures should be concentrated at first (to allow the audience to continue to build on their knowledge of the brand through successive exposures), and spaced further apart after the message content is fully realized. Finally, wear-out can be avoided by offering news, perhaps using the big idea described earlier.

MEASURING ADVERTISING EFFECTIVENESS FOR A BRAND

A variety of services are available to help advertisers assess advertising effectiveness. For television advertising, most services recruit consumers to watch television programming, where ads are tested alongside control ads. Prior to viewing these programs and ads, respondents are asked to indicate their brand preferences in several product categories, including the ones to be tested. Then they are shown the program with the advertising inserted as simulated commercial breaks. In some cases, respondents are asked to turn a knob to indicate their interest on a moment-to-moment basis while viewing the advertising. The parts of the ad that bring high interest are considered effective, whereas the low-interest parts are considered ineffective. However, recent research suggests that measuring whether interest increases or decreases over the full length of the ad, as well as measuring the level of peak interest, may be more indicative of ad effectiveness than the specific response to particular portions of the copy.[10]

When the presentation is complete, the audience is asked what they have learned about a brand and how they feel about it. One learning measure is *unaided recall.* It involves asking respondents to recall the advertising they have seen. If they fail to recall the target ad, they are given the target ad's category as a prompt (e.g., "Do you remember seeing an ad for automobiles?"). Advertisers typically receive the respondents' verbatim responses as well as a summary score reflecting the percentage of viewers who successfully recalled critical message information. The summary score is then compared to norms based on past scores for advertising in the particular product category. This information enables the advertiser to make changes to the ad as appropriate based on the test results.

In print advertising, respondents are usually asked to look through a magazine as they normally would. Then they are shown several different print ads and asked to indicate whether they had seen each of the ads in the magazine. These copy tests can provide valuable insights about people's reactions to advertising and how creative executions might be revised. However, these current approaches do not capture the full range of advertising effects. Depending on the objective of the advertising, different measures of advertising effectiveness may be appropriate.

Measures of Learning

Copy testing measures typically assess how well people remember the advertising message. Individuals are asked to recall an ad for a specific brand, and to play back the message content. The main advantage of these measures is that the intended outcome of the advertising can be unambiguously attributed to the specific campaign. Although recall of the advertising content can indicate how well a message has been learned, interpreting the impact of advertising exclusively from such an explicit measure of memory is problematic.

Recall is problematic as a measure of brand knowledge because people often have difficulty tracing the origin of their knowledge. People may have acquired information about a brand from being exposed to advertising, but they may not remember that the information came from a specific ad. As a result they do not report this information when asked to recall a message, which leads to an underestimation of learning. This issue may be addressed by administering measures that assess the extent of brand knowledge without making any direct reference to the ad. For example, in a brand recall task, people might be asked what they know about a brand. Responses of those who have been exposed to the advertising are compared to those who have not been exposed (i.e., a control group). Such brand recall reflects what people know about the brand, which is more likely to be predictive of their purchasing behavior than a measure of what they can remember about an ad.

Another concern in using recall measurements is that brand choice is often determined not by the information recalled but by the brand associations consumers have. For example, consumers may exhibit good recall of an automobile manufacturer's claim that a car comes with a complete tool kit because they associate this claim with the thought that the tool kit would be needed to fix the car's frequent breakdowns. In this case, good advertising recall is associated with a *dis*inclination to purchase. The implication is that attitudinal measures should also be used to assess advertising effectiveness.

Measures of Attitudes

Attitude measures probe how people feel about a brand. Message recipients are asked to evaluate a brand on general affective items such as like-dislike and superior-inferior, as well as more brand-specific characteristics such as price (e.g., value for money) and quality (e.g., effectiveness). Attitude responses are typically solicited without reference to the advertising. The advertising message is considered effective if respondents exhibit more favorable dispositions toward the brand than the no-ad-exposure control group. Attitude measures are most useful when the brand is new or when the advertising presents significant news. When brands are well-established, it is unlikely that one or even several exposures to advertising, which are typically used in tests of effectiveness, will affect people's judgments.

Direct measures of attitudes do not provide accurate predictions of brand choice if message recipients are unwilling to divulge their true sentiment toward the brand, perhaps due to social desirability concerns; or they may not be able to reveal their rank ordering of competing brands because of a lack of discernable difference in preference. These are situations when implicit measures of attitudes could be used to assess the impact of advertising on brand evaluations.

Implicit measures typically involve taking respondents' reaction time in response to certain pairs of stimuli. In a typical implicit test, the respondent may be asked to identify whether a string of letters presented on the computer screen is a word. The logo or the brand name of interest (e.g., Pampers) may be flashed subliminally on the screen prior to showing the string of letters (e.g., soft). The stronger the association between *soft* and *Pampers* in the respondent's mind, the faster the word *soft* will be identified. Such implicit measures that rely on response time can assess automatic, nonconscious attitudes that evade more traditional direct measures. Thus, by comparing the respondents' implicit attitudes to a control group, the impact of advertising on attitude formation or attitude change can be accurately assessed.

Indicators of Brand Choice

Copy tests often include measures of choice. Typically, respondents are asked to indicate their probability of purchasing the brand on some scale. The brand-switching potential of an ad is assessed by the change in purchase intent or brand preference as a result of ad exposure.

For many established brands, advertising is not likely to alter consumers' beliefs about the brand or their preferences. Nonetheless, advertising may serve as a reminder by enhancing the brand's top-of-mind awareness, and in turn increase brand choice probabilities. Measuring top-of-mind awareness involves using a category cue to prompt the retrieval of brand names. For example, consumers may be asked to list the brands of beer they would consider purchasing. An increase in top-of-mind awareness is indicated by the observation that people who have seen an ad for a particular brand (i.e., Miller) include this brand in their list to a greater extent (or earlier in the list) than those who have not. This would suggest that the ad was effective in increasing the probability that Miller is included in the consumers' consideration set.

Top-of-mind recall is particularly useful when the choice process is memory-based; that is, when consumers are asked to select an alternative from memory. For a stimulus-based choice that involves consumers picking a brand from a competitive set, perceptual measures that assess the ease of brand identification would be more relevant. Some common perceptual measures include brand name identification (e.g., respondents are asked to identify Bullseye, which is being presented very briefly (50 msec) on a computer screen), and product recognition (e.g., the time respondents take to pick out the brand from a collage of competing brands).

In sum, advertisers are interested in what customers know about their brand and how favorable this knowledge is. For these purposes, we suggest a greater reliance on implicit measures. Implicit measures of knowledge capture what people have learned from the advertising even though they may have forgotten where they got the information. Thus, customer knowledge can be tapped by asking message recipients what brands they can recall, what brands they would consider in a category, and what they know about the target brand. In addition, customers' disposition toward a brand should be assessed using message recipients' self-reports of overall and attribute-specific attitudes as well as brand choice. In addition, implicit measures of attitudes that rely on message recipients' reaction time are warranted when attitudes are not otherwise accessible. When customers' ability to recognize information such as brand name and packaging is of interest, perceptual measures such as brand name completion, brand name identification, or product recognition may be used.

CONCLUSION

Effective advertising for a brand requires that message recipients elaborate on the decision-relevant information presented in an ad and link that information to the brand being advertised. Advertisers can facilitate this process by prompting consumers through devices such as message repetition and humor. Effective advertising also includes creating copy and selecting media that resonate with the target's goals. Content and formats should be chosen that fit with consumers' regulatory orientations (achievement vs. safety), and by emphasizing shared interests and values beyond those immediately related to the brand. In assessing the effectiveness of advertising, focus should center on what people know about the brand and how they feel about this information, rather than on what they can recall about the advertising.

Brian Sternthal is the Kraft Professor of Marketing and is a past chair of the Marketing Department at the Kellogg School of Management. He received a BSc from McGill University and a Ph.D. from The Ohio State University.

Angela Y. Lee is associate professor of marketing at the Kellogg School of Management. She received a BBA from the University of Hawaii, an MPhil from the University of Hong Kong, and a Ph.D. from the University of Toronto.

NOTES

1. Higgins, E. Tory (1997), "Beyond Pleasure and Pain," *American Psychologist* (November), 1280–1300.

2. Lee, Angela Y. and Jennifer L. Aaker (2004), "Bringing the Frame into Focus: The Influence of Regulatory Fit on Processing Fluency and Persuasion," *Journal of Personality and Social Psychology*, 86, 205–218.

3. Aaker, Jennifer L., and Angela Y. Lee (2001), "I Seek Pleasures and We Avoid Pains: The Role of Self Regulatory Goals in Information Processing and Persuasion," *Journal of Consumer Research*, 28, 33–49.

4. See note 2.

5. Lee, Angela Y., Jennifer L. Aaker, and Wendi L. Gardner (2000), "The Pleasures and Pains of Distinct Self-Construals: The Role of Interdependence in Regulatory Focus," *Journal of Personality and Social Psychology*, 78, 1122–1134.

6. Wänke, Michaela, Gerd Bohner, and Andreas Jurkowitsch (1997), "There Are Many Reasons to Drive a BMW: Does Imagined Ease of Argument Generation Influence Attitudes?" *Journal of Consumer Research*, 24, 170–177.

7. Tybout, Alice M., Brian Sternthal, Prashant Malaviya, Georgios A. Bakamitsos, and Se-Bum Park (2005), "Information Accessibility as a Moderator of Judgments: The Role of Content versus Retrieval Ease," *Journal of Consumer Research*, 32, 76–85.

8. See note 7.

9. Lee, Angela Y. (2002), "The Effects of Implicit Memory on Memory-Based versus Stimulus-Based Brand Choice," *Journal of Marketing Research*, 39, 440–454.

10. Baumgartner, Hans, Mita Sujan, and Dan Padgett (1997), "Patterns of Affective Reactions to Advertisements: The Integration of Moment-to-Moment Responses into Overall Judgments," *Journal of Marketing Research*, 34, 219–232.

CHAPTER 8

RELATIONSHIP BRANDING AND CRM

EDWARD C. MALTHOUSE and BOBBY J. CALDER

Relationship branding is a *strategic* approach aimed at making consumers feel a sense of relationship, or personal connection, with a brand. By contrast, customer relationship management, or CRM, is largely an *operational* approach to managing customer relationships. Oddly enough, by the mid-2000s, there had not been a great deal of overlap between the two. Using an integrated marketing perspective, we outline a process for combining the two approaches to the advantage of each one. We show how the *process of subsegmentation* can become the link that enables companies to use a relationship brand to design CRM programs and in turn to use CRM to build the relationship brand. First, we will define relationship brands and highlight how relationship branding can add to the success of a brand. We then give an overview of CRM, and finally, we focus on combining CRM and relationship branding through the process of subsegmentation.

RELATIONSHIP BRANDS

Relationship branding is usually defined in terms of mass customization and market segmentation—a relationship brand is an offering tailored to a small segment of consumers. While this is true, we believe there is also much more to relationship branding. And in many ways the rhetoric of mass customization and targeting small segments (or even segments-of-one) is oversimplified. A more considered approach is necessary to realize the true potential of relationship branding.

The problem with the simple notion of relationship brands as mass customization is that almost all brand concepts or ideas are—at least to some extent—based on mass appeal. Overall they rely on the inherent appeal of shared experience. An example of this is branded diets, such as the South Beach Diet of the early 2000s. Part of the appeal of such diets is that everyone seems to be on them. Being on the latest weight-loss regimen is like joining a club, becoming part of a social group. It is the "next thing." Inherent in the very idea of the brand is its mass appeal. Once it loses this appeal, it is just another diet. The mass appeal of most brands is not as obvious as with the diet example. But think of a brand like Diet Coke. Part of the brand's appeal is surely that it is known, understood, and accepted by a large number of people—people who share something in common because of their experience with Diet Coke.

Thus most, if not all, brands are to some extent inherently *mass brands*—part of their appeal lies in their common appeal. The implication is that it may make sense to customize some activities around brands, but customization must be done carefully so as not to dilute the explicit or implicit mass appeal of the brand. The South Beach Diet may offer different meals for different customers, but the real appeal of the brand lies not in this customization but in the consumer's knowledge that she or he is one of the many people on the diet.

If relationship branding is not mere customization to segments, then what is it? Our view is as follows: *A relationship brand has a shared mass appeal that can be experienced in a more individualistic or idiosyncratic way by the consumer.* In the South Beach Diet example, the brand is an appealing idea or concept for a segment of consumers who are either on the diet or interested in it. But consider two *subsegments* of these consumers. One, mostly female, is always on a diet and is looking to use the diet for all her meals. Another, mostly male, is looking to diet at breakfast and lunch during the workweek (these males figure to "relax" at night and on weekends). If the marketer finds a way to allow each of these subsegments to experience the brand in their own way, the brand becomes a relationship brand. This could be as simple as giving the first subsegment a set of meal planning tips covering all meals and the other a set focusing on just the workday. Both subsegments share the same idea of the brand, and this is part of its appeal. They both buy into the diet, but they are able to relate to the brand in their own way.

To illustrate the concept another way, think of the brand as a person. We both know Mary. Now Mary is Mary, but we each have a different relationship with Mary because we have our own experiences with her. Indeed, this is what having a relationship is all about. We should think of relationship branding in the same way. Viewed as such, the key to relationship branding is

to allow subsegments of consumers to experience the brand in a more individualistic, personal way. And this leads directly to using different contact
points with each subsegment to create different experiences, and hence the
relevance of CRM.

A useful way to think about this idea comes from an integrated marketing
perspective.[1] As diagrammed in Figure 8.1, the key notion is that the company must translate the brand idea into a series of *contacts* with the consumer
that in turn creates the experience that underlies the brand. From this perspective, relationship branding involves creating contacts for subsegments of
consumers that produce a more idiosyncratic experience than would be the
case if the same contacts were used for all consumers.

CUSTOMER RELATIONSHIP MANAGEMENT

Customer relationship management, or CRM, encompasses every interface
between consumers (or customers) and a company. CRM is the entire set of
interactions or contacts with the consumer, whether initiated by the company or by the consumer. For example, CRM activities occur when a cus-

Figure 8.1
The Integrated Marketing Paradigm

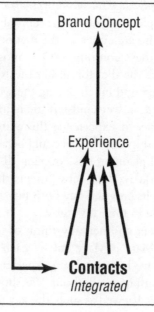

tomer calls with a service request or when a current customer is sent an offer for a related product.

CRM, however, is more than a label for these activities. In marketing circles, CRM has come to be defined as an *informed approach* to dealing with consumers. As practiced by leading companies (and as advocated by a host of consultants and vendors), CRM holds that the company should base its interaction with consumers on data specific to each customer. If a customer calls, the person answering the call should ideally have access to that customer's history of requests and their resolution. If the company attempts to cross-sell a consumer, the offer should be based on an analysis of that customer's previous purchases. CRM systems are thus designed to make interactions with consumers more data-based. The goal of CRM, as the name implies, is to turn interactions with consumers into ongoing relationships.

However, while the goal of CRM is to create a more informed end relationship with the customer, there seems to be wide agreement that in practice CRM is often very tactical in nature. Companies focus more on the hardware and software systems used in CRM than on the goal of making customer interactions more meaningful. This seems to be the case in the United States even more than in other countries. Indeed, there are even indications that interest in CRM has recently cooled (as of the mid-2000s). Although CRM expenditures will no doubt grow long term, increasingly it seems that companies and vendors have been driven too much by a tactical IT approach.

There have been two reactions to the current status of CRM. In the near term it appears that a number of companies have experienced more success by limiting CRM to smaller-scale projects.

> [Successful companies have] all taken a pragmatic, disciplined approach to CRM, launching highly focused projects that are relatively narrow in their scope and modest in their goals. Rather than use CRM to transform entire businesses, they've directed their investments toward solving clearly defined problems within their customer relationship cycle—the series of activities that runs from the initial segmenting and targeting of customers all the way through to wooing them back for more.[2]

Looking more at the long-term future of CRM, however, there is also a growing call for making CRM more strategic. Rigby and Reichheld,[3] for example, have sought to define CRM as "the bundling of customer strategy and processes, supported by relevant software, for the purpose of improving customer loyalty and, eventually, corporate profitability."[4] It is worth noting the emphasis on CRM as a way of turning strategy into activities.

More generally, Bligh and Turk[5] relate CRM to Michael Porter's framework for strategy. Porter stresses that strategy can no longer be approached as mere operational excellence (OE). Such excellence is necessary but not sufficient to sustain competitive advantage. Strategy is about either cost leadership or activities that differentiate the firm from competitors.

> CRM should be used to help maintain acceptable levels of OE on the customer side of the business. After all, a poorly designed service call center or poorly kept customer records would lead to a distinct disadvantage for most companies. But in most cases these improvements will be very similar to those provided by rivals, and so it is equally important that CRM is used to strengthen competitive advantage for the organization in the marketplace.[6]

If CRM is to be more strategic, it clearly needs to have a more strategic purpose. In Porter's terms, it needs to provide a competitive advantage in terms of cost leadership or marketplace differentiation. For example, CRM could be viewed as a way of reducing the total cost of dealing with consumers. By creating relationships with consumers, the company increases its efficiency in dealing with them. The line, however, between cost leadership and mere operational excellence is a fine one. To us, the most compelling way of approaching CRM more strategically is through seeking competitive advantage in the marketplace, though this has been relatively neglected in most discussions of CRM. But this still begs the real question of just how CRM can contribute to competitive advantage in the marketplace. How can it be a competitive advantage? We believe that companies need *to connect CRM and relationship branding by linking CRM to the process of designing contacts for subsegments of consumers, which allows these consumers to experience the brand in a more individualistic way.*

THE SUBSEGMENTATION PROCESS

A market *segment* is a target group (singled out from a larger universe or market) that is believed to be receptive to the brand concept or idea in a way that others are not. A segment may be defined in various ways (demographically, psychographically, attitudinally, behaviorally), but it is always a group of consumers who currently—or potentially—value the brand idea. These segments share a common receptivity to the brand idea.

Likewise, *subsegments* are the division of a basic segment into subgroups. By definition, a brand appeals to all subsegments of a market segment. Marketers use subsegmentation because they believe that the brand's appeal can be further strengthened by treating each subsegment differently. The marketer aims to allow different subsegments to experience the brand in a more individualistic or idiosyncratic way—a way that hinges on the uniqueness of their subsegment identity. In this manner, subsegmentation is integral to building a relationship brand as we have defined it.

The Case of Tesco

Tesco, the British supermarket chain, illustrates the way in which relationship brands can be built through successful subsegmentation and the use of CRM technology. As related by Humby and Hunt,[7] historically Tesco's strategy can be summarized in the words of its founder—"Pile it high, sell 'em cheap." The company has focused on cost leadership, promising to squeeze the most value out of a customer's weekly shopping trip. During the 1960s and 1970s this strategy took the form of a heavy reliance on green stamps (which customers pasted into books and redeemed for products like radios). This was followed by a rebranding around everyday low prices and a more downscale retail atmosphere. By the 1990s, however, Tesco still lagged behind its more upmarket competitor, Sainsbury, which contested its cost leadership.

Eventually Tesco embarked on a highly successful strategy of differentiating itself from both Sainsbury and emerging discount grocers by building a relationship brand. The core idea of the Tesco brand became, *Tesco allows you to buy more of what you want.* Operationally, the brand began with a CRM loyalty program called the Clubcard. By signing up for the card, consumers could earn points on their purchases. These points were converted periodically into vouchers that could be used to purchase items in Tesco stores. The vouchers were a way of thanking and rewarding consumers. The consumer experience of appreciation, resulting from the voucher contact, reinforced the brand idea of helping shoppers buy more of what they wanted.

As the brand strategy evolved, Tesco moved progressively further toward a relationship brand by actively exploiting the Clubcard program (a CRM initiative) through subsegmentation. One of Tesco's most successful subsegmentation efforts was the Baby&Toddler Club program started in 1996. Baby products had traditionally been an underperforming category at Tesco, despite the Clubcard. Then the supermarket offered pregnant women and mothers of young children a Baby&Toddler Club membership as part of the Clubcard program. Members periodically received coupons for baby and toddler essentials such as wipes and creams, which were a part of the basic Clubcard program (the original segment). But beyond simply using a CRM (operational) initiative to bring customers in, the Baby&Toddler Club aimed to relate to the special needs of new mothers. Tesco understood that most young mothers are not only trying to stretch their family's budget but are also simultaneously very concerned about taking the best care of, and buying the best products for, their babies and children. Their status as new parents brings an idiosyncratic aspect to the experience of stretching the family's budget. And this suggests special contacts for this subsegment. So the club's mailings (contacts) not only included coupons but also information and advice on topics such as pregnancy planning, immunization, and advice on when to call the doctor. Moreover, the mother received the coupons and advice on a time-dependent basis, reflecting the progress from pregnancy to baby to toddler (birthdate data was obtained when the woman joined the club). As reflected on the application form in Figure 8.2, the experience from these contacts was described as *help and offers* at *every little step of the way.*

Thus, through the Baby&Toddler Club, Tesco used CRM technology to build a relationship brand. Tesco formed a relationship with young mothers by allowing them to experience the brand concept—*Tesco allows you to buy more of what you want*—in a more individualistic or idiosyncratic way, helping young mothers stretch their budgets and meet the high standards of motherhood (*every little step of the way*).

But, why not think of the Tesco Baby&Toddler Club as simply a way to reach a different market segment, rather than as a way to reach a subsegment? This would seem more natural to many marketers, as consumers with young children are just another segment of the market. But here's the distinction: If the company planned to have a different brand concept or positioning for consumers with young children, then these consumers would be a separate market segment—the brand concept would be different in some way for them. But in the case of Tesco, the brand concept is the same for young mothers as it is for all others: *Tesco allows you to buy more of what you want.* The goal here was not to appeal to these consumers in an entirely different way, but rather *to create a relationship with the brand by allowing it to be experienced in a more individual way.*

Figure 8.2
Tesco Baby&Toddler Club

SUBSEGMENTATION AS A PROCESS

In our view relationship branding is best thought of as a *process* in which subsegments are identified and used via CRM operational structures to design contacts at the subsegment level. Keep in mind that subsegments are distinct from market segments. Brands should always be targeted at the *market segment(s)*. Subsegmention involves partitioning a market segment into smaller groups for the purpose of relationship branding.

The general process in which subsegments are identified and used via CRM operational structures to design contacts at the subsegment level is as follows:

1. Develop and profile subsegments.
2. Set measurable objectives for each subsegment.
3. Design and implement contacts.
4. Measure results.

We discuss each step in detail below.

Step 1: Develop and Profile Subsegments

The first step in the subsegmentation process is to partition a company's consumers or customers into subsegments and then profile those groups. The subsegmentation will be useful if the company can develop contacts targeted at the subsegments that are more effective than using the same contact for everyone. For example, Lexus might want to subsegment based on previous ownership of a Lexus automobile, and this group would profile as older. Advertising and other contacts targeted specifically to this group would likely be more successful than a generic appeal to all target consumers. But how can we think about these possible subsegmentation variables, like previous ownership, more systematically? We provide in the following a useful classification of subsegmentation possibilities.

RFM Subsegmentations   One way to subsegment customers is to use variables such as recency, frequency, and monetary value (RFM). Recency is the length of time since the most recent purchase. Current ownership (or not) of a Lexus is an example of a recency variable. Recency is often an important variable because it indicates whether a customer has lapsed. For example, a customer in an airline's frequent-flyer database who has not flown with that airline in two years is considered inactive, and that customer will require different contacts than someone who has flown more frequently. The airline might want to ask why the former customer has become inactive and address whatever is wrong with a special contact, one that would probably not be as relevant to the recent flier.

Frequency represents the number of previous purchases. Frequency is a natural measure of behavioral loyalty—the more often a customer has purchased from a company, the more loyal the customer is, at least in terms of behavior (attitudinal loyalty, on the other hand, is how the customer feels about the company and is often distinct from frequency-based loyalty). A first-time customer usually requires different contacts than a regular customer. Some hotel loyalty programs send new members a *welcome package* contact, which would not be relevant to a regular customer.

Monetary value, the amount that a customer has spent with a company in the past, is important because it is usually the best (available) predictor of future spending. Recency and frequency are good predictors of whether customers will be active in the future, but monetary value predicts how much they will spend if they are active at all. Big customers in the past are likely to be big customers in the future; little customers in the past are likely to be little customers in the future. Customers who have spent large amounts of money with a company in the past may deserve more expensive contacts than those with small historical monetary value. These customers may also expect recognition or appreciation to be part of their experience with the brand. Organizations that solicit donations often use monetary value to select a contact. For example, a symphony orchestra might invite its most generous donors to an exclusive concert or reception, while small donors receive only a direct mail solicitation for another donation. Airlines and hotels often give more expensive perks to high-tier customers (those with large monetary value and frequency in the recent past) than to normal customers. The Tesco supermarket chain has experimented with giving a "bigger thank you" to some customers.[8]

It is important for a company to consider RFM when designing contacts, but it should not stop at this. RFM is good for determining the objective of the contract and perhaps the size of the carrot, but RFM alone usually provides somewhat limited opportunities to achieve a more individualistic or idiosyncratic experience of a brand. The types of experiences that are relevant to a customer are often not related to RFM.

For example, RFM will not determine whether a supermarket customer is a gourmet cook, a junk-food addict, or a vegetarian. A contact that is meant to reward a best customer (low recency and high frequency and monetary) with relevant store coupons would be very different for the gourmet than for the junk-food addict. Each would require very different coupons, and probably a different voice in the message. Thus it is usually necessary to define subsegments based on other variables besides RFM.

Sociodemographic Subsegmentations   Defining subsegments based on sociodemographic variables—age, marital status, presence of children, education, income, and so on—is usually fairly easy for several reasons. For business-to-business companies, *firmographics* such as industry code, number of employees, and the like, play the same role. First, this information is easily available to companies in many different industries. Loyalty club applications often gather basic demographic information. For example, the membership applications of supermarket frequent-shopper programs should ask for age, number of children (living in the household), and marital status. The purchase patterns of a family with small children will be very different from those of an elderly couple, and the two subsegments will require different contacts. Humby and Hunt[9] suggest that life-stage subsegmentation "can avoid simple errors—for example, offering coupons for Coca Cola to tea-drinking pensioners [retirees]." Companies that do not gather this information directly from customers can purchase it from third-party data providers.

Second, subsegmentations based on sociodemographic or firmographic information are easy to implement in that the data analysis requirements are minimal (compared with the strenuous effort required to analyze previous purchase categories). It is easy to define business rules that classify customers into subsegments. For example, if a customer has one or more young children living in the household and the head of household is between the ages of 20 and 35, that customer is a member of the *Young Family* subsegment. If the head of household is over the age of 65 and there are no young children, it is part of the *Senior* subsegment. Customers who are single and between the ages of 20 and 30 constitute the *Young Singles*. Alternatively, several companies have developed general-purpose subsegmentations that can be overlaid onto a company's database. Examples include Cohorts, Personics from Acxiom, and PRIZM from Claritas.

Sociodemographic subsegmentations are easy to implement and help companies develop contacts that are more personally relevant. Another advantage of sociodemographic subsegmentations over those based on previous purchase categories is that prospective customers and new customers (who have little purchase history) can be classified into sociodemographic subsegments. Previous purchase categories, by definition, require previous purchase history, which is only available for more mature customers who have made several purchases. However, previous purchase categories, as discussed below, usually enable companies to develop more relevant contacts than sociodemographic variables. Not every senior buys prune juice and not every young family buys sugary breakfast cereals. Improved relevance, however, comes with a cost. It is usually much more difficult to process and analyze previous purchase history than demographics.

Subsegmentations Based on Previous Purchase Categories These subsegments are defined based on what a customer has purchased in the past. Subsegments can be found using traditional market research methods for market segmentation. This usually involves a two-step process. The first step in developing subsegments is to develop scales that measure a customer's interest in a particular type of merchandise, an approach used by the supermarket Tesco. For example, Tesco's *Adventurous* scale measures how often a customer (in the UK) buys adventurous food items such as extra-virgin olive oil or the ingredients for Malaysian curries,[10] while the *Fresh* scale measures how often a consumer buys fresh fruits and vegetables.

Another example is Rhenania, a German company that sells overstock books, mostly via catalogs. Rhenania set out to build a relationship brand through CRM contacts with customers. The company's first step was to include with every catalog a cover letter customized to subsegments, highlighting books that might be of interest to specific customers. The company then sought out a more ambitious contact structure by exploring the idea of creating specialized catalogs for individual subsegments. The first step was to develop *interest scales* that measured a customer's interest in various types of merchandise. These were general *types of books* (as opposed to types of readers). The company used a method called factor analysis to identify nearly a dozen interest categories,[11] which included such categories as *history, popular fiction, art, home and living,* and so on. Each customer was given a score that indicated his or her interest in each category, based on the number of books that a customer purchased of a particular type. A customer could have high scores in more than one category.

The next step in Rhenania's subsegmentation process was to find subsegments by applying cluster analysis to the above purchase interest scales. Cluster analysis (see box on the following page) is a method that groups customers into natural groups. For Rhenania, several natural groups were identified, including *Super Readers* (average purchases from all categories); *History Only* (substantially above-average purchases of history books, but below-average purchase levels in all other categories); *Music Only* (buys only classical and popular music CDs), and so on.

In sum, an effective subsegmentation creates contacts that appeal uniquely

---

What Is Cluster Analysis?

Cluster analysis refers to marketing research techniques that find natural groupings, or (sub)segments, of customers based on their characteristics. There are many versions of cluster analysis. The most commonly used method, *k-means,* groups customers so that their within-cluster variance is as small as possible. This means that the members of the resulting clusters are as similar to each other as possible. This also implies that the clusters are as different as possible from each other. This is exactly what marketers want to achieve with a (sub)segmentation. (Sub)segmentation makes sense whenever customers have different characteristics. Cluster analysis finds groups of customers such that the groups themselves have different characteristics, while the members of an individual group have similar characteristics.

---

to specific subsegments. RFM variables are useful for setting the behavioral objective for a group of customers. Demographic variables are useful because they are commonly available and easy to implement compared with the use of previous purchase categories. Previous purchase categories will usually yield more relevant contacts than demographics, but this approach requires substantially more analytical expertise to create and execute.

Step 2: Set Measurable Objectives for Each Subsegment

In this step, a company must specify what it wants to communicate to each subsegment and what it wants each subsegment to do. Often, different subsegments will have different objectives. Contacts follow from these objectives. In our Tesco example, many of the store's best customers do not shop in all departments. One group of customers buys a wide variety of food items, but does not purchase any wine or other alcohol at Tesco. An objective for these customers could be to educate them on the wide variety found in the wine section. Another group of loyal customers have babies but are not currently enrolled in the Tesco Baby&Toddler Club. The objective for this group might be to interest them in trying Tesco's baby-care products with contacts featuring high-end, more expensive items, perhaps even independently of the Club. It is important not only to define the subsegment but to define the company's objective for it as well.

Step 3: Design and Implement Contacts

After objectives have been set, the next step is to develop contacts to achieve these objectives. Recall that a contact is simply any interaction between the consumer and the brand, including traditional marketing communications. But contacts can include many additional activities. Anything that is associated with a brand and imparts the brand experience is a potential contact. Consider a resort hotel. The hotel van that collects guests at the airport and brings them back to the hotel produces a contact. While this contact is not normally thought of in terms of CRM, it should be. A van that is too large may not make a positive statement about the hotel for some subsegments. At check-in, the person behind the main desk makes another contact. This person's demeanor and attire communicate something about the hotel. The décor of the room, the hotel's restaurant and other facilities, the loyalty club statement, and even the doorman are all contacts. The accumulation of all such contacts ultimately defines the experience of the brand in the customer's mind. All of these contacts might be designed differently for different subsegments. Let us review two basic issues that often arise in thinking about designing contacts.

Proactive versus Reactive Contacts   Proactive contacts are not triggered by any specific event, while reactive contacts are triggered by specific actions or inaction, initiated either by the consumer or the company.[12] A proactive contact is mailing a catalog to existing and prospective customers (the catalog is not formatted as a response to any particular event). Another type of proactive contact is sending a weekly e-mail to an airline's frequent fliers that lists the bargain fares for that week.

Reactive contacts depend on trigger events. For example, when a customer lapses, a company might initiate a reactive contact designed to reactivate the customer. These reactive contacts generally are triggered by a specific business rule; for example, if a customer has not purchased in one year (the trigger event), then a contact letter is sent. Likewise, many loyalty programs have different membership tiers. When a top-tier customer falls into a lower tier (because of less activity), the company should initiate a reactive contact to help reenlist the loyalty of this customer.

With advances in CRM technology, reactive contacts can increasingly be automated so that the trigger event is transparent to the consumer. Book recommendations on Amazon.com are an example of a completely automated contact. Based on cookies or customer log-ins, Amazon makes cross-selling recommendations based on a variety of factors that are mostly transparent to the user (past purchases, unpurchased items in the shopping cart, wish list items, etc.). A computer algorithm, which is software and technology intensive, decides which items are of most interest to a particular customer.

Quid-pro-Quo versus Discretionary Rewards   Some contacts are designed to reward customers and are particularly common with loyalty programs. In a quid-pro-quo reward, the terms have been agreed on at the time of enrolling.[13] They are carrots—if the customer does something that has been agreed on (such as book a certain number of hotel rooms or fly a certain number of miles) the customer will receive a reward. Hotels and airlines offer quid-pro-quo rewards with their loyalty programs (free flights and rooms). The Tesco Clubcard program offers quid-pro-quo rewards to its members. A customer who has spent £200 during the quarter will receive a fixed percentage of this amount in a quarterly mailing. The defining characteristic here is that the company and customer agree on terms at the outset and the rewards are roughly proportional to consumption. Those who fly more get more free flights. Those who spend more get more savings.

Discretionary rewards are perks that the company *gives* to customers without any explicit agreement and without charging any points. These rewards are usually based on past consumer behavior. For example, hotels often leave a bouquet of flowers or a free bottle of wine in the room of a special customer. Some subsegments are sometimes even upgraded to a larger room. The customer and the hotel have no agreement that after a specified number of visits the customer will receive such a perk, and the customer does not have to spend any points. The hotel awards these perks to make certain customers feel good about the hotel and earn their loyalty. Collinger[14] calls such perks surprises and delights.

However, we believe that discretionary rewards are risky. Customers who have been loyal in the past may or may not continue to be loyal. Customers who have been marginal in the past can become best customers. For these reasons, we think that quid-pro-quo rewards, where the size of the carrot is linked to actual *future* behavior, should be the first choice for most such contacts. Discretionary rewards should be used when they (1) involve little or no cost to the company giving the reward, (2) are highly valued by the recipient, (3) can affect a customer's future behavior, and (4) fit well with the desired customer experience.

For example, suppose that an airline has an empty business-class seat on a four-hour flight. The airline should delight one of its customers with a free upgrade because the incremental cost in doing so is negligible. But which customer should receive the upgrade? In our view, the recipient should be someone who would place a high value on the extra benefits offered in business class (e.g., they need the extra space and power port so that they can work), *and* whose future behavior could be affected by the delight. Someone who flies frequently but spreads the miles across multiple carriers would be a good choice. Such a person would be more likely to experience a heightened sense of relationship due to the contact reward. The brand has chosen to do something for them that they had no reason to expect.

Step 4: Measure Results

One of the benefits of a CRM-based contact is its ability to measure results. In our Rhenania example, suppose we want to determine the effectiveness of sending a special cover letter to a subsegment of history book lovers. By assigning history lovers to two groups, one of which received the special letter and one that received a generic letter (the control group), we can measure the results of the subsegmentation contact. The difference in response rates, order amounts, and so forth, measures the effectiveness of the contact. The cost-effectiveness is then based on the expense of producing the special letter. Note that the control offer should include a generic letter (control customers should not receive just the catalog alone). It is important that both groups receive a letter so that the difference in response rates is not attributed to the mere fact of having *any* kind of letter (specialized or not).

Once evaluated, the entire four-step contact process should be viewed as iterative. After measuring the results of a contact, the company may want to return to any of the previous steps. For example, perhaps contacts work better for some subsegments than for others. It may be necessary to redesign the contacts for poorly performing subsegments (step 3). Once a company finds that some contacts work, it should explore the possibility of further improvement by introducing additional subsegments (step 1). Additional subsegments will incur additional costs, but they should yield more individually relevant experiences.

STRONG BRANDS MAKE GOOD RELATIONSHIP BRANDS

We conclude with a final example and an important principle. The principle is that the best candidates for relationship branding are brands that are already strong. Our example is a consumer magazine that is a very strong brand but not yet a relationship brand. It is a popular *country lifestyle* magazine. There are several magazines of this kind targeted at women, all variations on the brand idea: *In today's hectic, noisy, busy world, it is appealing to think about bringing simplicity and peacefulness to your life by getting back to the simpler ways of doing things from the past.* This is a strong brand concept. Can the brand become even stronger through subsegmentation?

To explore this idea we utilized research that asked readers about what they *experience* when reading a magazine. Recall the framework summarized in Figure 8.1—the experiences consumers have with a product define the brand in their mind. The research indicated that readers have a wide variety of experiences with magazines.[15] Two experiences that seem useful for the country magazine are *Using Advertisements* and *A Personal Time-Out*. A scale was developed for measuring each of these experiences. A reader who experiences Using Advertisements *agrees* with statements such as "I like the ads as much as the articles" and "I look at most of the ads," and *disagrees* with "I make a special effort to skip over the ads." Readers who experience A Personal Time-Out agree that "Reading this magazine is a quiet time," "It's an escape," "My goal is to relax with the magazine," "It takes my mind off other things," and "I feel less stress after reading it."

A cluster analysis revealed one reader subsegment of the country magazine that was low on the Advertising Usefulness scale and high on the A Personal Time-Out scale. To engage in relationship branding we therefore need contacts especially designed for this subsegment. For example, at least a certain percentage of articles in the magazine could be written with this subsegment in mind. These articles could enhance the time-out experience by being less informational, more pensive, and more visual. And possibly these articles should jump pages less so that they are not interrupted by ads as often. The point would be to create a contact point in the magazine that this subsegment would gravitate to, one that would allow them to experience the magazine in a more individualistic way. Acquisition mailings and other CRM contacts could obviously be designed for this subsegment as well. By adding contacts such as these to reflect and enhance the experience of this and other subsegments we can build on the already strong value of the brand precisely because there are already strong experiences to work with.

Even a weak brand could potentially be improved through subsegmentation that improves the experience of the brand. But brands that are already associated with strong experiences offer the possibility of building on and fine tuning these experiences through subsegmentation.

SUMMARY

The key to relationship branding and the strategic use of CRM is to subsegment your market. This will enable you to create contacts that allow specific subsegments of consumers to make a more personal connection to the brand—to enable them to experience your brand in a more powerful individualistic or idiosyncratic way. This is the true power of relationship branding and CRM.

Edward C. Malthouse is an associate professor of Integrated Marketing Communications at the Medill School of Journalism at Northwestern University. He also teaches in the Communication Systems executive program and at Aoyama Gakuin University in Japan. He received a BA from Augustana College, an MA from Southampton University, and a Ph.D. from Northwestern University.

Bobby J. Calder is the Charles H. Kellstadt Distinguished Professor of Marketing and professor of psychology at the Kellogg School of Management, Northwestern University. He is also a professor of journalism at the Medill School of Journalism. In addition, he serves as director of research for the Media Management Center at Northwestern University and is co-director of the Media program at Kellogg. Previously, he taught at the Wharton School, University of Pennsylvania, and the University of Illinois. He is co-editor of Kellogg on Integrated Marketing *(Wiley). He received his BA, MA, and Ph.D. degrees from the University of North Carolina at Chapel Hill.*

NOTES

1. Calder, Bobby J. and Edward C. Malthouse (2003), "What Is Integrated Marketing," in Dawn Iacobucci and Bobby Calder (eds.), *Kellogg on Integrated Marketing,* New York: Wiley, pp. 6–15.

2. Rigby, Darrell and Dianne Ledingham (2004), "CRM Done Right," *Harvard Business Review* (November), 118–129.

3. Rigby, Darrell, Frederick Reichheld, and Phil Schefter (2002), "Avoid the Four Perils of CRM," *Harvard Business Review* (February), 101–109.

4. Ibid., p. 102.

5. Bligh, Philip and Douglas Turk (2004), *CRM Unplugged: Releasing CRM's Strategic Value,* New York: Wiley.

6. Ibid., p. 63.

7. Humby, Clive and Terry Hunt (2003), *Scoring Points: How Tesco Is Winning Customer Loyalty,* London: Kogan Page.

8. Ibid., p. 216.

9. Ibid., p. 109.

10. Ibid., p. 156.

11. Malthouse, Edward C. and Ralf Elsner (2004), "Customization with Crossed-Basis Sub-segmentation," under review at *Journal of Advertising*.

12. Malthouse, Edward C. (2005), "Detecting Trigger Events Using Survival Analysis," working paper, Department of Integrated Marketing Communications, Northwestern University.

13. Malthouse, Edward C. and Robert C. Blattberg (2005), "Can We Predict Customer Long-Term Value?" in press, *Journal of Interactive Marketing*.

14. Collinger, Tom (2003), "The Tao of Customer Loyalty: Getting to 'My Brand, My Way,' " in Dawn Iacobucci and Bobby Calder (eds.), *Kellogg on Integrated Marketing*, New York: Wiley, pp. 16–38.

15. Malthouse, Edward C., Bobby J. Calder, and Wayne Eadie (2003), "Conceptualizing and Measuring Magazine Reader Experiences," *Proceedings of the Worldwide Readership Symposium*, Cambridge (October), pp. 285–306.

CHAPTER 9

BRAND STRATEGY FOR BUSINESS MARKETS

JAMES C. ANDERSON and GREGORY S. CARPENTER

Every business, whether its customers are individuals or businesses, manages a brand. Although businesses that sell to firms, institutions, or governments may have a relatively small number of customers, and they may not rely on television advertising and other traditional brand building media, they have brands nonetheless. In fact, brands are one of the most common elements of modern markets. Complex, high-technology products such as microprocessors or jet aircraft engines, intangibles such as financial advice or management consulting, and even the simplest commodities, such as water or oxygen, can be—and, indeed, are—branded.

Managing brands in business markets does present unique challenges in comparison to the more traditional consumer branding. First, within consumer goods organizations, the concept of brand management is widely accepted. In business markets, brands are of more recent interest, experience with brands is more limited, and the benefit of devoting time, effort, and resources to brand building is less well understood. Second, in consumer markets, purchasing typically involves few decision makers, and the process can be very unstructured. In business markets, purchasing can be a simple process limited to one individual, but it also can involve many individuals with specialized expertise participating in a highly structured process. Third, business

---

This chapter incorporates material from James C. Anderson and James A. Narus (2004), *Business Market Management: Understanding, Creating, and Delivering Value,* 2nd edition, Upper Saddle River, NJ: Prentice Hall.

and consumer brands differ in their architecture, that is, the structure of multiple brand offerings. In consumer markets, managers have access to the full range of brand options. In business markets, organizations have less flexibility. If Boeing decided, for instance, to create a new line of airplanes, creating a brand for a range of airplanes that has no association with Boeing would be extremely difficult.

In this chapter, we discuss how powerful business brands can be created, recognizing their differences from consumer brands. We illustrate the financial value of business brands, explore the basis for their value, and identify three types of brand strategy that are commonly effective in business markets: creating a brand associated with superior performance, differentiating brands, and building brands on unique bundles of products. We discuss the sources of brand equity created through that process and the impact brand equity has on price sensitivity and competition.

THE POWER OF BUSINESS BRANDS

Brands are symbols of the value that an organization creates and delivers to its customers. Symbols have value. Indeed, brands are strategically endowed with value through the actions of the organization. In developing a unique value proposition, by communicating that position within the organization, and by implementing a strategy to deliver the promised value, an organization's actions convey a brand's value to customers. Every action taken by an organization that touches a customer—every communication with customers, whether verbalized or not—influences how that customer sees the organization. That knowledge in turn contributes to the overall value of the unique symbol of the organization, its brand.

There are many ways to measure the value of brands.[1] One measure of the power and importance of brands can be found in estimates of their financial value. Figure 9.1 shows estimates of the value of a sample of consumer and business brands. It shows that Coca-Cola is the most valuable brand, reaching nearly $70 billion, but that Microsoft, IBM, and GE are also exceptionally valuable brands, with values ranging from $40 billion to nearly $70 billion. The analysis includes a few surprises. Consumer brand powerhouses such as Nike and Starbucks are overshadowed by many business brands, such as Goldman Sachs, Pfizer, and Hewlett Packard. Contrary to the view that brands are fundamentally a phenomenon of consumer good markets, Figure 9.1 shows that brands can be valuable in both business and consumer markets, and that brands in business markets can be even more valuable.

The power of brands is derived from the dual roles they play. Externally,

Figure 9.1
Estimates of Brand Value in Billions of Dollars

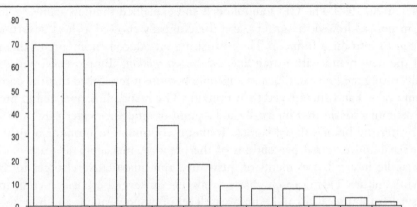

brands convey to customers the value that can be expected from doing business with an organization. If well managed, a brand can be a powerful symbol to current and potential customers of that organization's promise. Internally, a brand becomes a beacon for organizing the firm's activities. By necessity, organizations consist of groups of individuals performing different functions, ranging from sales and production to R&D and finance. Each has measures of success and each has functional objectives. Salespeople seek volume, R&D pursues innovations, and finance seeks high return on investment. These differences, however important, can be divisive as well. A brand, as a symbol of the value the organization is intent on delivering to its customers, can align internal efforts and increase the impact of the organization's resources. Infineon's experience of developing its new brand illustrates the importance of a brand's internal and external roles.

Infineon   In 1999 Siemens, a diversified 160-year-old German corporation, decided to spin off its semiconductor business as a separate corporation. To create an identity for the new firm, senior managers organized workshops in Europe and in the United States, asking participants to brainstorm what the defining attributes of the new company ought to be, based on reality as well as aspirations. Using the results from these workshops, Seimens chose to brand the new corporation *Infineon,* which is a blend of *infinity, eternity (eon* in Greek), and *new (neon* in Greek). To announce the new brand and use it as a catalyst for launching a new culture, Seimens organized a huge party at each of its sites worldwide, inviting the 25,000 Infineon employees to celebrate on March 26, 1999. The CEO announced and explained the new name, senior managers addressed the groups, and the company showed a short advertisement to introduce Infineon. The advertising introduced an important theme of the new brand with its tag line: *Never stop thinking.* Employees found the advertising tag line exciting and engaging because it reinforced that the company valued and encouraged their thinking. The brand, thus, operated to provide both a focal point internally and a point of difference externally.

After the brand's initial launch, Infineon continued to monitor both the internal and external perceptions of the brand. A management team made periodic internal assessments of qualitative and quantitative changes in the firm's culture. This research charted progress on several criteria, such as internal communication and employees' level of empowerment and how they felt about the impact of their jobs on the company. The team documented its findings in a report entitled "Cultural Mirror of the Company," which was shared with all employees. External perceptions of the brand were tracked through an annual "Brand Tracking Survey." Infineon interviewed customers as well as managers at target companies (prospective customers) to understand what they thought about the brand and how their perceptions of Infineon have evolved since 1999. The Infineon brand thus became the guiding principle for internal coordination, spanning the range of functions, and it also became a symbol of the value customers could expect from the new organization.

CREATING BRAND EQUITY

The process of creating powerful, meaningful, unique brands involves making decisions in three key areas, as shown in Figure 9.2. The first decision focuses on what positioning the brand will adopt. Crafting a compelling position requires focus—selecting target customers and choosing the value that the organization will deliver to them. A brand must then be situated in the

Figure 9.2
A Process for Creating Brand Equity

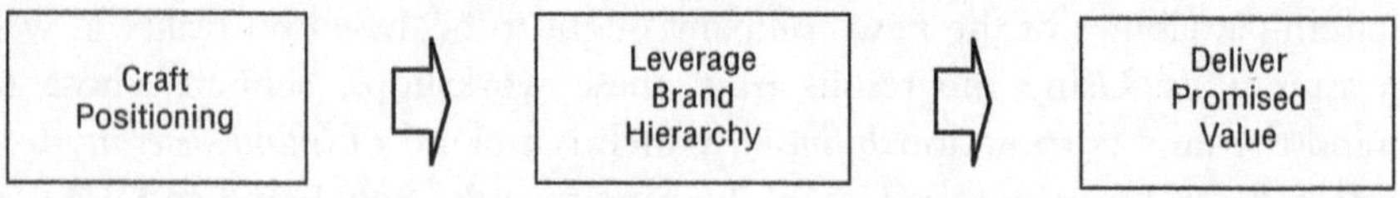

| Craft Positioning | ⇨ | Leverage Brand Hierarchy | ⇨ | Deliver Promised Value |

organization's brand hierarchy (its array of brands). Finally, the organization must act to fulfill the promise established in the value proposition.

Craft Positioning

The foundation of branding is *positioning*. It provides the conceptual corner-stone for the actions that inevitably flow from it. The critical components are the target, offering concept, and value proposition. The *target* specifies the customers whose business the organization seeks to win. For example, "itin-erant, Generation-X professionals" might be specified as the target for some advanced, intelligent-network telephone services, such as single-number reach. The *offering concept* component specifies the essential attributes of the market offering for the selected target, out of the potentially larger set of at-tributes that an offering may possess.

The *value proposition* expresses the points of difference and, sometimes, the points of parity of the market offering relative to the next-best-alternative of-fering. The value proposition should be a persuasive one- or two-sentence answer to the customer question: "Why should I do business with your firm and not your competitor?" Although managers often correctly believe that their offering provides many different types of value, we advise managers to focus on the one or two points of difference that are most valuable to the tar-get customers.[2] These points of difference may be supplemented by a point of parity in order to establish that the supplier's brand performs comparably on a value element relative to the next-best-alternative offering.

Successful value propositions share three characteristics. First, they focus on value meaningful to target customers. The positioning statement should be expressed in the everyday language of target customers. Both target cus-tomers and everyone within the supplier firm should readily grasp its exact meaning. Positioning statements that contain hackneyed words or phrases, such as "highest performance," "best quality," or "world class," lose any true meaning with target customers and within the supplier's own workforce. Second, the positioning statement conveys the value of the brand, succinctly and effectively. Business market managers must strive to make the value proposition precise, tangible, and credible for target customers. Third, the value promised in the proposition must be consistent with the goals of the business unit as a whole. Senior management as well as other functional area managers must be willing to support the actions needed to attain that posi-tioning in the marketplace. Finally, it provides a foundation for creative exe-cutions of business marketing communications, such as advertisements and sales presentations.

Viewed in this way, the positioning statement can serve as a guiding beacon for the agreed-on market strategy and, especially, as the answer to the question: "What do we want to accomplish?" It puts into sharper focus which firms the supplier regards as relatively important customers, what the supplier wants to emphasize about the market offering, and what promise the supplier is making to customers about the value they will receive. Everyone in the supplier's workforce needs to have a good grasp on these issues. Yet, not everyone in the firm may want the greater direction and focus that positioning statements provide. For example, some may want to avoid positioning statements, or to write only vague ones, because they fear that customers might find out the supplier does not consider them the targets for an offering. They would rather have the customers, and their own sales force, believe that all customers are equally good prospects! This not only dilutes sales force efforts but can also have negative consequences when customers purchase an offering that was not designed to meet their requirements.

Leverage Brand Hierarchy

Once the positioning has been identified, an organization must decide where to place the brand within its hierarchy of existing brands or its brand portfolio. Every organization has a wide range of brands operating at different levels. The potential levels of a brand hierarchy, from highest to lowest, would be: corporate brand, family brand, individual brand, and modifier. IBM ThinkPad X30 offers one example of a brand hierarchy. *IBM* is the corporate brand, *ThinkPad* is the family brand for all notebook computers (as contrasted with desktop computers), *X Series* is the individual brand that refers to extra-light, extra-small, and ultraportable notebooks, and *30* is the modifier that refers to the Ethernet connection models (as contrasted with wireless network connection models, *31*).

The brand hierarchy enables a firm to leverage previous investments in brand building. The investment required to successfully gain awareness and purchase of the IBM ThinkPad G Series is much less because of the previous brand building for the IBM corporate brand and ThinkPad family brand. Brand equity that has been built in one offering category also can be leveraged to launch a brand extension in another offering category. The brand equity 3M Company has established for its Post-it Notes was a resource to enable 3M to enter the market for flipchart pads with its Post-it Self-Stick Easel Pads.

The value of a supplier's brand is reflected in the acquisition prices paid by firms in business markets. Citigroup acquired Grupo Financiero Banamex-

Accival in 2001 for $12.5 billion, the largest ever U.S.-Mexico corporate merger. Less than six months later, an integrated Citibank Mexico and Banamex began operating under the Banamex brand name. The acquiring firm must adroitly manage the newly acquired brands, deciding how best to fit them within the existing brands, brand hierarchy, and brand architecture of the firm. GE, which has extensive experience in this, provides a noteworthy case.

General Electric   In 2000 and 2001, GE acquired 200 companies each year, at a pace of about four acquisitions a week. In order to have a coherent approach to managing this brand portfolio, GE applied its proprietary *acquired-affiliate naming scheme*, which is part of GE's Identity Program.

Because GE's overall brand strategy has historically been technically monolithic—focusing on GE as the only core identity—this process encouraged linking GE with its acquisitions, but it also considered the external variables that influenced the degree to which a particular acquisition should be associated with GE. Therefore, the objective of this five-level naming scheme was twofold: to protect the equity of the GE brand and to leverage the brand equity of the acquired company, where appropriate. The levels were as follows:

- *Naming Level 1* represented the highest level of identification and the strongest association with GE. The acquired company's name would become a combination of *GE* and a succinct generic name describing the business. An example of this level is Thomson CGR, which became GE Medical Systems Europe in 1987.
- *Naming Level 2* associated GE with the main name of the acquisition. This was done when the acquired name had a high degree of brand equity and when a lesser association with GE was desired. For example, because Fanuc had strong brand equity in the industrial automation market, the company was named GE Fanuc. By contrast, at GE Medical Systems, the acquired brands with equity such as OEC (surgical C-arms) and Lunar (bone densitometry) saw their names placed below the GE Medical Systems name in the GE logo format (called a *graphic signature*).
- *Naming Level 3* corresponded to a logo endorsement, where only a strong visual association was desirable. The acquired brand name was used in the GE logo format. When GE Medical Systems acquired Marquette Medical Systems in 1998, the brand had such recognition in the cardiology market that the existing Marquette logo was transitionally incorporated into the GE logo format.

- *Naming Level 4* created only a verbal association with the acquired company. The acquired company's existing name and logo were kept (the GE logo format was not used) and were combined with a reference to GE in a tag line. An example is Transportation International Pool, *a GE Capital Company.*
- *In Naming Level 5,* GE would be invisible, because there was no benefit in associating GE with the acquired brand. An example is media conglomerate NBC, which is a GE company but retained its own separate identity.

GE determines the appropriate naming level for an acquired business by considering three types of issues, each requiring subjective judgment. *Business issues* focus on management control (Does GE control the company?) and commitment (Does GE have a long-term commitment to this company?). *Industry issues* deal with the image value of the industry (Is the industry perceived to be dynamic and innovative?) and performance expectations (How well is GE expected to perform in this industry?). *Identity issues* are tied to the equity of the existing brand (Is it strong?) and the impact on GE (What is the impact when the new brand is associated with the parent company?). GE uses these kinds of questions as sequential steps of a decision tree to determine the best naming strategy.

The scheme described above is designed to integrate and manage *newly* acquired brands. With time, brands evolve and may move up the ladder of association with GE after a transitional period. The Marquette example mentioned earlier illustrates this point. In 2000, approximately two years after the acquisition of Marquette (when the Marquette logo was integrated into the GE logo format), the company was renamed *GE Medical Systems Information Technologies* and given a new logo. *Marquette* no longer appeared as part of the name of the company or in its logo. Instead, it was transitioned to be an umbrella product brand. Eventually, it was phased out completely.

GE's acquired-affiliate naming scheme provided branding guidance that could be applied consistently across a firm as vast and diversified as GE. The structured alternatives enabled GE to protect and build its brand equity, yet leverage the existing equity of acquired brands. Through this process, the company gained the greatest return on its brand resources.

BUSINESS BRANDING OPTIONS

Brands can be created using a wide range of unique aspects of value. We will focus on three—superiority, differentiation, and bundling.

Brand Superiority

The most obvious and appealing concept for a brand in many firms serving business markets is one built on *product superiority*. Brand superiority relies on beating the target competitors on some key, established, recognized element of competition. It can mean having the fastest clock speed of all microprocessor brands or the highest gloss of all pigment brands.

Developing a brand based on product superiority can create a compelling position. Within the organization, it has great appeal. Creating a better mousetrap is almost always recognized as a useful source of competitive advantage. Customers can easily evaluate features, leading to fast adoption, producing strong results in the short term. So, product superiority brands are favorites of organizations.

Customers like them, too. The question is, how long can a supplier pursue this strategy? Over time, the marginal gains associated with increasing any one of these product-based advantages can decline. Moreover, meeting product advances has become relatively easy for many competitors. Like the organization that initially offers them, its competitors like product advantages as well. By building brands on product superiority, one possible outcome is to create something of an arms race on superiority. In other words, it can lead to an escalation of performance, even beyond that which customers require, simply to claim superiority. On the other hand, if competitors are unable or unwilling to respond in the short or medium term, gaining an advantage on product superiority can have widespread appeal and be a powerful brand position. The power of brand superiority can be greatest when one organization breaks out of a pack of commodity suppliers, as illustrated by the branding efforts of Mondi Paper Company.

Mondi Rotatrim   To most white-collar professionals, paper is simply paper. It is a commodity. In South Africa this was the case until Mondi Paper Company took a novel approach to paper production in the 1980s. At that time, paper companies cut paper using the guillotine method. Although efficient, this method can produce a curled edge on the paper as well as rough edges or burrs. These features of the cut paper can lead to more frequent jams in copiers, particularly with high-speed machines. Mondi Paper was the first company to move away from the guillotine cutting method to rotary cutting, which is more precise and consistent (the method puts no pressure on the edge of the paper and cuts through only four or five layers of paper at a time). Based on this innovation, Mondi created the Mondi Rotatrim brand. The company built a strong reputation for high-quality paper based on an accurate and uniform sheet size that translated into customer benefits: increased copying quality; better faxing and printing; and reduced machine downtime, lost time, and paper waste from fewer paper jams.

In the 1990s, all major competitors moved to rotary cutting. By that time, Mondi had built a significant market share, but the company no longer enjoyed a technological advantage over the competition. Building on its previous innovation, in 1997, Mondi once again improved its product. Rotatrim moved from an acid-based to an alkaline-based formulation. As part of this change, Mondi used precipitated calcium carbonate, which is eight times less abrasive than the ground calcium carbonate that competitors continued to use. Mondi Rotatrim became a significantly more environmentally friendly paper, and the brand gained a new technological advantage over the competition. The South African Bureau of Standards tested Mondi's paper as well as its rivals'. Rotatrim met the standards for superior paper for business application, and it was the only brand to attain such a high quality rating.

After that time, Mondi aggressively supported the brand through advertising. Rivals, disadvantaged with lower prices and smaller volumes, were unable or unwilling to match Mondi's spending. These advertising efforts continued to reinforce the central proposition of the brand. At the beginning of the twenty-first century, Mondi Rotatrim enjoyed a stable and comfortable 35 percent market share. Its perceived superior performance enabled Mondi Rotatrim to sustain a pricing premium in certain markets while maintaining its customer share.

Brand Differentiation

Brand differentiation seeks to define the value associated with a brand as fundamentally different from its rivals. The distinction between differentiation and superiority is critical. Both approaches have the same ultimate goal: building a more attractive brand to the customer. But they go about it in fundamentally different ways. *Superiority* focuses on being *better* than competitors on well-established, conventional dimensions of competition. AMD, for instance, might seek to make microprocessors that are faster and less expensive than similar Intel microprocessors. By contrast, *differentiation* seeks to offer value on a dimension that is *inventive* or *unconventional,* but is nonetheless valuable to target customers. Of course, a differentiated brand must be adequate, though not necessarily superior, on the conventional dimensions. Combining adequate value on the customary dimensions with unique value on a novel dimension can produce a decidedly more attractive offering.

Dalloz Safety Products   Differentiation is well illustrated by Dalloz Safety Products, a maker of safety glasses. Safety glasses are designed to protect workers' eyes from foreign substances, and infrared and ultraviolet light. By protecting workers' eyes, safety glasses provide an economic benefit to the firm in terms of fewer lost days and lower insurance premiums. One option for suppliers in this market is to offer safety glasses with ever-increasing levels of protection. Dalloz, however, took a different approach—fashion. For a firm to obtain the benefits of fewer lost days and lower insurance premiums, workers must actually wear the glasses. Some workers, particularly younger ones, felt that safety glasses make them look like a dork, and so they might not always wear the glasses when they should.

Thus, Dalloz began offering a range of safety glasses that look like designer sunglasses. They had contoured wraparound frames and came in a variety of colors and tints. They exceeded minimum requirements on foreign substances and ultraviolet and infrared light, but their main appeal was that workers actually enjoyed wearing them, increasing compliance. Increased compliance delivers more value to customers and thereby made the Dalloz brand more valuable.[3]

Bundling

Brand bundling represents a very attractive option when being better or being different is unsustainable. This is often the case in what are regarded as commodities, such as supplying oxygen. If a company cannot be better or different, what is left? One option is to bundle a group of commodities together to create uniqueness, not through any one commodity, but through a collection of them. The items can't be better or different, *but the particular assortment and supplementary services can*.

Building a brand through the bundling of commodities is a risky venture. The individual components of the bundle may be readily available to many, and the specific bundle created may appeal only to a limited market. So one obvious issue is, should an organization create a bundle that can be imitated yet limits market appeal? Moreover, for any one element of the bundle, another rival may have either a superior alternative or a comparable alternative at a lower price. Bundling many products together furthermore reduces the impact of innovation in any one product. The value is derived from the entire bundle, watering down any impact of innovation.

Despite these real risks, bundling has many advantages. First, it changes the nature of the comparison between competitors. A commodity is a commodity because customers have come to believe, rightly or wrongly, that there is no meaningful difference between brands. As a result, price is the only remaining basis for choice. By bundling commodities together, one creates differences where none existed. Suddenly the basis of comparison must shift from price. It is no longer the only difference. If customers are in fact purchasing bundles but doing so one product at a time, bundling can save time, reduce transaction costs, and increase the role of brand name in choice. By shifting the attention away from any one product and price, it also makes the bundled brand less vulnerable to price competition and innovation.

Texas Instruments   A classic bundling strategy can be illustrated through Texas Instruments (TI) in semiconductors. Principally treated as a commodity, semiconductors have historically been subjected to price and profit cycles as a result of their commodity nature. TI grew tired of profit swings and chose to focus its efforts on one type of microprocessor, the digital signal processor (DSP) bought by makers of cellular phones. These companies, such as Nokia, were locked in a fierce price struggle, so they bought DSPs, core to their technology, on price. TI recognized that for them speed was perhaps more important than price, and the key to speed was providing not simply DSPs but bundles of DSPs, software, development tools, and other related services to makers of cellular phones. Based on that insight, TI transformed itself. According to its former CEO, Thomas Engibous, that transformation led to a fundamentally new TI: "We've focused our energies and resources where we have leading industry positions that we can maintain and widen. This puts TI in a unique position to provide total solutions. It's the difference between making a spark plug or building the engine." Making that transformation has placed limits on TI's strategic options. For example, by focusing on DSPs, TI reduced the number of customers it can serve. But in exchange for those limits, its margin, sales growth, market share, and profits have all grown faster than rivals' as it moved from a commodity microprocessor maker to a dominant player in DSPs. More important, its market capitalization has increased fivefold since it began the transformation.

THE IMPACT OF BRAND BUILDING EFFORTS

As a result of a successful positioning, placing a brand within an existing hierarchy, and implementation, brands become endowed with value. Brands are intellectual assets—the thoughts, feelings, and images that a brand evokes in customers' minds. Brand value, or *brand equity,* is derived from the impact that those thoughts, feelings, and associations have on customers' behavior and, ultimately, their purchases. Brand associations can be divided into three categories as shown in Figure 9.3.

Focal Associations

The most obvious associations, but not always the most powerful, are the focal associations that define a brand. These are the most salient, obvious aspects of a brand. Apple computers are seen as easy to use, Caterpillar tractors are supported with excellent service, and AMD microprocessors are associated with excellent performance at low prices. In the minds of customers these associations are the most accessible, and most easily recalled. In consumer markets, focal associations can range from product functionality to more abstract, emotional associations. Nike running shoes, for instance, are associated with ultimate performance, and Haagen-Dazs ice cream with indulgence. In business markets, focal associations are more typically linked to product functionality and to prices, as in the case of Caterpillar tractor and AMD microprocessors.

Figure 9.3
Hierarchy of Brand Associations

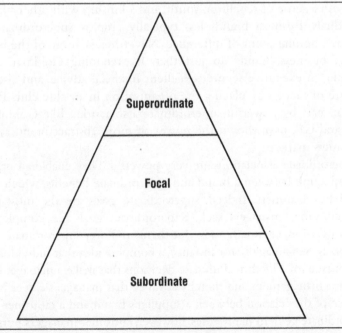

Focal associations are valuable because they enable purchasers to link a brand to an important focal benefit, such as faster diagnostic results for a medical instrument. As a general rule, focal benefits are derived from a functional aspect of the product, such as higher performance. Customers are highly conscious of these benefits, and customers expect to derive these benefits over a moderately long time. In choosing a microprocessor, for instance, computer makers will consider the current performance of the chip and the impact on future development plans of selecting a specific supplier.

Superordinate Associations

Some brands create more abstract, higher-order associations. These superordinate associations are often based on emotion or feeling that derives from some focal association that defines the brand or, through the brand, its purchaser. Apple Computer is associated with innovative thinking ("think different"), Caterpillar tractors are associated with high productivity and low risk as a result of their excellent service, and Texas Instruments is seen as a valuable ally by its customers as a result of its successful bundling strategy. Consumer brands very often rely on superordinate associations as their point of difference. Evian bottled water is French and all that is linked to the concept of being French. Harley-Davidson is associated with a sense of rebellion, youth, and a kinship with other like-minded individuals. Business brands less typically employ superordinate associations as a unique point of difference. Nevertheless, some of the best examples of business brands do just that. By retaining Goldman Sachs, for example, an executive secures excellent financial advice, and also signals a measure of success by placing the organization in an elite club. Brands defined in part by powerful superordinate associations, like Goldman Sachs, IBM, and GE, have shown the power of more abstract brand associations in business markets.

Superordinate associations are very powerful. They enable an organization to build a link between a brand and superordinate benefits, which are highly valued by customers. Indeed, superordinate goals are the most important goals customer managers seek. Superordinate goals are complex and are sought over longer time frames. But there are fewer superordinate goals than focal goals. Self-image is, for instance, a complex idea that individuals continually pursue for a lifetime. Purchase decisions that make a manager look good to senior management and thereby advance that manager's career is a specific instance of the relation between a supplier's brand and a customer manager's superordinate goal. In many cases, however, customer managers pursue superordinate goals subconsciously. These associations are enduring, are competitively distinct (creating greater differentiation), and are difficult to imitate by rivals. Much potential remains for many other business brands, however. Many organizations dismiss creating such associations before understanding the real power they offer in business markets.

Subordinate Associations

Many brands are defined by a vast range of less important associations. Caterpillar tractors are yellow, IBM uses a distinctive typeface to distinguish its products, and Apple Computer uses a unique sound to indicate the startup of its operating system. These associations are uniquely linked to a brand, but customers are often less aware of them without prompting. They are linked with less important benefits in the minds of customers, they are easier to imitate, and as a result they are less enduring over time.

Impact of Brand Associations

Brand associations have a profound impact on competition, sales, and ultimately profit. Customer knowledge defines the nature of the competitive game. It defines how customers compare alternatives, on what dimensions they place importance, and through what process they make a choice. Research on the impact of brands demonstrates that branding affects the perceptions of product quality, the confidence with which people purchase, their sensitivity to price, and the acceptance of new products by members of the distribution channel.[4]

Product Performance and Confidence   Customers in business markets often make a diligent effort to assess the functionality and performance of what they purchase. Aircraft engines are exhaustively tested for performance, fuel consumption, reliability; even lightbulbs are analyzed. Any analysis, however thorough, is incomplete. No customer, however determined, can assess full knowledge about the performance of a product and its supplier. Limits on time, resources, or knowledge make eliminating all ambiguity, uncertainty, or risk impossible. Performance is subjective, in some measure, in every market. Value is, therefore, to some extent subjective. Brands help reduce that subjectivity and convey to customers information that they cannot easily observe through testing or analysis. What, for example, will be the supplier's responsiveness to any unforeseen or unanticipated problems that occur in the customer's usage of the supplier's offering? Greater brand familiarity also creates more confidence in the minds of customers, increases purchase intentions, and can even overcome negative experiences.

Price Sensitivity It follows directly that if customer perceptions of performance, their confidence, and their purchase intention are related to brand recognition, then brand recognition influences price sensitivity. And, as one would expect, research finds this effect.[5] Brand leaders tend as a result to ask for and obtain higher prices. But the effect of brands on price sensitivity reaches further. It influences the response of customers to price changes both by the firm and its rivals. Brand leaders tend to be better able to increase prices without losing business, compared to rivals with weaker brands.[6] Leading brands also are more immune to price cuts by rivals. In contrast, one might predict that leading brands have the most to lose and, therefore, would lose most when a weaker rival cuts price. Yet, research shows that price cuts by rivals tend to draw the most share not from the powerful brands but from the weakest.[7]

CONCLUSION

Everything is branded—from oxygen to airplanes—and all customers use brands to make purchase decisions. Brands are increasingly critical in business markets for creating competitive advantage. Creating powerful brands in business markets requires understanding customers deeply, focusing resources, developing compelling value propositions, creating brands that leverage established hierarchies, and delivering on the promise of the brand. Doing so effectively can help exploit one of the most valuable assets many organizations own, yet one that is neglected far too often.

James C. Anderson is the William L. Ford Distinguished Professor of Marketing and Wholesale Distribution and professor of Behavioral Science in Management at the Kellogg School of Management. He is the program director of the Business Marketing Strategy executive program. Before joining the Kellogg School faculty, he was a member of the marketing faculty of University of Texas at Austin. Earlier in his career he worked at E.I. duPont de Nemours and Company, Inc. He earned a BA from Western Illinois University and a Ph.D. from Michigan State University.

Gregory S. Carpenter is James Farley/Booz Allen Hamilton Professor of Marketing Strategy and director of the Center for Market Leadership at the Kellogg School of Management. He served on the faculties of the University of California, Los Angeles,

Columbia University, and the Yale School of Management before joining the Kellogg School faculty in 1990. Carpenter received a BA from Ohio Wesleyan University and an MBA, MPhil, and Ph.D. from Columbia University.

NOTES

1. Rust, Roland T., Tim Ambler, Gregory S. Carpenter, V. Kumar, and R. Srivastava (2004), "Measuring Marketing Productivity: Current Knowledge and Future Directions," *Journal of Marketing*, 68 (October), 76–89.

2. Anderson, James C. and James A. Narus (2004), *Business Market Management: Understanding, Creating, and Delivering Value*, 2nd edition, Upper Saddle River NJ: Pearson Prentice Hall.

3. Anderson, James C. and Gregory S. Carpenter (1998), "How to Escape the Commodity Trap in Business Markets," *Financial Times, Mastering Marketing* supplement (November 2), 5–6.

4. Keller, Kevin Lane (2002), *Branding and Brand Equity*, Cambridge: Marketing Science Institute.

5. Simon, Hermann (1979), "The Dynamics of Price Elasticity and Brand Life Cycles," *Journal of Marketing Research*, 16, 439–452.

6. Sivakumar, K. and S. P. Raj (1997), "Quality Tier Competition: How Price Changes Influence Brand Choice and Category Choice," *Journal of Marketing*, 61, 71–84.

7. Carpenter, Gregory S., Lee G. Cooper, Dominique M. Hanssens, and David Midgley (1988), "Modeling Asymmetric Competition," *Marketing Science*, 7, 393–412.

CHAPTER 10

SERVICES BRANDING

AMY L. OSTROM, DAWN IACOBUCCI,

and FELICIA N. MORGAN

Brand managers of services often find that they have much in common with brand managers of consumer or durable goods. For both, brands serve as information and are very important in customer expectations, which contribute to customer satisfaction. Yet challenging issues arise in the brand management of hotels, airlines, retail outlets, advertising agencies, consulting firms, and other service firms.

This chapter focuses on the unique issues that arise in branding services. First we provide a brief overview of brands in general (namely, the purposes of brands and their roles in customer expectations and evaluations). We then delve into the *key differences* between goods and services, including the intangibility and heterogeneity of service delivery systems. We describe the strategic and tactical implications of these differences on branding, including the premise that, for services, frontline employees are typically a firm's strongest brand signal. Finally, we provide a variety of prescriptions for the services brand manager.

BRANDS AS INFORMATION

Consider the purposes of brands. Brands serve as names or identity. In ancient times, generations of descendants of the Biblical Levite family were known to be holy priests. In less ancient times, a family might name their son John with the hopes that the name imbued the young boy with qualities associated with a saint. When that young man grew up, his son was known as John's son, or soon, Johnson. Other families in the village were known as the Tailors, the Carpenters, the Candle/Leather/Wood-Smiths, and so on (the current concept of marketing oneself is not so modern). Still others were known from their points of origin: "No, not that Leonardo, the one from Vinci." Identities acclaim knowledge: "That's the family who made my shoes; those are the people who are good at building barns; that's the family that came from the North," and so forth. These reputations and familial brand associations were many families' primary assets, and normative behaviors instilled the distinction between bringing honor or shame to a family, concerns that still exist in some cultures today.

Brand extensions are similar to human progeny, and an ill-performing extension is pulled from the market as quickly as possible so as not to destroy the family/brand name. Test marketing brand extensions looks for the answer to the question, "Is the new product to be launched worthy of the brand name?"

Brands also depict ownership, whether it is the iron-brand on cattle or the Hoosier's T-shirt brand on chattel: "That's my cow, that's my mailbox, that's my kid's camp clothing." Brands from the simple to the upscale serve these purposes. For example: "I, Armani, designed that suit"; "I, Michael Jordan, approved those basketball shoes"; "I, Paul Newman, (oversaw those who) stirred that vat of spaghetti sauce"; "I, J.Lo, am being paid to lend my name to that perfume."

The Role of Brand Information

As brand names come to carry information, that information contributes to a customer's expectations about the product (goods or services) being purchased. A company's communications to the marketplace help create both brand name associations and customer expectations. The company's communications can come in the well-known form of advertising, or in the cues suggested by prices, or in whether guarantees are offered for services rendered.

Customers' expectations are also informed and updated throughout their experience with the brand. Some experience is direct. For example, customers' ideas about what to expect on a Southwest Airlines flight might be informed partly via their previous flights on Southwest. Other experience is indirect, which in this case might include flights with other airlines or comments heard via word-of-mouth from other customers. These indirect experiences might also include the Southwest flight experiences of friends, family members, and co-workers.

Customers compare their purchase, such as their Southwest flight service encounter, to their expectations. If the experience exceeds those expectations, customers are thought to be *delighted*. If the experience merely meets those expectations, customers are thought to be *satisfied*, and if the experience falls short of the expectations, they are *disgruntled*. Thus, customer expectations are extraordinarily important in marketing. Managing those expectations, just like managing brands, is more difficult in services than for goods.

KEY DIFFERENCES BETWEEN GOODS AND SERVICES

There are a number of differences between goods and services. We will focus on those that have the most impact on branding. These differences include the intangibility of services, their complexity, their heterogeneity, and their process nature.

Intangibility

In the undergraduate, MBA, and executive Services Marketing courses we teach, students reliably offer intangibility as a key distinction between the purchase of goods such as blue jeans, shampoo, laptops, and cars versus their service sector counterparts such as dry cleaning, beauty salons, consulting, and car repair. When a customer buys a pair of shoes, the customer receives something to show for the purchase. By comparison, when a customer gets a car tuned up, the most tangible elements of the service are the customer's interactions with the frontline employees, the waiting room, and the bill. The customer hopes the service will make the car run more smoothly. If the car had been making noises prior to service or had been unresponsive in some manner, there may be tangible evidence of the quality of service as the car is driven off the service lot (e.g., if the ping is gone or the braking more responsive). But a good deal of automotive service is preventive, such as an oil change, and in such instances the customer is left with merely an intangible hope that the service improved the car.

Goods and services are typically conceptualized as lying along a continuum from tangible to intangible. But indeed, there is much overlap on the continuum—that is, most purchases have some tangible elements (e.g., clean clothes returned from the dry cleaner) and some intangible elements (e.g., financing an automobile purchase). Nevertheless, the intangible elements dominate in services.

Tangibility is not inherently superior to intangibility, but intangibility makes it difficult for customers to evaluate the service experience. If a customer purchases a certain brand of shampoo, the customer makes a purchase point evaluation of price and likely value, tries the product at home, and reaches a conclusion as to whether the hair treatment is good enough for subsequent repurchase. Contrast this purchasing of physical goods to the hiring of a service such as an attorney: First, a search for an attorney begins (probably by reaching out to friends and co-workers for advice). Then a selection is made among attorneys on ill-defined choice criteria. The attorney is contacted and met, a contract is purchased, and advice is given and paid for. But after the entire process, the client typically has insufficient expertise to evaluate the purchase. Hence, the customer looks to other environmental cues, such as the professionalism of the attorney and the attorney's staff, the appearance of the offices, and so forth. These cues may or may not correlate with the soundness of the advice just purchased.

Some marketers have implicitly acknowledged the difficulty that intangibility brings to the customer's evaluation of a service and have sought to enhance the tangible evidence and symbols of quality. For example, few purchases are more intangible than insurance, and insurance companies have brilliantly tried to communicate tangible symbols of their intangible services (e.g., State Farm's good neighbor, Prudential's rock, Allstate's good hands, the Traveler's umbrella, Merrill Lynch's bull, MetLife's Snoopy (signaling friendliness perhaps?), Aflac's duck (hmm)).

Of course, just as we've described goods and services as lying along a tangibility continuum, marketers of familiar goods have had to reach to intangible qualities for brand distinctions among commodity-like purchases. These tactics include different spokespeople for soft drinks and imagery advertisements for perfumes and cars. These marketers can afford to reach toward such abstract qualities because their core offering is inherently tangible. By contrast, services marketers begin on the intangible end of the continuum and enhance their communications to customers by integrating more tangible qualities.

Complexity

Admittedly, the shampoo and attorney examples vary in other ways in addition to their tangibility. For example, hiring an attorney is likely more complex than the purchase of a shampoo. Typical customers purchasing an attorney's services are not trained in law, so the evaluation of the core purchase is beyond their abilities. Hence, they look to the cues that are within their realm of expertise (e.g., the friendliness of the receptionist, the ease of making an appointment, the price charged, etc.). By comparison, customers can judge whether their hair feels cleaner or bouncier after shampooing. Still, some goods are quite complex. For instance, most of us do not understand the inner workings of our laptops or automobiles. And, by contrast, some services can also be straightforward, where the biggest decision looming is whether "you want fries with that?" The psychological and economic explanation for this complexity is that goods are composed more of *search* qualities (those that may be evaluated even prior to purchase, e.g., price, color) and *experience* qualities (those that may be evaluated after some trial or consumption, e.g., dinner at a restaurant). Services tend to be comprised more of experience and *credence* qualities (those that are difficult to judge even post-consumption, e.g., whether a cavity has been filled properly at the dentist's).

The more complex the service, the more difficult it is for customers to judge quality and satisfaction, and therefore they need assistance. When a brand signals quality, the customer relaxes about judging every component of the service and begins to trust that the brand name brings credibility and an assurance of the service providers' competence and overall standards of excellence.

Heterogeneity

Another important means by which goods and services differ that will impact branding is the heterogeneity of service processes. Service processes inherently vary across consumers as well as within one consumer's experiences with the service over time. Consider a service that is purchased frequently enough to make comparisons, such as a visit to a barber or beauty salon. A customer might make an appointment every six weeks with the same hair stylist and even ask for the same haircut, yet the customer is highly likely to have an experience that differs at least slightly with every visit. The haircut might be subtly different, the stylist might be more or less friendly or efficient, and the demeanor of other customers in the salon may vary as well. By comparison, many consumer packaged goods are so constant in their formulation, appearance, and performance that companies can strive for quality standards as precise as the Six Sigma of Motorola. That precision surely dominates a typical call-center's goal of "We pick up the phone within three rings."

We maintain that heterogeneity is the biggest source of difficulty in branding services.[1] If a purchase is not consistent in its customer experience, the information the brand conveys is fuzzy. As a result, a brand can mean one thing to one customer and something else to another customer. Indeed, in such scenarios, brands are not serving their fundamental purpose of conveying information precisely. Given the integral role of brands and expectations in judgments of satisfaction, the heterogeneity of branded services can ultimately create customer dissatisfaction, which in turn affects downstream results such as loyalty and profitability.

Services Are Processes

The final distinction between goods and services is that services may be characterized as processes that unfold in real time. Unlike manufactured goods, for which oversupply can be handled via inventory and storage, services are perishable—and yield management is both a science and an art. For example, consider the tremendously complex differential pricing of airline seats. Airlines use this pricing in an attempt to ensure that as many seats as possible are filled before takeoff, given that the unused seats are thereafter irretrievable. Similarly, the empty table at a restaurant on a Thursday afternoon cannot be regained for Friday's rush; hence demand is managed with reservations and queuing for Friday, and perhaps price discounts or another value-added novelty for Thursday. Professional service providers such as consultants have the same 24 hours in a day every week; time desired during peak demand seasons cannot be borrowed against slower periods.

Services are perishable, and they are processes that unfold in real time. For many services, the service provider is simultaneously producing the service while the customer is consuming or experiencing the service encounter. The hair stylist cannot begin cutting a customer's hair until the customer appears. The tax consultant cannot begin to craft a tax return until W-2 forms have been received and its (possibly procrastinating) customers have brought their records into the tax office. Some service providers position themselves to take advantage of the real-time production, whereas others seek to manage the service delivery system more like inventorying goods. For example, fine restaurants prepare meals upon order placement so that the real-time production ensures freshness and high quality. By contrast, fast-food restaurants stash burgers under heat lamps with less concern for freshness and more focus on speed and convenience—qualities fast-food customers seek.

Note also that the simultaneity of production and consumption has implications beyond service duration and demand management—the customer is frequently inherently involved in the consumption episode.[2] The client at the hair stylist gives directions regarding preferences, sometimes resulting in a substandard outcome in cut or color according to the service provider. The restaurant patron may ask for an exquisitely prepared dish to be smothered in catsup. Thus, the quality of the haircut and the meal are not entirely under the sole control of the provider (though the customer may be satisfied nevertheless). The service provider can make suggestions and offer advice but ultimately cannot always save customers from themselves.

The process element of services also contributes to the complexity of the service encounter experience. Customer evaluation becomes the sum of many factors—some under a firm's management and some not. A service provider might think that the firm's competitive advantage will be noticed and appreciated by the customer, but the customer's experience is more complicated than that. For example, a travel agency might believe it offers the best advice and prices. Its management and frontline employees might believe that if a customer walks in and is given excellent advice and prices, the customer will leave happy. But the customer's experience began when he or she flipped through the *Yellow Pages* to find a travel agency. It continued as the customer drove around the block to locate the office and a parking spot; waited in line at the office; interacted with the agent who might have had to field phone calls and co-worker inquiries; and finally left the office in the rain, only to find a ticket waiting on the car. The vacation trip the customer just booked at the travel agency might indeed be excellent, the travel agent's advice sound, and the agency's prices reasonable. But a problem might occur with billing, or the airline might lose the customer's luggage. Is it fair that customers judge the travel agency on all these *moments of truth*? Perhaps not, but they do.[3]

In sum, services are different from goods. Services are typically comprised of more intangible elements. They tend to be both more complex and more heterogeneous. Services are also processes that unfold in real time. All of these differences have implications for branding services.

THE ESSENCE OF BRANDING A SERVICE

If marketing managers have a tough time branding toothpaste and laundry detergent, imagine the complications they face in branding a service. Remember that the primary purposes of a brand name are to convey information and to help formulate and maintain a customer expectation. Couple those goals with a purchase that is intangible, complex, heterogeneous, and process-like (all of which contribute to making quality control difficult), and the result is the challenge of services brands.

The Company as Brand

Many service organizations must confront the fact that the name of the company serves as the focal brand for all of its offerings. Granted, the company name can serve as the primary brand for some manufacturers as well (e.g., Ford). It is also true that some service organizations have multiple brands that reach different segments (e.g., Gap Inc.'s brand portfolio of Old Navy, Gap, and Banana Republic), thus further complicating matters. However, for many services, the *company as brand* concept is vital. For example, in professional services, it is difficult for consumers to differentiate between companies' service offerings.[4] The company name is central to its brand identity. When the company name is the umbrella brand for all of its services, anything that impacts perceptions of the company—good or bad—will influence customers' perceptions of the service offerings.

The Frontline Employee *Is* the Brand

It is well-known that a customer's personal experiences with a company far outweigh the company's own communications to the customer (e.g., advertising). By far, *experiences* dominate the formation of customer evaluations (e.g., perceptions of quality, satisfaction, value, loyalty) and expectations for subsequent service encounters.[5] The result is the fundamental principle of branding in services: *The frontline employee is the brand* for the customer. It is the employees who deliver the service, which conveys the brand to customers. Whether it is the attentive and accommodating staff at a Ritz Carlton, the efficient UPS drivers, or the competent, empathetic, and patient-focused employees at Mayo Clinic, it is the individuals on the frontline who bring the brand to life for customers during each service encounter.

While all employees contribute to the success of a company, the individuals who interact with customers are key to establishing and maintaining customers' perceptions of the brand. Consider the implications of that simple finding: that in many service settings, a million-dollar advertising campaign can be completely undermined by the inability or indifferent attitude of a minimum-wage frontline service helper.

For example, in air travel, customers are not focused on United's friendly skies, American's leg room, or Southwest's free-for-all boarding. Instead, a customer's flight experience is based on a series of interactions, predominately with personnel. The service process effectively begins with a customer interacting with a web site or a customer service agent for booking. It continues on the day of travel as the customer interacts with automated or assisted check-in, ground personnel, and gate personnel. Once boarded, the customer then encounters flight attendants serving soft drinks and pretzels, pilots mumbling over intercoms, and staff saying goodbye as customers depart. The flight can be convenient and timely, but a customer may leave dissatisfied if a flight attendant was rude. Never mind that the flight attendant might have been having a bad day, or that that bad day may have been initiated by a previous customer who was even more rude. Customers expect the frontline service people to function perfectly in their roles, without regard or recognition of the human performing that role.

As the flight service unfolds, the process nature of the service assures that customers interact with multiple frontline employees. In fact, they interact with several of them multiple times. Thus, the service personnel have multiple opportunities with each customer to perform well or poorly. Zero defects would require each of those interactions (across employees or within an employee over time) to be smooth, effective, and pleasant. That's a tall order. Heterogeneity naturally enters into the service delivery system, given the varieties of competence and extraversion of the frontline staff.

Internal Marketing

Given that frontline employees comprise the majority of a customer's impressions, a corollary fundamental principle in branding services is this: Marketing the brand to employees, or *internal branding,* is critical.[6] Research suggests that the behavior of employees is the most influential aspect of a service in determining customer brand preferences.[7] Hence, employees need to understand their importance, and they accordingly must be treated with respect. Those in management who believe that minimum wage employees are not worthy of such effort and expenditure fail to understand the critical role frontline employees play in service branding. In fact, the critical role of these boundary-spanning employees suggests that attracting and keeping quality frontline employees is an important step for successful service branding.

When frontline employees understand their partnership role in satisfying customers, world-class excellence in service quality can result. Customer satisfaction follows, along with retention and profitability.[8] When the brand is effectively communicated to all company employees, the end goal of high-quality service for the customer becomes paramount. Communication between functional roles and departments is streamlined to meet this goal, as opposed to employees worrying about bureaucratic lines drawn around arbitrary roles of responsibility. A proactive, customer-oriented mentality becomes ingrained in frontline employees, which is the result of consistent internal marketing from management leadership. This allows for a higher likelihood of quality service, as employee empowerment enables quicker recovery in the (inevitable) occurrence of subpar service. The employee knows the goal is to please the customer, and he or she works through the service delivery process with the customer, facilitating the customer's progress through the process.

This philosophy is evident at Zane's Cycles, which, with only one location (Branford, Connecticut), was one of the top 10 largest bicycle dealers in the United States in 2005. The firm's success has been due in large part to its position as an internationally recognized leader in customer service. Owner Chris Zane realized early on how to ensure high-quality frontline service for his customers: He paid his employees well and thanked them for providing great customer service. And he made working at Zane's Cycles a fun experience.[9] He and his management team have worked to ensure that employees keep having fun by providing them trips to an amusement park or a week of driving a cool, company-owned car (e.g., a new VW Beetle right after the car was introduced).

Self-Service

In many service sectors, customers receive service wholly or in part through technology. These encounters with self-service technologies (SSTs) can impact customers' evaluations of a service and their perceptions of the brand. Brand information transmission occurs through tangible aspects such as the look of a kiosk or web site and also through customers' experiences when using them.

The increased prevalence of technology in service delivery systems (which surely will continue to rise) can decrease heterogeneity. An automatic check-in machine at the airport does not exhibit mood or exhaustion (until the paper or toner runs out), so every customer's experience with the machine is theoretically standard and consistent with the next person's. However, just as with the diffusion of other automation (e.g., bank ATMs), there can be mixed reactions among customer segments. The complexity of the airline check-in service might be simplified for a segment that might also appreciate other by-products including a decreased wait time. However, technophobic users might perceive the system to have become more complicated, less friendly, and therefore less satisfying.

In contrast to robotics replacing factory jobs, service machines can make the remaining human employees *more,* not less, valuable. For example, the frontline may now require even greater expertise to be capable of assisting customers when the technology malfunctions or does not suit the customer's needs. A machine that creates dissatisfaction must be alleviated by the human service recovery system. Clearly, the successful coordination between technology, recovery actions, and people within the service process becomes an important part of managing customers' perceptions of the brand.

Service Networks

A relatively new area for services marketing research is found in the interconnectedness of service providers in service networks.[10] When customers rent cars, they often do so through partner airline-affiliated web sites. When they pick up those cars, they often sign for insurance provided by partner financial firms. When customers relocate, they may begin by seeking a realtor, but they also find a mortgage company, a moving company, a home insurance provider, and a carpet cleaner in the mix. When the realtor recommends a carpet cleaner, even if the cleaner is differentially branded (e.g., Prudential vs. ServiceMaster), the quality of the cleaner becomes in part reflected on the perceived quality of the realtor.

Thus, heterogeneous service scenarios that were already complicated on their own are now exacerbated. Substantial risks and rewards may result from partnering with other firms. The issue of brand compatibility arises when deciding what firm(s) to partner with and how strongly to associate with them. If customers' experiences with a partner firm can spill over and affect their perceptions of other service firms in the network, then brand management also implies partner management.

WHAT'S A SERVICES BRAND MANAGER TO DO?

The differences between goods and services clearly have implications for managing services brands. Branding services is more difficult, but not impossible. Here we offer prescriptions for the services brand manager.

In this day and age, it is not an answer to suggest that a services marketing manager not brand the service. Even implied brands are brands. The mom-and-pop grocer on the corner reflects that mom and pop. A high-end, highly customized architectural firm that operates on low-volume, nonscaleable jobs (e.g., selectively choosing projects with little likelihood of direct repeat purchasing) nevertheless wishes to retain a reputation of high quality. Reputation as brand is in part shared in the marketplace via word-of-mouth. The reputation of the grocer or the architectural firm brings us full circle to the notion of brand as identity, with name and reputation being a most precious resource. Thus, regardless of the content of the service a firm provides, every service firm is branding, whether that fact is explicitly acknowledged or not, and whether the branding oversight is managed well or not.

Given that most firms wish to successfully manage their brands (and don't want to leave branding to chance) there are several steps that can be taken. First, in situations in which the company is the brand, it is important to be particularly sensitive to any company actions that can affect a customer's brand expectations and perceptions. This may include everything from sponsored events to the ethical behavior of the firm and its employees. Because brand meaning is created for the customer with every brand experience, it is critical that the company message be consistent across the presented brand. The company must control communication of its identity as well as the customer's actual experience in consuming the brand. For example, through its advertising, telecom company Qwest's customers have been exposed to its tagline, "Spirit of Service." It is important that customers' experiences with the company and its representatives live up to that promise.

Second, service marketing managers need to manage customers' experience with their services across touch points. This means managing the service process. A useful tool for diagnosing the strengths and weaknesses of a service delivery system is service blueprinting, a literal mapping of the process. Process mapping includes the elements that the customer sees (the so-called *front stage*) as well as the operational support (the *back stage*).[11] A blueprint is often useful for diagnosing bottlenecks in the system—for example, places where service slows down or more mistakes are made. Blueprinting also makes all the steps in the service delivery process clear from the customer's point of view. Ideally service blueprints include all of the moments of truth that take place between the customer and the firm (as well as the physical evidence), customer contact points that can impact customers' perceptions of the service.

By thoroughly understanding the service process customers go through, a firm can understand and help manage the types of brand associations that are created throughout the experience. Companies deliver on their promises and distinguish themselves in the marketplace through these aspects of the service process (e.g., moments of truth, physical evidence). Therefore, beyond making sure that advertising and other external promotions are consistent with the brand positioning, service marketing managers should consider the following: "Are we doing all we can to convey our brand positioning during customers' moments of truth throughout the service experience?" "Are the tangibles we have in place consistent with the positioning of our brand?"

Doing all of these things well is consistent with what has been referred to as *orchestrating the clues* for customers. These include the functional clues (those that show the service is reliable and delivered well); the mechanic clues (the sights, sounds, and smells, etc. that make up the tangible aspects of the service experience); and finally the humanics clues that involve people (such as the demeanor of employees).[12] While the importance of mechanic and humanics clues tends to be more commonly overlooked by some companies,[13] others not only understand their significance but demonstrate great skill at providing such evidence to customers. For example, Mayo Clinic's "patients-first" philosophy has always been clearly conveyed through its facilities, which were carefully designed to reduce emotional stress and make patients and their families feel well cared for. The clinic's philosophy was also carried out through its employees, who were hired, trained, and rewarded so that their behavior was consistent with the Mayo founders' credo, "The best interest of the patient is the only interest to be considered."[14] As this example makes clear, managing the evidence or clues of a service is what helps create the desired brand meaning in the mind of consumers.[15]

The third prescription for services branding success is that there needs to be a constant focus on frontline employees. While blueprinting can help a firm strategize about how to create its brand in the mind of consumers, it is the frontline employees who will ultimately convey the brand. For frontline brand management to be successful, frontline employees must not only understand the brand vision but accept it and feel passionately about it.[16] Therefore, internal branding is critical. The meaning of the brand must be marketed to employees just as it is to external customers. The right service culture, tools, and reward system must be in place so that employees can live the brand day in and day out, thereby communicating it to customers.

Fourth, self-service technologies (SSTs) should also be evaluated to determine the extent to which they favorably impact evaluations of the service and perceptions of the brand. Doing so may involve studying the design of the SST, its look and functionality, and the service recovery processes that are in place in case customers have problems using the technology. When an SST is used as one aspect of a service experience (e.g., self-service check-in at a hotel), the extent to which the SST is smoothly integrated into the service process should also be examined to make sure that the encounter is evaluated positively by customers and that it fits with the brand.

And finally, in situations in which a service firm is part of a service network, it is important to carefully select partners whose brands are compatible. When other service firms are specifically recommended, there is even a greater likelihood that their performance may reflect on the recommending firm. Hence, relationships with partners in the network should be managed so that any spillover effects positively reflect on the brand.

There is no question that marketing services is much different from marketing physical goods. Thus, service firms that are committed to building and maintaining a successful brand over time have a difficult task ahead of them. It requires thinking about how customers perceive company actions and closely examining how customers interact with firm employees and partners, physical evidence, technology, and a host of other aspects of the service. It also requires significant effort to ensure that a consistent impression of the brand is formed each and every time the customer comes in contact with the firm. Companies must work diligently to ensure that they are creating deliberate associations in the minds of customers, maintaining the brand's integrity at each point of service contact.

Amy L. Ostrom is associate professor of marketing and an Honors Program Ford Faculty Fellow at the W. P. Carey School of Business at Arizona State University. She received her Ph.D. from the Kellogg School of Management.

Dawn Iacobucci is professor of marketing at the Wharton School of the University of Pennsylvania. She was professor of marketing at the Kellogg School of Management from 1987 to 2004, and she was the Coca-Cola Distinguished Professor of Marketing and head of the Marketing Department at the University of Arizona from 2001 to 2002. She edited Networks in Marketing, Handbook of Services Marketing and Management, Kellogg on Marketing, *and* Kellogg on Integrated Marketing, *and she is co-author on Gilbert Churchill's lead text on* Marketing Research. *She received her MS, MA, and Ph.D. from the University of Illinois at Urbana-Champaign.*

Felicia N. Morgan is an assistant professor of marketing at Ohio University. Prior to earning her Ph.D. at Arizona State University in 2004, she spent over 12 years in marketing, finance, and management within the services sector. She also enjoyed an early career as a professional musician. She received a BA and MBA from the University of New Orleans.

NOTES

1. de Chernatony, Leslie and Francesca Dall'Olmo Riley (1999), "Experts' Views about Defining Services Brands and the Principles of Services Branding," *Journal of Business Research*, 46, 181–192.

2. Moorthi, Y. L. R. (2002), "An Approach to Branding Services," *Journal of Services Marketing*, 16(2/3), 259–274.

3. Tax, Steve and Amy Smith (2003), "What's Fair Is Fair, or Is It? Assessing Failures in the Service Network," presented at the *12th Annual Frontiers in Services Conference*, Washington, D.C.

4. See note 1.

5. Berry, Leonard L. (2000), "Cultivating Service Brand Equity," *Journal of the Academy of Marketing Science,* 28(1), 128–137; Padgett, Dan and Douglas Allen (1997), "Communicating Experiences: A Narrative Approach to Creating Service Brand Image," *Journal of Advertising,* 26(4), 49–62.

6. Berry, Leonard L. and Neeli Bendapudi (2003), "Clueing in Customers," *Harvard Business Review,* 81 (February), 100–106.

7. Berry, Leonard L. and Sandra S. Lampo (2004), "Branding Labour-Intensive Services," *Business Strategy Review,* 15(1), 18–25.

8. Mackay, Marisa Maio (2001), "An Application of Brand Equity Measures in Service Markets," *Journal of Services Marketing,* 15(3), 210–221.

9. Zane, Christopher J. (2000), "Creating Lifetime Customers," *Retailing Issues Letter, Center for Retailing Studies,* Texas A&M University, 12(5), 1–5.

10. Tax, Stephen and Felicia Morgan (2004), "Toward a Theory of Service Delivery Networks," working paper, Arizona State University.

11. Zeithaml, Valarie and Mary Jo Bitner (2003), *Services Marketing: Integrating Customer Focus Across the Firm,* 3rd edition, NY: McGraw-Hill.

12. Berry, Leonard L. and Sandra S. Lampo (2004), "Branding Labour-Intensive Services," *Business Strategy Review,* 15(1), 18–25; Carbone, Lewis P. (2004), *Clued In: How to Keep Customers Coming Back Again and Again,* Upper Saddle River, NJ: Financial Times Prentice Hall.

13. Carbone, Lewis P. (2004), *Clued In: How to Keep Customers Coming Back Again and Again,* Upper Saddle River, NJ: Financial Times Prentice Hall.

14. See note 6, page 102.

15. See note 6.

16. Mitchell, Colin (2002), "Selling the Brand Inside," *Harvard Business Review,* 80(1), 99–105.

CHAPTER 11

BRANDING IN TECHNOLOGY MARKETS

MOHANBIR SAWHNEY

The importance of building strong brands is well understood in traditional consumer packaged goods markets. In fact, firms like Procter & Gamble have often described themselves as "being in the business of creating and building brands."[1] However, technology firms find it more difficult to accept the importance of brand building. According to Derrith Lambka, ex-corporate advertising manager at Hewlett-Packard, "It is very hard for technology companies to embrace branding because technology and branding are complete opposites. To me, branding is consistency, consistency, consistency, and technology is change, change, change."[2] Technology firms believe that success in technology markets is driven by technological innovation, product feature enhancements, and improving price performance.[3] As a result, they tend to focus their marketing efforts on developing and marketing innovative products. The marketing organization emphasizes product management as opposed to brand management.

Yet, the concept of using brands to develop and sustain competitive advantage has never been more important for technology firms. Competing based on *feeds and speeds*—a relentless improvement of price performance—quickly becomes a competitive rat race with no winners. As technology markets mature, product differentiation becomes difficult to sustain because competitors can often imitate new features quite rapidly. And adding new features to products produces diminishing marginal returns beyond the point where technology products become good enough for most customers.[4] Technology firms must look elsewhere for ways to set themselves apart from competitors and to inspire loyalty among their customers.

Building strong brands offers an attractive avenue for technology firms to insulate themselves from competition and commoditization pressures. Powerful technology brands like IBM, Microsoft, Hewlett-Packard, Kodak, Sony, and Nokia have traditionally offered customers the assurance of quality, performance, reliability, and style that have allowed them to command a premium price. These corporate brands are valuable intangible assets. In fact, in 2004, four of the world's 10 most valuable brands were technology brands: Microsoft (number 2 at $61.4 billion), IBM (number 3 at $53.8 billion), Intel (number 5 at $33.49 billion), and Nokia (number 8 at $24.04 billion).[5]

Consider the success of Apple Computer's iPod personal digital music player. Despite being a late entrant in the personal digital player market, the Apple iPod's superior user experience and brilliant marketing propelled Apple to a leadership position in the digital music business. In the fourth quarter of 2004, revenues from the iPod accounted for 35 percent of Apple's total revenues, and almost 4.6 million iPods were sold. Additionally, the iPod was largely responsible for a sharp increase of 24 percent in Apple's overall brand value to $6.85 billion in 2004, up from $5.55 billion in 2003.[6]

Brands can be a valuable anchor of stability amid the change, uncertainty, and confusion that is so pervasive in technology markets. As new technologies emerge, markets collide and products become more complex. Customers find it difficult to sort through the flood of information and conflicting claims when making buying decisions for technology products. Instead, they rely on brands they know and trust to cut through the clutter and complexity. Therefore, building strong brands is as important for technology firms as it is for consumer packaged goods (CPG) firms.

However, there are important contextual differences between technology markets and CPG markets. These contextual differences in turn pose a unique set of challenges when creating and managing brands in technology markets. In this chapter, I discuss these challenges by contrasting branding in technology markets with branding in CPG markets, and use these points of contrast to derive implications and insights for branding in technology markets. The reason for choosing CPG markets as a reference point is that most of the literature on branding focuses on CPG products, and the CPG market context is most familiar to managers. Further, CPG firms like Procter & Gamble epitomize the state-of-the-art in brand management.

The differences between technology markets and CPG markets from a branding standpoint can be categorized into differences related to the market, differences related to products, differences related to customer behavior, and differences related to channels and ecosystems. I use this categorization scheme to discuss the challenges and principles of branding in technology markets. Figure 11.1 summarizes the key contextual dimensions that form the basis of contrasting branding in technology markets with branding in CPG markets.

DIFFERENCES RELATED TO MARKET CHARACTERISTICS

Technology markets are characterized by rapid change and evolution. In contrast with CPG markets, where product categories evolve slowly and new category creation is rare, category boundaries are constantly shifting and blurring in technology markets, and new categories are created relatively frequently. Venerable CPG products like Dove soap, Tide detergent, and Kellogg's Frosted Flakes have existed for decades or even centuries as exemplars of the soap, detergent, and breakfast cereal categories. These product categories have been relatively stable over several decades, with gradual incremental improvements like liquid detergents and cereal bars. By contrast, just since the 1990s, we have seen the creation of new technology product categories and subcategories like digital televisions, personal digital assistants, web browsers, digital cameras, and digital personal music players. The creation of new categories and the rapid evolution of existing categories have important implications for branding of technology products.

Branding the Company, Not the Product

The ephemeral and fluid nature of product categories in technology markets makes it difficult to closely associate technology brands to a specific product or even a specific product category. While Tide has been associated with detergents and Colgate has been associated with oral care for decades, technology brands are rarely associated with specific products. While CPG firms focus on branding the *product,* technology firms focus on branding the *company.* Technology firms tend to rely more on the "branded house" or the "sub-branding" approach to brand architecture, relative to the "house of brands" approach favored by some CPG firms like Procter & Gamble.[7] The driver brand for most technology firms is the corporate brand, and not the product brand.

Figure 11.1
Branding in Technology Markets versus Consumer Packaged Goods Markets

Contextual Factor	Consumer Packaged Goods Markets	Technology Markets	Implications for Managing Technology Brands
Market Characteristics	Relatively mature markets. Emphasis on market share within existing categories.	Rapidly changing and evolving markets. Emphasis on shaping demand and creating new categories.	• Branding the company, not the product • Pre-market branding in emerging opportunity arenas • Using abstract, not descriptive brand names
Product Life Cycle	Long. Product categories are relatively stable and evolve slowly.	Short. Products diffuse rapidly through the adoption life cycle and successive product generations are introduced rapidly.	• Managing dynamics of brand positioning across the technology adoption life cycle • Migrating from category-level competition to brand-level competition • Managing dynamics of brand positioning across successive product generations

Product Complexity	Low. Product have a few easily understood features.	High. Products may have hundreds or thousands of features.	• Product as focus instead of brand as focus • Abstracting from features and functions to benefits and emotional benefits
Product Architecture	Simple. Product is usually one integral unit.	Complex and modular. Products consist of several components from many providers.	• Importance of brand hierarchy and brand architecture • Importance of co-branding and ingredient branding
Customer Behavior	Relatively simple customer decision-making process (DMP). Simple decision-making unit (DMU).	Complex DMP with many steps and many sources of information. Complex DMU with multiple audiences and influencers.	• Brand as total customer experience across diverse touch points and steps in the buying cycle • Managing integrity of the total customer experience with the brand
Channels and Partner Ecosystem	Mostly vertical channel relationships—distributors and retailers.	Vertical as well as horizontal relationships—complementors, VARs, ISVs.	• Managing brand experiences mediated through partners • Managing conflicts of interest in co-branding with ecosystem partners

In cases where technology firms have created brands that have been too product-specific, they have been forced to abstract the brand name into a less descriptive acronym. For example, International Business Machines became IBM, American Telephone & Telegraph became AT&T, and the Belgian American Radio Company became BARCO. Likewise, technology firms tend to favor brand names that are neologisms (a made-up word that has no meaning in any language) because neologisms can be infused with any meaning that the firm seeks, and their meaning can be adapted over time as the brand's position evolves. Some of the most famous fanciful brand names have been created by technology firms—Xerox, Kodak, Google, Adobe, Amazon, Cisco, and eBay.

Pre-Market Branding for Thought Leadership

Technology firms often face the challenge of pioneering new-to-the-world product categories. For example, the communications firm Motorola pioneered the creation of pagers, cellular phones, and personal digital assistants.[8] Pioneering new categories poses a difficult branding challenge, because marketing communication activities may begin well before the products have even been created. Technology markets often go through a long "pre-market" stage where standards are being debated, products are being developed, and technologies are being perfected. At this stage, the actual product or markets don't even exist. The battle for market share has yet to begin. However, the battle for *mind share* may have begun in earnest. Pioneering technology firms need to vie for *thought leadership* at the pre-market stage by positioning themselves as leaders in markets of the future.[9] This requires them to associate their brands with an *opportunity arena,* which is a set of potential markets of the future.

Consider two examples. Sun Microsystems pioneered the Java programming language and the concept of *network-centric computing* as early as 1987 with its famous slogan, "The Network Is the Computer." When it began the campaign, Sun had few concrete offerings to back its claims. However, it was able to position itself as a thought leader in the emerging market for network-centric computing, which took off in earnest in the late 1990s. These early positioning efforts allowed Sun to become a leader in the market for web servers—the large computers that run web sites over the Internet. Sun successfully associated itself with the opportunity arena of web-based computing, even before the market actually existed. In early 2004, IBM began promoting the concept of the *on-demand business,* hoping to position itself as the leader in the emerging arena of business process outsourcing and computing as a utility-like service. While the market for the *software as a utility* of *business processes on demand* delivered over a network was in its infancy in 2004, IBM was well on its way to associating its brand with these emerging trends.

Pre-market branding requires a very different set of principles relative to branding in CPG markets. First, the object being branded is not a product. It is a concept or a vision about future possibilities enabled by technology. IBM, Sun Microsystems, and Nokia were not promoting specific products when they talked about *on-demand business, network-centric computing,* or the *mobile lifestyle.* Rather, they were promoting their vision about how the future might unfold, and the role that these companies might play in enabling the future. Second, the target audience for the branding effort is often not end-consumers in the pre-market stage. Instead, the target is *key influencers*—partners who might create complementary products, developers who might write applications for the pioneering firm's technology platform, industry analysts who might influence customers, and even competitors who might be co-opted into adopting the technology platform. Third, the goal of pre-market branding is not to gain market leadership in existing markets, but to gain thought leadership and share of opportunity in markets of the future. And finally, pre-market branding carries the risk of being perceived as hype or *vaporware* promotion if the market does not evolve as quickly as expected, or if the technology fails to deliver.

For example, Oracle aggressively promoted the *network computer* as the next-generation paradigm in personal computing, but this vision was largely discredited as personal computers continued to be the dominant form of personal computing.[10] Similarly, Apple suffered a black eye in the early 1990s when its then-CEO John Sculley hyped the personal digital assistant (PDA) as a new category of digital computing devices with massive potential, only to see its Newton PDA fail miserably because it came to market before its time.

DIFFERENCES RELATED TO THE PRODUCT LIFE CYCLE

Technology products tend to have far shorter life cycles than consumer packaged goods. In contrast with CPG products, where the product life cycle can be infinitely long because products can be successfully adapted over several decades,[11] technology products move quickly through the adoption life cycle. This begins with innovators and early adopters, who together constitute the early market, and progresses to the early majority, late majority, and laggards who together make up the mainstream market.[12]

The short product life cycle in technology markets also means that technology products often progress through several successive generations or versions, with each generation providing better performance, new features, and lower prices. The microprocessor firm Intel is a classic example of this relentless march of technology, following the famous Moore's law, which predicted that microprocessor performance would double every two years on the average. Intel introduced a series of successive generations of microprocessors in the x86 series, starting with the 8086 processor, followed by the 80286, the 80386, and the 80486 generations. It then adopted a nonnumeric brand name called the Pentium, and has since launched the Pentium II, the Pentium III, and the Pentium IV generations. The short product life cycles of technology products mean that the brand value proposition for technology products cannot be static. The brand name and the brand value proposition need to be adapted across the technology adoption life cycle within a generation, as well as across successive generations of products.

Dynamics of Brand Positioning across the Adoption Life Cycle

In CPG markets, marketers choose a specific set of customer segments to focus on, then develop a positioning strategy that appeals to the chosen target segments. Once this positioning strategy is chosen, it can be maintained for a long time because the product category and the segments are relatively stable over time. For instance, Ivory Soap used the slogan "so pure it floats" and Pepsi-Cola used "choice of the new generation" for many years. Even in consumer durables, brands like Maytag have used reliability as a positioning theme for a long time, with their use of the unemployed Maytag repairman. Over time, CPG marketers attempt to grow revenues by deepening the penetration and increasing the usage of their brands within the chosen target segments.

However, technology products go through a well-defined *adoption life cycle* as they diffuse through the marketplace, which requires the brand value proposition to be adapted over time to match the needs of various adopter segments. In the early stages of category evolution, technology products are targeted at early adopters, who value cutting-edge performance and innovative features. At later stages of evolution, the same products are targeted at the mainstream market, which may value ease of use and convenience, and may not care as much about innovative features.

Consider direct broadcast satellite (DBS) systems. In the early stages of this category's evolution, the value proposition of DBS systems focused on the rich choice of sporting and movie content, as well as on availability in areas not served by cable TV systems. However, as DBS attempted to broaden its appeal to the mainstream market, the value proposition had to be adapted to emphasize ease of installation and the inclusion of local broadcast channels. This dynamic adaptation of the brand value proposition poses difficult challenges, because the benefits that appeal to early adopters are very different from those desired by later adopters.

Technology firms can adapt their value proposition to address the mainstream market by creating multiple brands or multiple sub-brands that appeal to different adopter segments. Effectively, they migrate customers from the brands that signal cutting-edge performance to brands that signal benefits valued by mainstream customers. For instance, PDA maker Palm offered the Zire range of handhelds for the mass market that preferred low-cost and easy-to-use devices, while its Tungsten and Treo brands targeted customers who valued cutting-edge performance and multifunction devices respectively.

Another shift that technology firms need to manage as they navigate their brands across the adoption life cycle is the shift from differentiation at the *category level* to differentiation at the *brand level*. This occurs as products move from the early to late stages their life cycle. At the early stages of category evolution, the primary competition for a technology product is *nonconsumption,* because the category is largely untapped. Further, there may be only one early entrant—or at most a few. Therefore, the brand positioning tends to emphasize the benefits of the new category relative to existing substitutes in other categories in the early stages.

Consider the case of wireless phones. In the early stages of their evolution, wireless phones were positioned against wired phones (pay phones or landline phones), as their name suggests. The initial positioning of wireless phones tended to emphasize the mobility benefits of wireless phones relative to landline phones. However, as the product category evolved and competitors entered the marketplace, the positioning strategy needed to shift to emphasizing *brand-specific* differentiation. By the mid-2000s, competitors in the wireless handset markets focused on brand-specific unique features and benefits, because the category-level benefits were no longer a source of differentiation. Technology firms must manage these transitions proactively, or they may find their differentiation eroding as the points of differentiation for competition at the category level become table stakes for competition at the brand level.

Dynamics of Brand Positioning across Successive Generations

As technology products progress rapidly through several generations, the brand positioning also must be adapted across multiple generations to address the evolution of the product's features and benefits over time. Unlike CPG products, where the product's basis feature set remains fairly stable over a few years, technology products are constantly being made cheaper, better, and faster. Therefore, the brand value proposition needs to be *dynamically adapted* across generations in a way that preserves consistency in the brand's positioning over time, while accommodating the significant evolution in the product features and benefits.

To create more coherence and consistency in brand positioning across generations, technology firms need to choose a *vector of differentiation* (VOD) for their products.[13] In technology firms, a vector of differentiation represents the unique way that a product or a brand will be successful over several generations. A VOD is a deliberate choice by the company that defines how a firm will continue to enhance performance or sustain competitive differentiation. Thus, a VOD provides a clear direction for the evolution of the brand value proposition over time. A well-defined VOD can help a technology firm increasingly distance itself from competitors along the dimensions that it has chosen.

Consider the example of the enterprise software firm SAP. Over several generations, SAP chose a VOD that it called "increasing breadth of functionality" (see Figure 11.2). This involved progressively increasing the scope of functional areas that SAP's Enterprise Resource Management (ERP) suite covered. In its first generation, SAP's ERP suite included manufacturing and accounting modules. In the next generation, the ERP suite was expanded to include purchasing and order processing, while human resource management and sales force automation were added in the third generation. In subsequent generations, SAP added supply chain management and customer relationship management functionalities. While the features and functions of each of SAP's software generations changed, SAP stuck to the overall positioning theme of increasing breadth of functionality. By adhering to this VOD, SAP was able to distance itself from competitors in the enterprise software arena.

Similarly, Apple Computer pursued the VOD of "usability and superior customer experience" across several generations of its Macintosh products. Every subsequent generation of its products offered further improvements in usability, and most of its innovations have traditionally been focused on creating a better out-of-the-box user experience. On the other hand, Microsoft has focused on a VOD that it calls *integrated innovation*—the promise that Mi-

Figure 11.2
How SAP Uses Vectors of Differentiation to Manage Dynamics of Brand Positioning across Generations

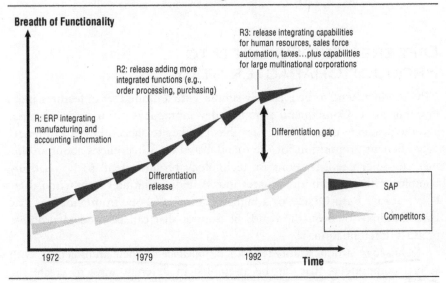

Source: Michael E. McGrath, *Product Strategy for High Technology Companies* (2nd Edition), New York: McGraw–Hill, 2000.

crosoft products work better together than products from any competing vendors. This is a powerful promise that allowed Microsoft to leverage its strong market position in operating systems to applications, databases, server products, and mobile devices that all worked as an integrated system.

VODs may sustain differentiation across several generations, but they do run out of steam as the marginal returns to providing even better performance inevitably diminish, once sufficient progress has been made on any particular dimension. For instance, Apple's lead in usability shrunk as Microsoft's Windows operating system caught up in usability improvements. Similarly, Intel's chosen VOD of "increasing microprocessor speed and performance" became less compelling over time, because the performance of a PC was no longer constrained by the microprocessor, but by the speed of the connection between the PC and the Internet. When a VOD begins to produce diminishing marginal returns, technology firms need to make a conscious decision to switch to a new VOD. This is a very important strategic decision. Starting in 2001, Apple switched to a new VOD of "digital media experiences," with its suite of multimedia software and hardware offerings like iPod, iTunes, and iMovie. And Intel made a significant switch to promoting a new VOD of mobility with its Centrino microprocessor and the "Unwire" advertising campaign.[14]

DIFFERENCES RELATED TO PRODUCT CHARACTERISTICS

CPG products tend to be relatively simple, with a limited set of features and a low unit price. Consequently, product development is not too complicated, and the products are technically feasible. The key to success lies in a differentiated benefit proposition for the brand, based on a hypothesis about an unmet customer need. By contrast, technology products tend to be relatively complex with a large number of features. A high-end router from Cisco, database software from Oracle, or a high-end camera phone from Samsung may have hundreds or even thousands of features that can be used to promote product differentiation.

Technology products also tend to be *modular* in their architecture, with several components that can be assembled in different ways to create the overall offering.[15] These components are often created by several independent firms that collaborate to create technology products based on a common technology platform. The importance of modularity and platforms in turn means that technology standards and network externalities play a key role in marketing and development.[16] Technology firms don't compete on a product-to-product basis. Rather, they compete on an ecosystem-to-ecosystem basis.[17] For instance, in the mid-2000s, Microsoft and its ecosystem of partners competed with PalmOne and its partners in the mobile devices market. Similarly, IBM and its partners competed with Microsoft and its ecosystem of partners in the enterprise software market. These product differences have several important implications for branding of technology products.

Product Management versus Brand Management

CPG firms created the concept of the *brand manager* as the person responsible for the planning, coordination, and monitoring of a brand's performance. In CPG markets, brands are closely associated with specific products, so brand managers are responsible for all marketing activities for the products that use the brand name. Brand management is almost synonymous with product management in CPG firms, because brand managers are responsible for the brand's inbound (product development) as well as outbound (product marketing) activities. Further, the brand is the central asset that the brand manager manages. The brand is the hero, not the product.

Technology firms, on the other hand, make a big distinction between brand management and product management. Given the fact that technology products are complex and often require a long and technically demanding development process, the *product* becomes the focal unit of analysis for a product manager. At technology firms like Microsoft, the brand management role is exclusively *outbound* in nature, with a focus on managing marketing communications to build the equity of a specific brand. These brands can be a product brand (like Xbox), a platform brand (like Office System), an ingredient brand (like .NET), or the corporate brand.

Brand management in technology firms is typically the responsibility of corporate marketing, especially for the higher-level platform brands and the corporate brands. Brand advertising is fairly centralized in technology firms, because most of the advertising spending is done at the level of the corporate brand. Increasingly, technology firms like IBM, Samsung, Hewlett-Packard, DuPont, and Microsoft have been putting a larger percentage of their advertising dollars behind the corporate brand instead of promoting product-level brands, to gain economies of scale. This is very different from the highly decentralized nature of brand advertising in CPG firms, where brand managers responsible for specific products control the advertising budgets and formulate brand advertising campaigns for their products. In essence, brand managers in CPG firms function like general managers for their brands, with revenue and profit responsibility. By contrast, brand managers in technology firms rarely have revenue responsibility because the brands are not closely tied to a specific product or products.

Brand Hierarchy and Architecture

In technology markets, products in a product line and in the overall product portfolio often have some common components, common features, or common technologies. So the product portfolio for technology firms is more than a collection of disparate products. Instead, it is often a product *family* that is built on a common platform. This relatedness therefore suggests that the products portfolio can be organized into a *product hierarchy*, with some common features that are shared across the entire family, and some features that are unique to specific products. This hierarchical nature of a technology product family in turn suggests that the brand portfolio for technology firms should also be organized into a *brand hierarchy* reflecting the brand architecture for the firm.

The brand architecture for technology firms can be thought of as a pyramid, with the corporate brand at the top, followed by platform or range brands, and product-specific brands at the lowest level of the hierarchy. For most technology firms, the corporate brand is the *driver brand*—the brand that is most important in driving customers to purchase the product. The corporate brand is followed by two or more sub-brands that reflect different levels in the hierarchy. At the lowest level, specific products or models are often designated by alphanumeric names. Consider the IBM ThinkPad T23 laptop computer. This brand consists of three levels—the corporate brand (IBM), the range brand (ThinkPad), and the model-specific brand (T23). Generally, the range brand tends to be the most descriptive, while the product-specific brand is deliberately a meaningless alphanumeric code.

Creating a multilevel brand hierarchy allows technology firms to overcome the dilemma of reconciling the consistency demanded by branding with the change demanded by technology evolution. As Figure 11.3 illus-

Figure 11.3
How Brand Architecture Helps Reconcile Consistency with Change in Technology Branding

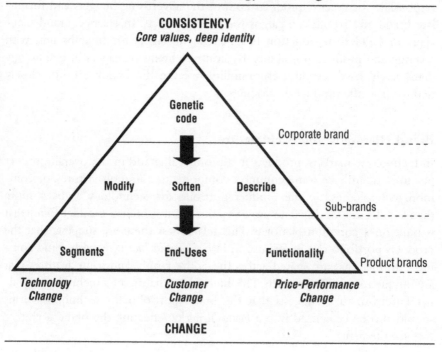

trates, the corporate brand provides the anchor of stability and consistency in branding technology products. The corporate brand serves as an umbrella with a common set of brand values that all of the firm's products must embody. The corporate brand is not subject to change, and the equity in the corporate brand helps every product that the company offers to its customers. At lower levels in the hierarchy, the brands can be more dynamic to accommodate the rapid changes in technology, customer needs, and price points. Sub-brands can be created to target specific segments or specific price points. These sub-brands can modify, soften, or further describe the corporate brand position for specific segments or price points.

The challenge in creating an effective brand architecture is to devise an umbrella positioning strategy for the corporate brand that is flexible enough to accommodate a diverse set of sub-brands, and yet is focused enough to be distinct and differentiated from the competition. For instance, in 2003, the Microsoft corporate brand promise was to "enable individuals and businesses around the world to realize their fullest potential by using Microsoft technologies." Under the corporate brand, Microsoft had several sub-brands, platform brands, ingredient brands, and product-specific brands that allowed it to target specific segments and audiences (see Figure 11.4 for the Microsoft brand architecture in 2003). Each of the sub-brands under the corporate brand needed to complement the Microsoft corporate brand promise and make it relevant to specific segments and audiences.

Ingredient Branding and Co-Branding

Technology products are often a composite system consisting of several component products or ingredients. In fact, some technology firms like Dolby Labs (consumer electronics), Intel (microprocessors), DuPont (intermediates in chemicals and plastics), and Gore-Tex (insulation) only make ingredients that are used in a final product sold by another company. Therefore, technology products often consist of a branded ingredient that may have its own brand equity, which is used to enhance the equity of the host brand. This co-branding approach, called *ingredient branding*, is fairly common in technology markets. The most famous example of ingredient branding is the "Intel Inside" branding campaign that made Intel a household name and one of the world's most valuable brands, despite the fact that very few end-users had ever seen an Intel product. Intel invested billions of dollars over the years in co-marketing dollars to build the equity in the Intel brand.

Ingredient branding makes sense when the branded ingredient enjoys

Figure 11.4
Microsoft Brand Architecture in 2003

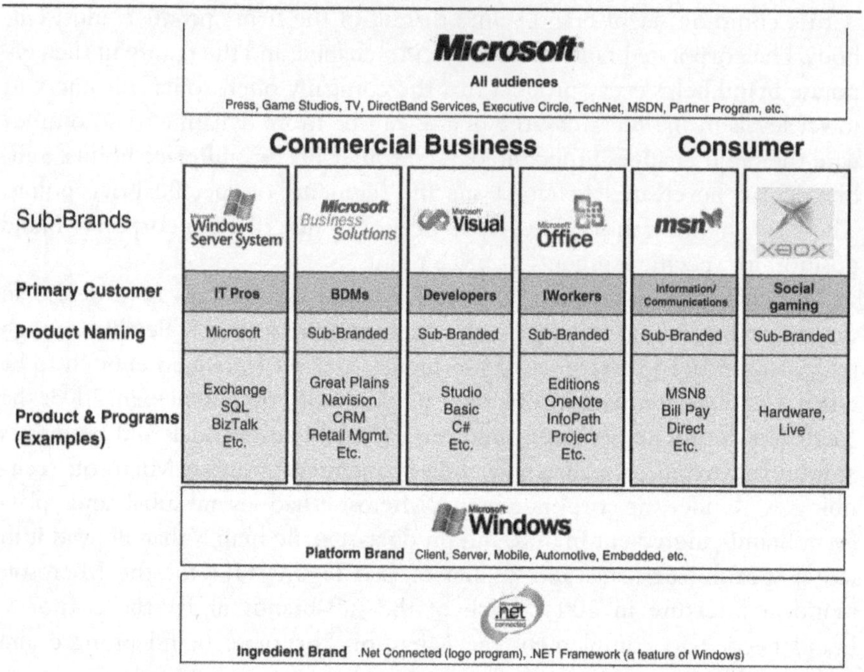

	Microsoft®					
	All audiences					
	Press, Game Studios, TV, DirectBand Services, Executive Circle, TechNet, MSDN, Partner Program, etc.					
	Commercial Business				**Consumer**	
Sub-Brands	Windows Server System	Microsoft Business Solutions	Visual	Office	msn®	XBOX
Primary Customer	IT Pros	BDMs	Developers	IWorkers	Information/ Communications	Social gaming
Product Naming	Microsoft	Sub-Branded	Sub-Branded	Sub-Branded	Sub-Branded	Sub-Branded
Product & Programs (Examples)	Exchange SQL BizTalk Etc.	Great Plains Navision CRM Retail Mgmt. Etc.	Studio Basic C# Etc.	Editions OneNote InfoPath Project Etc.	MSN8 Bill Pay Direct Etc.	Hardware, Live
	Windows					
	Platform Brand Client, Server, Mobile, Automotive, Embedded, etc.					
	.net					
	Ingredient Brand .Net Connected (logo program), .NET Framework (a feature of Windows)					

Source: Microsoft Corporation.

more perceived value than its host product. If the host product is new, if it has low awareness, if the product category is commoditized, or if the ingredient brand can provide the product with a legitimate quality advantage over its competition, ingredient branding can benefit the host brand. Conversely, ingredient branding is less beneficial if the host product enjoys a premium image, has high awareness, or is highly differentiated. This is true because the ingredient brand may overshadow the host brand, reduce its uniqueness, add additional licensing costs, and potentially conflict with the equity of the host brand.[18] In Intel's case, well-known PC manufacturers like IBM, Hewlett-Packard, and Dell would benefit less from co-branding with Intel as an ingredient brand, while relatively unknown white-box PC manufacturers would benefit from the Intel brand equity. So ingredient branding can be a double-edged sword.

Besides ingredient branding, technology products often involve co-branding with multiple brands belonging to different partners who collaborate to create the offering. Consider the Motorola MPx220 Smartphone that a sub-scriber would receive from Vodafone (a European cellular carrier). The phone was manufactured by Motorola, the operating system came from Microsoft (Windows Mobile), and the carrier also had its brand name on the product. So there were at least three brands vying for the relationship with the end customer. Further, the interests of the three partners may not be aligned. Vo-daphone would like the carrier's brand to be the driver brand, while Mo-torola and Microsoft in turn would like the device and the operating system respectively to be the driver brand. In fact, Vodaphone demanded that all de-vice manufacturers create a Vodafone-branded, icon-driven menu and user interface that would be consistent across all Vodafone wireless devices. This was an attempt by Vodafone to downplay the partner brands and to take con-trol of the brand relationship with the end customer. These conflicts of inter-est are endemic to technology markets, and we are likely to see more such incidents where the existence of multiple co-branded elements of a technol-ogy product results in a jockeying for position among the various component brands.

DIFFERENCES RELATED TO CUSTOMER DECISION MAKING

Technology products tend to be complex and plagued with technology risk. They also tend to be far more expensive than CPG products, particularly in business-to-business technology markets where a single purchase can run into millions of dollars. Therefore, the customer decision-making process (DMP) for buying technology products tends to be far more complex, and the customer decision-making unit (DMU) tends to include several actors who influence the purchase decision, besides the end users. In fact, in busi-ness-to-business technology markets, the end users rarely are the people who make the purchasing decision. The complexities of the customer DMP and DMU have important implications for branding of technology products.

Marketing to Multiple Audiences in Business-to-Business Markets

Technology products sold to businesses need to be marketed at two levels—to the organization, as well as to the specific audiences within the organiza-tion. For instance, GE Healthcare, when marketing its Digital Ultrasound products, might segment its market and create focused value propositions for community hospitals, teaching hospitals, and rural hospitals. However, within each hospital, it also must create focused value propositions for hospital administrators, physicians, and nurses. This means that technology brands need to be marketed simultaneously to multiple audiences, who may have different needs and may desire very different outcomes.

For instance, physicians may want the most sophisticated and innovative features in ultrasound equipment, so a brand value proposition that emphasizes cutting-edge performance and innovation may appeal to them. However, nurses who actually conduct the ultrasounds may care about ease of use and convenience of the device, while hospital administrators may care about the capital and operating costs of the equipment. Therefore, technology firms must create multiple *audience-specific* value propositions for their brands that speak to the needs of each audience that makes up the DMU. While these audience-specific value propositions should be focused, they still need to have a cumulative logic with common themes that unify them into a broader umbrella value proposition.

Consider the 2003 Microsoft brand architecture in Figure 11.4. Microsoft's commercial business sub-brands at that time (MBS, Office System, Windows Server System, and Visual) not only needed to be targeted to specific types of business customers, they also needed to be targeted to specific audiences within a business customer's organization. Each sub-brand had a primary audience, but it also had to appeal to secondary target audiences. For instance, the Office System sub-brand's primary target audience was information workers (iWorkers), while the Windows Server System sub-brand was targeted to information technology professionals (IT Pros). However, other audiences, including business decision makers (BDMs) and developers were also secondary targets for these sub-brands. Therefore, in creating the brand promise for each sub-brand, Microsoft had to think about the *segment-specific* value propositions (for instance, small business versus enterprise customers) as well as the *audience-specific* value propositions (for instance, IT Pros and BDMs). These value propositions in turn needed to ladder up to the overall corporate brand promise of *realizing potential*.

For instance, the brand promise for Windows Server System needed to articulate how this sub-brand could help the audience of IT pros realize their potential—possibly by making them more productive or empowering them to manage their IT assets more effectively. Similarly, the Visual sub-brand, whose primary audience was software developers, needed to convey how the Visual family of products allowed developers to realize their potential by helping them to write software code more efficiently or manage software development projects more effectively.

So brand marketing for business-to-business technology products takes on a dual nature, consisting of segment marketing as well as audience marketing. This duality is unique to business-to-business brands, and it introduces a layer of complexity that is not found in CPG brand marketing.

Going beyond Feeds and Speeds

In technology firms, the engineering group tends to dominate the organization. Engineers developing new technology products are driven by the belief that innovative product features and improved product performance are the drivers of competitive advantage. Consequently, technology firms emphasize functional characteristics of their products in development as well as in marketing. This emphasis on product features often spills over to the brand marketing efforts, with a strong emphasis on functional aspects of the brand promise. This tendency of technology firms to emphasize features and functional performance in brand positioning is sometimes called *feeds-and-speeds* marketing. A simple glance at advertising for personal computers conveys the pervasiveness of feeds-and-speeds marketing. Most advertising for PCs is little more than a laundry list of features and detailed comparison tables highlighting how one manufacturer's PC outperforms its competitors on a number of technical features. Rarely are the features linked to benefits or customer-desired outcomes.

Enlightened technology firms realize that they need to go beyond feeds-and-speeds marketing in two important ways. First, even if they talk about features and functions, the emphasis should be on the *functional benefits* that the brand offers and not the features per se. Functions are what the brand does, while functional benefits are what the brand does *for the customer* in terms of outcomes that it enables. For instance, Apple's iPod offered a unique click-wheel feature that allowed users to quickly scroll through their collections of songs. The functional benefit of the click-wheel is the ease of use and the increased speed of searching the music collection. Moving from feature-based positioning to benefits-based positioning is an art that few technology firms have mastered. A stellar exception is the personal and small business financial software company Intuit. According to Intuit's founder Scott Cook, a key functional benefit that Intuit constantly seeks to offer is products that are "drop-dead easy" to use. There may be several features that enable ease of use, but Intuit does not focus on the features as much as on the outcome—software for financial management that is easy to use.

Enlightened technology firms also move beyond feeds-and-speeds by realizing that there is more to customer benefits than functional benefits. They focus on two additional dimensions of benefits—*economic benefits* and *emotional benefits*. This three-dimensional view of benefits reinforces the importance of converting functional benefits into economic value (time and money for the customer) and the importance of making an emotional connection with customers. Figure 11.5 shows the three-dimensional view of benefits in positioning technology brands. The diagram deliberately places emotional benefits at the top, to emphasize the fact that technology firms need to climb the ladder from a brand promise centered around functional and economic benefits to a brand promise that includes emotional benefits as an important aspect of the brand value proposition.[19]

Economic benefits speak to economic buyers, particularly in business-to-business settings, by quantifying the brand's economic value to the customer (EVC) and the total value of ownership (TVO) over the entire ownership life cycle. Emotional benefits speak to the psychological and relational rewards that customers can expect from owning and using the brand. In consumer

Figure 11.5
Three Dimensions of Benefits in Positioning Technology Brands

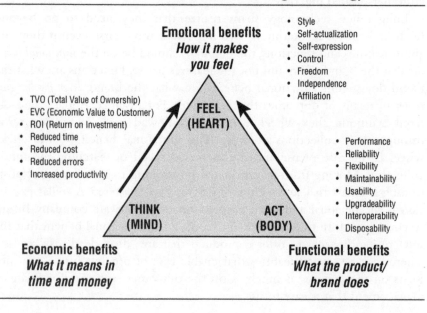

technology markets, these emotional benefits can include self-expression, self-actualization, association with a desirable reference group, or enabling a desired lifestyle. Brands like Apple, Palm, Nokia, Samsung, and Intuit have succeeded in making a powerful emotional connection with customers and have benefited tremendously from the brand loyalty that follows. In business markets, emotional benefits can include freedom, empowerment, a sense of control, and a valued relationship with the vendor. For instance, IBM and Cisco have competed effectively based on their promise of peace of mind and the strength of the relationships they build with their business customers, as evidenced by the famous adage in the computer industry—"Nobody got fired for buying IBM."

Technology brands that progress beyond functional and economic value to emotional value can extract a significant price premium and effectively insulate themselves from feature-based competition. But few technology brands are able to make this transition, and as a result, they stay stuck on the feature treadmill—running faster and faster to stay on the same spot. To rise above the fray, technology brands need to go beyond feeds-and-speeds and make an emotional connection with their customers.

The Brand as the Total Customer Experience

The customer decision-making process (DMP) for technology products, particularly capital goods purchased by business customers, tends to be a complex process with many players. The DMP consists of a number of steps, and customers can get informational input about technology brands from a diverse array of touch points. Further, the customer's brand experience does not end with the acquisition of the product—customers go through a number of post-purchase steps over the ownership and usage life cycle of the product.

A useful way to understand the customer's total experience with a technology brand is the "Circle of Customer Experience" (see Figure 11.6), which shows a 360-degree view of the sequence of stages in the customer experience. It also shows the different touch points through which customers might experience the brand. Blueprinting the customer experience this way allows technology firms to diagnose the experience that customers have at each stage in the buying and ownership process, and to find opportunities for improving the customer experience at each stage.

For instance, Hewlett-Packard defined the "Total Customer Experience"

Figure 11.6
The Circle of Customer Experience

in terms of the following stages and desired customer outcomes for customers of its large enterprise systems:[20]

1. Aware: "I know who you are and what value you offer."
2. Choose: "I can easily find the right products and services for my business."
3. Order: "I can get all HP products easily from one place at competitive prices."
4. Install: "I can easily integrate your solution into my business environment."
5. Learn: "You provide me with the information I need and allow me to learn in the way I want."
6. Use: "Your solution is easy to use and manage within my business environment. It feels familiar; everything I did yesterday I can do today."
7. Support: "You provide me access to knowledge to quickly solve my problems—plus, you're only a phone call or click away."
8. Dispose/Upgrade: "It's easy for my business to grow with HP."

By mapping these stages in detail, HP can diagnose the customer experience in great detail and ensure that the customer's brand experience is consistent and coherent and embodies the brand values that HP promotes. The consistency of the customer experience should be evaluated on the following dimensions:

- *Consistency across touch points.* The brand experience should be consistent across the various channels and modes of communication that customers may use to interact with the brand. All touch points should reinforce the same brand values.
- *Consistency across buying stages.* The brand experience should be consistent across the entire customer buying and ownership cycle. Handoffs from stage to stage should be managed carefully, to ensure that customers are able to progress through the end-to-end process without any disconnects or problems.
- *Consistency across partners.* The brand experience should be consistent across all the firm's partners who participate in bringing the brand experience to life. For instance, a technology firm's partners may be responsible for installation, delivery, or support. The challenge for the firm is to ensure that the experience that customers have with each partner is consistent and coordinated.

When well orchestrated, the total customer experience becomes a powerful and multifaceted approach that enables technology firms to create a differentiated brand experience.[21] Given the intensity and the richness of customer interactions, there are multiple avenues for differentiating the brand as experienced by customers that go well beyond the product itself.

CONCLUSION

Technology firms have been late to embrace the concept of branding, partly because of the cultural bias in technology firms toward engineering and feature-based product differentiation. However, the dynamic and uncertain nature of technology markets, the complexity of technology products, and the difficulty of choosing among conflicting technologies and claims mean that brands play an important role in technology markets as an anchor of stability and a source of assurance. To exploit the full power of brands, technology firms must learn from the CPG firms (the state-of-the-art in brand management), which originated the concept of brands and brand management. However, the principles of branding need to be adapted by taking into account the contextual differences between technology markets and CPG markets. The information presented here should give technology firms a deeper understanding of these contextual differences and their implications for managing technology brands. Additionally, the frameworks, examples, and best practices provided in the chapter can serve as a roadmap for improving the state of the practice in managing technology brands.

Mohanbir Sawhney is the McCormick Tribune Professor of Technology and the director of the Center for Research in Technology & Innovation at the Kellogg School of Management. He has been on the faculty since 1993. He is co-author of three books on technology marketing. He received a BTech from the Indian Institute of Technology, an MBA from the Indian Institute of Management, and a Ph.D. from the Wharton School of the University of Pennsylvania.

NOTES

1. "P&G: New and Improved," *BusinessWeek* (July 7, 2003).

2. Pettis, Chuck (1995), *TechnoBrands*, New York: AMACOM, p. 39.

3. For a good discussion of the popular myths and misconceptions about branding in technology markets, see: Ward, Scott, Larry Light, and Jonathan Goldstine (1999), "What High-Tech Managers Need to Know about Brands," *Harvard Business Review*, (July–August), 85–95.

4. In fact, when technology firms keep pushing the frontier of technology performance beyond the level of performance desired by customers, they may alienate themselves from customers and become vulnerable to attacks from disruptive technologies. This idea is discussed in detail in Christensen, Clayton (1997), *The Innovator's Dilemma*, Harvard Business School Press.

5. Source: www.interbrand.com/best_brands_04/league_table/BGBleaguetable_final.pdf.

6. "Apple Brand Value Jumps 24 Percent on iPod," *MacCentral* (July 23, 2004).

7. For an excellent discussion of brand architecture and the brand relationship spectrum, see Aaker, D.A. and E. Joachimsthaler (2000), "The Brand Relationship Spectrum: The Key to the Brand Architecture Challenge," *California Management Review*, 42(4), 8–23.

8. For a detailed case study on the challenges faced by Motorola in creating new-to-the-world product categories, see Monrone, Joseph G. (1993), *Winning in High-Tech Markets*, Harvard Business School Press.

9. The concept of the "battle for intellectual leadership" in the pre-market stage was first presented in Prahalad, C.K. and Gary Hamel (1994), *Competing for the Future*, Harvard Business School Press.

10. Berinato, Scott (2001), "7 Reasons the PC Is Here to Stay," *CIO* (June 1).

11. The Product Life Cycle concept has been criticized as not being applicable to CPG brands, because brands can live on forever. See, for instance, Dhalla, K. and S. Yuspeh (1976), "Forget the Product Life Cycle," *Harvard Business Review,* 54 (January), 102–112.

12. For a detailed discussion of the adoption lifecycle, see Moore, Geoffrey (1999), *Crossing the Chasm: Marketing and Selling High-Tech Products to Mainstream Customers,* New York: HarperBusiness.

13. The concept of vectors of differentiation is explained in detail in McGrath, Michael E. (2000), *Product Strategy for High Technology Companies* (2nd Edition), New York: McGraw Hill.

14. Hesseldahl, Arik (2003), "The New Cool Chip in Town," *Forbes* (January 9).

15. For a discussion of the principles of modularity and platforms design, see Baldwin, Carliss Y. and Kim B. Clark (2000), *Design Rules, Vol. 1: The Power of Modularity,* Cambridge, MA: MIT Press; and Meyer, Marc H. and Alvin P. Lehnerd (1997), *The Power of Product Platforms,* New York: Free Press.

16. An excellent discussion of the role of network externalities in the evolution of technology markets can be found in Shaprio, Carl and Hal R. Varian (1998), *Information Rules: A Strategic Guide to the Network Economy,* Boston: Harvard Business School Press.

17. The principles of ecosystem-level competition are discussed in Hagel, John III (1996), "Spider versus Spider," *McKinsey Quarterly,* 1.

18. Source: "Ingredient Branding: Does What Is Inside Really Matter?" Available at: www .landor.com.

19. For a slightly different visual depiction of this idea, see the "Brand Pyramid" in Ward et al. (1999), "What High-Tech Managers Need to Know about Brands," *Harvard Business Review* (July–August), 91.

20. For details of Hewlett-Packard's Total Customer Experience (TCE) initiative, see Sato, Stephen and Andrew Panton (2003), "Using a Change-Management Approach to Promote Customer-Centered Design," *ACM,* 1–58113–728–1.

21. The concept of differentiating along different stages of the customer experience can be applied to other contexts too, including consumer products and services. For an excellent discussion of such differentiation strategies, see MacMillan, Ian C. and R.G. McGrath (1997), "Discovering New Points of Differentiation," *Harvard Business Review,* 75(4) (July–August), 133–138.

CHAPTER 12

BUILDING A
BRAND-DRIVEN ORGANIZATION

SCOTT DAVIS

On June 9, 2003, financial services giant UBS launched a rebranding effort. The company set out to brand its new consolidation (under the UBS moniker) of all the private bankers, wealth managers, asset managers, and investment bankers it had acquired around the globe over the previous 10 years. The move overtly signaled the success of UBS's business strategy to integrate the pieces to create a virtual juggernaut in the financial marketplace.

An important part of the initiative, as most marketers would expect, was the launch of a multimillion-dollar global ad campaign around the theme of "You and Us" heralding the changeover. But just as critical—if less showy— was a simultaneous internal initiative to integrate the new brand throughout the organization. One of the key aspects of the internal initiative was to ensure that employees who interacted with customers (e.g., the financial advisors and money managers) clearly understood the new brand, as these employees were ultimately the front line representatives of the brand.

Thus, UBS launched an all-out internal effort to engage employees and customers directly in the new brand. In the United States, the rebranding meant that the respected PaineWebber brand, which had briefly been renamed after its 2000 acquisition as UBS PaineWebber, would be replaced entirely. After first training members of the organization on the mission, vision, and promise of the emerging UBS brand, a one-month campaign was designed to roll out the official adoption of the UBS name. Every financial advisor, money manager, and financial planner in every office was given one month to contact each client to personally tell them about the change, what it signified, and to thank them for being loyal clients over the years. A check for $500 per broker would be donated to the designated charity of each office that reached 100 percent of its clients.

Not only was more than $4 million donated to various charities, but a wave of fresh cash flowed into UBS, as the initiative to market and reinforce the UBS brand around this direct customer touch point proved out. As Jestyn Thirkell-White of UBS pointed out, "The fact is that in the wealth management business, our financial advisors are the key customer touch point. But the pressure to increase results can easily turn into a focus on bringing in *new* business. Brokers say, 'Why spend more time with one client when it's a numbers game? I need to be spending more time calling *more* people to increase my base!' In fact, UBS's financial advisors found that by spending a little more time with their existing clients, as the campaign showed, they built the brand as standing for something more than just the stereotypical brokerage churning and burning, and increased business levels at the same time."

Much of UBS's internal and external brand building efforts began paying off immediately: In 2004, UBS was ranked, for the first time ever, among the top 50 most powerful brands in the world, according to *BusinessWeek*.

CARRYING THE BRAND BANNER INTERNALLY

The approach taken by UBS as it continued on its path to better integrate its brand and business strategy illustrates an emerging critical tenet among businesses that have—or aspire to have—the strongest and most valuable brands: *An internal culture must first be created that makes upholding the brand and its implicit promises and representations everyone's very raison d'etre.*

It's increasingly understood that brand is about far more than just advertising and logos. It's about the relationship forged between an entity and its products and services—represented by the brand—and customers. How well customers' experiences measure up to what's implicitly and explicitly being promised by the brand shapes their perceptions and creates bonds of loyalty (or not).

Loyalty, of course, is one of many results of building a strong brand that is linked to tangible business benefits. Various studies have shown that in some categories, an increase in customer loyalty of just 2 percent is equivalent to a 10 percent cost-reduction program, while an increase of 5 percent in loyal customers can deliver 95 percent greater profitability over the lifetime of each customer. Moreover, other studies have shown that customers are willing to pay as much as 25 percent more for a brand to which they have loyalty. It all combines to create both top-line and bottom-line business growth.

Building a brand-based culture goes beyond the creation of a short-term buzz to the development of a genuine and ongoing commitment to the organization's brands. The benefits are many:

- Employees are provided a tangible reason to believe in a company, keeping them motivated and energized.
- Employees can see how they fit into the overall plan to deliver the brand vision and promise to customers—and how their efforts affect the fulfillment of business goals.
- Employees develop a high level of pride that is tied to fulfilling the brand's promise.
- Recruitment and retention are strengthened.
- A common focus on the customer and brand heightens a cohesive and productive environment.

Making brand the central focus of the organization helps clarify on-brand and off-brand behaviors and decisions for all employees—whether they're in the field or in the executive suite—which makes it easier to make the right strategic decisions from an overall business perspective. Applying a brand lens to the decision-making process can influence product developers, who might otherwise focus more on making new widgets rather than thinking about what the brand (and therefore its products) promises. For example, as an innovative leader in the mobile phone industry, Nokia's brand has historically dictated that its phone design must be sleek as well as a point of differentiation from competitors. Brand also plays a role with pricing. John Deere has always charged a premium for its farm equipment because its name is commensurate with the product's value and with the brand's promise. Brand also plays into strategic acquisitions, which can help build the value of the brand. An example is FedEx's 2004 acquisition of Kinko's, which was aimed at helping FedEx expand the scope of what its brand stands for in the marketplace.

An internal branding program is also critical for a business's ability to better mine the value of the touch points (or points of customer interaction, such as customer service department) with the brand. Touch points are the interactions where the customer relationship with the brand is either made or broken. And, to a significant extent, that relationship's success is cemented by employees as much as it is by static messaging.

Think about it: During the pre-purchase experience (Figure 12.1), the initial phone call with a customer service representative that gains you more information on a product is just as important as the advertising or sponsorships

Figure 12.1
The Brand Touch Point Wheel

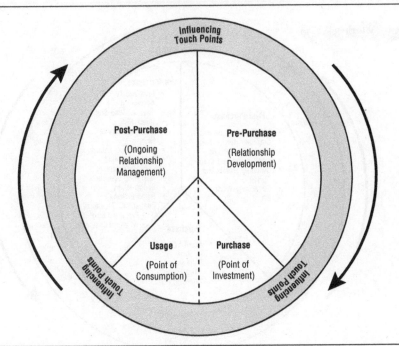

designed to build awareness. During the purchase phase, the politeness, speed, and accuracy of the retail clerk or the know-how and helpfulness of the salesperson are more influential in shaping the customer experience than all the best-designed point-of-purchase displays. And, after the transaction has been completed (when encouraging repeat business is the end goal) the responsiveness of the call center employee to customer questions as well as the timely arrival of polite and efficient technicians are just as integral to cementing loyalty as are frequent buyer programs, user groups, or other value-added services. The Whirlpool example in Figure 12.2 shows the various touch points (both the human touch points as well as the communications touch points) that Whirlpool must manage over time.

Turning your organization into one that is more brand-driven, where the customer focus is embraced by the entire culture, is a process that evolves over time. This chapter is designed to show you the various steps that are required to get started on this path. We begin with the leadership team and specific players who must lead the initiative; then we describe the specific

Figure 12.2
Whirlpool's Touch Point Wheel

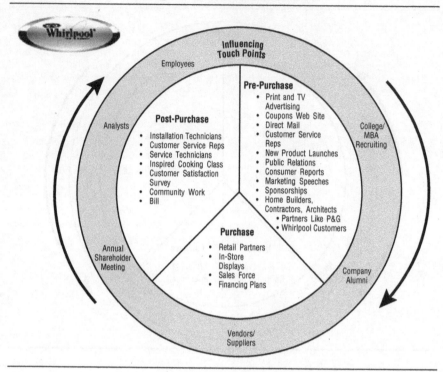

requirements of an assimilation program and the underlying tenets that should be followed to gain the best results; and finally, we discuss the importance of measuring the progress and successes you're achieving along the way. Additionally, we also point out common stumbling blocks and mistakes that can keep your program from achieving the highest level of success.

THE ROLE OF SENIOR MANAGEMENT

Participation at the organization's most senior levels is critical. Organizations that intend to fully reap the benefits of becoming brand-driven need to work to create the internal culture that encourages and supports on-brand behaviors. Like any form of organizational change, affecting it begins at the top and filters down from there. Bringing the brand to life requires key participation from top-level executives, and it also requires marketing to play a leadership role by stepping out of its silo to form teams with various influential nonmarketers in the organization—from operations executives to the human resources decision-makers. And the same focus and consistency that is brought to external branding programs must exist behind the internal branding programs to bring about cultural change.

The process of creating a brand-based culture begins, necessarily, at the top—at what is commonly known in business circles as the *C-Level* (for *chiefs* of units or functions in organization, such as CEO, COO, CFO, etc.). A company's chief executive officer is the company's ultimate brand builder. When you ask CISCO Systems CEO John Chambers who runs the brand there, he is emphatic: "I do!" Consider other great brands and the CEO brand builders behind them: Meg Whitman at eBay, Fred Smith at FedEx, Herb Kelleher at Southwest, Steven Jobs at Apple, Andy Grove at Intel, Jeff Bezos at Amazon, Howard Schultz at Starbucks, Richard Branson at Virgin Records.

None of these individuals came into the job to build a brand; none came from a classical marketing position. Their common ground was the desire to build or strengthen a company and differentiate their organizations from the competition by creating a value proposition that could be delivered consistently and in a customer-centric way.

The CEO ultimately sets the tone, enforces the development of a true brand-based culture, and determines whether the necessary resources to accomplish this goal are registered as investments or expenses. But since the CEO's reach into the organization is necessarily limited, it's also incumbent on him or her to empower other C-level executives as change agents, to ensure that brand-building receives adequate human and financial attention.

The chief operating officer, for example, is an increasingly critical brand enabler; this is the individual who owns the employee base and thus has the ability and credibility to direct employees to bring the company's brand promise to life. By the same token, the chief financial officer has an important role to play: The CFO ultimately holds the purse strings to fund brand building and must understand not just the rationale for brand building, but also the commensurate return on investment.

The chief information officer controls the ability to get the right information and make sure the supporting systems and processes are in place to enable smart, brand-driven decisions. The senior human resources executive is integral, given the cross-functional and company-wide nature of the HR department. This executive is critical for his or her ability to identify and reward those employees who support the brand, to build the brand into recruiting initiatives, and to facilitate the training process throughout the organization.

And, of course, the chief marketing officer has the potential to be the greatest enabler in driving this cultural shift. The most successful companies realize that not only must they create a great brand-driven plan to help guide the company to increased awareness, trial, and penetration, but they must also lead others in the organization to better understand and buy into their roles in the brand's success. This involves framing the conversation in a jargon-free context understood by all (potentially discussing *cultural* practices rather than *branding* approaches) and including others in any rewards and recognitions that come for brand-building successes.

It's essential that all these key players (the C-levels) take active roles in leading the brand-based cultural shift from the top. Without senior-level support and accountability across the organization, the brand strategy will likely be undersupported and assimilation will not take root. The talk must be walked. Take, for example, the seven most senior-level executives of Sheetz, a Pennsylvania-based convenience store chain, who got actively involved in the internal launch of a new brand and business strategy around a new store concept. In a sneak preview to employees, each of the seven dressed up as characters from the movie trilogy "The Matrix." They also embarked on a 26-region roadshow to personally introduce the store concept, "Sheetz Revolutionz," to 3,000 employees. There is no more powerful way to prove to the rest of the organization the executives' investment in the branding process than to have the top seven personally carry the torch on the road.

One way to bring about the requisite level of senior executive involvement is through the formation of executive brand councils (EBCs). The idea behind these councils is to create a team of heads of business units and functional areas that takes on a cross-disciplinary ownership of brand, tackling many of the tough issues that can arise. The charter of EBCs is generally to guide and direct the brand and to manage brand impact. Members' involvement also increases their level of ownership in the assimilation process.

Just as importantly, EBCs are highly visible within the organization. As such, they help send a tangible message that brand management and ownership is an organization-wide responsibility—not just a marketing priority. Serving as a virtual board of directors for the CMO, the responsibilities that fall to these councils vary from organization to organization. Generally, though, they are charged to provide oversight and approval of specific brand-related strategies and changes to policies tied to brand. Typical issues requiring the EBC's involvement can range from company name changes to dealing with rationales and justifications for acquisitions and divestitures of brands to overseeing new creative in support of the brand.

Visa's executive brand council is a great example of a team of executives that represented Visa's major competitive markets and many of its critical functional areas. This team got together several times a year to discuss, debate, and decide on many brand-based issues that impacted the organization at large. These meetings were strategic, anchored around the business strategy, and always focused on what Visa was trying to create with its brand on a global basis.

As important as senior-level involvement is, it's equally important to identify and train key employees from the rank and file who are best suited to becoming individual brand ambassadors. These employees are capable of imbuing the brand mindset through the middle and lower reaches of the organization. Taking their cue from senior executives, these individuals can be a powerful force in teaching and reinforcing the best brand behaviors among their peers. They can provide tremendous day-to-day insight on the brand and lend help to any functional area, creating buy-in and participation around brand-building behaviors. Once the right ambassadors are identified from each functional area of the company, they should be brought together quarterly to provide input and insights on progress of the internal brand-building initiatives.

BUILDING THE BRAND-BASED CULTURE: THE ASSIMILATION PROCESS

When employees inside a business deal with key customers, prospects, or other stakeholders, they gain the best results when they think, speak, and behave in ways that create the kind of customer experience and lasting impact that the brand aspires to deliver. For employees to become passionate brand advocates, they must understand what a brand is, how it is built, what their organization's brand stands for, and what their role is in delivering on the brand promise.

The process starts with the presentation of a compelling argument about the value of brand. The presentation also includes segments that ensure employees understand the impact of the brand and its positioning on their individual activities. This isn't a one-time initiative; the link between the brand and employee behaviors needs to be reinforced consistently over time until employees become passionate advocates of the brand and until the idea of *living* the brand becomes an instinctive mindset (see Figure 12.3). It's a matter of education, leading to inspiration, and finally, execution on a daily basis. Importantly, effecting this sort of shift requires a reevaluation of current systems

Figure 12.3
Brand Assimilation

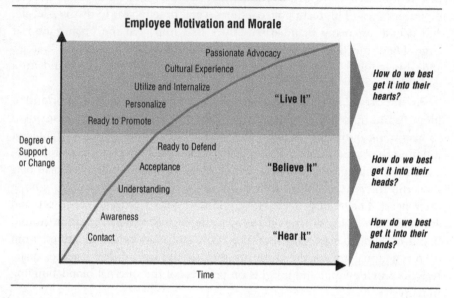

and structures that may present an impediment to success. It also requires development of a brand assimilation plan that is implemented over an 18-month to two-year period, and attention to the tactical components of the plan to ensure it is reinforced over the longer haul.

A key first step is to conduct a strategic, employee-based segmentation (much like you would a customer needs-based segmentation) that will drive the scope, depth, pace, and timing of brand assimilation activities. There are multiple ways to segment your employees. One approach is to segment by an individual's level in the organization; another approach is to segment by the extent to which they interact with customers. Each segment has a different set of expectations from the assimilation initiative and plays different roles in its implementation. The more specific and tailored the behavior-change need is for each segment, the more beneficial it is to call that group out as a separate segment.

Specific types of communications and experiences can be targeted and tailored for each, and timing and intensity is similarly varied. Alternatively, if a company is dealing with limited time and resources, some firms have achieved success in the assimilation process by executing broad education initiatives via existing communication vehicles or meeting schedules.

Employee-based segmentation is valuable for helping to define and prioritize the right brand assimilation programs for your organization and for your employee base. With segmentation understood, a three-phase structured assimilation approach can be put in place.

Phase 1: Strategic Development

During this phase, a brand assimilation framework is designed that ensures key employee segments will buy into, support, and understand the brand strategy and positioning. If an internal cultural identity isn't easily communicated (e.g., in an employee values document), a means for codifying and communicating it should be developed through employee focus groups or interviews. A detailed assimilation roadmap that identifies—by segment—key objectives, messages, vehicles, and timing needs to be developed. In this phase, key managers who can serve as change agents to help champion the initiative are identified as well.

Phase 2: Foundation-Building

This is the stage when much of the heavy lifting occurs, in terms of developing the right brand messages and content within each segment. In order to secure buy-in for the initiative and to increase the understanding of the brand positioning, a series of educational brand workshops needs to be held with the key managers and change agents who have already been identified. At this stage, employees are also encouraged to articulate what brand means for their respective areas. Here, understanding is developed on how employees' behaviors, activities, and mindsets may need to be modified to support the brand moving forward.

Phase 3: Implementation

While the workshops are underway in the foundation-building phase, another team should be working on key communications, events, and other experiences that will be instrumental in supporting the implementation phase company-wide. Here, tactics will be varied, from interactive communication (regional meetings, webcasts, and conference calls) to training and workshops as well as other activities, such as games, contests, and team-building activities.

SIX GUIDING PRINCIPLES

Throughout this three-phased assimilation approach, six underlying principles should be followed to establish and reinforce the desired behaviors, and to ensure that tactics achieve the desired behaviors among employees over the longer term.

Principle 1: Make the Brand Relevant

One of most critical principles is to make sure the brand is relevant to employees. Each employee in each functional group or unit of the company must understand not just what the brand stands for, but how they as individuals can embrace its meaning and represent it publicly. Only employees who understand the brand can help support it and use it to guide decision making. Nordstrom is an excellent case in point: This renowned retailer has traditionally been known for the quality of its shopping experience, which rests on outstanding customer service. Nordstrom shaped the relevance of such brand promises with employees by pioneering a unique policy: Sales associates were given the authority to approve customer purchase exchanges without the store manager's approval. This policy helped employees understand how everyone played a role in shaping the customer experience, and it empowered them to do so.

Brand relevancy can be imparted tactically in a variety of ways—from workshops geared to developing ideal behaviors that are aligned with the brand promise to giving employees (particularly those with direct customer interaction) the ability and tools to solve problems and resolve issues.

Principle 2: Make the Brand Accessible

If employees are to live and breathe the organization's brand, they must be equipped with the information and tools they need to understand it. Giving employees the ability to make brand-supporting decisions means that they must have ready access to answers to questions. Without creating that kind of access, the organization risks creating employees who are disinterested or frustrated with the task. Here's how one of the Big Four accounting firms, Ernst & Young, supported its goal of creating employees who would present a consistent and professional image of the firm: It launched what it called "The Branding Zone," a central, web-based source of information on its branding, marketing, and advertising programs. In addition to other components, the site contained a discussion area where employees could access information on

Ernst & Young's marketing strategy, pose questions to its global branding and marketing team, and offer suggestions. Intranet sites are ideal for this purpose. Brand training tools and toolkits—an elevator pitch (i.e., a two-minute description of what the brand stands for), wallet-sized brand cards that describe key aspects of the brand, training decks, and so on—can also be helpful.

Principle 3: Reinforce the Brand Continuously

For brand to become a cultural underpinning of the organization, employees must be continuously exposed to its meaning, far beyond the initial rollout of the internal branding program. Take Southwest Airlines as an example. In seeking to internally apply the attributes of its brand promise, "A symbol of freedom," Southwest's people (or HR) department teamed with other such departments as public relations and marketing to create an internal branding campaign around employee freedom. As part of the campaign, support was fostered through tactics such as having the carrier's in-house publication highlight employee freedoms, having employees write about how they personally took advantage of freedoms, and renaming the intranet site "Freedom Net."

Newsletters and the intranet can be invaluable communication tools that help keep brand identity elements, successes, and updated information on the brand strategy top-of-mind for employees. Other tactics can include the rollout of such brand-related tools as laminated identity cards and brand trading cards.

Principle 4: Make Brand Education an Ongoing Program

It's particularly important that new employees are grounded in the brand culture and inspired to believe in what the brand represents. Putting these processes in place helps newcomers better understand the brand's role and impact on the business, and it gives them the tools and the frameworks they need for their day-to-day decision-making. Additionally, the investment the company makes in training new employees speaks volumes about its level of commitment to them. Training has always been integral to Ritz-Carlton's emphasis on creating a connection between the internal and external brand. The hotel chain has emphasized training because its top priority was the satisfaction of its guests—and it knew that employees were critical to delivering on that promise. Each new employee went through an intensive orientation called *The Gold Standard,* which was comprised of principles created to support the brand. These brand precepts were reinforced in daily departmental meetings attended by all employees. *The Gold Standard* provided the basis for all ongoing employee training. Not so coincidentally, Ritz-Carlton became a hospitality industry leader in training, providing 120 hours of training per employee per year.

Principle 5: Reward On-Brand Behaviors

An incentive system rewarding employees for exceptional support of the brand strategy should be tied to the rollout of the internal branding program. This not only helps create and maintain excitement in the program, but it underscores, through individual recognition, the kinds of behaviors that need to be supported. Rewards also help demonstrate the organization's commitment to the brand and the program while creating a tangible model that helps employees better understand how they, too, perform on-brand. Continental Airlines created an employee reward program called "Working Together" under its new emphasis of promising on-time service as a key component of its brand promise to customers. Under the program, each employee received $65 for every month that the airline ranked in the top five on the U.S. Department of Transportation's list of on-time airlines. Other programs tied demonstrable support of the brand to annual performance goals for each employee and also offered special initiatives, such as employee-of-the-month recognitions for individuals exhibiting behaviors aligned with the brand strategy.

Principle 6: Align Hiring Practices

Because the success of a brand assimilation program hinges on employees' ability and capacity to embody the brand spirit, it's also important that HR and marketing work together to develop basic screening procedures that ensure new hires will fit with and support the company's brand culture. This can be accomplished through a variety of tactics, starting with the incorporation of the core and extended brand identity elements into the process of evaluating prospective employees. Over time, job descriptions should be rewritten to incorporate these same brand identity traits into the list of expected employee behaviors. Pret A Manger, a London-based chain of sandwich shops, not only revised its screening procedures to reflect desired, on-brand cultural characteristics of prospective employees, but it also revised its hiring policy so that other employees decided whether a store should extend an offer to a candidate. As such, the company only hired 20 percent of all candidates, and it ensured that only those who shared its spirit became part of the team.

MEASURING AND TRACKING PROGRESS

Several years ago, Spokane, Washington–based Itron relaunched its brand, successfully repositioning itself as the leading global solutions provider and source of analytical knowledge for electric, gas, and water usage and delivery information. A brand assimilation program was part of the initiative. Importantly, Itron's leaders realized that without the right internal metrics to measure progress, neither employees nor management would be able to evaluate how well they were progressing on their brand-building activities. Internal and external measurements were put into place.

Internally, Itron understood that rewards needed to be in place for on-brand behaviors, which led to one metric that tied brand-building efforts to profit sharing. Under this metric, employees created a plan for how they would live the brand, essentially setting up a contract with senior management for achieving the goal. At the end of the year, they were evaluated against this contract to determine what level of profit sharing they would receive. Another metric involved regularly measuring employee morale, which was based on the belief that brand-building initiatives should create a positive shift in employees' attitudes about and belief in the company and the brand.

Externally, a variety of gauges were put into place at Itron, ranging from year-end customer satisfaction surveys to tying stock price appreciation to brand-building efforts. Although it's generally difficult to isolate the role of brand in achieving stock price and profitability gain, the company believed that, in its case, there was a cause-and-effect relationship.

The metrics have shown gratifying results at Itron. Internally, the company reported that employee morale and belief in the company continued to reach new highs. Moreover, its stock skyrocketed from $3.70 per share since the rebranding started to over $18.50 per share, while the company's marketing capitalization went from $200 million to $388 million.

Insightful metrics must go beyond the traditional measures of awareness and recall in order to address such issues as price premiums, intent to purchase, and returns on brand investment. These measures are critical to determining the role that brand plays in reaching and supporting the business's long-term, external, or customer-focused goals and objectives.

But it's also important to measure progress of internal branding initiatives in addition to external efforts. In fact, many participants in our best practices study said that brand should drive investment in continuing employee education and training.

Interestingly, when Prophet, a management consultancy that helps clients create and implement integrated business, brand, and marketing programs, surveyed over 100 senior marketing executives and other C-level decision-makers on best practices in branding in the late 1990s, only one-third of the participating companies measured the performance of their brand. Those who don't measure their performance are missing out on reaping the most benefits from their brand strategies.

For those companies that do make the internal investment that's required to truly become—and reap the benefits of—a brand-driven business, there are seven key brand metrics that should be considered when assessing the effectiveness of the brand assimilation program:

1. *Business understanding.* How well employees understand the philosophical and historical underpinnings of the organization, as well as how it makes money, who its customers are, and its current-year financial goals.
2. *Brand understanding.* How well key valued and differentiated elements of the brand are articulated.
3. *Brand influence.* How well the specific ways that employees have an impact on the customer experience are defined, communicated, and upheld.
4. *Brand trust.* A gauge of the trust level that employees have in the company leadership's ability to do the right thing relative to the values of the brand.
5. *Brand credibility.* Measurements that indicate whether employees believe that the company is capable of *delivering* on its promises to customer and employees.
6. *Brand delivery.* Measurements of whether employees believe that the company *fulfills* its promises to customer and employees.
7. *Brand preference, advocacy, and satisfaction.* Measurements that show the extent to which employees prefer to work at the company rather than its competitors and the degree to which they are comfortable referring friends and family to their employer. It is also important to track employee retention and turnover and internal satisfaction relative to the brand assimilation process.

Such findings can be gained through a variety of tactics. Employee focus groups, internal surveys, mentoring, and performance reviews are popular vehicles. Another approach is to set up suggestion boxes—and closely monitor their contents—that allow employees to provide informal feedback. Detailed questionnaires should also be provided at the end of all brand-training sessions.

THE PITFALLS—AND HOW TO AVOID THEM

Working effectively from the inside out ultimately helps all facets of the overall brand-building agenda. The true test of a brand lies less in a successful advertising campaign and more with the customer's direct interaction with the brand and the people representing it. In fact, how well employees fulfill customer expectations *is* the brand's moment of truth. Despite the best intentions, however, programs designed to infuse internal audiences with the brand spirit can often derail.

One of the most common reasons that internal branding programs do not effectively take hold is because they've been rooted in the *broadcast*—the internal communications model. This means that the organization simply launches brand roadshows to get their message out to employees, rather than systematically going about creating real behavioral change. While the brand is defined and communicated under this model, the internal conditions, processes, and resources needed to allow employees to deliver the corresponding experience to customers have not been developed. Additionally, this shortsighted approach underestimates the time that's involved to develop a genuine and ongoing commitment to the brand. It's not all about creating short-term buzz, but instead it's about creating long-lasting brand impressions, perceptions, behaviors, and performance that will ultimately drive top- and bottom-line results.

Failure can also result when the same resources, support, and planning that are devoted to external marketing efforts are not allocated to the internal initiatives. Today's external marketing is all about intricate, segmented, and targeted communications, with considerable care given to global, cultural, and industry nuances that require fine-tuning in marketing and brand strategy. But internal communications around brand tend to remain a blunt instrument. Employees are a different audience than customers, but many of the core external marketing principles hold true in reaching them: audience segmentation, tailored messages, careful timing, multimedia channels, performance incentives, and technology utilization.

Another reason that an internal brand education may fail is the seduction of sexy new ad campaigns, new names, or logos. It's too easy and too common to use the external messaging as primary vehicles for internal brand education, without communicating the implications in terms of employee behaviors that will support the implicit promises of the campaign. This can also prove to be a dangerous path: Particularly in the business-to-business realm, it's the *post-purchase* use and service experience that can make or break a brand (which hinges on the involvement and buy-in of internal employees), not the pre-purchase promises of advertising and imagery.

Another mistake many organizations make is failing to integrate brand-building programs into their other internal initiatives, such as their vision, mission, and culture programs. As a result, employees may well view brand building as yet another flavor-of-the-month initiative. Companies do a disservice to employees by not connecting the dots for them—they must show how the pieces fit together and clarify expectations about what employees should focus on and do.

Finally, many companies have a tendency to overrely on technology as an instrument to disseminate the word about brand-building programs. Intranets and the Web can be powerfully effective tools to communicate brand into the farthest reaches of the company and help to expand brand awareness and understanding. But if the technology is not supported by tools to support the vision or to translate the received knowledge into actionable behavior, then the medium only compounds the problems of the broadcast model of communication.

CONCLUSION

As is obvious throughout this chapter, the degree to which you can expect to achieve external brand success is 100 percent proportional to the degree to which you achieve internal brand success. If employees fully understand what your brand is trying to accomplish, if they understand the required changes in behavior needed to live the brand, and if they embrace it equally in their heads and hearts, then there is a high likelihood that you will achieve your brand goals. Carefully considering, planning, executing, and operationalizing your internal brand assimilation plan will not only guarantee you an employee base of brand ambassadors, but it will most likely guarantee you brand success.

Scott Davis is managing partner of the Chicago office of Prophet, a management consultancy specializing in the integration of brand, business, and marketing strategies. He is author of Brand Asset Management: Driving Profitable Growth Through Your Brands *(Jossey-Bass, 2000) and co-author of* Building the Brand-Driven Business: Operationalize Your Brand to Drive Profitable Growth *(Jossey-Bass, 2002). He received a BS from the University of Illinois and an MBA from the Kellogg School of Management.*

CHAPTER 13

MEASURING BRAND VALUE

DON E. SCHULTZ and HEIDI F. SCHULTZ

There's an old saw that suggests: "If you don't know where you're going, any road will get you there." That old saw rings true for measuring and evaluating brands. While a number of methodologies exist for tracking, measuring, and evaluating brands, they vary widely in purpose, scope, definition, and outcome. The first challenge to measuring and evaluating brands is defining the specific questions: What are we trying to evaluate or measure? What yardstick will we use and for what purpose? Are we attempting to determine the current market value of the brand if we placed it up for sale? Or, are we interested in estimating the firm's financial returns on the investments it makes in the brand? Are we trying to determine the value customers put on the brand, which might influence their future preferences? Or, are we trying to measure or evaluate something else?

Clearly, all these questions (plus many others) could be posed by brand owners at various times. But each measurement methodology serves a different managerial purpose. Some track the brand as it is seen and perceived by the customer or prospect, providing guidance for managing brand communication activities. Others are analytical techniques for establishing and monitoring brand performance in the marketplace. And still others are tools for understanding the brand's contribution to the organization's shareholder value or asset base.

So, the primary questions are: What information is needed; what metrics are required to determine the value or importance of the brand; and what audience(s) will be measured? Until the objectives are clearly defined, brand measurement is like a dog chasing its tail—lots of action and activity but few useful results.

This chapter is devoted to helping managers understand the measurement options available, and more important, helping them learn when, where, and how to apply each to their brand. We sort through the differing views of brand measurement and evaluation and give an overall view of the various ways of assessing the impact of various brand investments. We also identify a variety of measurement approaches, discuss what they can and cannot do, and attempt at the end to suggest some directions for the future of brand evaluation and brand measurement.

THREE PATHWAYS: A CONCEPTUAL MODEL TO PROVIDE A FRAMEWORK

This chapter is based on the Three-Pathway model of brand measurement illustrated in Figure 13.1. The model represents what we consider to be the three primary methods of measuring, tracking, and evaluating brands over time. Each pathway has distinct goals and management information objectives. The challenge, of course, is determining which one to use and for what purpose.

Within each pathway, there are a number of analytical tools and approaches.

Figure 13.1
Three-Pathway Model for Measuring Brands

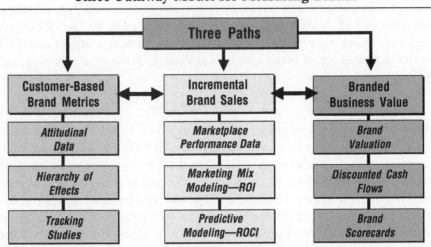

Before getting to these underlying methodologies, however, we briefly describe each pathway below.

Pathway 1: Customer-Based Brand Metrics

Pathway 1 consists of quantitative and qualitative measurement approaches to understanding the consumer's or brand user's awareness, understanding, and relationship with the brand. The most common approach is to measure current brand perceptions, knowledge, and understanding, then track changes over time. These changes are then related to the marketing communication programs conducted on behalf of the brand.[1]

Pathway 2: Incremental Brand Sales

Pathway 2 consists of measuring short-term incremental sales or cash flows generated by the brand. These measures are primarily behavioral, consisting of known past consumer behavior or likely future preferences. In addition, the measures used in Pathway 2 are financially oriented, seeking to identify the incremental financial returns the brand generates as a result of marketing activities and investments.[2]

Pathway 3: Branded Business Value

Pathway 3 measures the financial value of the brand to the firm over the longer-term. These approaches generally treat the brand as an organizational asset in which investments can be made and returns achieved. Typically these measures provide a valuation or appraisal of brand assets for use in mergers and acquisitions, taxation, and licensing. Brand valuation is often conducted at the request of senior management to provide guidance on the strategic use of corporate resources.[3]

★ ★ ★ ★

With this general framework in mind, we can now discuss the various tools and processes found in each of the pathways. It is worth noting that each pathway offers a number of specific methodologies by a variety of vendors, but we won't cover those in much detail—the goal of this chapter is to provide a general overview. Thus, the examples are not intended as a set of detailed instructions or an endorsement for any particular provider. Instead, we illustrate what can be measured under each pathway, how the research is most often conducted, and how the results can be best applied.

PATHWAY 1: CUSTOMER-BASED BRAND METRICS

The measures used in Pathway 1 are generally designed to identify the awareness, attitudes, preferences, likes, dislikes, and other perceptions that consumers hold about the brand and its value to them. The first pathway is the most closely related to traditional marketing, advertising, and communication measurement techniques, and thus it is generally the most widely used.

The brand measurement methodologies used in this pathway have their roots in traditional marketing and communication tracking systems. These tools have been adapted almost directly from various consumer behavior and mass communication concepts developed over the past century or so. Therefore, in many cases, their popularity stems as much from the fact that brand, marketing, and communication managers are familiar with the techniques as it does from their capability to provide the answers to brand measurement requirements.

The Underlying Premises of Pathway 1

The measurement approaches used in Pathway 1 stem from the marketing philosophy that attitudes, opinions, and beliefs drive consumer brand behaviors. Thus, if the consumer or prospect holds certain marketer-generated *right* attitudes and beliefs about the brand, they will most likely behave in the *right way* toward the brand. Likewise, if the consumer's attitudes, opinions, and beliefs about the brand are not positive, they will likely purchase or use a competitive brand. Thus, the principal question underlying Pathway 1 is whether the marketing organization has successfully created, reinforced, or changed the attitudes, opinions, and beliefs of its consumers and prospects.

Much of the support for this approach stems from the development of what is now called the Hierarchy of Effects model developed by Lavidge and Steiner[4] and simultaneously by Colley[5] in the early 1960s. These individuals hypothesized that consumers move through a measurable, linear attitudinal development process on the way to making a purchasing decision. Thus, by asking customers about various levels of awareness, knowledge, preference, and conviction, the advertiser can measure the impact of communication activities in moving prospects along a continuum toward eventual purchase behavior. The Hierarchy of Effects model has been used to explain and illustrate the impact and marketplace effects of advertising for nearly 50 years. More recently, it has been widely adapted for use in brand measurement, and in one fashion or another, it underlies many of the brand tracking systems in place today.

Beginning in the mid-1980s, financial and marketing managers became interested in the future earning power of the brand. That is, the recognition that a brand, if properly managed, could create future value and income flows for the firm. By the early 1990s, David Aaker[6] and later Kevin Lane Keller[7] began to develop their concepts of brand equity. Aaker published his first book titled *Managing Brand Equity*[8] in 1991, and Keller followed with a more extensive treatment of the subject with his *Strategic Brand Management*[9] text in 1998. In it he included a specific definition of brand equity as seen from the customer's point of view—what he calls *customer-based brand equity:*

> Customer-based brand equity is the differential effect brand knowledge has on the customer response to the marketing of that brand. Equity occurs when the consumer has a high level of awareness and familiarity with the brand and holds some strong, favorable, and unique brand associations in memory.[10]

The basic premise that underlies this view is that the consumer determines and drives the value of the brand. That is, the consumer essentially creates an image of the brand on a personal level, based on the way he or she takes in, assembles, and retains information about the brand. Therefore, to determine the level of *consumer equity,* or value of the relationship, the marketer must measure the attitudes, opinions, and beliefs the consumer has attached to the brand over time.

Keller's underlying assumption is that if *strong, favorable, and unique* associations about the brand are held by the consumer, those associations will at some point lead to favorable customer behavior toward that brand (i.e., purchase, trial, continued use, etc.). However, as we will see, most Pathway 1 measurement approaches stop short of actually linking changes in attitudes to changes in behaviors.

Current Status of Customer-Based Brand Equity Measures

In response to the growing interest in brands, a number of approaches have been developed to understand, measure, and track customer attitudes over time. Many major advertising agencies and market research companies have developed a proprietary model or methodology. Some of the more widely accepted are Millward Brown's "BrandDynamics,"[11] the Y&R "Brand Asset

Valuator,"[12] and the Taylor Nelson Sofres approach, licensed from Hofmeyr, which is called the "Conversion Model."[13] However, there are a multitude of other research options in this pathway. They range from the quantitative survey methods designed to statistically identify levels of awareness, preference, product usage, satisfaction, and acceptance to the more qualitative methodologies such as focus groups and in-depth interviews, which attempt to identify consumers' impressions, feelings, and perceptions.

Generally speaking, most of the approaches used are based on defining and tracking levels of awareness, familiarity, and attitudinal change over time. While there are differences in nomenclature, methodologies, and output, all have a common goal of measuring changes in consumer attitudes, opinions, and beliefs that result from brand communication programs. To illustrate the methodologies under this pathway, we will explore the Millward Brown BrandDynamics method as just one example of the type of information services available in Pathway 1.

The Brand Dynamics Model

As shown in Figure 13.2, the BrandDynamics model is based on a hierarchal methodology designed to measure consumer attitudes, opinions, and beliefs about the brand. Consumers or prospects are surveyed and asked such questions as: "Do you know about the brand?" "Does it offer you something?" This approach defines five levels of relationship with the brand, each believed to depict a stronger connection between the consumer and the brand: Presence, Relevance, Performance, Advantage, and Bonding, with Bonding being the most powerful relationship of all.

By measuring consumer attitudes over time using the BrandDynamics methodology, the marketer can see changes in the relationship between the customer and the brand, and he or she can trace those changes to various marketing and communication activities. The example in Figure 13.3 illustrates the net change in scores on each level for a brand measured at two points in time.[14]

As shown in the example, the levels of Presence, Relevance, and Performance have increased while the measures of brand Advantage and Bonding have declined. This result might occur if a brand has been heavily advertised and promoted, but evidently in a way that has managed to alienate some previously loyal (Bonded) customers.

Additionally, BrandDynamics compares the marketer's brand with those of competitors to provide a comparison of consumer perceptions of all alternatives in the category. This type of brand information can be invaluable to

Figure 13.2
BrandDynamics

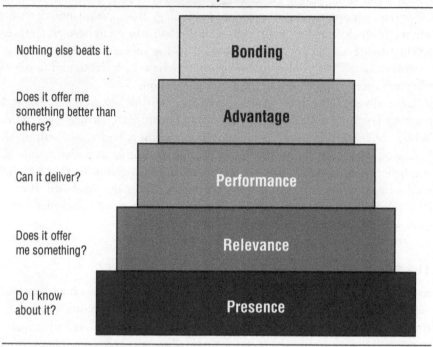

Nothing else beats it. — **Bonding**

Does it offer me something better than others? — **Advantage**

Can it deliver? — **Performance**

Does it offer me something? — **Relevance**

Do I know about it? — **Presence**

Source: Millward Brown.

the marketer in terms of adjusting and adapting brand marketplace activities, including communication and messaging. Indeed, the greatest value of this type of brand measurement or valuation generally occurs within this marketing task.

The usefulness of the BrandDynamics approach is that the marketing organization can see where the brand is improving and where it is declining. Those measures are intended to provide guidance to the brand manager in where to change, adapt, or enhance brand positioning, messaging, and marketing efforts.

While we have used the Millward Brown BrandDynamics approach as one example of a Pathway 1 methodology, many other approaches fall in this category. In addition to the awareness, perception, and preference research mentioned earlier, other relevant customer-based brand metrics within Pathway 1 include methods to identify and track customer value drivers, customer satisfaction, and customer perceptions of quality.

Figure 13.3
BrandDynamics

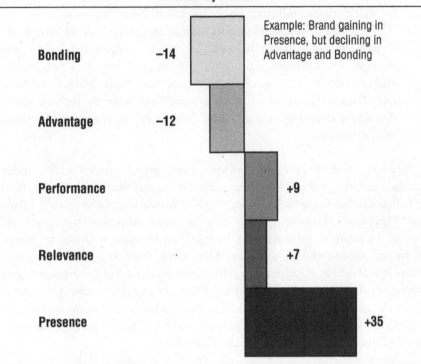

Bonding	–14	Example: Brand gaining in Presence, but declining in Advantage and Bonding
Advantage	–12	
Performance	+9	
Relevance	+7	
Presence	+35	

Source: Millward Brown.

Summary of Pathway 1: The Three Pillars of Customer-Based Brand Metrics

To summarize Pathway 1, most methodologies are focused on three pillars of customer-based brand metrics:

1. The Pathway 1 measurement approaches are based on this assumption: Consumers create brand equity for themselves based on the attitudes, opinions, and beliefs they create about the brand for themselves over time. In this view, the development of brand equity occurs as a result of the observations, exposures, and other brand experiences developed and communicated by the marketing organization. Thus, the marketing organization can, through its messaging and marketing activities, directly impact the level, type, and strength of brand associations held by the consumer.

2. The Pathway 1 measurement approaches assume that strong feelings or associations with the brand will, at some point, result in positive brand behaviors, that is, purchase, repurchase, switching, and so on.

3. The Pathway 1 approaches also assume marketers can determine the impact of their marketing communication programs by measuring changes in consumer attitudes, opinions, and beliefs. Thus, positive changes can be determined, and in some way these changes can be related back to the activities of the organization, based on the assumption that those organizational activities contributed to the positive changes that occurred.

Inherent in these types of customer-based brand metrics is the understanding that the changes that have occurred in consumer attitudes, opinions, or beliefs can be quantified in some way. The primary problem with the Pathway 1 measures, however, is that they generally stop short of connecting changes in awareness and attitudes to attendant changes in consumer behavior or any resulting financial impact. Thus, while the first pathway does what it says it will do (track changes in customer awareness and perceptions), great difficulty often arises in relating those measures to what consumers actually do in the marketplace. The solution to this problem is commonly found in Pathway 2, which measures incremental product sales and income flows as a result of marketing and communication activities.

PATHWAY 2: INCREMENTAL BRAND SALES

Pathway 2 is focused on identifying the short-term incremental financial value, generally increased sales volume, premium pricing, or other outcomes that can be attributed to brand activities. The measurable impacts are commonly related to how those activities influenced the brand's demand. Obviously, this pathway is heavily focused on the economic and financial aspects of brand management and measurement, as opposed to the attitudinal orientation of Pathway 1.

In this section we will focus on the two basic methodologies in Pathway 2. While both are focused on determining the financial impact of branding investments, the time frame in which the measurement is conducted separates them:

1. *Marketing mix modeling* is used to determine historical brand return on investment (ROI). These measures help a firm determine the extent to

which different activities (advertising, promotion, special events, etc.) impact sales volume, revenues, and profits over time.

2. *Predictive modeling* forecasts potential returns on future branding activities. These tools project the likely impact branding activities may have in the near term, usually the current fiscal year. Typically, predictive methods rely on forecasts of what specific customers or groups of customers might do in the future.

The primary difference between determining historical brand investment returns (marketing mix modeling) and predicting future returns (predictive modeling) is this: In historical analysis, understanding the customers who created the returns is not a critical issue—it is the aggregated marketing activities that are relevant. By contrast, in predictive modeling, the primary concern is more often about which customers are the most valuable or the most likely to respond, which can be used to forecast future returns.

Thus, in marketing mix modeling, the brand owner is interested in learning the impact and effect of the various brand marketing tools employed in the marketplace, regardless of which customers responded. Predictive modeling, however, focuses on the customers who will likely respond and the level of response that might be expected.

Marketing Mix Modeling

Marketing mix modeling is a statistical technique that enables the brand owner to determine the incremental financial returns generated as a result of brand investments in certain marketing activities made over a given set of time periods in the past.[15] Since the methodology is somewhat complex, in this section we will focus our discussion on the managerial aspects of the approach, not on the specific techniques used. One excellent source that is not overly technical is the web site www.santella.com/marketing.htm.[16]

The general purpose of marketing mix modeling is to separate or parse out base brand sales from actual measured sales, generally through the use of correlation analysis and various types of regression equations. The goal is to isolate the base sales that likely would have occurred had brand promotion activities not been used and to set those apart from the overall returns that were actually recorded. In this way, the brand manager can understand the incremental bump, or increase in sales, generated by the various marketing activities used during the period.

The analyst initially inputs the historical brand sales data for a certain period of time, typically monthly or weekly data for the past two to three years. Then, the analyst inputs investments made in brand marketing or promotional activities during the same period, recording as much detail as possible regarding the timing and level of expenditures. At this stage, the raw data are adjusted to control for variations such as seasonality, unit pricing, and similar factors that could otherwise distort the outcome.

The analyst then creates a baseline of the brand's sales for the period analyzed. This is done by iteratively correlating brand sales and marketing investments during the relevant time frame to find the best data fit. The result is a base dollars estimate of the sales volume that would have been likely had no marketing activity been employed during the period. This baseline is then subtracted from the total sales to isolate the *incremental volume,* usually dollars, that can be attributed to the various marketing activities. A simplified example is illustrated in Figure 13.4.

In most cases, however, the brand owner is commonly employing more than one brand building activity at a time (i.e., television advertising plus radio plus magazines plus sales promotion). In such cases, the brand owner generally wants to know the specific impact of each activity. Through another statistical technique—generally some form of multiple regression analysis—the analyst can determine the approximate impact of each marketing investment. An example of this type of outcome is illustrated in Figure 13.5, where

Figure 13.4
Parsing Out Incremental Returns from Base Sales

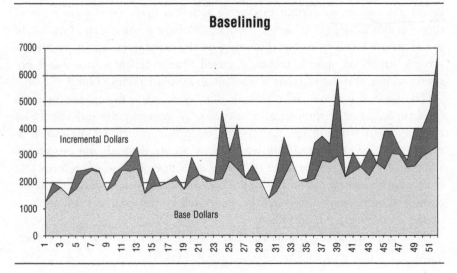

Figure 13.5
Measuring Media and Promotion Impact (*Retail Example*)

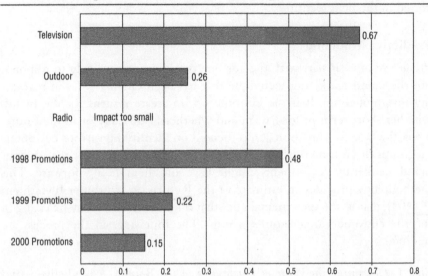

the relative impacts of television advertising, radio advertising, and various annual sales promotion activities have been estimated. In Figure 13.5, a regional retailer sees that television advertising had about three times the impact of the investments made in outdoor advertising. In addition, the results show that negligible returns were received from radio advertising. The chart also illustrates the impact of the various brand promotions over the same period, with the 1998 program generating the greatest returns.

While marketing mix modeling represents a backward-looking analysis of historical data, it can be quite useful in understanding which activities produced returns and which did not. Thus, many marketers have found marketing mix modeling to be quite helpful in identifying ROI on previous investments. For this reason, it is one of the most widely used analytical tools employed by brand marketers, particularly among consumer product companies.

Yet, in spite of its popularity and widespread use, marketing mix modeling has definite limitations. Most importantly, it is a historical analysis of what has happened, not what might happen. Marketers generally want to predict what might occur in the future, particularly in the short-term future (often the coming fiscal year). To determine these predictions, the second technique in Pathway 2 is used: an estimate of future returns using a technique called Return-on-Customer-Investment (ROCI) analysis . This is discussed in the next section.

Predictive Modeling

Predictive models start with the customers who are most likely to respond, not the brand marketing technique that has been employed (as in marketing mix modeling). It is the customers who create returns for the brand, whether short term or long term and whether historically or in the future. Thus, the base for this approach is focused on identifying various customers or groups of customers, then estimating the impact and effect that various brand marketing investments might have on them going forward. This methodology provides an estimate of the Return on Customer Investment (ROCI), that is, the incremental sales that might be achieved by investing in specific customers or customer groups. The four steps in the process are outlined here.

Step 1: Determine the Value of Customers to the Brand A predictive brand return model starts with the customers or prospects the brand owner knows or believes will respond to the planned program. The goal is to determine the level of Customer-Brand Value (CBV—the economic value a customer represents to the brand being developed). This estimate takes the form of the financial returns the program is estimated to generate in the future. One such approach is based on the formula:

$$CBV = P \times BR \times SOP \times M$$

where:

CBV = Customer-Brand Value

P = Penetration (i.e., percent of the marketer's brand users compared to overall number of users in the category)

BR = Buying rate (i.e., the average number of units per customer being bought in the product category on an annual or other periodic basis)

SOP = Share of purchase (i.e., the percentage of purchases the brand achieves among its customers versus competitors) (Note: This is not the same as share of market, but rather looks only at the behavior of the brand's existing customers and the proportion of purchases they direct to the brand.)

M = Margin (i.e., the brand's gross contribution margin)

By determining the number of customers who buy the brand, multiplying the number of units the average customer purchases by the contribution "Margin" (M) of the brand, an estimate can be derived of the approximate value of an average customer or what we call the Customer-Brand Value (CBV).

Step 2: *Aggregate Customers by Value or Objective* If the marketer has some knowledge of individual customers, it quickly becomes apparent that some customers are more valuable than others. Thus, the second step in this methodology is to aggregate customers in some way by value or by potential behavior.

If the aggregation is done by customer value, a common strategy is to use a ranking technique such as quintile or decile analysis. This methodology sorts all customers in descending order based on their value to the brand as determined in step 1. The marketer typically discovers that a relatively small number of customers account for a disproportionately large percentage of the brand's total volume or profits (the 80/20 Rule). This is often a critical element in understanding the value of customers to the brand and their potential for future response.

An alternative approach is to aggregate customers on the basis of the goals established by the marketer (i.e., customer acquisition, retention, migration, and so on). By estimating the value of customers within each of these groups, the total potential financial value of the various customer groups can be determined. This provides another effective way to quantify the brand marketer's objectives and provides a yardstick for estimating the potential returns that might be obtained from various brand marketing activities. This approach can be a useful tool for defining which customer groups the brand should pursue and in which groups marketing investments should be made.

Step 3: *Employ a Closed-Loop Brand Investment Process* The *closed-loop* brand investment process enables the marketer to clearly determine the impact of brand marketing programs on specific groups of customers. For example, if the marketer knows the value of a group of customers from the analysis discussed previously, then relevant investment decisions can be made. The closed-loop process (Figure 13.6) allows the manager to relate marketing investments to measurable changes in customer behavior and relate financial investments to financial returns.

The importance of the closed-loop process is that it uses a financial yardstick to measure both the inputs to the marketing program as well as the measurable changes in customer behavior. Thus, the marketer obtains a

Figure 13.6
Closed Loop Investment System

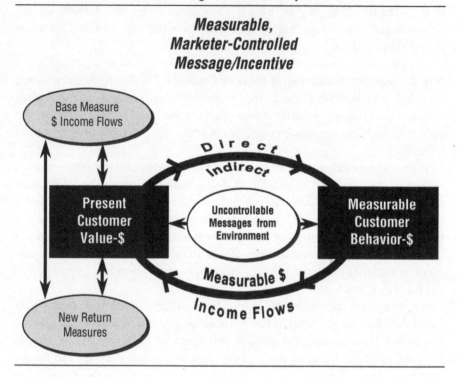

Measurable, Marketer-Controlled Message/Incentive

Base Measure $ Income Flows

Direct

Indirect

Present Customer Value-$

Uncontrollable Messages from Environment

Measurable Customer Behavior-$

Measurable $ Income Flows

New Return Measures

reasonable indication of what level of investment could or should be made against specific customers or prospects, and has some expectation of the potential return on investments made in those groups. This calculation, obviously, is critical to the entire measurement process.

Step 4: Develop a Probability Model   In the final step in an ROCI analysis, marketers use the information in the earlier steps to develop a probability model to estimate the future value of a customer or group of customers. There are a number of ways to develop this forecast, ranging from predictive modeling to the use of Markov chains, a statistical technique used to predict future results when currents results are known. Once the customer value is known, the model can be further adjusted to determine the probability of the customer responding to the brand's marketing programs as well. Thus, using historical data, we can create a forward-looking probablility model that can be used as the basis for investment decisions or can be used as the calculus for estimating returns on future brand investments.

One simple example of such a predictive model is shown in the Return-on-Customer-Investment chart in Figure 13.7. In this example, customers have been aggregated based on their past behaviors (i.e., Present Customers, Competitive Users, and New and Emerging Customers). The ROCI process is simply a scenario-modeling approach containing some basic, underlying response estimates as the model drivers. Using this methodology, the analyst can develop various investment scenarios against various customer segments and play what-if games to determine the best brand investment strategy.

Clearly, the assumptions underlying the ROCI methodology are critical, but they can be easily adjusted if the brand marketer has additional research

Figure 13.7
Basic ROCI Process

	Present Users	Competitive Users	New and Emerging Users
1 Present Income Flow in Category	$	$	$
2 Share of Requirements	%	%	%
3 Customer Income Flow to Brand	$	$	$
4 Contribution Margin %	%	%	%
5 Contribution Margin $	$	$	$
6 Income Flow without a Brand Communication Program	$	$	$
7 Contribution Margin without a Brand Communication Program	$	$	$
8 Income Flow with a Brand Communication Program	$	$	$
9 Gross Contribution Margin with a Brand Communication Program	$	$	$
10 Brand Communication Investment	$	$	$
11 Net Contribution Margin	$	$	$
12 Difference in Contribution Margins with and without Brand Communication	$	$	$
13 Incremental Gain or Loss	$	$	$
14 Return on Investment	%	%	%

or analytical data. The ROCI approach enables the brand manager to estimate future returns that might accrue to the brand if certain decisions were made and certain brand marketing programs were implemented.

Summary of Pathway 2

The two approaches presented for Pathway 2 (marketing mix modeling and the predictive ROCI approach) are fairly well established in the research community. In addition, there are a number of other methodologies available in the marketplace. For the most part, however, they are based on some adaptation of one of these two primary approaches.

Great strides have been made in the methodologies of Pathway 2. That said, however, there is still much work to be done on using historical performance and predictive forecasting. The data necessary for the calculations are sometimes difficult to obtain. Additionally, a dynamic marketplace does not always perform or react as it has in the past, since it is dynamic and continuously changing. Thus, variations in results may occur that cannot be fully explained. And, finally, all these methodologies rely to a great extent on management judgment, statistical techniques, and various subjective decisions. So, while the tools do provide useful and usable answers to the questions of brand measurement, they are subject to the same challenges of any business decision.

The primary challenge of the methodologies used in Pathway 2 is that they are all short-term measures of the returns on marketing investments. That is, most identify only the results of certain periods in the brand's history or predict returns for only a limited future time. So, while these measurements have great value, they are limited when it comes to understanding the total financial value of the brand. To fully understand that, it is necessary to view the brand as a corporate asset. Pathway 3 illustrates that view.

PATHWAY 3: BRANDED BUSINESS VALUE

In the previous two pathways, the goal was to measure the impact of specific, identifiable investments in the brand and the results those investments might generate (i.e., measures of the short-term returns on brand investments). Thus, Pathways 1 and 2 are essentially tools for judging the effectiveness of various brand and communication strategies and tactics.

The goal in Pathway 3, however, is to understand the brand as a separable, organizational asset—that is, to understand the economic worth of the brand to its owner. This economic worth is calculated using one or more methods of brand valuation discussed later in this section. However, this calculation is not a defined statistical process, such as the marketing mix and predictive modeling approaches discussed earlier. Instead, it is a process based on combining hard financial data, market research, industry benchmarks, and generally accepted accounting principles to arrive at an estimated valuation for a brand under a given set of assumptions.

Why Brand Valuations Are Conducted

The practice of brand valuation has existed for many years, although only recently has the practice gained increased senior management attention and visibility. For many years, brand valuation was done primarily for technical or financial purposes and typically was somewhat distanced from the marketing function. The most obvious instance of this traditional approach is valuation done to arrive at a purchase price at the time a brand is sold or acquired. However, brand valuation also occurs in a range of other circumstances, such as litigation, trademark defense, financing, licensing, tax planning, and so on.

In the past few years, changes in U.S. and international accounting rules have brought the question of brand valuation to the forefront. With recently adopted Financial Accounting Standard Board guidelines now in place, particularly FASB 141 and others, U.S. practices have been brought in line with international practices concerning the acquisition of intangible assets (i.e., the difference between the actual purchase price for a business and the total of its tangible assets such as cash, inventory, plant fixtures, and so on). Beginning in March 2004, based on international accounting standards, U.S. companies were required to begin recording all identifiable intangible assets of an acquired business at fair value, rather than lumping everything under a single goodwill figure as in the past.

Brands are often a significant portion of acquired intangible assets, and this rule required that the value of the brand be recorded and reported on the balance sheet separate from the other intangible assets acquired, such as patents, copyrights, customer lists, licensing agreements, and so on.[17]

But beyond accounting rules, and perhaps even more importantly, there is another reason for conducting a valuation of the brand: to improve the long-range management of the brand and to provide a framework for determining and measuring increases (or decreases) in brand asset value over time. In this view, the estimated value of the brand at any point serves as a basis for judging how well a brand is being managed as a key strategic asset. This shifts the focus away from the traditional cost-oriented view of marketing as a series of expenditures in advertising, sales promotion, events and the like to an emphasis on how the organization can optimally invest in and increase brand asset value, and thus, shareholder value over time.

This managerial view of brand valuation will be the primary focus of our discussion of Pathway 3. The legal, technical, and financial details of valuation can become quite complex; thus we will attempt only to provide a general overview of the process behind the valuation systems most often used for managerial purposes.

As will be seen, brand valuation is not something that can generally be done by nonfinancial managers. It requires substantial accounting and financial experience, as well as an understanding of the applicable tax laws. Thus, brand valuations are most often conducted by specialized external consulting companies such Interbrand, Brand Finance, FutureBrand, or a number of management consulting and accounting firms. While each may have developed proprietary tools and methods, the approaches are fundamentally similar, since they generally must be able to withstand scrutiny from external bodies such as the courts, tax bureaus, the SEC, and the like. For purposes of illustrating the basic logic and issues in brand valuation, we utilize the approaches and terms used by Brand Finance, a London-based brand valuation provider.

What Is Being Valued?

The first step in any valuation approach is to define precisely what is being valued. There are essentially three levels of valuation:[18]

1. *Trademark valuation.* This valuation focuses on appraising the value of a specific trademark, name, logo, or other identifying element. This is the most basic definition of a brand and the narrowest view of valuation. For example, such a valuation might look at the value of the trademark for purposes such as tax planning, licensing, or entering into a joint venture where the trademark will be used by a strategic partner.

2. *Brand valuation.* This valuation expands the work to encompass broader range of intellectual property rights and identifying elements of the brand, such as design rights, domain names, trade dress, packaging, copyrights, and secondary elements such as colors, smells, sounds, advertising materials, and so on.

3. *Branded business valuation.* This valuation is a corporate or organizational brand and includes not just the trademarks, names, logos and so on, but also the culture, people, and programs that combine to create the brand

experience for customers. Typically, this level of valuation is more reflective of the totality of the brand than an analysis conducted only on the outward identifying elements.

From legal, technical, and financial standpoints, all three levels of valuation are important and useful in a wide range of circumstances. However, to address the strategic and marketing issues of this chapter, branded business value is generally more relevant and aligned to the management goal of enhancing total shareholder value. Thus, our focus will be primarily on conducting branded business valuations.

A General Model for Brand Valuation

The general Brand Finance model for brand valuation (Figure 13.8) is based on the idea that the financial value of the brand is a function of the level of profitable earnings it will provide over some future time period. Thus, the process of brand valuation essentially determines the portion of earnings attributable to the brand and the likelihood those earnings will continue into

Figure 13.8
A General Model for Brand Valuation

1. Financial Forecasts   2. BVA—the Brand's Contribution to Demand   3. Risks Attached to Future Earnings

Financial Data   Market Data   Demand Drivers   Risk Factors

Brand Forecasts

Economic Value Added

Brand Value Added BVA® Index   BrandßSeta® Analysis

Brand Value Added

Brand Value   Discount Rate

4. Valuation and Sensitivity Analysis

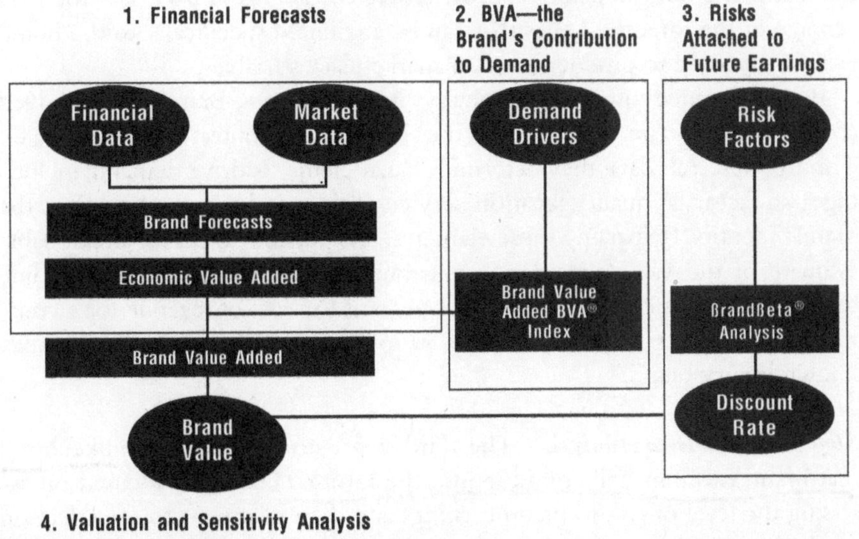

Source: Brand Finance plc.

the future, and then calculates the discounted cash-flow value of those brand earnings over some future period of time, generally five years.

There are four steps in the Brand Finance methodology. From these four steps, the brand manager or owner should have a working understanding of the overall process.

Step 1: Financial Forecasts   The first step is to review the brand's historical financial performance, typically for the previous three to five years, and to include the firm's forecasts of its future volume, revenues, costs, and profitability, also generally five years into the future. Additionally, the relevant market data are taken under consideration to assess overall category trends, the brand's strength relative to competitors, the levels of customer awareness and preferences, and so on. At this stage, an analysis is usually conducted to determine the relevant business or customer segments, since commonly the brand has a greater role as a driver of purchase behavior in some segments than in others.

Step 2: Brand Value Added (BVA)—the Brand's Contribution to Demand
While the total earnings of the product or unit are important, the primary valuation goal is to determine what portion of those estimated earnings can be attributed to the brand. Thus, the second step is to separate out the contribution to the forecasted sales that the brand is expected to contribute. Similar to the determination of the base and incremental sales estimates we saw in the marketing mix modeling approach, here the goal is to parse out the percentage of the forecasted sales that can be attributed specifically to the brand itself, as opposed to product or other marketplace variables.

Brand Finance uses a proprietary methodology—Brand Value Added (BVA)—to estimate how much the brand contributes to overall sales. Through research data, they determine what elements drive demand, including such factors as quality, location, service, variety, and so forth, as well as the brand's identity. By parsing those elements, it is possible to derive a reasonable estimate of the value the brand contributes to the estimated product line earnings. This value can be as low as 1 percent (or less) of revenue for a commoditized, industrialized product, or 50 to 70 percent (or more) for a well-known luxury brand.

Step 3: Brand Beta Analysis   The third step is to determine the likelihood that brand earnings will continue into the future. This step is focused on assessing the level of risk to brand earnings and then relating it to the selection of an appropriate discount rate.

Brand Finance relies on another proprietary model, the Brand Beta Analysis, to assess earnings risk. This analysis is conducted by identifying a range of factors that could influence future performance, then assessing and scoring the brand in the context of its competitive set. Such an analysis typically includes factors such as distribution, yield, market share, and position as well as other drivers of brand demand. The goal of the Brand Beta assessment is to compare the brand against its competitors. Once these factors have been scored, they are applied against the forecasted sales to provide the appropriate discount rate to be used in determining future brand earnings.

Step 4: Application of Discount Rate and Estimation of Brand Value The final step in the process is to develop a long-term estimate of projected brand earnings using a net present value calculation, as shown in the simplified durables product example in Figure 13.9.

Figure 13.9
Durables Example (Simplified)

Discounted Future Earnings Method		Year 0	Year 1	Year 2	Year 3	Year 4	Year 5
Net Sales		500	520	550	580	620	650
Operating Earnings	a	75.0	78.0	82.5	87.0	93.0	97.5
Tangible Capital Employed		250	260	275	290	310	325
Charge for Capital @ 5%	b	12.5	13.0	13.8	14.5	15.5	16.3
Intangible Earnings	c	62.5	65.0	68.8	72.5	77.5	81.3
Brand Earnings @ 25%	d	15.6	16.3	17.2	18.1	19.4	20.3
Tax Rate		33%	33%	33%	33%	33%	33%
Tax		5.2	5.4	5.7	6.0	6.4	6.7
Post Tax Brand Earnings	e	10.5	10.9	11.5	12.1	13.0	13.6
Discount Rate		15%					
Discount Factor	f	1.0	1.15	1.32	1.52	1.75	2.01
Discounted Brand Earning	g	10.5	9.5	8.7	8.0	7.4	6.8
Value to Year 5	h	**50.8**					
Annuity	i	**45.1**					
Growth 0%							
Brand Value		**95.9**					

Source: Brand Finance plc.

The methodology used to develop this long-term estimate is called the economic value calculation of the brand. It is an estimate of what the brand might earn, and therefore it is an estimate of a brand's value to an organization that wishes to buy or sell the brand.

As can be seen in Figure 13.9, the future estimated sales and earnings for the next five years in this product example make up the base of the model. The brand is estimated to generate $75 in earnings in the base year, growing to $97.5 in year 5.

From the figure, we see that the organization has $250 employed in tangible capital to support the brand. A charge for capital is made by the firm to the brand at a rate of 5 percent per annum. That charge is deducted from the estimated earnings each year.

The intangible earnings of $62.5 provides the base for the balance of the analysis. In this particular example, the Brand Value Added assessment indicated that 25 percent of the brand's intangible earnings could be attributed specifically to the brand, separate from the other elements of the offering. As shown, that amounts to $15.6 in the base year, growing to $20.3 in year 5.

Clearly, earnings from the brand are liable for taxes. Those taxes are estimated at the rate of 33 percent per year, which are deducted from the brand earnings. As a result, the post-tax earnings are calculated to be $10.5 in the base year, growing to $13.6 in year 5.

The only remaining calculation is to apply the discount factor to the post-tax earnings. From the Brand Value Added calculation, this discount factor has been determined to be 15 percent. In other words, the post-tax earnings estimated for the brand will be discounted by 15 percent each year on an accumulated basis to account for the time value of money. Thus, the discount factor is 1.15 in year 1, growing to 2.01 percent in year 5. Those figures are then applied to the post-tax brand earnings. The figures then show a discounted cash flow of $9.5 in year 1, declining to $6.8 in year 5.

The final step is to aggregate the discounted cash flow for the brand for the five-year analysis period. When combined, the total is $50.8. Since the estimate has been developed only for the next five years, it is necessary to add what is called the *annuity factor*. This is a financial estimate of what the brand would likely earn if the estimate were taken to perpetuity. In this case, that amount would be $45.1. When that amount is added to the five-year estimate, a total estimated brand value of $95.9 is determined to be the value of the brand at that point in time.

There are, of course, other ways to arrive at a brand valuation estimate. For example, it might be possible to add up all the investments made in the brand since its inception and determine an investment value. Or, it also might be possible to estimate what the cost of replicating the brand might be given current economic conditions. Both of these methods, while having obvious flaws, are often used by the courts and tax authorities as an objective point of reference, even when more sophisticated—and subjective—valuation approaches have been developed.

The most common alternative method, however, is called the *royalty relief* method. The premise for the royalty relief calculation is simply this: If the brand owner did not own the brand, the firm would likely have to either pay a franchise fee or a royalty rate to the brand owner to use the brand in the marketplace. Thus, royalty relief is simply the value of the brand to the company that owns the brand, which is then relieved from paying the royalty rate or franchise fees to another brand owner going forward.

Having explained the general method by which brand valuations are conducted, the question now becomes: What is the corporate value of knowing that the brand has a certain economic value?

Now That We Know the Brand Value, What Do We Know?

Clearly, if the brand owner is planning to buy or sell the brand, the knowledge of the brand's value is important. But, if the brand is being managed for growth and profit, what then is the importance of a brand valuation, especially given the high cost and labor-intensive nature of most valuation projects? There are, in fact, several benefits of brand evaluation for the brand owner:

- Knowing the financial value of the brand allows management to compare it against other tangible and intangible assets and consider how best to apply finite resources to create additional value. Typically, the brand is one of the most valuable assets the firm owns, so it only seems prudent for management to have a clear idea of the brand's financial worth.
- If the brand has definable financial value, then the investments and returns against it can and should be measured. A brand valuation provides a starting point for any determination of whether investments being made in the brand are providing a reasonable return to the firm.
- In many cases, brands often enter into various types of licensing arrangements, co-branding agreements, joint promotional programs, and so on.

Knowing the value of the brand provides an important negotiating tool when working with other companies in developing the terms of such arrangements.

- Brand value is a key element in shareholder value. If the value of the brand is increasing, the value of the shareholder's holdings in the firm is doubtless increasing as well. Clearly, the value of the brand is a key element in identifying shareholder value.

- Brand valuation can provide the base for development of an ongoing *brand scorecard* to track financial progress over time. Typically, the scorecard pulls together many of the attitudinal and market performance elements discussed in Pathways 1 and 2. It also serves as a framework for focusing organizational attention on the most important factors in the brand's long-term success. Properly developed and executed, a brand scorecard serves as a valuable management tool to adjust and allocate scarce and finite corporate resources to the best benefit of the brand and the organization.

With this discussion of the benefits of brand valuation, we have provided a fairly complete discussion of Pathway 3. The only issue left is to consider the future of brand measurement.

WHERE DO WE GO FROM HERE?

Having discussed the three primary methods of measuring and evaluating brands, the obvious question is: What is next? Quite honestly, a fairly clearcut but challenging agenda remains in terms of finding solutions to measurement and valuation of brands and their relationship to marketing activities.

As shown in the Three-Pathway model, three separate and distinct brand measurement and valuation measurement approaches exist. Clearly, each provides the answers to the questions being asked: What are the impact and effects of brand investments and activities on consumers (Pathway 1)? What does short-term, incremental financial value of the brand marketing investment provide (Pathway 2)? How might the brand be valued as a corporate asset (Pathway 3)? The problem, of course, is that each pathway is separate and distinct. The pathways can't be easily combined, and if they can, the results tend to favor one measure over another. So, clearly, the pathway that the brand owner or manager chooses determines the results that will be obtained. But, the answer the manager derives from his or her research may not be the one being sought. Or, it may be only a partial answer to a larger corporate or management question.

The solution, clearly, is to find some way to integrate the various measurement approaches and to better understand the cause-and-effect relationships between the three pathways. The challenge is clearly shown in Figure 13.10.

The difficulty, of course, is that developing an integrated measurement system requires the capability of combining attitudinal data, behavioral data, and financial data. It also requires the ability to measure all three sets of results historically, and to forecast or estimate what the future outcomes might be. This is a challenging task indeed. While there are some innovative measures being developed at this time, there is no clear solution on the horizon. So, the challenge of the brand owner or brand manager is to have a clear idea of what he or she wants to measure and then select the proper pathway. The pathway will give the results being sought, but only if the manager knows clearly what he or she is trying to measure or evaluate.

Figure 13.10
Three-Pathway Model for Measuring Brands

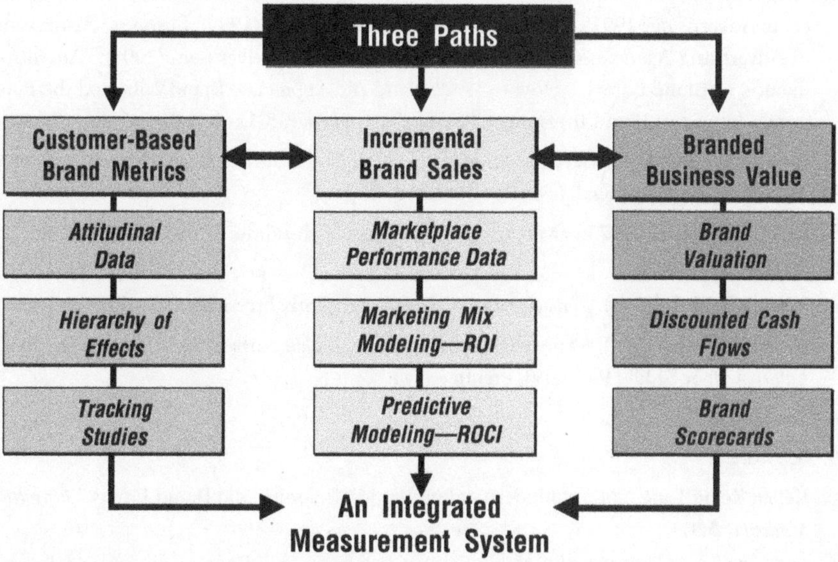

Don E. Schultz is professor of Integrated Marketing Communications at the Medill School of Journalism, Northwestern University. He is also president of the consulting firm Agora, Inc. Schultz is the author of 13 books, including his latest, Brand Babble: Sense and Nonsense about Brands and Branding, *which he wrote with Heidi F. Schultz. Early in his career he worked at Tracy-Locke Advertising and Public Relations. He received his BA from the University of Oklahoma and a Ph.D. from Michigan State University.*

Heidi Schultz is executive vice president of Agora, Inc., a marketing and branding consulting firm based in Evanston, Illinois, and a lecturer in Northwestern University's Department of Integrated Marketing Communications. Prior to joining Agora, Schultz was publisher of Chicago *magazine. She received a BA from the University of Southern California School of Journalism and an MBA from the Kellogg School of Management.*

NOTES

1. Aaker, David A. (1991), *Managing Brand Equity,* New York: Free Press; Keller, Kevin L. (1998), *Strategic Brand Management: Building, Measuring and Managing Brand Equity,* Upper Saddle River, NJ: Prentice Hall.

2. Schultz, Don E. and Heidi F. Schultz (2003), *IMC: The Next Generation,* New York: McGraw-Hill.

3. Haigh, David, *Brand Valuation: A Guide to Current Best Practice,* UK Institute of Practitioners in Advertising (1997); Institute of Canadian Advertising (1999); European Association of Advertising Agencies (2000); Australian Federation of Advertisers (2001); "An Introduction to Brand Equity—How to Understand and Appreciate Brand Value and the Economic Impact of Brand Investment," *Interactive Marketing,* 5(1) (July–September 2003).

4. Lavidge, Robert J. and Gary A. Steiner (1961), "A Model for Predictive Measurements of Advertising Effectiveness," *Journal of Marketing,* 25(6).

5. Colley, Russell H. (1973), *Defining Advertising Goals* (7th Edition), Association of National Advertisers, Inc.

6. Aaker, David A. (1991), *Managing Brand Equity,* New York: Free Press.

7. Keller, Kevin L. (1998), *Strategic Brand Management: Building, Measuring and Managing Brand Equity,* Upper Saddle River, NJ: Prentice Hall.

8. See note 6.

9. See note 7.

10. Keller, Kevin Lane (2003), "Understanding Brands, Branding and Brand Equity," *Interactive Marketing* 5(1).

11. "BrandDynamics Online Information," millwardbrown.com, 2005.

12. Young & Rubicam (2002), "White Paper on the Brand Asset Valuation," yr.com.

13. Hofmeyr, Jan and Butch Rice (2001), *Commitment-Led Marketing: The Key to Brand Profits Is in the Customer's Mind*, New York: Wiley.

14. See note 11.

15. Ibid.

16. Ibid.

17. Haigh, David and Jonathan Knowles (2004), "So You Think You Need a Brand Valuation?" Unpublished manuscript.

18. Ibid.

SECTION IV

BRANDING INSIGHTS FROM SENIOR MANAGERS

CHAPTER 14

USING POSITIONING TO BUILD A MEGABRAND

MARK R. GOLDSTON

Chairman, CEO, and President, United Online

Positioning is a critical question for every brand, but it is particularly important for new brands. Maintaining a consistent positioning while dealing with the rapid changes that face new brands is a challenge—for that reason, managers must be able to adapt quickly while preserving the brand's core essence.

This is a story about how a tiny, unknown startup company called Net-Zero went from zero to megabrand in just five years. Along the way, NetZero was forced to adapt its positioning to address major changes in market conditions. While making these changes, however, NetZero preserved its core value positioning and its brand identity. As a result, the brand became one of the dominant brands in the Internet market.

THE BEGINNING

In 1998, NetZero was simply a rough concept for a free Internet access service (free ISP). The idea was to give consumers a free dialup connection to the Internet in exchange for placing a small, persistent banner advertising window on the computer screen above the browser. The ad window would run banner ads every 30 seconds throughout the consumer's online session. These ads were a way of "monetizing" (Internet speak) the online session and offsetting the cost of the telecom required to keep the online connection going. If the users tried to close the window, the Internet connection would cease. If they saw an interesting ad, a click anywhere in the ad window would take them to the advertiser's web site.

275

In essence, NetZero had visions of creating the Internet equivalent of network television or radio, where consumers were not charged for the service and the cost was offset by advertising revenue. If this sounds a little crazy, it's not, really. Your radio doesn't need quarters to operate, and your network television stations don't send you a bill. We felt that your Internet access should be free, too.

NetZero was launched in October 1998 with little fanfare and much ridicule. In entering the multibillion-dollar Internet service provider (ISP) market, NetZero took on several of the largest brand goliaths in the world, including America Online (AOL), Microsoft, and AT&T. NetZero did so with a distinct positioning: value. America Online was the clear market leader, with more than 50 percent of the dialup market. AOL was charging $21.95 per month *and* advertising to online users. MSN, AT&T, Earthlink, and others were also charging between $19.95 and $21.95 for the same basic access that NetZero was providing for free.

BETTING ON THE POSITIONING

NetZero's initial results were strong; within the first five months, tiny Net-Zero had signed up nearly 250,000 people for its national free ISP.

However, the business soon was at an early crossroads. The company had roughly 50 employees and a rapidly declining bank account; it was burning cash like an incinerator. This situation was not that unusual for an Internet startup circa 1999. But there was a more fundamental problem: The cost of keeping a free user on the Internet was approximately $.45 per hour, and the amount of advertising revenue sold to offset that expense was just a small fraction of that, because NetZero could not deliver the scale advertisers needed.

In March 1999, with cash running low and advertising sales barely ringing the register, NetZero was forced to make some bold moves. The company's venture capitalist backers were getting antsy for their promise of Internet IPO riches. In order to generate revenue, NetZero needed a critical mass that would be appealing to advertisers.

The NetZero team decided that critical mass could be achieved through a marketing campaign that would quickly bring in large numbers of users. The team decided to invest its remaining funds behind NetZero's unique value positioning.

The marketing plan we created was called "Defenders of the Free World." Essentially, the campaign would invoke cold war imagery to indicate that NetZero was a company that would defend the free world by introducing it to free Internet service. We would augment our already successful *viral marketing* plan (online web site listings) with a cohesive television, outdoor, and print campaign to raise our profile as a disruptive force in the emerging ISP market.

NetZero began its first national advertising campaign in August 1999 with a paltry budget of less than $5 million; the company had not yet raised large amounts of capital through an initial public offering. We wanted to create the illusion of size, which we felt was very important to consumers who were looking to potentially switch from the likes of AOL, MSN, AT&T and others. But due to our limited cash, we could not afford to spend the requisite $750,000 to $1 million for producing high-impact television spots. In addition, we didn't have the money to run a 30-second television campaign that would break through the clutter and drive people to sign up for NetZero.

And so we developed revolutionary 10-second television spots and placed them in-program on key sporting events, game shows, and other programs during traditional voiceover announcement time. The 10-second ad idea enabled NetZero to run a large number of spots at a fraction of the cost of a conventional 30-second ad. Thus, the relative impact of the television media spend was almost *five times* what it would have been with 30-second spots. But more importantly, this strategic decision made the brand appear to be much larger and more ubiquitous than it had a right to be with the actual ad dollars we spent.

We needed to find a way to create 10-second commercials that looked epic in size but were produced at a fraction of the cost. We decided to focus on the cold war era of the 1950s and early 1960s to drive home the concept of "defending the free world." We utilized stock cold war film footage that we could rent very inexpensively. We ran it in black and white encased in a frame of red borders, which contained our web address and our toll-free number. The images were of Roswell-like flying saucers, early NASA testing, military drills, and people doing the Twist. The ads featured sci-fi music with no voiceover and a large "Defenders of the Free World" banner emblazoned across the screen images. These ads were very inexpensive and utilized very efficient media units. And, they created an industry firestorm and were successful beyond our wildest expectations.

The NetZero IPO occurred just one month after the ad campaign's launch, and it raised $184 million of fresh capital. The NetZero IPO was the third-largest in 1999, and the buzz surrounding our controversial business model was a marketing tool in itself. We were ready to compete at the national level with the powerhouse competitors (albeit with a fraction of their spending level), so NetZero engaged in a full-fledged guerilla marketing effort. This effort encompassed many different strategies, but all were built on putting the "Defenders" cold war imagery in front of as many people as we could reach. We put "Defenders" ads on high-traffic billboards in major cities. We dressed people in early 1960s spacesuits and had them pass out NetZero software CDs in major downtown areas. We purchased two-page color spreads in *USA Today* and the *Wall Street Journal*. We purchased taxi toppers and bus wraps in the top 10 U.S. markets. We utilized over 10,000 wild postings (advertising posters affixed to construction site façades across the country). We placed seven-foot-tall displays in 1,000 movie theaters across the country, passing out NetZero CDs to every movie patron and printing up NetZero popcorn bags.

Our guerrilla tactics made us the Achilles heel for major competitors like AOL and MSN, who used the business and consumer press to deride our business concept as a fool's errand and to challenge the quality and longevity of NetZero's offerings. Our competitors' thesis was that we were going to "punch ourselves out" and go down in a blaze of glory, and that we would have no ability to sustain the losses created by a still-developing Internet advertising business and the high cost of telecom.

As we moved toward the 1999 holiday season, we produced a series of 30-second television ads with our new-found cash. These "Defenders" ads were designed to be epic in nature. We reenacted the scenes from the famous McCarthy hearings of the late 1950s and had a female defendant (or defender) in one spot and a male in another, testifying in front of a 50-person Congressional committee that free Internet service was a fundamental right. These ads looked like a black-and-white feature film, with our red borders framing the screen. The concept was that "free access to the Internet was a fundamental right, and if the committee were to keep the defendant there forever, NetZero would still give it away!"

The ads were highly acclaimed and enabled NetZero to sign up more than 100,000 people per day over three days during December 1999. In addition, NetZero signed on to become the official halftime sponsor of the NBA on NBC with "NetZero @ The Half." This sponsorship gave NetZero massive exposure, because the entire 15-minute halftime report on every nationally televised NBA game on NBC featured a NetZero "Defenders of the Free World" stage set and several 30-second TV spots.

The "Defenders of the Free World" television, radio, print, outdoor, and guerilla marketing efforts turned the ISP category on its ear. NetZero was the fastest-growing ISP in history and was becoming a true force to be reckoned with. By February 2000, NetZero had more than 3 million subscribers to its free ISP service, and it was starting to build brand awareness both off-line and online.

EVOLVING THE BRAND

Unfortunately, the euphoria didn't last long. Having built a powerful brand utilizing the free ISP positioning as a true advantage versus the premium-priced ISP brands, NetZero faced another major crossroads with the decline of the advertising market in mid-2000 as a result of the crash of the Nasdaq. The core element of the free ISP business model revolved around utilizing advertising sales to offset the cost of keeping people online for free. The crash of the Nasdaq and the subsequent nuclear winter that fell over the online advertising market put a pall over our efforts at NetZero. After the bursting of the Internet bubble one basic fact emerged: In a seriously depressed advertising market, advertising revenue alone was not sufficient to cover the costs of providing service and delivering a profit to our investors.

So we began to reassess our product and brand. We analyzed the category and determined that the majority of dialup ISPs were premium-priced, and there was no value-priced product available (other than free ISPs like our own NetZero). To generate revenue and profit, the NetZero brand needed to evolve; we couldn't just offer an ad-supported free service and remain in business given the prolonged depression in the online advertising market. NetZero decided to branch out and position itself as the value-priced alternative to premium-priced ISPs, utilizing feature set differentiation as the basis for having both a free ISP and a value-priced ISP. Importantly, the core of NetZero's brand remained: It was an advocate for the value-conscious consumer.

Accordingly, we began thinking about how to create a vertical segmentation structure of the ISP market that consisted of free, value, and premium offerings. We created a value-priced niche with a new product, NetZero Platinum, at $9.95 per month for unlimited access with *no banner ads*. NetZero Platinum's value proposition was that it was *better* than the free product because it was unlimited and did not show banner ads.

NetZero Platinum was launched in late March 2001. All "Defenders of the Free World" advertising was halted, and we focused spending on the launch of the $9.95 NetZero Platinum product. The NBA playoffs and finals featured NetZero Platinum ads and branding on the set of "NetZero @ The Half" on NBC, and all TV spots were switched to the $9.95 Platinum product. NetZero Platinum quickly became one of the most successful introductions in the history of the ISP market, as NetZero signed up over 140,000 paid sub-

scribers from a brand that had previously been 100 percent free. By continuing to emphasize a value positioning, NetZero was able to launch a new
product that was not free but that had many of the powerful value elements
that were true to its legacy as a free ISP.

The fundamental unique selling proposition of NetZero Platinum was that
it was just as good as AOL, served no banner ads, and was less than half the
price (AOL was then priced at $23.90 per month). It appeared as though one
of the most difficult challenges in branding had been successfully accomplished: leveraging a brand up the pricing strata within the same category.

Buoyed by the success of its foray into the paid ISP market, NetZero approached its archrival Juno Online Services about a merger in June 2001. The
combination of NetZero and Juno, which offered both free and value-priced
pay ISP services, would create the largest value-priced ISP in America. The
merger was completed in late September 2001, and the new company, called
United Online, Inc., featured the NetZero and Juno brands of value-priced
Internet access. Going forward, it was decided that while United Online
would maintain a portfolio of value-priced Internet access brands (we later
acquired Bluelight Internet from K-Mart in November 2002), the major advertising and marketing thrust would be against the flagship NetZero brand.

EXPANDING THE PORTFOLIO

To address changing market conditions, NetZero expanded its brand portfolio in 2003. At this time, broadband providers were targeting the premium
dialup user. Broadband providers sold the consumer market on the *need for
speed*. To address this market opportunity, NetZero launched HiSpeed dialup,
which promised dialup service that was five times faster than standard dialup.

In terms of market segmentation, NetZero was now able to provide a
good (free), better (Platinum), and best (HiSpeed) product portfolio. Importantly, NetZero continued to embrace value across all its product offerings.
Even at $14.95 per month, NetZero HiSpeed was almost 40 percent cheaper
than AOL . . . and faster as well. At a 50 percent price premium to the $9.95
per month NetZero Platinum product, NetZero HiSpeed had very attractive
profit margins and was still priced as a superior and inexpensive alternative to
the premium ISPs.

We focused the NetZero marketing budget on the new HiSpeed product.
We created the NetZero HiSpeed Challenge television campaign, which
showed two computers side by side connected to the Internet. One utilized a
standard dialup connection, and the other utilized NetZero HiSpeed. In the
ads, it was clear that the HiSpeed product was about five times faster than

standard dialup. We also used consumer testimonials in the ads to make our point, highlighting the fact that for $14.95 a month, consumers could get a much faster Internet connection over dialup lines at an attractive price. Most importantly, the NetZero HiSpeed product was available immediately, with none of the waiting and special equipment typically associated with signing up for broadband services.

As a result, NetZero HiSpeed signed up approximately 1 million subscribers in its first year of service. As usual, other competitive dialup companies followed suit and launched accelerated dialup products of their own. But the NetZero HiSpeed product continued to grow, thanks to the NetZero HiSpeed Challenge advertising and our innovations in quality and speed.

RESULTS

NetZero delivered outstanding results. *Advertising Age* named the NetZero television spots among the top recalled ads on all of television numerous times, and *Adweek* listed NetZero as one of America's *megabrands* in June 2004. At the end of 2004, the NetZero aided brand awareness registered 87 percent. And, J.D. Power and Associates ranked NetZero ahead of brands like AOL, MSN, AT&T, SBC Yahoo! and many others in 2004 for overall customer satisfaction.

Financial results were very positive as well. In 2004, United Online, which owns NetZero, had revenues of almost $500 million and profits of over $100 million, with the NetZero brand being a major contributor to the success of United Online.

LESSONS LEARNED

The story of building the NetZero brand is a modern-day version of how David beat Goliath. Three lessons emerge. First, when challenging large, well-established, and well-funded competitors, start with a tangible point of difference that resonates with consumers. The concept of free ISP clearly differentiated NetZero from its competitors and was readily understood and embraced by consumers.

Second, create the impression that you are bigger than you are. Everyone loves to root for the underdog, but they won't put down their money if it is unclear how long a company will be around. NetZero was masterful in making a relatively small advertising budget create a big impression. And it did so by thinking beyond traditional approaches to advertising, illustrating that necessity is often the mother of invention.

Finally, be nimble in responding to changes in the marketplace, but be true to your basis for differentiation as you extend the brand. When NetZero launched Platinum and HiSpeed services, these extensions maintained NetZero's value positioning in new ISP segments.

NetZero is an example of a brand that utilized a brilliant positioning and creative marketing to deliver tremendous brand awareness, share growth, profitability, and shareholder value—and all in just five short years.

Mark Goldston is chairman, CEO, and president of United Online, parent company of NetZero. He joined NetZero as chairman and CEO in March 1999, when the company was a start-up. Previously, he was chairman and CEO of the Goldston Group, a strategic advisory firm. Earlier in his career he was president and CEO of Einstein/Noah Bagel Corporation, president and chief operating officer of L.A. Gear, and president of Faberge USA. He is the author of The Turnaround Prescription—Repositioning Troubled Companies *(Free Press, 1992). He is a member of the Kellogg School of Management Dean's Advisory Board. He received his BS and BA from The Ohio State University and his MBA from the Kellogg School of Management.*

CHAPTER 15

MARKETING LEVERAGE IN THE FRAME OF REFERENCE

MARK SHAPIRO
Principal, New England Consulting Group

Frame of reference is a powerful strategic tool often overlooked by marketers. Having worked with developing brand positionings for some 25 years, I believe that organizations and their advertising agencies rarely give development of the frame of reference the attention it warrants.

Alice Tybout and Brian Sternthal define frame of reference in Chapter 1 of this book. According to Tybout and Sternthal, frame of reference is "a statement of the target's goal that will be served by consuming the brand. . . . The frame of reference may guide the choice of targets, identify situations in which the brand might be used, and define relevant competitors (i.e., brands that claim to serve the same goal)." Frame of reference is one part of a brand's positioning; the other three parts are target, benefit, and reason to believe.

Marketers often invest considerable time and research dollars developing a brand's positioning, but in most situations the focus is on the target, benefit, and reason to believe. Brand managers generate and test dozens of different benefits to identify those with the greatest leverage. Research teams often segment and resegment consumers, looking for the most promising target. All too often, however, the frame of reference component is simply an afterthought in positioning. The result is a throwaway in many positioning statements, where the frame of reference is simply the obvious product or service category.

This is opportunity lost! Leveraging the frame of reference is a real opportunity to get consumers to think about your brand beyond its original category. In many categories, products are very similar, so differentiation is

283

difficult. Defining your competitive set in different ways can drive growth by helping consumers to think about the brand in a new way.

This chapter presents three ways marketers can use frame of reference as a tool for strategic advantage. These approaches include broad category definition, gold standard comparisons, and "I am what I'm not." The chapter closes with an example of one company that is thinking broadly about the frame of references of its different brands.

BROAD CATEGORY DEFINITION

Frame of reference that focuses on category membership, or placing a product in its logical competitive set, can be effective. Indeed, for new products, it is essential to clearly place the product in a relevant and logical category. However, brand managers should consider establishing a frame of reference that goes beyond the obvious competitive set. Done properly, embracing a broad competitive set can push a marketer to think expansively about the business, thereby opening up growth opportunities.

For example, the obvious frame of reference for a sports car is, of course, sports cars. However, it is not the only possible frame of reference. Sports cars fulfill many different goals, and marketers can embrace any of these as frames of reference. BMW did this successfully; instead of positioning itself against sports cars, BMW compared itself to automobiles, a much broader frame of reference. This broad frame let the brand claim and own the powerful benefit of "The ultimate driving machine."

Online auctioneer eBay's success can be attributed to its technology, branding, and the fun and unique experience it provides in matching buyers with sellers. But the scale of this company's success is also due to its vision in broadly defining its competitive set, or frame of reference. eBay started as a venue for hobbyists and collectors, but it quickly expanded its frame of reference to include virtually anything an individual might want to sell or buy. The company broadened itself further by entering the business-to-business space, expanding its frame of reference even more. Expanding this set drove the company's growth.

Gillette, historically the world's leading razor manufacturer, similarly embraced a broad frame of reference. Gillette's expected category membership would be razors. However, this frame would be limiting; Gillette was already the leader in razors. Gillette went beyond razors, promising to be "The best a man can get." Was this the best shaving experience, or the best feeling a man can have? By using the broad frame of reference, Gillette has been able to own a powerful benefit.

Diamond giant DeBeers brilliantly embraced a broad frame of reference to drive growth. The logical frame of reference for DeBeers is diamonds. However, embracing diamonds as a frame of reference would limit the company's growth; DeBeers already had a high share position in diamonds. As a result, DeBeers embraced the broader frame of gifts, thereby opening up substantial growth opportunities. The company first built the category of diamonds with its "Diamonds Are Forever" campaign. DeBeers then took this approach to the next level by embracing the line, "Diamonds, a gift like no other." DeBeers later took the frame one step further to include self-gifts, by encouraging women to purchase diamond rings for their right hand, with the idea, "Left hand says we, right hand says me."

GOLD STANDARD COMPARISONS

Identifying the consumers' perceived gold standard and utilizing this as the brand's frame of reference is perhaps the greatest way to create leverage. When done effectively, this strategy raises perceptions of the brand to levels above its competitors. Importantly, the goal is not always to steal share from the gold standard product. Often the goal is to indicate relative quality and steal share from others.

Kraft's DiGiorno brand of frozen pizza has been a terrific example of this. Kraft launched the DiGiorno brand in 1995. DiGiorno had a unique technology; it was the first frozen pizza with a crust that would rise during baking. As a result, it was a clearly superior product. The obvious frame of reference for DiGiorno was frozen pizza. However, rather than claim superiority over other frozen pizzas, Kraft brilliantly identified the consumer gold standard and compared itself to delivery pizza, with the line: "It's not delivery, it's DiGiorno." The results were stunning. DiGiorno, first introduced in 1995, catapulted to the number-one position *and* grew the category.

Visa is another example of a brand that grew by including a gold standard in its frame of reference. In the mid-1980s, Visa was at parity with mainstream competitor MasterCard in virtually every area: ubiquity of acceptance (the category benefit), attributes (credit terms), card issuers (same banks), card users (same demographics and similar psychographics), and market share. Going head to head with MasterCard was destined to be a tough fight for Visa; the products were essentially identical. At the time, American Express was the prestige player in the category. Instead of embracing the obvious frame of reference—mainstream credit cards—Visa focused its frame of reference on American Express, the consumer-perceived category leader in quality, if not market share. Visa then identified a claim that it could make against American Express: broader acceptance. This led to a powerful marketing campaign where Visa compared itself to American Express on the broader acceptance benefit, and in the process owned this benefit across the entire category, even though MasterCard offered exactly the same amount of acceptance. The "It's everywhere you want to be" campaign ran for almost two decades and drove strong growth. Curiously, Visa probably did not take business from American Express; by comparing itself to the category gold standard, American Express, Visa took share from its direct competitor, MasterCard.

Tropicana orange juice has been another example. Tropicana's primary competitor was frozen concentrate. Instead of positioning itself as better than frozen concentrate, Tropicana focused on the gold standard, fresh squeezed. In making this comparison, Tropicana rose above frozen concentrates. The support, "not from concentrate," served to further distinguish the brand. And Tropicana has continued to remain the leader in orange juice. Interestingly, Minute Maid orange juice also offered juice "not from concentrate," but Tropicana effectively co-opted this benefit as its own.

"I Am What I'm Not"

Marketers can use their frame of reference to grow by clearly stating what they aren't. This seems somewhat counterintuitive, but the approach can differentiate products in a parity category and establish innovative new products.

HBO is a good example of the power of this approach. To be successful, HBO had to convince people to pay a premium for content. To do this, it needed to differentiate itself from free programming—a challenge compounded by the fact that its product was delivered precisely through the same medium as its free competitors. HBO succeeded by developing proprietary television programming (*Sex and the City, The Sopranos, Curb Your Enthusiasm*) to complement its feature movie schedule. HBO then brilliantly positioned itself by pushing away from the logical set of competitors with the slogan, "It's not TV, it's HBO." This strategy, supported by its own programs, effectively differentiated HBO as not only different, but superior, so as to justify the demanded premium price.

It is possible to even position against yourself, through comparisons to your historic positioning. Sears successfully did this. In an effort to drive sales of its clothing line, Sears compared itself to its hard-goods line with the line "Come see the softer side of Sears." The claim communicated that

Sears's soft goods were of the same superior quality as its well-known hard goods lines.

AN EXAMPLE

In 2005 Procter & Gamble was an example of a company using frame of reference to drive growth. Indeed, P&G appeared to be systematically rethinking the frame of reference on all of its core brands, an indication of the company's belief in the leverage behind frame of reference.

Crest is just one of P&G's brands leveraging frame of reference. For many years, P&G considered Crest to be toothpaste. This seemed quite obvious. The category membership of toothpaste is toothpaste. The result was a series of growth initiatives within toothpaste, as Crest introduced dozens of different varieties all designed to do the job toothpaste is expected to do: fight cavities. However, in the early 2000s, P&G began revising the frame of reference of Crest, moving to a much broader frame of oral care. With a broader frame, the benefit became a much bigger, healthy, happy smile.

The result of this shift in frame of reference was dramatic growth. Crest embraced higher-order and more powerful benefits in its advertising, and it launched a series of successful new products including the Crest Spinbrush and Crest Whitestrips. The broader frame likely played a role in Crest's acquisition of Glide dental floss, as well.

P&G seems to be rethinking its frame of reference in other categories, too. P&G used to play in laundry detergent, but it began embracing a broader frame of reference of cleaning of all clothes with the introduction of Dryel. The Mr. Clean brand used to be a floor cleaner; P&G broadened the frame to include all cleaning. This in turn led to innovative new products including an item to erase marks on the wall and a product for cleaning the car.

By rethinking the frame of reference on all its core brands, P&G was able to find ways to grow its very established businesses.

CONCLUSION

Frame of reference is an important tool for generating strategic advantage and growth. Yet frame of reference is an area that is more often overlooked than it is explored. As agencies and clients embark on the positioning development process, frame of reference should be given the same priority and resources as target audience, benefit, and reason to believe, and perhaps more.

Smart marketers and smart brand managers understand the importance of leveraging frame of reference to build their brands.

Mark Shapiro is principal at the New England Consulting Group. Prior to joining the firm, he spent 18 years at the Quaker Oats Company, where he managed businesses including Gatorade and Rice-a-Roni before becoming a corporate strategist. He started his career in marketing at General Mills. Shapiro is a member of the Kellogg School of Management Alumni Advisory Board and received his BA from Union College and his MBA from the Kellogg School of Management.

CHAPTER 16

FINDING THE RIGHT BRAND NAME

CAROL L. BERNICK
Chairman, Alberto-Culver Company

Before you begin to read this chapter, you decide you're a bit hungry. So you pick up your local Yellow Pages—I'm in Chicago—and hunt for pizza, trying to remember that place where you got the fantastic pizza a couple of months ago (Pizza Broker? Pizza Capri? Pizza Factory? Pizano's Pizza? Pizza Kitchen? Pizza Metro? Pizza Nova?) Better just go back to Giordano's; you'll be able to remember that name the next time.

Now you've made your pizza decision, but you're still feeling you want to upgrade the evening a bit, so you turn to florists (Flower Bucket? Flower Box? Flower Cart? Flower Cottage? Flower Island? Flower Stop? Flowers First?). How creative can these people be . . . *not!* Then your eye falls on the more distinctive and creative KaBloom.

Welcome to the world of—and the importance of—the name in your brand's life story.

In the process of branded product development, the selection of a name can be the most creative and the most critical aspect of the process. If your brand name is distinctive and memorable, it can and will make the difference in winning at the shelf. It can and will make a major contribution to the longevity of the overall concept. It can and will make your advertising dollars work harder, and it will create more attention and provide more value to your consumer.

As marketers, it's far too easy to get too close to our brands. What seems obvious to us can be confusing to the consumer. A great name is the chance to bring definition, clarity, personality, and, ultimately, trial to a new idea just taking shape.

Each of these names has specific meaning to you: Jell-O, Godiva, McDonald's, Mercedes, Wal-Mart, Cheerios, Subway, Pepsi, Nike, KFC, Kodak. Establishing those meanings has taken a great deal of thought, hard work, and great advertising, and yet in the end some of these iconic names may fail.

The new brand faces daunting odds—crowded shelves stocked high with competitors' products, the huge advertising budgets of global players that in turn bring with them a larger presence on retailer shelves, and a greater concentration of in-store display and advertising support. And yet each year new entrants carve out niches and sometimes a considerable presence in both new and established categories.

In part this is because the playing field is a bit more level than it may appear. A consumer watching a television commercial or reading a print ad does not know, nor particularly care, whether the company behind that message is a start-up or a global powerhouse. At that moment she may be convinced by a message—more specifically a unique selling proposition convincingly communicated. Whatever shelf space you are allotted, a powerfully communicated benefit—your *unique selling proposition*—coupled with an outstanding, memorable, ownable name and personality can still reach the shopper. But the time for a product to prove itself is short and continually shrinking, and the need to move a consumer with a single message as opposed to 10 is increasingly critical.

It is hard work to create the right name, promote that name, and link that name to your brand's personality and benefit. But I believe there are certain principles that, while not guaranteeing success, can at least give focus to the process.

First, your name must be memorable and ownable. If a five-year-old child can remember your name after hearing it several times, you might be onto something. I don't mean simplistic names, but rather distinctive names like Fritos, Nintendo, or Nickelodeon. The name must be broad enough that you can imbue it with a meaning that resonates with consumers. Review the list of iconic brand names given earlier. There is nothing inherent in the word *Mercedes* that means car. There is nothing in the word *Nike* that stands on its own for shoes, and furthermore, very few consumers would initially associate *Nike* with athletics in general. But Nike has grown the brand—and the brand meaning—from shoes to every piece of athletic sportswear imaginable. The link for each of the brand names above has been made through communication to the consumer, and now those names not only have iconic standing but are so unique that they will never be treated generically by any manufacturer of autos or athletic apparel.

At the same time, you must be very careful of descriptive names. *Pure, clear, soft, clean, natural,* and the now-ubiquitous *carb* are all appealing words that have a meaning to your consumer. They are also words that can be replicated by another company or a generic brand in a moment's time. When a trademark attorney gives you the go-ahead because the name you want is so generic no one can challenge it, you should get rid of it. Unless you are purposefully planning a short-term hit, the brand name must have the capacity to withstand the changes that will occur in the marketplace. Equally important, you cannot own generics: Pure & Clear, Soft and Natural, Flower Box, Flower Bucket, Flower Cart—too much potential for mass consumer confusion. Go instead for something distinctive. Create something!

CarbNot, LoCarb, Single Carb, Carb-o-Lite, SmarterCarb, CarbSense, CarbOption, Bella Carb, SlimCarb—in the early 2000s, clearly something was breaking out in the low-carb market, but it was not a rash of smart branding. Pick the bread from the above, or the snack bar, or the drink, or the combination. The fact of the matter is that for a short-term hit, many of these names will probably work, but none is distinguishable from the other. The only brand with a product differentiation will be the one with the lowest price.

How-to names present problems as well. While an instant pancake mix can sell under the name Shake & Pour for a time, Fast Shake or Pour 'n' Flip are not far behind, and you find you have helped to define a category but not establish a brand. Your television advertising is likely building your competitors' sales as quickly as your own.

You must also be careful of fads. For those of you who can remember the television show *Laugh In,* the phrases "Sock it to me" and "Verrrry interesting" probably have some meaning. If you once wore bell-bottom trousers, the term *groovy* probably brings a rush of memories. But brands that tie themselves to fads fade very quickly in the marketplace. If there are brands still carrying the name *millennium,* they must have something else going for them. In its brand name, any product that ties itself to the cultural zeitgeist in this way is destined for a short shelf life. Earthborn, Farrah Fawcett shampoo, and Body on Tap are long gone. Maxwell House, Tide, Alberto VO5, and Skippy endure.

In short, a brand name must be able to stand the test of time. Mercedes has been able to morph from a brand synonymous with racing vehicles to one that invokes safety first and back again without disturbing the cachet of the name. Whatever the trend at any given moment in shaving, Gillette has remained a market leader.

Pepsi has shown the staying power to adapt. From a stimulant drink with heavy sugar in the fifties, it has evolved to an iconic drink for the "Now Generation" and now has a low-carb formula. Consumers believe that Pepsi can bring taste, quality, and refreshment to a wide range of their diet and health concerns, and they give it permission to do so. They give Pepsi permission to add flavors because they trust the brand name. And from time to time, consumers give Pepsi permission to fail and move on. There is no better definition of a strong brand name, identity, and personality. The brand is capable of withstanding the test of time, and a company like Pepsi stays abreast of changing trends and has the ability to turn them to the benefit of the brand and the company.

As Pepsi demonstrates, a strong brand must be extendable. Several of the brands on our iconic list have struggled. McDonald's has broadened its name to mean hot sandwich rather than just burger, and in the mid-2000s the company came to mean salads as well, but many of the company's forays into cold sandwiches or pizza or chicken have met with less success. The Subway name became so identifiable with a type of sandwich that it was difficult to push the parameters out much, but they began to make a sustained effort to do so. Does this mean either brand is not successful? Of course not—a billion burgers served at McDonald's; several thousand locations opened by Subway— these are strong testaments to the strength of these names. But there are cautionary lessons here for the entrepreneur or the new product manager: Choosing a name that defines a single product benefit too narrowly or too specifically may only be successful in a much smaller category.

Kentucky Fried Chicken has spent tens of millions of dollars trying to move to the more general *KFC* as fried foods have lost some of their consumer appeal. Boston Chicken changed its name to Boston Market to attempt to broaden its appeal. When you choose a brand name, make sure you think beyond what is popular today.

In our iconic list mentioned earlier, Jell-O has withstood competitors' advertising attacks, changing tastes and diets, and changes in hand-prepared versus all-convenience meals. The Jell-O brand has demonstrated time and again its ability both to change with the times and to extend the line. Today Jell-O offers single-serving cups in the cooling case as well as pie fillings and puddings, and—for better or worse—the brand has had several runs in bars as Jell-O shots, a fad of the moment. Jell-O's flavors have shifted, and from time to time so has the company's seriousness in its communications, but the brand has continued to recreate and extend itself.

The brand and its name must convey a personality. One of the most ruggedly competitive aisles in the supermarket is the cereal aisle. Major companies have come and gone in this space. Major brands have peaked and faded. Store brands have created generic corn flakes and brans and a wide variety of fruit-flavored and chocolate-flavored cereals.

Clearly, market research shows cereal makers that crunchy cereals are preferred by consumers, and the variants on these types of cereals have come and gone for years. And yet Cap'n Crunch has continued to endure. In fact, the brand has not only endured but flourished, adding the occasional berry or novelty and continuing to be major player. Why? I believe it is because the brand—and the brand's name—has a personality. Cap'n Crunch was not strictly an ingredient story that could be copied, nor did it focus on a particular diet or regimen. But the cereal has established a fun identity that resonates with its consumers (and their mothers), and it has for several generations.

In the same aisle, despite oat fads that have come and gone, Cheerios has both prevailed and claimed a large piece of real estate. The brand's name and its personality have allowed it to remain a market leader, and, and as a result, consumers have given it permission to range far afield. Cheerios has expanded from oats to multigrain; it has expanded from primarily a health cereal to a line that has included several sweetened products. This brand equity has allowed Cheerios to add fruits and other ingredients but keep its name and personality—as conveyed through its unique shape, which has always anchored its success.

One final point (which is helpful although there are many exceptions) is the shorter the brand name, the better. We live in an age of the 30-second television commercial or the 15-second television or radio spot, and we at Alberto-Culver believe that a brand name should, optimally, be mentioned at least three times. For this reason, a long name is simply a heavy burden to carry. We own a product named Alberto VO5 Hot Oil Treatment. That takes a lot of beats in your TV commercial, and so it gets shortened, to VO5 Hot Oil and occasionally to just Hot Oil. That works for us (sort of) because it is a leading brand in its category, and bringing the consumer to the category increases the sales for the brand. But we've learned . . . a shorter, punchier name would have been stronger. Nickelodeon is a mouthful, and I-Can't-Believe-It's-Not-Butter certainly violates this rule, and yet both are successful because the personality trumps the length. But in general, for memorability, for punch, for the economy of time in your ad messages, shorter is better.

Let me demonstrate how all this came together when I created a product for our portfolio named Mrs. Dash.

Mrs. Dash has always sold in the spice aisle of grocery stores, which traditionally has operated in an opposite manner from of many of the categories we have discussed. The spice aisle has always been bought, paid for, and stocked by the spice giant McCormick, with some 350 single-note spices and blends under various McCormick banners. Other entries in the category have played at the edges, vying for consumer attention. This has never been a category of brands—it is a category of descriptors: oregano, thai basil, lemon pepper. And yet we created a brand that started as a single SKU and showed the ability to expand into different flavors and additional categories. Today, in the mid-2000s, Mrs. Dash regularly ranks in the top five of all spices. Let's discuss the reasons why.

As a company, Alberto-Culver has always been close to the consumer. We were in her kitchen and poking around in her bath long before this became an accepted research technique. As a result, in the early 1980s we were seeing a confluence of factors: concern about salt (the market was being flooded with a collection of not-very-good, similarly named salt substitutes—NuSalt, No Salt, Veg-It); a greater concern about healthy eating both in the general population and among those with specific health concerns such as diabetes; and the desire for convenience in cooking while preserving a personal homemade touch—a step back from TV dinners, but not all the way to meals from scratch.

A prepared blend of herbs and spices, the Mrs. Dash unique selling proposition—14 savory flavors to shake your craving for salt—provided a unique-to-the-market answer to each of those concerns, but it presented a branding challenge. In essence, Alberto-Culver needed to create a new category, that of spice-blend salt alternatives. We were creating a standalone brand that would not be carried under a corporate umbrella—a whole different approach for the category—so a distinct name and personality were key.

While we expected a significant portion of the early trial for Mrs. Dash to come from recommendations from doctors and dieticians, it was important that the product not be seen as medicinal or limited to people with health concerns. We addressed this through name and color. The Mrs. Dash name had a number of positive connotations for us. The word *dash* had both suggestions of speed and convenience, but also got very positive feedback from women who cooked—they described the recipe as meaning "a dash of flavor" or a "dash of salt." The *Mrs.* in the name (as opposed to using Dr. Dash or just Dash), personalized the brand and gave it a bit of an irreverent, fun tone.

So here we had a name that was quickly identifiable without being descriptive (no reference to "no salt" here), was clearly ownable, and was memorable. It conveyed a personality while leaving some room for us to define that personality, and it was short and punchy enough that we could display it prominently on a very small package and repeat it often in television advertising.

To reinforce the fun and zest we wanted consumers to associate with Mrs. Dash and to move us further away from any medicinal connotation, we chose primary colors—a distinctive bright yellow field with a red logo and a bright, yellow-colored cap. As we extended the line with additional flavor choices and flanker products, different color caps became an important part of the flavor identifier. Spices had traditionally been packaged in muted fit-in-any-kitchen colors, so the new Mrs. Dash brand look was also distinctive.

In television advertising for the brand (featuring this short, punchy name) we went with the signature of an upbeat musical jingle and a fun rolling parade of vegetables and spices to further communicate great taste, strictly avoiding a message to sick people.

Finally, while we were convinced that we had struck the right tone, we rigorously monitored the consumer's uses of the product and her perception of the brand's equity. As health concerns change, as diets and dieting patterns change, as meal tastes evolve, it is crucial that the brand remain relevant, and we have constantly taken steps to assure that, which we believe proves Mrs. Dash will stand the test of time.

From perhaps the second year of the Alberto-Culver Company's history—and we turned 50 in 2005—the question has been asked: How can you expect to compete against the Procter & Gambles and the Unilevers and the other giants in the packaged goods world in specific categories?

Our ability to develop brands—brands with a unique selling proposition convincingly communicated—is the key reason Alberto-Culver continues to remain strong today. Our brands around the globe (Alberto VO5, TRESemme, St. Ives, Motions, Soft & Beautiful, Alberto European, Get Set, Molly McButter, TCB, Mrs. Dash, FDS, Consort, Just For Me, and many more) have all followed these principles and have continued to be top players in their categories as well as market leaders in important niches within those categories.

And frankly, luck plays a role. I created a unique product back in my first year in marketing and named it Static Guard. In 2005 it was still very dominant in its niche with a market share of over 90 percent. The truth is that Static Guard is not much of a name—too easily copied, too much of a descriptor—but fortunately the brand met a consumer need and got off to a running start, which has carried the day.

In summary, given several hundred million dollars and the ability to sustain heavy levels of spending behind a brand, you can make a generic, descriptive, uninteresting name stand for something and sell at the shelf—sometimes.

Absent that, once you have a product that you believe has a unique selling proposition and can perform as you promise, the day you select the brand's name and establish its personality can be the day that puts you on the road to success.

And recognizing that is just the start. All those who have developed the iconic names we have used recognize that you must have distinctive, relentless, single-minded communication to build the identity that is the essence of your brand. Then, like a seedling, the brand identity needs to be nurtured, reinforced, perhaps transplanted occasionally, and given enough nutrients to grow, but you have captured the essential first step.

Good luck, good branding, and good selling.

Oh, and if the pizza has arrived, a sprinkle of Mrs. Dash Extra Spicy (red cap) will give it special zing.

Carol L. Bernick is chairman of the Alberto-Culver Company. Prior to becoming chairman, she was president of Alberto-Culver Consumer Products Worldwide. Bernick has worked at Alberto-Culver for 30 years in various positions. Bernick is a member of the Kellogg School of Management Dean's Advisory Board. She received a BA degree from Tulane University.

CHAPTER 17

BUILDING GLOBAL BRANDS

BETSY HOLDEN
President, Global Marketing and Category Development, Kraft Foods

In recent years, building and leveraging global brands has become an important avenue of growth for many companies. Many factors are contributing to this trend, including the explosion in media and global communications, the convergence of consumer trends and needs, and the worldwide expansion of global retailers such as Carrefour and Wal-Mart. Consumers are growing increasingly aware of global brands, and the infrastructure for reaching them is improving.

As a result, a global approach to branding is now more feasible and attractive for many companies. If you've got a brand with a superior product and positioning, it can be more efficient to take it into a new international market than to create a whole new brand. There are real competitive advantages here. By taking your existing brand into a global marketplace, you have more opportunities to leverage your company's scale, expertise, and core competencies. You can benefit from the cross-pollination of ideas across countries. You can fine-tune and continually improve your best practices. By benchmarking around the world, you can also find terrific opportunities to save money and reduce costs.

At Kraft, we have been continually working to build many of our brands globally, including Tang, Philadelphia, and Oreo. But not all brands and categories have global potential. Food is more challenging to drive globally than some categories because of its link to local customs and rituals. We have found that categories such as beverages and snacks travel more easily than meal products. For example, most consumers in China do not have ovens, making it difficult to succeed there with a product that needs to be baked, such as pizza.

When we think about taking a brand global, we assess whether the brand addresses a global consumer need, whether it can be adapted to differences in eating behaviors and income in different cultures, and whether the magnitude of the opportunity offsets the challenges.

To do this, we must answer a host of questions. We first explore the category attractiveness. How big is the category? What is its potential? What is the projected growth? How competitively concentrated is it? How likely are we to get to a number-one or number-two share? How profitable is the category? Additionally, we assess our ability to win, the fit with our brands, and our category expertise. We also consider our technology, assets, capabilities, sales, and distribution. We look at our management capabilities and depth.

Then, we assess the country we are considering entering. How big is the country? What is the projected population growth? What is the projected economic growth? What's the average income level? How many households will be at a particular income level by what time frame? What's the composition of the population? How much is rural, and how much is urban? If it is a very rural population, simply getting the product to the consumers can be challenging. How established are the trade infrastructure and the distribution channels? What's the sociopolitical stability? What sort of infrastructure do we already have in the market? All of these factors determine which markets we will enter and which brands we will take globally.

BEST OF GLOBAL, BEST OF LOCAL

One of the key challenges of building global brands is balancing the best of both global and local branding practices. The goal is to complement global standardization with local customization.

But there is no one right way to find that balance. It depends on the company, category and geographic strengths, development, and strategy. You must optimize both the global and local elements and find the balance that works for your business.

In general, the product or service and its unique relevant positioning should be *driven globally and adapted locally.* The global oversight will provide consistency, while the local adaptation in pricing, distribution, and integrated marketing will allow for flexibility to address local needs.

We have found it best to drive the superiority of a product or service at the global level. We find that our brands are often at a price premium to local brands, and we need to justify that. Philadelphia, for example, is superior in quality to other competitive cream cheeses in its markets. It performs better in key usages such as cheesecake. When compared to the broader frame of other spreads, such as butter, Philadelphia has superior nutrition (an important factor in developing markets). Tang, too, has superior flavor and nutrition to other powdered beverages. It has superior nutrition to colas, and superior flavor to a lot of fruit juices and fruit-ades.

Consumers have very high expectations of these and other global brands. They expect them not only to be recognizable, but also to be seen as the best. They trust that you will consistently deliver superior quality, and if they don't see the difference, you will not be successful. Furthermore, when you introduce a global brand, you are usually asking consumers to switch from something else, or you are approaching them from an entirely different frame of reference. If you are not delivering something that they believe is better than what they are currently buying, they won't buy your product.

The global level is also the place to define the essence of the brand and the overarching positioning. Ideally, this creates a relevant emotional connection to consumers that transcends borders. If you are consistent with your brand essence, you can make minor adjustments to your positioning in a particular market and not be inconsistent with the total brand personality.

Your brand essence must be represented consistently over time, geography, and brand extensions. The positioning itself may flex a bit—it specifies the target consumer and the frame of reference; it identifies a key point of difference; and it clarifies the reason for that difference. The positioning can also be adapted as needed to address a changing frame of reference and competitive set, as well as new brand extensions and cultural differences.

Kraft's positioning with Oreo is a good example. Our core consumer is mothers who value and enjoy moments of togetherness with their families. Our insight is that only Oreo can turn an ordinary moment into one of special, fun connections. We have built our campaign around parents teaching their children how to eat an Oreo cookie, passing on the "Twist, Lick, and Dunk" tradition. In a market such as China, where Oreos do not carry the same pass-it-down tradition, we flipped the interaction and portrayed a little boy teaching his father how to eat an Oreo. Our most successful advertising has focused consistently on the various ways you can eat an Oreo, and especially on the connection between Oreo and milk.

To ensure this consistency across time, geography, and brand extensions, it is critical to articulate and communicate the brand essence and positioning guidelines globally. This clarity helps managers in local markets protect the brand essence. We have found it useful to have a *brand equity keeper*—someone who is responsible for a brand worldwide. On our key global brands, we have a person who develops the advertising with the local markets to ensure consistency. It is also helpful to have a person in a parallel role at our advertising agency, so that one person at both the company and the advertising agency is responsible for those brands globally.

What's best driven at the local level? Market pricing strategies are among the most important decisions to be made locally. Your product must offer a clear price value relative to local competitors, which often serve as consumers' natural frame of reference. In any market we enter, we evaluate the market structure so that we know our product's competition and can monitor the relative pricing. We have found that Tang, for example, must be priced relative to other powdered beverages to succeed. It also must be priced appropriately relative to the larger beverage frame of reference, which includes colas and fruit drinks. You have to keep looking at the right frame of reference in each market for the brand.

Sizes and pricing should be consistent with the key channels of distribution. Affordability is a critical issue. When people in developing markets are only earning $200 a month, they can buy one or two cookies or one beverage, but they can't afford to buy large quantities (and thus, they don't *want* to buy in bulk). You must make sure you are offering the appropriate sizes for affordability in a particular market.

In addition, the local distribution system must be profitable and competitive. Getting the product to the consumer can be one of the biggest challenges, particularly in developing markets.

We often use a two-tiered segmentation approach. When we go into a market, we will either buy or build a mainstream or value brand, and then we will bring in our global brands as the more premium brands. This enables us to get scale in the category. It also enables us to weather economic downturns, when consumers trade down from our premium brand to our mainstream brand. When we went into Russia, for example, we bought a confectionery company called Stollwerck, which gave us a strong position in the market with a mainstream confectionery brand. Then we brought in Milka as our premium confectionery brand.

In some categories, such as powdered beverages, we will segment the market based on consumer targets. Tang, for example, is positioned to families. Crystal Light or Clight, is positioned to women. Combined, the brands give us sufficient scale in the category.

Alternative formats are growing and changing the rules in many areas. In developing markets, the modern trade—the Wal-Marts and Carrefours of the world—has been expanding, while the traditional trade is stable or declining. Even so, the traditional trade is still the largest percent of outlets in those markets, and in 2005 it still represented collectively about 50 percent of sales. In some markets it has been as high as 70 percent of sales. In Russia, for example, a lot of groceries are sold in open markets at kiosks. Each kiosk sells a different product. You may go to the coffee kiosk, then to the meat kiosk, and then to the confections kiosk. Each kiosk only carries a select number of products.

You must find an efficient way to get to those local outlets. You need sizes and distribution suitable for both the traditional trade as well as the modern trade. You need scale within a category, or you need enough categories so that the distribution system is profitable. You may need to employ a variety of ways to distribute your product, including partnerships, joint ventures, and unique distribution relationships. This can make or break you, particularly when you're entering a new country or a new category. It doesn't matter whether you have the best product or the best marketing in the world. If you don't have a system for profitable competitive distribution, you will not be successful.

Another local key is integrated marketing. You need to be consistent in your execution of the selling idea across time and geography, and you need to be sure that you are supporting it adequately. You want to surround the consumer with multiple relevant tactics. If what the consumers are seeing in the store, in print, and on outdoor advertising venues is consistent with what they see on television, you will get a lot more bang from your marketing dollars.

We've seen improved effectiveness due to programs that are specifically targeted to the interests of the core users or particularly relevant to the brand positioning. Our Milka brand of chocolate, for example, has continued to be a ski sponsor in Europe, because its heritage revolves around alpine milk. That link to the Alps and to skiers has proven successful for that particular brand.

This approach helps you combat media fragmentation in developed markets, where there are so many alternatives for consumers. It also gives you an opportunity for breakthrough. Through integrated marketing, you build emotional bonds with consumers and allow them to have experiences with the brand. Local events are key in building those bonds, enabling you to build some of the local relevance that you are seeking as a global brand. We might use event marketing, the Internet, in-store promotions and sampling, or bus, park, and outdoor advertising, among other media vehicles, to reach consumers. We have found when building a new category, like Tang in developing markets, sampling is essential. We will give consumers dry samples (the mix) direct to homes, through magazines, and in cross promotions. We also offer consumers already made product in-store during the summer season. Getting consumers involved with your brand in many different and integrated ways (not just relying on television) is absolutely critical in building global brands.

A CASE STUDY IN GLOBAL BRANDING

Philadelphia cream cheese was launched in the United States in the 1880s as an ingredient cheese product. The brand quickly became known as a superior rich dairy ingredient. We extended the product to a soft spreadable form to capture growing spreading behavior. We then extended to a range of sweet and savory flavors and nutritional alternatives such as reduced fat. We have extended the brand into more convenient forms such as snack bars and dips to capture new uses and occasions.

As a result, in 2004 Philadelphia generated over a billion dollars in revenue a year across 90 countries.

Philadelphia's brand proposition is that it is a superior rich, creamy white cheese. It is positioned to women as a superior eating experience because of its rich taste, creamy texture, and dairy credentials.

The global insight that drives our marketing is that Philadelphia is a little bit of pleasure or reward every day. Philly inspires busy women to take a few moments to treat themselves. The ritual of spreading the product on a bagel, bread, or crackers is an important part of the pleasure.

We are consistent with these insights in our advertising. The campaign is set in Heaven, with the clouds as metaphor for Philly's rich, creamy taste. In humorous stories, the main character, an angel, is always rewarded with her Philadelphia cream cheese. The tag line is, "A Little Taste of Heaven." Luscious spread shots and appetizing foods visualize the consumer ritual.

The Philadelphia oval plus silver, white, and blue colors are key brand equities. The brand values are authentic, light-hearted, and engaging. As captured in its brand essence, Philadelphia "makes everything a little bit more special." It causes women to "slow down during their otherwise active day. But emotionally, Philadelphia lifts them up because of the simple pleasure it brings them."

After success in the United States, Philadelphia was expanded into western and central European markets with a high development of cheese consumption and spreading behavior. It was then expanded into some Latin American markets and developed markets in Asia Pacific, such as Japan and Australia. We have continued to expand Philly into developing markets with established cheese consumption and spreading behavior.

The best of global with Philadelphia is our clear, consistent leveraging of the Philadelphia brand and its key equities. We leverage our superior dairy technology to deliver a superior product and a full innovation pipeline. We have leveraged our global insight that women view Philly as "a little taste of heaven every day" into a global campaign.

The best of local with Philadelphia is the flavors and local brand extensions. The usages and frame of reference capitalize on local behavior. The personality and humor of the Philly angel reflect local cultural norms. Our integrated marketing draws on the best of our local insights as well.

KEY LESSONS IN GLOBAL BRANDING

- *Global standardization must complement local customization.* The global oversight will provide consistency, while the local adaptation in pricing, distribution, and integrated marketing allows for needed flexibility.
- *The superiority of the product and its unique positioning are best established at the global level.* These brand qualities must be communicated clearly to local business teams.
- *The brand positioning must be delivered consistently, over time, geography, and brand extensions.* This positioning can be adapted to the local market, but it must be consistent with the global message.
- *Market pricing strategies are best made locally.* The product must offer a clear price value relative to local competitors, which often serve as consumers' natural frame of reference. Decisions about prices and sizing must be made with an eye toward what is affordable at the local level.
- *Category scale is critical for efficient distribution.* A two-tiered approach, involving the purchase or building of a mainstream or value brand, combined with the introduction of the global brand as the premium brand, can be an effective way to achieve critical mass.
- *The traditional trade still comprises a large percentage of outlets in global markets.* The distribution system must reach those outlets for a global brand to attain a leading share in a market.
- *It is critical to have a full innovation pipeline.* Consumers expect global brands to continue to lead innovation in their categories and to be first and best to market.
- *Integrated marketing offers opportunities to break through to consumers in new markets.* Experiences with the brand help build relevance and emotional bonds with consumers. Programs that are specifically relevant to the interests of the core users or to the positioning are particularly effective.

Betsy Holden is president of global marketing and category development at Kraft Foods. In this role she is responsible for leading growth initiatives across the company's five global consumer sectors. She has more than 20 years of experience in the food industry. Holden started her marketing career at General Foods, which later merged with Kraft. She is a member of the Kellogg School of Management Dean's Advisory Board. She received a BA from Duke University, an MA in education from Northwestern University, and an MBA from the Kellogg School of Management.

CHAPTER 18

BRANDING AND
ORGANIZATIONAL CULTURE

GARY A. MECKLENBURG

President and CEO, Northwest Memorial HealthCare

$\mathbf{I}$n most industries, businesses know that having a positive brand image is critical to building a loyal customer base. Those of us in the highly complex healthcare field recognize that our image and reputation are based on the first-hand experiences that patients and families have at a time when they are most vulnerable. Sensitivity and compassion as well as professional competence are both essential elements of our brand.

Many believe that a successful brand image is the product of marketing and advertising initiatives that present an organization's attributes to the outside world. Based on 35 years as a hospital executive, I believe the most successful brands, especially in healthcare, begin internally with a strong, accepted, and omnipresent organizational culture. And, at its core, that culture needs a clearly articulated and lived mission that captures the commitment of every person in the organization.

My own realization of this principle began in the early 1980s when I was asked to lead St. Joseph's Hospital, the largest Catholic hospital in Wisconsin.

I met a woman named Emma during my tenure as president and CEO. Emma was like many people in Milwaukee—very ethnic, very religious, and very industrious. She was an older woman whose features and carriage exhibited a life of hard work. Emma was the housekeeper responsible for cleaning the main lobby where a large statue of St. Joseph stood to welcome visitors. Even though the building was 60 years old, the floors shined, the windows sparkled, and nothing was out of place.

As I got to know her, I realized that Emma worked not only for a paycheck but also to help fulfill her responsibilities to her faith. It wasn't the hospital's lobby, it was God's lobby. Emma kept it spotlessly clean for Him as He healed our patients.

Over time, I learned that most of our staff, regardless of their religious affiliation, were just like Emma. They worked harder and longer, volunteered for extra assignments, and came in on weekends and holidays because they fundamentally believed in the importance of the organization's work and their personal role within it.

At St. Joseph's, the founder's purpose and the employees' goals had become one. Our strategies, decisions, and allocation of resources emanated from our mission and values, which resulted in a clear direction and focus throughout the organization. Seemingly difficult decisions not only became obvious, but they actually became easy. Emma and the others at St. Joseph's taught me what business we were in. They also taught me that having a tangible, believable, and unwavering mission and shared values are fundamental to long-term success.

These individual and collective beliefs were obvious to the patients and families we served and were the essence of our attractiveness to the community. Thus, long before the concept of *branding* became popular in healthcare, I learned that a positive brand image begins with day-to-day service excellence provided by committed employees. Employee dedication can only be achieved by building a strong, accepted culture.

PATIENTS FIRST

When I arrived at Chicago's Northwestern Memorial Hospital in 1985, the question facing me was whether the principles I learned in a religious, community-based organization could be effectively translated into a large, secular, multidimensional, academic medical center.

At that time, Northwestern Memorial was still digesting its merger of two leading community teaching hospitals. It had a reputation for excellent physicians and nurses, but it was only one of several leading hospitals in Chicago. Even though the hospital was financially sound, its high cost structure was not sustainable. Its facilities were old, technologically obsolete, and inconveniently spread across the downtown Chicago campus. The management team was unfocused. It was not difficult to recognize that the organization needed a clear sense of direction as well as a sense of purpose.

After months of meetings, discussions, and drafts, we developed a strategic plan including a mission that captured Northwestern Memorial's sense of purpose—a 120-year history of service to all the people of Chicago and a more recent but essential affiliation with Northwestern University's medical school.

The mission began with and reflected the core reason for our existence: *Northwestern Memorial Hospital is an academic medical center where the patient comes first.* The mission still stands today, 20 years later, and it is more than our responsibility; it is our passion and our promise, as well as a direction for the future.

Over the next few years, we shaped programs and invested in our staff—from entry-level service workers to top management. We placed a high priority on hiring those who shared our organizational values and mission and who could bring them to life. We created a lapel pin as a visible reinforcement of our *Patients First* motto, which has continued to be worn proudly by our employees and medical staff. The words on that pin have become a simple yet very powerful credo for our organization. (See Figure 18.1.)

Then and today, our mission and values drive everything we do, from how we treat our patients, to how we develop and implement our strategic goals, to how we hire and train our workforce, to the design, construction, and furnishings of our buildings. It guides how we honor our history and celebrate our successes, as well as the design of our signage. As a result, Northwestern Memorial today enjoys a consistent reputation—an image, a *brand*—for patient-centered care. We've been recognized as Chicago's most preferred hospital every year for a decade.

Figure 18.1
Patients First **Lapel Pin**

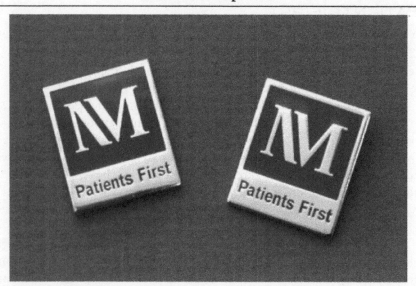

Source: Northwestern Memorial Hospital.

People Make the Difference

A few years ago I was asked to chair a national commission to develop an action plan to address hospitals' large and growing workforce shortage. As we crafted the report, it became increasingly clear that success in both healthcare and human resources was closely interrelated. Healthcare is a human business, and success is based on the institution's employees and the caring they demonstrate for their patients. People select health careers because they want to make a difference in others' lives. In the absence of a strong patient-focused culture, the staff does not have a meaningful work experience, which results in decisions to work elsewhere—or even to leave healthcare—which further contributes to a shortage of workers.

Recognizing the importance of our staff as stewards of our brand, Northwestern Memorial continues to place great emphasis on strong human resource management, from compensation and benefits to on-site child care. As CEO, I participate in new employee orientation by providing a session describing our history, mission, strategy, and values.

We have initiated a number of programs to celebrate our success. We publicly recognize and reward perfect attendance—the record is 42 consecutive years. Each month, one exceptional employee receives a "Patients First—One of Our Finest" award and is featured in a cafeteria display. Believing that experience and continuity is important, we celebrate the longevity of our workers through annual receptions for those who have 5 to 45 or more years of consecutive service. Our Quarter Century Club has grown from 30 to 478 individuals in 20 years, a valuable reservoir of those who are the true caretakers and champions of our history, traditions, and mission.

Because we believe so strongly that the success of our strategies is based in our employees, each year, top management takes a week to meet with and report to the organization. In less than four days, 5,000 people attend meetings and hear directly from the CEO and senior management about the current year's accomplishments and goals for the next year. Since 100 percent of our workforce is eligible for incentive compensation, everyone has more than a passing interest in the achievement of goals. The meetings include a candid dialogue with the CEO—every question is answered directly.

At Northwestern Memorial Hospital, we hire those who emulate our values of integrity, Patients First, teamwork, and excellence. If we can get the right people doing jobs that create value for the hospital, our patients, and their own personal development, then we will have created an institution where every job counts. And, we will have a team that will continually support our culture.

REDEVELOPMENT PROJECT

In the late 1980s, it became clear that our three antiquated inpatient buildings and the absence of ambulatory care space were the greatest single barrier to achieving our vision of greatness. The decision to construct a $600 million, two-million-square-foot complex was not an easy one. It was a huge bet on the future, and the financial planning was complex. We felt strongly that the facility should not only include all the contemporary technology to support a leading academic medical center, but it should also reflect our Patients First mission.

After meeting the essential requirements of building codes and complex medical equipment, our new hospital would be built from the patients' perspective. During the planning stages, user groups of patients and families, as well as caregivers and employees, worked with management and the architectural team to design the new hospital. We not only learned what patients wanted in a contemporary hospital, but we also learned about the many frustrations and irritations that led most to *dislike* hospitals.

The new facility, opened in 1999, is not only an advanced technological marvel, but it is also the embodiment of our mission. Consistently, the first reaction is, "It doesn't look like a hospital." The warm, friendly design uses light, space, color, texture, and art to create a calm, welcoming environment. The building is easy to navigate with elevators near the front of the building, visitor corridors with windows, and excellent bilingual signage. With automated registration, there is no admitting department—patients can proceed directly to their point of service without the inconvenience of waiting to be admitted.

The spacious, all-private rooms are the epitome of a calm, positive setting with large windows and artwork that contribute to a healing environment. The patient/family zone in the room includes two chairs and a window seat that pulls out into a bed to enable a family member to spend the night.

The building also includes the Health Learning Center, a consumer medical library that promotes health education and wellness by providing up-to-date information to patients and families. Everyone, including the community-at-large, has free access to one of the largest healthcare consumer education centers in the country, staffed by a full-time medical librarian and reference staff.

While none of these elements were a medical necessity, they were important in creating a facility that responded to our patients' needs and helped to differentiate us in the marketplace. We built a hospital that is a physical manifestation of our brand and mission. For our staff, the facility reinforces our Patients First culture and is a great environment in which to work. For our patients and our community, the building is a reflection of who we are.

The facility has supported business success. Since its opening, Northwestern Memorial has experienced dramatic growth. Inpatient admissions have grown by 34 percent, visits to the emergency department are up by 27 percent, and births are up 47 percent. We are among the lowest-cost teaching hospitals in Chicago and one of four hospitals nationally with a top bond rating. Thus, a consistent commitment to our mission, values, culture, and brand has resulted in extraordinary performance.

"ENJOY YOUR HEALTH"

We take our brand image seriously and recognize that it must be constantly nurtured and monitored. We perform market research routinely to gauge any changes in key attributes, both internally and externally. We use third-party surveys, patient questionnaires, national and local rankings, and patient feedback as indicators of market perceptions, brand image, and recognition.

In healthcare, direct patient feedback is one of our most important resources. Early in my career, I learned the value of reading, sharing, and responding to each patient letter. I have found that these letters provide a window into the organization and are extremely sensitive to both positive and negative changes in our daily activities. These firsthand accounts help us validate new initiatives, identify areas for improvement, and acknowledge those on the front line who have exceeded a patient or visitor's expectations.

Thus, when faced with the prospect of creating a new advertising campaign in 2001, we naturally focused on those we served. At that time, our census was near capacity, our unaided awareness remained high, and we continued to rank as Chicago's most preferred hospital. Yet, we wanted to protect our leading position in the marketplace and differentiate ourselves from other hospitals.

Most hospital advertising is not unique, and it generally speaks to consumers from an inside-out perspective. Understanding this, we decided to create a campaign that would stand out, be meaningful, and most importantly, remain credible to our community. Prior to developing new ads, we conducted brand image research and learned that many of the attributes we assigned to ourselves matched those from our consumers. They included trust, stability, and having a compassionate and talented workforce. They said, "We already know you are good; you don't have to tell us." We also learned that consumers were indifferent to most hospital advertising because either it wasn't relevant to their healthcare needs or it appeared as a direct solicitation.

Coupled with our market position and this intelligence, we created a branding campaign that spoke to consumers in a friendly manner about the importance of enjoying life regardless of their health status. Entitled "Enjoy Your Health," we provided consumers with a humorous and sometimes direct

Figure 18.2
Example of "Enjoy Your Health" Advertising

Source: Northwestern Memorial Hospital.

reminder to keep life in perspective. In so doing, we have continued to build our reputation as an organization that cares about each patient as an individual. The campaign has generated positive attention and recognition. (See Figure 18.2.) We have developed many internal and external brand extensions since inception.

Admittedly, we could not have embarked on an exclusive campaign had we not already developed a strong brand reputation to support this initiative.

CONCLUSION

Northwestern Memorial Hospital's brand has matured and endured. At its heart, it speaks to our continued promise to provide the best quality care, in the best environment and with the best staff—and to do so in a manner that differentiates us from every other medical center.

As a high-touch service organization, our brand is tied to the experience that our patients and their families—our customers—have when they receive care within our institution. They know they will receive compassionate, quality care, and each positive encounter further reinforces our image as an organization that truly promotes the best patient experience.

While healthcare today is a complicated business, it is really very simple at its core: Healthcare is people taking care of people. Northwestern Memorial Hospital has been able to demonstrate an honest and passionate commitment to fulfill our mission. We are recognized because our employees and medical staff truly believe that the work they do makes a difference.

No matter the industry, the product, or the service, a brand must be built on a sense of purpose; and that mission must be real, seamless, and ring true to your customers. At Northwestern Memorial, we learned early on that our mission is the core of the institution and that a strong, positive culture is built slowly, one person at a time. It is not something that can be dictated from top management. It has to be practiced and modeled every day. Each employee at all levels of the organization must understand the importance of his or her individual role as an ambassador and caretaker of your mission. In doing so, any organization can create a powerful, sustainable, and effective brand.

Gary A. Mecklenburg is president and chief executive officer of Northwestern Memorial Hospital's parent organization, Northwestern Memorial HealthCare. Prior to joining Northwestern Memorial, Mecklenburg was president and chief executive officer of St. Joseph's Hospital and Franciscan Health Care, Inc., in Milwaukee, Wisconsin. Early in his career he worked at Stanford University Hospital and Clinics and the University of Wisconsin Hospitals. He is a past chairman of the American Hospital Association, a member of the Board of Directors of Becton, Dickinson and Company, and a member of the Kellogg School of Management Dean's Advisory Board. He received a BA from Northwestern University and an MBA with a concentration in Hospital Administration from the University of Chicago.

CHAPTER 19

BRANDING AND
THE ORGANIZATION

E. DAVID COOLIDGE III
Vice Chairman, William Blair & Company

In an established enterprise, how do you link the brand to the organization and the organization to the brand? What role does organizational culture play in the mix? As CEO of William Blair & Company, I asked myself these two important questions as our financial services firm began a lengthy branding initiative in 2002.

As we began this year-long branding process, I communicated to our team my strong feelings that for any company, the brand must reflect the organization's culture and its reality. If it does not, the brand is a fraud. Branding alone cannot change a large, impersonal company into a personal, hands-on firm with a small-company feel. But branding can and should call direct attention to the unique characteristics that sets a company apart from its competition.

With these tenets in mind, the initial part of our brand research work began internally. And it began at the top of the organization. If the marketing department had been the sole champion of our branding effort, our employees and principals would have viewed it as a marketing project, and it would have been compartmentalized. Once again, I felt strongly that we were not signing up for a marketing project; we wanted to affect a significant change in how we nurtured and sustained our unique brand positioning in the marketplace. The goal was to integrate the marketing and branding strategy with the business strategy.

As an independent, employee-owned private firm (with fewer than 1,000 employees in 2005), William Blair & Company is a unique entity, especially in the world of investment banking and money management, which is dominated by large, publicly traded financial conglomerates. William Blair & Company has survived and prospered for 70 years as a smaller, more personal financial services firm. In the current era of consolidation in financial services, the ability to endure and prosper requires a focus, a will, and a strategy that keep clients and employees happy and loyal. Additionally, to combat the ubiquity of well-known brands in the financial services industry, a small firm needs a distinct brand identity, communicated through its people, its electronic and printed publications, and the media.

OUR COMPANY'S HISTORY AND REPUTATION

William McCormick Blair founded William Blair & Company in 1935 at age 50. Launching a financial services firm during the Great Depression and just before World War II was not a risk-averse undertaking. But Mr. Blair wanted to be a catalyst for helping companies, institutions, and individuals manage their way out of a rough economic environment. His firm was founded on a set of strong principles: integrity, investment performance, lasting relationships, and civic commitment. Mr. Blair also had a strong penchant for independence.

During its 70-year history, William Blair & Company has always had a terrific reputation. Through the years, we accepted the positives of our reputation (integrity, stability, business ethics, and caring about clients), and we shrugged off the misperceptions that went along with that reputation (that we were an old-school, white-shoe firm). In 1935, Mr. Blair had established a business with a distinct culture. But it was not until nearly 70 years later that our organization began to embrace, articulate, and manage our brand as a distinct asset.

As a company, we began this process in 2002, when we first established a central marketing department. Until that time, the firm's partners had been satisfied with each department's handling of its own marketing. These efforts were, unfortunately, often ad-hoc and not strategically developed. This approach is common in a professional services organization, where the product is intellectual capital provided by a professional such as a banker, portfolio manager, or trader. In many such companies there is often no marketing person in the business mix. But when William Blair & Company established its new marketing and branding effort with senior-level talent, it quickly became clear to everyone that our marketing professionals needed to be a vital part of the business mix. It also became clear that the process of marketing and branding is part art and part science—with more science than we had imagined.

BRANDING IN THE FINANCIAL
SERVICES INDUSTRY

The consolidation of financial services firms is a global phenomenon, and the pervasiveness of the large corporate names—some of which by 2005 had become household words as never before, such as Goldman Sachs and Citigroup—serves to reinforce those brands. But the very consolidation phenomenon eliminated a huge cadre of independent firms whose focus was serving small to midsize entities and emphasizing investment performance. In addition, this consolidation often caused relationships to suffer when firms were acquired or merged, due to excessive employee turnover and strategy shifts. This in turn affected these companies' brand images.

The power of large, well-known brands is significant, and size can create countervailing power and entities that are *too big to fail*. In his book, *American Capitalism: The Concept of Countervailing Power*, renowned economist John Kenneth Galbraith discusses the need for organizational scale so that corporate entities can go toe-to-toe with their corporate, customer, union, or governmental regulatory body counterparts. Large financial institutions that have recently run afoul of regulators have paid big fines, but there was never a thought to put them out of business, because of their large employment bases and their impact on the capital markets. Some of these brands have suffered mightily, but they are still significant, well-capitalized competitors of both larger and smaller firms like William Blair & Company.

With all that said, we at William Blair & Company know that succeeding without scale is possible; in fact, it is often preferable. And independence, combined with an intense focus on investment performance and serving a market niche, stands out more distinctly today than ever before. And so it became mission critical for us to communicate this brand and what it stands for. Thus, as our branding initiative officially got off the ground in 2002, I continued to ponder the essential questions of branding—how to link the brand to the organization and the organization to the brand, and how to integrate organizational culture into the mix.

I have found that some organizations may do their branding research and conclude that the marketplace and their customers describe them as large and impersonal. This research drives the company to reposition its brand as personal, hands-on, high-touch. But no one bothers to examine the company's existing culture, and so the branding effort eventually fails. Here's why: In a large organization of 50,000 employees, it would be extremely difficult to let the research drive a new brand positioning effort without effecting significant changes in the existing organizational reality as well as in the company's business structure. Advertising campaigns alone are not the brand—the everyday culture of the company is the brand. Branding is a matter of all employees understanding the brand they represent and fulfilling the brand promise to the customer every day. When steps are not taken to accommodate the internal culture of the organization, the branding effort can (and usually will) fail.

These important premises related to William Blair & Company's branding effort in two significant ways. First, the desired attributes of William Blair & Company were a very close match to how both the internal and external brand research respondents perceived our firm. We did not need to change our customer's perceptions of us in any radical way. And second, we are a smaller firm, which allowed us to communicate the branding effort throughout the enterprise thoroughly and efficiently.

BRANDING IN A SMALL FIRM

As we began our branding process, our extensive research with employees, clients, and prospects showed us that aspects of the firm resonated well with all audiences. These themes were, not surprisingly, consistent with the culture Mr. Blair established in 1935: independence, performance, and long-term relationships.

In many ways, the timing of our branding initiative was auspicious. In the early years of the twenty-first century, the business world had been rocked by corporate and financial institution reputation scandals. But we have always believed that it is necessary to emphasize the importance of values and beliefs in building an enduring enterprise, especially from a smaller-scale firm's vantage point. The truth is, it is immensely easier to maintain values and focus in a smaller organization.

As we began the branding process, we were thankful for the opportunities our smaller organization afforded. Implementing a branding program is easier in a smaller firm, because decision making is far simpler in an organization with fewer people. Additionally, concentrated, centralized locations make communications and a broader understanding of the issues and the enterprise goals common knowledge among the internal players. Innovation and creativity are easier to encourage, through both formal and informal communications.

Our small size is also an advantage in recruiting, which helps us keep the quality of the brand consistently high by continually recruiting the best and the brightest employees. We do this by infusing our brand with the idea that smaller operations are more fun to be part of. The operative words are *be a part of*—employees feel a greater sense of belonging and loyalty to a small firm. Not all qualified business school graduates want to join a huge firm. I certainly did not when I joined William Blair & Company 35 years ago, when the staff totaled 60 people.

BRAND RESEARCH RESULTS

The results of our brand research matched both the internal and external perceptions of our firm's image. And given the timing of the research (just nine months after September 11 and amid national scandals involving investment banks, research analyst practices, and broker fraud), our persona was the one clients were seeking to do business with. Words like *independence, stability, relationships, performance, trust,* and *integrity* were important to clients and the marketplace in general. The brand attributes our research turned up mirrored the image we had of ourselves. Fortunately, we were not named in any of the high-profile investigations and settlements, so as we began our branding launch, our message rang true and people noticed.

Once the research was completed and final recommendations accepted, our team began working on creating the communications themes, for the firm as a whole and for each of our main business lines. This was done with consideration of every client interface and touch point in mind: our web presence, our pitchbook materials, our *Annual Review* and other publications, account forms, and so on. We considered every aspect of the client's experience with William Blair & Company. The team spent about five months from the proposal's approval until the actual brand launch.

BRANDING LAUNCH AND IMPLEMENTATION

We took advantage of the positives of our small firm when we launched our branding effort in March 2003. For the official launch, we gathered together nearly all employees in one location, where we shared the results of the research and the direction we were headed as a business and a brand. Leading up to the launch, we used our employee web site to communicate. More important, many employees had been involved in the entire branding research process—many had participated in the internal interview process or helped recommend clients for independent researchers to interview.

I believe that the close-knit and geographically concentrated nature of our firm helped to build momentum and create genuine curiosity around our branding endeavor. The speakers at the launch were the top three leaders at our firm and two of the consultants from the independent research team. This presentation was choreographed specifically to show the top-level support of and commitment to our brand strategy. After the firm-wide launch, each department had a specifically targeted brand meeting.

A major aspect of our brand implementation involved the visual and messaging elements of the brand identity: colors, logo usage, tag line, message points, and so on. Our collateral materials from all departments of the firm received a unified look and feel. This effort is a large part of presenting the brand, but it is not the only effort. And it is secondary to the understanding, internalization, and ownership of the brand by all employees.

As time has marched on, we have continued to provide updates to the organization. Periodically, employees ask about the latest news on the branding front, and responses from the CEO are published in the employee newsletter. Our company also has a "Learn the Firm" program, and through this initiative we update employees on the continued marketing and branding strategy. We have instituted daily brand messaging to internal (and external) audiences through our web sites. We inform our clients, employees, and the public with our media coverage, speaking engagements, and new collateral materials, products, and services—all of which reinforce the brand.

An important hurdle we did face, however, was proving to a group of conservative professionals (our own people, many of whom are owners of the firm) that the brand and marketing approach would have a positive impact on business results. But the execution by our marketing professionals made this a nonissue. If I had to sum up the branding implementation in one word, it would be *consistency,* and this consistency did have a positive impact on our business results. For the first time, we published our firm's beliefs and values statements—the principles that sustain us through the ups and downs of business and life and allow us to endure. We simply articulated what everyone already knew. We incorporated our three platforms—Independence, Performance, and Relationships—from the research study into our daily language. Our mission statement and our tag line, "Committed to Client Success Since 1935," are consistent with words that Mr. Blair uttered more than a half-century ago—"When our clients succeed, the firm's success will follow"—a client-centric philosophy that is a big part of Mr. Blair's ongoing legacy that has led to the firm's long-term success. The culture is the brand, and fortunately, we already had the culture in place.

So while the extensive communication program for the new brand position was different from what employees were accustomed to, there was something familiar and even comforting in the message. The culture, our beliefs and values, our mission statement, our business strategy, and the brand are now virtually interchangeable. What we are on the inside is reflected back out to the marketplace. We have no inconsistencies between what we say and what we do and who we are as an organization. This seamlessness between the brand and the culture makes it possible for everyone in the organization to fulfill the brand promise to our clients. The clients' expectations are met by their overall experience with William Blair & Company. And I know everyone in our firm is capable of and committed to reflecting our high-quality brand to our clients. It does require a continuing effort, however, because new people are hired every day. And even longer-term employees need to be reminded of who we are and what we stand for. A core concept of branding is repetition: If it is a worthwhile message, then it is worth repeating.

After surviving the Depression, World War II, the back-office crunch of the 1960s, the bear markets of the 1970s, 1980s, and 1990s, and the dot-com era, we know we can survive and prosper for many years to come as an independent firm. We know who we are: We are focused on our clients, and we are fiercely protective of a business and a brand that we believe in. Our brand and our culture cannot be separated. We may be a smaller player in a rather large pond, but we own a distinct identity and a competitive advantage that have served our clients and our firm well for 70 years and will serve us well into the future.

BRANDING: LESSONS LEARNED

Knowledge acquisition is a part of our business at the firm, and our branding initiative has provided us with several key lessons learned. Here are a few of them:

- *Match the brand to the internal culture.* This principle is key to any organization that strives to achieve a consistent and genuine brand experience for its clients and achieve buy-in from its employees.
- *Involve senior management in the process.* High-level championship of the branding effort is crucial. In the case of William Blair & Company, senior-level involvement went beyond mere sponsorship: We made a business case for making branding work for the organization. The concept was pitched to an executive committee and accepted after one year. This was a substantial investment for our firm—in time, money, and energy. Moreover, we decided to undertake this initiative in 2002, a low point for the securities business. Senior management truly believed that this shift would positively affect our business.
- *Manage the brand actively with marketing professionals.* Consumer products companies are sophisticated in their marketing efforts because

they employ sophisticated marketing talent that drives their business. A financial services firm will never be driven by marketing, but we have learned that there is an important place for marketing in our business strategy.

E. David Coolidge III is vice chairman of William Blair & Company. He was CEO of the firm from 1995 until 2004, and he has worked at the firm in various positions for more than 35 years. Coolidge is a member of the Kellogg School of Management Dean's Advisory Board. He earned a BA from Williams College and an MBA from the Harvard Business School.

CHAPTER 20

INTERNAL BRANDING

ED BUCKLEY
Vice President, UPS
and
MATT WILLIAMS
Senior Vice President, Martin Agency

At its most basic level, a brand is simply a promise a company makes to the market. But when building their brands, too often companies overlook the audience most vital to the successful delivery of that promise—their employees. In most cases, branding is viewed only from a market-facing perspective and often is too narrowly focused on advertising, packaging, logos, and colors. The result: millions spent defining and making the promise, only to have it broken by a disappointing experience delivered by uninformed employees.

Capturing the true business-building power of a brand by engaging employees may be the biggest missed opportunity in branding today. If employees understand and internalize the objectives established for the brand, they can become an army of brand ambassadors, as opposed to inadvertent brand saboteurs. Creating brand ambassadors means marketers must keep employees in mind as they develop their brands. This is the perspective we took when we redefined the UPS brand in 2003.

BRAND BUILDING AT UPS

For almost 100 years the UPS brand has been synonymous with reliable package delivery. And our expertise has made us the world leader. But as our customers' businesses evolved to be increasingly interconnected and complex, UPS focused on targeting a bigger opportunity: to establish a deep portfolio of transportation and supply chain services that can be efficiently and seamlessly combined into service bundles based on the needs of individual customers. Today, our services range from global package delivery, service parts logistics, international air freight, and customs brokerage to managing customers' entire inventory and distribution systems. The goal is to enhance our customers' supply chains so that they can focus their attention on other things that will make them more successful, rather than spending time stitching together the services they need from multiple logistics providers. Built on the foundation of this business strategy, we called the new brand promise "Synchronized Commerce."

In 2002, when the marketing team at UPS began the process of more thoroughly developing the company's brand, we believed that the company's strategy was sound, but that the vision, the message, and, most importantly, the array of benefits offered by the company were not fully recognized or understood by the market. Customers had heard us talking about things beyond package delivery, but they didn't understand what we were saying. To them, UPS still seemed like the traditional package delivery firm they'd relied on for years. They didn't understand what else UPS could do. To expand their view of UPS's capabilities, we introduced advertising built around the tag line "What can Brown do for you?"

Additionally, although UPS employees were loyal, hardworking, and experienced, many of them lacked a clear understanding of the corporate strategy. While UPS people had a deep knowledge of their business units and jobs, they were relatively unfamiliar with the newer capabilities of the firm. As a result, it was difficult for employees in one part of the business to fully appreciate what their counterparts in other areas of the company did or how their roles could relate to one another. So, when managers heard UPS's strategy of enabling global commerce, they rarely understood how that vision came to life in the unique combination of capabilities across the company. Ironically, due to an incomplete understanding of the company's capabilities, employees' response to the strategy mirrored the response of the market. Changing that situation became a key focal point of UPS's internal brand repositioning and education process.

MARKETING THE BRAND PROMISE TO EMPLOYEES

From the beginning, the marketing team set out to engage all 360,000 UPS employees as it launched the brand development program. Many of the company's managers and employees still viewed brand building as something that only consumer product companies needed to worry about. We had to change their thinking and help them understand that brand building was a discipline central to achieving success at UPS. The key was elevating the brand to become a core pillar of the company's culture. UPS always had a strong corporate culture, so incorporating the brand as a vital element of the organizational identity was a logical path.

As the marketing staff worked through issues such as brand positioning, brand architecture, and the development of a new identity system, we treated the creation of a brand education program for employees as an equal priority. We knew that it was never a good idea to use a firm's strategy statements as external marketing messages, and early on we received confirmation that strategy statements were equally ineffective in communicating to our own people. Consequently, we focused on developing an internal messaging platform linked to UPS's external positioning and advertising, adapting it specifically for the employee audience. One result of this was the development of an internal tag line: "One Company. One Vision. One Brand."

Just as the advertising was designed to explain UPS's capabilities to our external audiences, this internal tag line captured the essence of the broader story that needed to be shared with employees. Firms undertaking an internal branding effort should not underestimate the value of devices such as tag lines, which are common among external marketplace branding efforts but are often overlooked when communicating to employees. The value of crisply stating and reinforcing key message points is as important inside your company as it is outside.

LAUNCHING THE EVOLVED BRAND

As planning progressed toward the launch of the evolved UPS brand, we never lost sight of the internal audience. At UPS, it was clear that we needed to help employees understand the vision for the company and for the brand in a way that they could internalize it and act upon it. Additionally, it was clear that we had an opportunity to orchestrate the launch itself to be inclusive, to galvanize all employees, and to reinforce the concept of synchronization—the core of the company's evolved positioning.

As a result, celebratory events were scheduled for all UPS employees around the world, with preparations carried out largely in secret. As business started around the globe on launch day, the level of energy indicated that this was no ordinary day. Work groups covering all of UPS's 360,000 employees were introduced to the evolved UPS brand with launch events led by senior managers. Unveiling ceremonies were held at all locations. Delivery centers revealed the redesigned delivery trucks and drop boxes. And at our air hubs, we held ceremonial landings of aircraft bearing the new livery. Employees also received a gift box containing a pin with the new logo design, a letter from the chairman, and a document that explained the purpose of the company's brand transformation centered on an explanation of the business and the brand strategies. The dramatic breadth of the brand program was readily apparent to all employees at launch, and the fact that all of the elements secretly came together around the globe in support of the launch was arresting in and of itself.

But more importantly, the launch was used as an opportunity to reinforce the meaning of the company's new strategy and positioning. From the staging of launch events to the production, assembly, and distribution of all associated materials and gifts, the launch provided a prime example of the level of synchronization UPS aimed to provide its customers. The human resources and marketing teams also developed a host of communications for employees, which explained that while the firm was divided into separate operating units, it would go to market as a single entity. Employees were asked to learn about the broader capabilities and services of the company and to find ways to collaborate with their partners in adjacent business units. The brand strategy was also clearly explained, helping employees understand that independent or endorsed brands of UPS subsidiaries would be eliminated in favor of a master brand approach. Employees learned that the entire company would benefit from the strong equity that exists in the UPS brand. The internal tag line ("One Company. One Vision. One Brand.") did a masterful job of reinforcing these points in a way that was easily remembered and often repeated by employees throughout the company.

Discussions were then held with each work group, where teams began to jointly explore how they could contribute to the successful execution of the brand strategies. These discussions were critical to helping employees understand the new brand strategies and begin to implement them in their own jobs. Managers completed this process with their work groups within a week of the launch to ensure that all employees were fully engaged.

Immediately following the launch celebrations, the 30,000 members of the management team received additional training and a book entitled *One UPS: A Roadmap for the Future*. The plainspoken text of the book explained the business and brand strategies in greater detail and provided the rationale for why they would be successful. Platitudes and marketing-speak were pointedly avoided (something all companies should keep in mind when launching a brand initiative to employees).

LAUNCH RESULTS

This high-energy internal brand launch helped employees immediately understand that the new brand strategy was much more than a new logo and paint job. It meant nothing less than a company-wide change in perspective. In addition to engaging and educating employees throughout the corporation, the launch activities elevated the UPS brand from the limited domain of the brand communications department to center stage in the company. The brand was recognized as an essential asset that needed to be built, protected, and leveraged to achieve organizational success. Along with this realization came the recognition that the value of the brand is either enhanced or diminished each time a customer interacts with a UPS employee. As a result, everyone at UPS began to understand that they played an essential part in shaping and building the brand, and more importantly, that they were responsible for delivering on the brand promise.

Admittedly, it isn't easy to find ways to engage hundreds of thousands of people and prompt them to reflect on a specific topic, especially one as foreign to many of them as branding. While these launch efforts and materials effectively supported the effort at UPS, other companies must find their own appropriate mechanisms to accomplish their internal communications objectives. Obviously, the methods must fit the company's culture. Whatever the method, the common goal is to create a constructive disruption that causes people to pause, think, and absorb the brand message—and then to begin to think differently about the brand.

POST-LAUNCH STRATEGIES

To replicate the level of understanding that was established among existing employees through these initial launch efforts, it became standard practice to deliver brand materials and training at all new-management orientations.

In addition, to sustain the brand's new position of prominence among employees, all internal materials and communications were uniformly and simultaneously rebranded. These materials included newsletters, training materials, benefit brochures, PowerPoint templates, posters, and paychecks. By consistently applying the brand design system as rigorously to internal materials as it was applied to external communications, the linkage between our people and the brand was continually reinforced.

Clearly, advertising also is a central component of the brand development process, and this, too, can be leveraged with employees. In the past, UPS employees would generally see new company advertising at home while watching television—right along with the rest of the viewing public. We recognized that as stewards of the brand, our people wanted and needed to understand our brand messages prior to release. So, now we routinely preview all new advertising with employees, explaining the strategy behind the ads while relating it back to the broader corporate strategy. As a result, employees began to take great pride in the company's advertising and are now prepared to discuss it with customers, friends, and families. This has had an enormous impact on sustaining and building employee engagement with the brand.

There is an additional benefit to engaging employees in the advertising process. Because employees have a better understanding of the UPS business and brand strategy, each time they view a UPS ad it becomes a reminder of what UPS is promising to do for our customers—and their role in keeping that promise. The prominent question asked in the UPS advertising campaign, "What can Brown do for you?" reminds employees that they need to serve our customers in unique and effective ways. From an employee and customer perspective, this is a vastly different message than the one the company was sending years ago with our old tag line: "The tightest ship in the shipping business."

RESULTS

Many things have been accomplished as a result of these brand building efforts among employees, but none more important than the understanding and resolve that is routinely demonstrated by our people at every level of the organization. Moreover, the "One Company. One Vision. One Brand." internal tag line created an atmosphere focused on organizational success rather than divisional wins. This focus is essential, since effective cross-organizational coordination often requires managers to contribute to corporate-level solutions that may occasionally appear to generate suboptimal results at the regional or business-unit level. Such situations can take a variety of shapes; one example is space allocation on a cargo flight.

Imagine a cargo manager is faced with the choice between machine parts or a garment shipment to fill the remaining space on an aircraft. Since charges for cargo shipments are usually based on weight, the heavy machine parts would seem to be the obvious, profit-generating choice. But if the manager were to base his or her decision on the revenue and profit generated by the cargo alone, he or she could actually undermine corporate results. Perhaps the garment shipment was picked up at a factory, consolidated in a UPS warehouse with other merchandise for the same customer, tagged for retail sale, moved to the airport, and ultimately distributed across the destination country—all by UPS. By contrast, the shipment of machine parts is simply being moved between two airports.

If the manager chose to fill the cargo space with the lighter garment shipment, he or she would produce a higher total return for the company. He or she would be also engaging in business that more directly aligns with the company's strategy—one that delivers more value to customers, is differenti-ated from competitive offerings, and is not easily imitated. Encouraging this kind of decision making is what internal brand building is all about.

SUMMARY

Prior to the 2003 UPS brand initiative, most UPS employees were content to work hard and provide reliable service in their area of responsibility. They didn't always recognize the need to build bridges between business units or contribute to collaborative solutions for customers. And if they did, they of-ten dismissed the prospect as being too complicated. Today, in 2005, while it isn't always obvious how to accomplish the desired outcomes, virtually all employees demonstrate a sense of personal responsibility to explore and dis-cover new ways to develop synchronized solutions for our customers. Whereas in the past dozens (or perhaps more optimistically, hundreds) of se-nior managers really understood the corporate vision and worked tirelessly to achieve it, the company now has thousands of employees tackling those issues every day. In so doing, they are delivering on the brand promise. UPS's for-mer chairman, Jim Kelly, summed up this process well when he said, "Living out the brand promise doesn't come solely from mission statements. Or prod-uct differentiation. Or lower prices. Or snappy logos. It flows from the inter-section of culture and people. It flows from the living, breathing brand."

Ed Buckley is vice president of marketing at UPS, responsible for enterprise-wide service and product development. Buckley's experience at UPS spans virtually all areas of mar-keting within the firm. In his prior assignment as vice president of brand management and customer communications, Buckley led the company's brand development effort, in-cluding the introduction of the first new corporate identity and logo in over 40 years and the broadening of its global advertising. He is a member of the Kellogg School of Man-agement Alumni Advisory Board. He graduated from Purdue University with a degree in industrial management and received an MBA from the Kellogg School of Management.

Matt Williams is senior vice president, group planning director at the Martin Agency. He has managed and led strategic development for accounts including UPS, Bank One, GEICO Auto Insurance, and PING Golf Equipment. Prior to joining the Martin Agency, Williams worked at Ketchum Advertising. He received an under-graduate degree in marketing from the College of William & Mary and received an MBA from the Kellogg School of Management.

INDEX